MODERN
FIGHTER
AIRCRAFT
TECHNOLOGY AND TACTICS

As part of our ongoing market research, we are always pleased to receive comments about our books, suggestions for new titles, or requests for catalogues. Please write to: The Editorial Director, Patrick Stephens Limited, Sparkford, Near Yeovil, Somerset, BA22 7JJ.

MODERN
FIGHTER
AIRCRAFT
TECHNOLOGY AND TACTICS

Into combat with today's fighter pilots

Anthony Thornborough

PSL

Patrick Stephens Limited

First published in 1995

British Library Cataloguing-in-Publication Data:
A catalogue record for this book is available from the British Library

ISBN 1 85260 426 3

Library of Congress catalog card No. 95-78112

Patrick Stephens Limited is an imprint of Haynes Publishing, Sparkford, Nr Yeovil, Somerset BA22 7JJ

Typeset by J. H. Haynes & Co. Ltd.

Printed in Great Britain by Butler & Tanner Ltd, Frome and London

CONTENTS

Introduction   7

Chapter 1 Modern Technology & Tactics: An Overview   9

Chapter 2 Launch   29

Chapter 3 Air Superiority   53

Chapter 4 Target Ingress   101

Chapter 5 Recovery   169

Chapter 6 Future Technologies   179

Glossary   195

Index   201

INTRODUCTION

Designing, building, maintaining and flying modern fighters has become an incredibly complex and expensive business, and one which is becoming increasingly mind-boggling in its breadth. This has as much to do with the ancillary technology stuffed into, and strapped onto, modern military aircraft as the inevitable technological growth in airframes and propulsion, creating a veritable minefield of terminology derived from increasingly compartmentalized sciences.

Tactics at the sharp end, too, constantly being reshaped by these new technologies, continue to grow at such a pace that only a privileged few are able to keep up with the multifarious developments around the world. And in the aftermath of the Cold War, it is becoming increasingly clear that East and West created many diverging rather than copy-cat technological solutions in response to each other's real and perceived military developments, further complicating the issue! Hopefully, the NATO-Russian Partnership for Peace deal signed in June 1994 will be the harbinger of an exciting new era in cooperative development, however good competition might be at preserving the technical edge.

This book sets out to unravel some of that technology, and how it has evolved since the Vietnam War, hopefully in an entertaining fashion. My brief from the publisher was to make this book accessible. In attempting to do this, I was astounded by how much has been taken for granted in past works, or simply skipped over without adequate explanation and, as a result, how little (at the outset, at least) I actually knew myself given the breadth of the subject matter. Many past works have been written by engineers for other engineers, by pilots for other pilots, or by politicians, analysts and planners for other like-minded folk, with plenty of scope for laymen to become all too quickly lost in the quagmire of technical and professional terminology. Much of this book, therefore, is written in layman's terms for fellow enthusiasts or those enquiring into the subject for the first time: everything you wanted to know about modern military aviation, but were too afraid (or embarrassed) to ask. In many instances I myself started from scratch and asked a lot of seemingly unintelligent, stupid questions until it was possible to piece together what I hope is an accurate (albeit simplified in places) representation of the technology, procedures and tactics employed in modern air warfare. American leading-edge technology and tactics dominates, but many comparative illustrations are offered with competing British, French and Russian hardware, which in some instances has surpassed massively financed American ingenuity or has built upon it.

The initial and closing sections of the book take a broader view of developments of the recent past and future developments, respectively, while sandwiched in-between is a series of essays describing the various missions and hardware, beginning with pre-flight planning and ending, appropriately enough, with aircraft recovery. Psychological and physiological aspects of flying modern high-performance fighters, including some of the thrills and spills (ultimately the real face of tearing about the sky), are also given thorough scrutiny within the confines of this work.

Much of this should prove equally fascinating to budding aviators and engineers taking their first glimpse at modern aerial warfare. It is also hoped that readers' eyes are not glazed over too much by the extensive use of terms and acronyms. These are explained as they crop up and are reproduced in the Glossary. Partly owing to the multi-national flavour of this book which requires the use of some generic terminology, and partly because of the current acronym disease plaguing the Pentagon in Washington, DC, this ultimately proved unavoidable; there simply was no alternative if the narrative was to incorporate analytical perspectives, and there was much of this to be accomplished in the light of the Gulf War, and more recent developments.

Incidentally, many of the arguments reproduced within these covers are intended to reflect the often differing opinions held by the professionals, some of whom remain at loggerheads over certain issues. As I am not privy to much of the detailed classified information (nor do I pretend to be) which might assist me in being unequivocal about these matters, both sides of the debate are presented wherever possible, albeit sometimes isolated. It is then up to the reader to choose which camp he or she belongs to on any given issue. In any event, many of the arguments and case studies contained in this book should be of equal value to professional aviators and analysts too; sometimes, as the old saying goes, it is all too easy to lose sight of the woods for the trees. The inherent simplicity of the approach taken within these pages, in going back to basics on many occasions, should help provide a clearer overall perspective of how technologies and tactics are shaping today. And shaping they most definitely are.

In closing, it can be boldly asserted that there exist four glaringly obvious factors remoulding the nature of modern air warfare, all of which feature strongly throughout the book. The first is the impact of modern microprocessors in everything from engines and flight control systems, to weapons and defensive systems. The emerging range of new fighters, and their upgraded derivatives, are nothing less than computers with wings on them, including many of the latest previously besmirched but otherwise superb fighters of Russian origin. Similarly, it is interesting to reflect that most of the Precision-Guided Munitions (PGMs) now being perfected in the West bear unit costs comparable in real terms to early jet fighters, and are arguably more technologically sophisticated!

The second factor is low-observable stealth fighter technology, and the impact this is having on current force planning. It appears that a small force of such silver bullets is able to replace a much greater number of conventional fighters and their support entourage.

The third advance is in data-linking and communications, and the fourth, allied to this, is the increasing use of space satellites. The explosive effect that these latter two are having on a broad range of technologies and tactics, from navigation to weapons employment, is best summed up by the slogan of the recently formed Space Warfare Center at Colorado Springs in the western United States: 'In your face from outer space'!

Had this book been compiled 12 years ago, very little of these sweeping changes would have been included in the study at all. Quite how much will change over the next 12 years remains to be seen.

Fathoming out the material for this book was a long and rewarding process, but would have been impossible without the generous assistance of many people, too numerous to list in full, who freely helped with ideas, information and illustrations. I would, however, like to give special thanks to Bruce Benyshek, Craig Brown, Jim Chamberlain, Peter E. Davies, Dale Donovan, Andy Evans, Douglas S. McCurrach, Denny Lombard, Lois Lovisolo, Tim Perry, Jim Rotramel, James M. Shaw, and my father Dick Thornborough. Mention must also be made of some of the organizations behind some of these names which responded specifically to help tie-up some loose ends on this project, including Aérospatiale, Dassault-Breguet, GEC-Marconi, Hughes Missiles and Radar groups, Lockheed Advanced Development Company, Martin-Baker, Martin-Marietta, the MoD Photographic Workshop, Northrop Grumman, RAF Strike Command, Rockwell-Collins, Texas Instruments, USAFE 3rd Air Force, Mildenhall, and the US OASD in Washington, DC. Thanks also to Bob Munro, and my publisher Darryl Reach at Haynes Publishing and his diplomatic editorial assistant Alison Roelich, who patiently put up with numerous delays in completing the project.

Anthony M. Thornborough
Bristol, England, March 1995

Chapter One

MODERN TECHNOLOGY & TACTICS: AN OVERVIEW

The lightning air war in the Gulf in the opening months of 1991 arguably represented the first true application of air power as a decisive factor in modern warfare. As Gen Merrill A. McPeak, USAF Chief of Staff, noted, Operation *Desert Storm* represented 'the first time in history that a field army has been defeated by air power'. In the United States, its success represented the pinnacle of two decades of relatively quiet and subdued military re-equipment and preparation, which finally exorcized the Vietnam ghost.

The will to succeed in the Gulf, considerably aided by a multi-national Coalition sanctioned by the United Nations to use force which effectively encircled its enemy, was an ingredient sadly all too lacking in the embroilment of the US in the long and troubled civil war in South-East Asia. The former Soviet Union encountered much the same problems during its lengthy and internationally condemned incursion into Afghanistan which similarly ended in withdrawal with little net accomplishment.

The fighting ground and weather conditions also favoured success in the Gulf. There were no tropical monsoons to blanket out radar or electro-optic (E-O) sensors for half the year (*Desert Storm* was quite deliberately initiated at the height of a cool, clear desert winter). Overall, the clear, open tracts of sand and rocky terrain, with the Iraqi opposition laid out or entrenched in the field (as opposed to being dispersed into thousands of elusive pockets of low-value targets cloaked by vegetation, many of which were underground, as was the case in South-East Asia) also played a significant part.

But the overriding factor in the success of *Desert Storm* was the employment of overwhelming air power, *ab initio*. It was a well-orchestrated aerial ballet which involved up to 3,000 carefully interwoven sorties each day, following much along the lines of what sacked USAF Gen Dugan had indiscreetly outlined to the Press beforehand. When Coalition forces gave the enemy a temporary respite, it was because movements and developments needed evaluating for the next thrust, not because the political or military will to engage had run out of steam. And such respite could be measured in minutes, so that the enemy was kept constantly guessing.

The ceaseless, rolling 'gorilla packages' used around the clock in the Gulf – as opposed to piecemeal strike packages employed on a stop-go basis against North Vietnam – were honed for maximum mutual protection and quickly established air superiority deep over enemy lines. A significant portion of the responsibility for drawing up specific target assignments rested in the hands of the theatre commanders, who knew best where and when to strike. It gave the enemy no leeway. Vital ingredients such as surprise and stealth (in the broader sense of the word) thus became bywords for success, as did the concept of establishing and maintaining air superiority at the earliest opportunity, which can be accomplished with relatively little actual action.

In contrast, the air war in Vietnam escalated very gradually, stripping the American forces of any element of surprise. This permitted the North's regime to re-equip after every major skirmish, while US air superiority (a transitory thing) only reached temporary crescendoes in 1967–68 and 1972, before petering out again. Maintaining this tempo over such a long time was totally impracticable – and North Vietnam was prepared to sit it out. In the end, the US lost to hostile fire through August 1973 (discounting personnel and aircraft stricken by operational causes, and helicopters), a staggering 2,475 fixed-wing aircraft[1].

---

[1] Source: US DoD OASD, dated 17 Oct 1973

Combat over North Vietnam was conducted in strike packages which gradually evolved a host of mutually-supportive fighter concepts – reconnaissance, defence-suppression, strike and CAPs – supported by a backstage fleet of EW, AEW and C³ aircraft. The concept proved successful during the Linebacker II *offensives of 1972. Here, a pair of F-4E Phantom IIs, mainstay fighters of the era, cruise to the target with bombs, fuel drop tanks and ECM. The success of* Linebacker II *facilitated a not entirely ungracious withdrawal from the intractable, protracted conflict. (via Jim Rotramel)*

During the Gulf War, total US and Coalition losses attributed to enemy action amounted to just 43 aircraft of all types – less than half those Gen Dugan feared would be incurred during the *first week* of air operations! Overall, more Coalition casualties accrued to heatstroke than to enemy action.

However, several gains did emerge from aerial operations over North Vietnam. Airborne weapons, targeting devices and electronic countermeasures (ECM) matured rapidly in what was seen at the time as a great testing ground, effectively coming of age long before they became showpieces during *Desert Storm*. The giant coordinating eyes in the sky such as the E-3 Airborne Warning & Control System (AWACS), which proved crucial during the Gulf conflict, also evolved from their piston-powered humble beginnings in South-East Asia as airborne early warning platforms. Also matured in Vietnam was the use of coordinated action by mutually protective air power. However, this package was not employed properly until May 1972, seven years into the war, when President Nixon ordered massive air reinforcements to the theatre (primarily in response to the North Vietnamese invasion of the South). Interdiction strikes were unleashed with full fury against the Hanoi regime to thwart its war-making capacity, obliging its wily diplomats back to the negotiating table in Paris. Initially code-named *Freedom Train*, and then *Linebacker I*, the

composition of these packages remained confidently constant throughout the campaign, which endured until October that year.

Each of the new American strike packages comprised a core of 50–60 fast jets, in various roles. Typically, eight F-4E Phantom IIs as 'chaff bombers' were at the apex of the strike package, which would dispense clouds of radar-reflective metal strips to cloak the precise whereabouts of the oncoming waves of aircraft behind them. To ward off or destroy enemy fighters, a MiG combat air patrol (MiGCAP) was included, comprising eight F-4D armed with AIM-9 Sidewinder and AIM-7 Sparrow air-to-air missiles (AAMs), and some gun-equipped F-4E models sent in as *Constant Guard* reinforcements, their engines retuned for operations in the muggy Orient, with a further eight nestled close to the main wave as strike escort. Radar suppression was carried out by four F-105G *Wild Weasels* toting *Iron Hand* radar-homing missiles and cluster munitions to locate and neutralize the North Vietnamese radar-guided anti-aircraft artillery (AAA) and surface-to-air missile (SAM) threat. Reconnaissance was provided by four RF-4C dedicated reconnaissance models of the Phantom II for pre-strike and post-strike comparative target battle damage assessment (BDA), working in pairs, and preceded by one or two more fast jets engaged purely in pre-strike weather recce duties to determine cloud cover and wind factors over the target area. As the major component of the bomber force, there were eight Flights of four F-4D/E Phantom IIs, with each Flight typically toting up to 12 tons of either dumb free-fall or smart precision-guided bombs.

Backstage, armadas of KC-135A Stratotanker air-to-air refuelling (AAR) tankers kept the force topped-up with fuel at pre-established coordinates *en route* to and from the target. Several EB-66C Destroyers provided spot-noise radar-jamming and SAM launch warnings. Piston-powered EC-121 Warning Stars code-named *Disco* used their giant airborne radars to help keep track of overall movements and vector the MiGCAP Flights against enemy fighters. Further assistance was provided by a *Red Crown* US Navy radar picket ship.

The use of such packages proved highly effective. By 22 October, when the strikes were suspended, most road and rail links to Communist China through which the North received war supplies had been severed (including 106 bridges), and a hefty percentage of its railway marshalling yards, electricity-generating and petroleum, oil, lubricants (POL) storage facilities had been smashed. Somewhat astonished by this sudden onset of resolve, the North Vietnamese promptly sued for peace, and began to draw up a nine-point plan until this, sadly, ended in stalemate – interestingly enough, within weeks of the US once again having suspended its aerial campaign.

Viewed objectively, the *Linebacker I* package concept remained experimental. Many new weapons systems (described later in this book) were employed in quantity for the first time, notably the new range of modular smart bombs and their allied targeting systems developed under numerous Precision Avionics Vectoring Equipment (*Pave*) efforts. Similarly, dogfight-capable AAM variants of the mainstay Sparrow and Sidewinder families were also developed, and some allied, esoteric avionics bearing fanciful names and acronyms like *Combat Tree* and Target Identification System Electro-Optical (TISEO) also came into being. These assisted the stand-off use

The US Navy's contribution to Vietnam-era smart bombing, a concept which became a standard feature of INT aircraft engaged in Desert Storm *duties two decades later, included the A-6A Intruder Pave Knife. The banana-shaped pod (centreline) housed an LLLTV boresighted with a YAG laser which would be squirted at targets to mark them for LGBs. (Loral)*

of the AIM-7E-2 Sparrow III where this AAM weapon worked best: *Combat Tree* worked by picking up enemy *Odd Rods* identification friend or foe (IFF) codes, and TISEO provided a magnified, long-range TV image of the bogey. These gave some shape to the otherwise nondescript blip displayed on the radarscope. For the first time ever, crews could use medium-range stand-off missiles for beyond visual range (BVR) work.

Linebacker I effectively laid the groundwork for the second round of operations. This, ordered into action after the Peace negotiations had reached a stalemate, ensued as *Linebacker II* during December 1972 – the infamous 11-day Christmas bombing campaign – and it was here that the strike package truly came of age. Operations were extended into the night hours using heavier firepower in the form of F-111A Aardvark and B-52D/G Stratofortress bombers, while packages of USAF F-4s and US Navy jets

Israel's Heyl Ha'Avir was the first air arm to utilize the impressive GBU-15 E-O glide bomb. This Phantom II brandishes two of them, along with an ECM pod (right of the nose landing gear) and TISEO E-O (protruding from the port wing leading-edge). TISEO could be slaved to radar to provide long-range identification of aerial bogeys at BVR distances. (Rockwell)

worked by day. These made increasing use of different timings and headings to confuse the enemy in a series of focused attacks, along with greater use of low-level, under-the-radar flight. Increasing use, too, was made of the evolving airborne warning systems and IFF avionics so that the MiGCAP Flights were able to put up rudimentary BVR 'kill box' barriers around the strike waves, protecting them around the clock from all but the worst ravages by MiGs. The results were devastating, obliging the Hanoi regime to resume negotiations, which culminated in a cease-fire on 23 January 1973.

But for President Nixon's untimely domestic political indiscretion (which unfolded in the American public eye in the form of Watergate just over a year later and which precipitated his resignation in 1974) the North Vietnamese would have scarcely dared to invade the South with the overwhelming force they employed in such a blasé fashion the following Spring. What the US had thus achieved three years previously came to naught, and gave the widespread impression that its military prowess was nothing more than a state-of-the-art tool of terror.

However, far from being totally perplexed by it all, American air power, which continued to lead Western orthodoxy, quietly prospered and further evolved the strike package concept. With the focus of attention having shifted to Europe and the North Atlantic Treaty Organization (NATO), with the Soviet Red Army as the key potential protagonist, the concept of all-weather air power soon matured. New advances were made in radar and E-O sensors designed to work in the sullen Central European climate where winter daylight averages 8 hours, cloud ceilings below 1,500 ft are prevalent for half the time between October and February, and low-level fog often persists for two to four days unabated.

New aircraft tailor-made for specific jobs also appeared in rapid succession, gradually supplanting the 'vanilla' variants of the do-it-all F-4 Phantom II. These included the Fairchild-Republic A-10A Thunderbolt II, built around a mighty 30 mm anti-tank gun for close air support (CAS). Another was the McDonnell Douglas F-15A/B Eagle dedicated air superiority fighter, with a thrust-to-weight ratio in excess of unity which permitted it to accelerate in a vertical climb. It introduced the concept of chin-up Hands-On-Throttle-and-Stick (HOTAS) whereby the pilot no longer needed to duck back down into the cockpit to reconfigure the radar or weapons. Deep interdiction was furnished by further improved models of the General Dynamics F-111 Aardvark, notably the definitive F-111F version, an attack machine with an all-up weight of 45 tons. This could operate at the edge of sound virtually automatically

down to heights of as little as 200 ft above ground level (AGL) over the roughest terrain, with an impressive warload and an even more prestigious radius of action. The stealth concept, developed under the *Have Blue* programme and designed to produce a fighter that would be virtually invisible to radar and infrared sensors by night, also matured under the top secret cloak of 'Black World' development. This was initially under a cadre of ex-Vietnam F-4 jet-jockeys who had access to a secret *Red Hat* squadron of American-owned MiGs. Simultaneously, newer and more lethal forms of defence-suppression systems came on line, such as the McDonnell Douglas/IBM F-4G *Advanced Wild Weasel*, Grumman/Eaton EF-111A Raven, and Texas Instruments AGM-88 high-speed anti-radar missile (HARM). Navy aircraft also pushed the boundaries out farther, in the shape of machines like the Grumman F-14A Tomcat with its 120-mile-range AIM-54 Phoenix AAM system, while European forces broke new ground with such novelties as the Vertical Short Take-Off & Landing (V/STOL) Harrier Jump Jet. All of these prospered during the 1970s.

Thus, the impressive array of hardware which seemed to have sprouted out of the blue during the opening night of *Desert Storm* on 17 January 1991, had in fact been a long time in the making, and was largely shaped by the lessons learned two decades previously in the fire-filled skies of South-East Asia.

Combat experience in Vietnam also spawned a whole new series of peacetime training initiatives, or built upon ones hatched late in that conflict. In 1976 the USAF inaugurated full-scale aerial exercises at Nellis Air Force Base (AFB), Nevada, designed to hone the strike package concept into a rolling series of integrated interdiction Flights for round-the-clock, all-weather, high-intensity combat in Europe: Red Flag. Following on the heels from this was Maple Flag, conducted over the testing snowy backdrop of Canada, and Green Flag, a dedicated electronic warfare (EW) version of Red Flag, where the new panoply of AAA/SAM radar-locating, radar-jamming and radar-smashing hardware could be wrung-out. Piecemeal initiatives such as the US Navy's Top Gun school, which originated in 1969, also spread. The spin-off USAF programme, initiated under Project College Dart, bore the banner Fighter Weapons School, with air and ground attack duties encompassed into its syllabuses. These combined to provide a completely new standard of training, as close to actual air combat as could be imagined; and from 1978 other NATO participants began to show up on a regular basis for the six-week manoeuvres and three-month courses.

The Tactical Aircrew Combat Training System/Air Combat Manoeuvring Instrumented (TACTS/ACMI)

The black-and-blue Sidewinder AAM-sized ACMI pods relay critical aircraft data from fighters engaged in mock air combat to the ground station to assist with computer-aided mission analysis at the ACMI/TACTS debrief . . . (Cubic)

. . . where the data can be replayed with sometimes embarrassing accuracy to demonstrate who did what right or wrong, so that the aviators can learn the subtle and complex art of aerial combat without even firing a shot. The technology was popularized in the movie Top Gun. *(Cubic)*

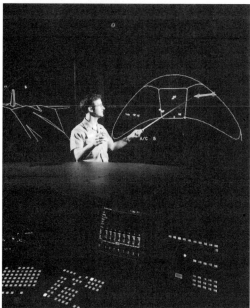

debriefing, replayed on giant computer-generated synthesized Display & Debriefing Systems (DDSs), could recount the day's or night's action with sometimes embarrassing accuracy.

Then there were the simple dynamics of the exercises. The chosen venues, situated in deserts, adjacent to large tracts of ocean, or out over icy barren wastelands, provided the opportunity for virtually unrestricted flight. For the first time, the crews could push the throttles to the firewall and 'turn and burn' virtually to their heart's content (with safety only, intervening where necessary). Such authenticity permitted the crews to quickly develop their skills without having to actually go to war, with dissimilar air combat fighters from the opposing force attempting to thwart progress to the target. Tearing about the sky in mock but ever-so-real combat with a full load of active seeker-equipped inert AAMs to play with was just about as close it was possible to get to the real thing. It was fighting for survival at the edge

ranges developed by the Cubic Corporation at Nellis Tactical Fighter Weapons Center (TFWC) and Yuma soon spread to new sites in the US, and foreign subscriptions quickly followed, including the establishment of further such installations at places as far-flung as Decimommanu in Sardinia (where NATO crews congregate each winter for air combat training), CFB Cold Lake in Canada, and Cheong-Ju in South Korea. These ranges could record the dynamics of the participants (by means of airborne pods and ground-based tracker-receivers) in such detail that the of the performance envelope in a gigantic, supersonic joust, with friendly villains on the ground firing mock arrows in the guise of 'Smoky SAM' surface-to-air missile simulators and flickering strobes for AAA, and employing multifarious jamming equipment, including some designed to fox communications, as if to thwart thought?!

It has brought with it a whole new lexicography of terms and acronyms, SA, or situational awareness, being one of the strongest attributes accredited to those who can survive the gruelling process and come out on top. Thus was born the modern fighter pilot's axiom: 'You fight like you train'! Many *Desert Storm* veterans attribute their cool nerves and swift success in combat to these manoeuvres, which realistically mirrored real war; panic, fright and a sweat-soaked flightsuit all included. Nothing quite so authentic was available during the 1960s. During the Vietnam War, crews were offered a quick series of live missile firings and bomb drops, as per practice camp, plus what was commonly described as 'two weeks of hell' undergoing jungle survival training, before being thrown into the bizarre war itself.

AWACS and J-STARS Appraised

The evolution of round-the-clock mutually supportive strike packages, and superb training, played essential parts in winning the Gulf War. However, there can be no doubt that a few genuinely new technologies played a very big part indeed in the Coalition's victory. In particular, the modern netted command & control system allied to the new all-seeing, all-knowing eyes in the sky – the Boeing E-3 AWACS and Grumman E-8 Joint-service Surveillance Target Attack Radar System (J-STARS) – played a huge role. These coordinated the aerial ballet while at the same time furnishing the performers with fresh target information in the form of big-picture perspectives for both air-to-air and air-to-ground work.

The 100-ton E-3 Sentry flying radar is the more mature of the two, evolving from the Vietnam-era EC-121 Warning Star but taking advantage of advances in airborne radar technology, computer processing, and commensurate developments in IFF, all installed on board Boeing 707-320-class jets. First flown as the EC-137D AWACS during February 1972, Boeing went on to produce 34 Sentries for the USAF and a further 18 for a NATO consortium, as well as for the air forces of France, Saudi Arabia and the United Kingdom. Later updated to E-3B/C standard (part of ongoing improvements fielded at regular intervals of between two and three years), these boast IBM CC-2E computers linked to a distinctive saucer-shaped rotating dorsal Westinghouse AN/APY-1 or AN/APY-2 Overland Downlook Radar (ODR) which is capable of interrogating all aircraft that come within its Big Eye. These are duly plotted on 14 individual situation

AWACS is the lynchpin in today's aerial Order of Battle, keeping track of friendly and enemy aircraft via its giant 'screwtop' ODR and conveying intercept vectors to the Cappers. JTIDS is making the information exchange between the two a purely electronic affair. Illustrated is one of seven E-3D Sentry AWACSs in service with the RAF. (RAF)

display consoles (SDCs) manned by personnel who receive two years of hands-on training before being handed a prime controlling job.

These machines and crews spend a good deal of their time pre-positioned around the globe as airborne controlling agencies to direct allied fighter, bomber, tanker and EW aircraft. They receive vectors to aerial intruders, and so-called 'picture calls' (updates regarding the disposition of friendly and enemy aircraft) over joint tactical information distribution system (JTIDS) Class 2 terminals. These terminals can feed the data direct to the recipient aircraft's computers via an improved data modem (IDM), or the crews can rely on scrambled verbal instructions sent by UHF radio, such as the Magnavox *Have Quick*. All are designed to improve SA – situational awareness.

AWACS was the lynchpin of modern power projection during *Desert Storm*. The Coalition forces launched up to 3,000 sorties each day, a massively complex affair which required intricate interweaving with tankers and EW support and deconfliction over the assembly and target areas to avoid mid-air collisions, ensure adequate AAR facilities were to hand, and that suppression of enemy air defences (SEAD) and MiGCAP cover was available over the right sectors. Computer-aided flight-plan mission-modelling made available in Bahrain, Saudi Arabia and Turkey was a boon, but AWACS 'bridged all the voids and kept things running smoothly'. Col Gary Voellger's 552nd AWACW contingent in Saudi Arabia maintained four aircraft in the air around the clock, one as an air spare and three to cover the eastern, central and western sectors. During missions of 16–18 hours' duration (with two full crews on board) the force controlled the entire Coalition Airborne Order of Battle. Many of the airborne kills achieved against Iraqi aircraft would not have been possible but for the timely and valuable assistance furnished by the E-3 Sentries and their crews.

A major dilemma regarding who should interpret target data is now beginning to confront the air-to-air community: the need for snap decisions to shoot from AWACS versus positive visual identification of the bogey prior to attack. It is no longer possible to have hundreds of high-performance fighters free-ranging over the war zone to confirm an AWACS-sighted bogey as a bandit relying solely on sightings by Mark 1 eyeball. In order to catch a fleeting enemy, and in the absence of support data, it is sometimes necessary to assume that lack of an adequate IFF transponder signal is sufficient indication that it is indeed hostile. In many instances this is tactically sound doctrine, enabling the bigger fighters to take advantage of their superior medium-range AAM weaponry before closing too near to their quarry, which in some instances may possess the ability to outgun or outshoot the heavyweights at close-quarters.

In the Gulf, E-3 Sentries and trusted IFF permitted many targets to be engaged without resort to visual identification, particularly in the opening stages of the campaign when the movements of every Coalition aircraft were known in advance. When much of the Iraqi Air Force chose to flee to Iran, stand-off shooting was thus the only way to catch them. However, tragedies will inevitably occur when excessive reliance is placed on remote sensing and interpretation of targets in lieu of visual identification, even if the fighters vectored to intercept them are assisted by onboard E-O sensors such as television camera set (TCS) or imaging infrared (IIR) – fantastic as they are – for a peek at the supposed bandit at arm's length. Concurrent advances in medium-range AAMs, such as the dual-mode radar/IIR versions of the AIM-120 advanced medium-range air-to-air missile (AMRAAM), will soon permit pilots to shoot well out of visual range of the target purely on the basis of a 'cleared to fire' from AWACS and a very fuzzy IIR silhouette of the quarry flashed-up on the cockpit cathode-ray tube (CRT) displays.

These potential problems came to the fore at

IFF MODES

Mode 1	military unit identification beacon interrogated by AWACS, GCI and friendly aircraft
Modes 2 & 4	special identification codes used by tactical aircraft in wartime, and never used during peacetime
Modes 3 & C	standard civil air traffic control beacon codes used to transmit flight call-sign and altitude

---

09:35L on 14 April 1994 when a pair of USAF F-15C Eagles deliberately shot down two United Nations UH-60A Blackhawk helicopters engaged on *Provide Comfort* duties. These were mistaken for Iraqi Mi-24 *Hind* gunships about to attack a Kurdish village. It seems that in this instance the fail-safe of visual sighting was given only cursory treatment by the Eagle pilots who did not come closer than half a mile of the supposed bandits. As neither they nor the AWACS received friendly IFF signals from the helicopters – the helicopter team's 'squawk box' beacon was turned off in the crucial military unit identification Mode 1 to avoid electronic overheating during their brief point-to-point inspection hops – there existed some kind of mutual understanding that the helicopters were hostile. Under the circumstances, as this was far removed from the opening night of a major aerial campaign, either the AWACS crew or the Eagle pilots should have attempted radio communication. Excessive reliance on the automation involved, allied to complacency, resulted in the unnecessary death of 26 United Nations personnel.

To underline the problems inherent in this new technology, a similar occurrence nearly took place the previous January. On that occasion, an E-3 AWACS authorized two US Navy F/A-18C Hornet pilots to fire on a supposed bandit flying south of the 32nd Parallel. The Navy pilots opted for a visual identification, only to discover that the assigned target was in fact a Sudanese airliner!

AWACS relies on a combination of IFF and five ODR radar-scanning modes, including passive detection, full-power beyond-the-horizon (BTH) and pulse-Doppler techniques (in elevation or non-elevation), each of which has its relative merits. For example, BTH gives extreme range but does not adequately track low-flying targets, whereas at the other extreme a pulse-Doppler elevation scan catches virtually everything within its sphere of influence, along with its height and velocity, but at much shorter ranges. The computer complex also relies upon a technique known as jet engine modulation whereby it can classify an aircraft based on the beat of the radar signals being reflected from the bogey's engine fan blades. Each engine has a unique characteristic which can help to identify it. Unfortunately, the Sudanese Boeing 727's T-tail shadowed the aft-mounted engines, preventing the E-3 from carrying out a full fingerprint, and the radar operator subsequently assumed it was an enemy fighter, possibly two in close formation! It has also since been disclosed that a lumbering jet transporter such as the C-5 Galaxy can, under certain conditions, be mistaken for a Flight of three jets, based on reflections from the tail and two wings (which similarly shadow the engines), each of which register as a separate target.

Clearly, the interrogating crews need to remain vigilant at all times. Crew fatigue and resulting complacency can result in the built-in electronic fail-safes breaking down too, even when target classification is sharp and accurate. Console operators in AWACS and J-STARS, hunched for hours at a stretch over soporific displays without the benefit of being able to take brief, rejuvenating strolls or proper siestas between shifts, lack the physiological stress relievers that keep the confined fighter crewmen alert. For fighter crewmen there are the more dynamic flight forces that keep the adrenalin pumping, the manual activation of a g-suit valve to massage the lower body, moments of complete uninterrupted silence, an invigorating drag on the oxygen mask, or the simple

stunning view from the driving seat. Yet it is these long-suffering console operators in the all-seeing airborne sentinels who are increasingly running the show.

Addressing the need for reliable target classification has provided the impetus for several post-Gulf War improvements to the AWACS fleet. In its emerging Block 30/35 updated format, equipped with four UTL Argosystems passive electronic support measures (ESM, or 'listening') radio-frequency receivers, AWACS can project its new ears out more than 260 miles to acquire a fighter's radar and deduce its intentions by detecting mode in which the potential quarry's radar is working: a wide-scan search of a fighter trolling for trade, or narrow-scan target tracking indicating an attack is underway. Such ESM can be used stealthily to provide raw data as to the target's height and speed, and also to classify it by type, based purely on a pre-flight updated library of information covering a broad range of radars and their unique characteristics. For example, search emissions characteristic of an NO-193 *Slot Back* would indicate the bogey to be a MiG-29 *Fulcrum*. Fused with radar returns from the Big Eye, the system can furnish very reliable information. At present, AWACS operators usually ascertain whether the bogey is friendly or hostile purely by means of IFF codes flashed up alongside the ODR radar returns, with friendly radar targets being displayed in green, and unknowns in yellow.

Work on helping to detect low-observable targets such as pseudo-stealthy fighters and cruise missiles is also progressing at speed, by means of new scan modes employing pulse-compressed wave forms which effectively provide greater clarity. But perhaps the best development of all, from the operators' perspective, are the updates directed at cleaning up the radar screens, and presenting the targets under scrutiny as icons (little aircraft symbols) coloured to represent their status (friendly, unknown or confirmed as hostile), instead of the sometimes frighteningly complex mass of nondescript four-digit identifying tags displayed at present. This will greatly simplify the operators' tasks.

Further refined computer processing will also enable AWACS to keep track of targets performing violent manoeuvres. Again, at present, such manoeuvring causes the radar to hiccup and temporarily lose track of its quarry for several crucial seconds, a loophole which the former Soviet Union exploited in its training manuals with Doppler-defeating Cobra and Hook manoeuvres that were apt to drive a Westinghouse AWACS ODR schizophrenic! By sieving out a lot of rubbish, the job of the teams sat at the SDCs will become more manageable, reliable, and survivable. But it is far from perfect.

Thrown into the thick of *Desert Storm*, even before they reached the teething stage, were two development Grumman E-8 J-STARS, also derived from the Boeing 707-300 series (from which the two prototypes and the follow-on 20 production conversions – mostly from second-hand airliner stock – are being converted). Their contribution led Gen Merill McPeak to say: 'We will not ever again want to fight a war without a J-STARS kind of system.' Army commanders reckoned that, by comparison, they had fought previous conflicts blindfolded.

The two E-8s flew 49 sorties of 10.4 hours' average duration during *Desert Storm*. Assigned to Col George K. Muellner's 4411th JSTARS Squadron (JSS), stationed at Riyadh alongside the E-3 Sentry AWACS fleet, the aircraft and crews – made up from a mix of Service personnel and Grumman contractors – proved capable of employing the big belly-mounted Norden AN/APY-3 phased-array radar to track Iraqi armour and other ground-based weapons at distances of up to 155 miles from the forward line of troops (FLOT).

The radar was used in two primary modes. In the wide-area moving target indicator (MTI) mode, sharpened by pulse-Doppler processing, clutter suppression interferometry and adaptive clutter cancellation (techniques used to pick up moving objects and plot their range, relative position and speed against the backdrop of the terrain), the package produced a real-time ground map covering 31,000 square miles at a stand-off range of up to 300 miles. This was displayed on 10 workstations (production E-8Cs will feature 17), plotted as dots which could clearly be seen moving along roads and other networks, based on their incremental movements following each separate radar scan. In the Synthetic Aperture Radar (SAR) mode, the Norden system generated a high-resolution ground map offering 3 ft resolving power to assist with the identification of high-value fixed targets. The two modes could be displayed on any of the workstation console screens, with the separate functions being furnished by computer.

The way the two modes complemented one another was best explained by Capt James Dew:

With MTI we would see very, very large numbers in convoys coming down a road. It was mind-boggling. In fact, sometimes there were so many you couldn't even count them all. Then, all of the sudden, you don't see any more traffic. What does that tell you? It tells you they left the road or stopped. Then you would use your SAR, and Shazaam! All of a sudden, you've got

Two E-8 J-STARS (the only ones extant at that time) were deployed to the Gulf under the 4411th JSS, stationed at Riyadh in Saudi Arabia alongside the E-3 AWACSs. A further 20 production examples are being produced. (Grumman)

the exact number of vehicles, and where they are parked.

That information would be relayed to fighters and Army rocket batteries so that they were able to address the situation quickly. This capability saved the day on 22 January 1991, picking up a 60-vehicle convoy grinding its way towards friendly positions. Fifty-eight tanks were knocked-out in the ensuing air strike. It saved countless lives in the Coalition ground forces according to Maj Gen Stephen Silvasy, US Army Deputy Chief of Staff for Concepts, by ensuring that the enemy could not outflank them. J-STARS similarly monitored the Iraqi retreat from Kuwait City,

J-STARS is the other great sentinel which proved its worth in the Gulf War. Console operators review SAR ground-mapping radar imagery and can acquire enemy ground forces on the move via an MTI capability. (Grumman)

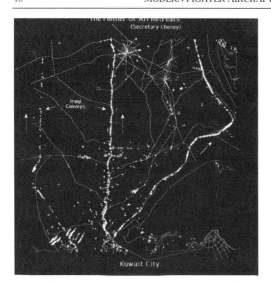

The Mother of All Retreats
(Secretary Cheney)

Iraqi
Convoys

Kuwait City

J-STARS imagery garnered during the closing stages of the Gulf War. The Mother of All Retreats refers to the Iraqi retreat up the road to Basrah, which turned into a turkey shoot before Coalition action abruptly ended on 28 February 1991. The use of air power in massive quantities effectively routed the Iraqi Army which was defeated and booted out of Kuwait in a four-day ground offensive! (US DoD)

setting them up for a 'gopher shoot'. However, as was the case with AWACS, there existed little scope for confusion during *Desert Storm*.

In a more intense conflict, with increased, intermeshed movements on the ground, there is much more scope for ambiguous target classification. Improved computer processing (J-STARS is fortunately a generation ahead of AWACS in this regard) will further aid the console operators' jobs by the time all 22 operational aircraft are fielded, in 2001. SAR resolution is being sharpened to 1 foot, while software programmes aimed at tidying-up the displays for clarity are being tested. These will offer clear colour coding for traffic density, and offer the option of compressed replay condensing minutes into seconds, to clearly indicate the speed, direction and numbers of advancing or retreating enemy ground forces, before committing fighters and Army rocket batteries to knock them out. The relaying of data will be performed by means of secure UHF radio and data modem links.

Most of the innovations to AWACS and J-STARS, such as data-fusion combined with refined displays, are designed specifically to overcome problems with human error. However, instead of using these emerging technologies to soften the taxing workload of the giant sentinels' crews, there are moves afoot to use the expanded processing capability to fuse yet more data into their systems, derived from remote off-board sensors far removed from the battle front. This will comprise Doppler radar, infrared and ultraviolet scans from satellites or an RC-135S *Cobra Ball*, which can pick up rapid movement or a rocket launch flash, and electronic intelligence (Elint) furnished by RC-135V/W *Rivet Joints* which can plot enemy radars and their status. Fusing this data with

spotlighted areas of interest coming under the watchful eye of AWACS and J-STARS may be the only fail-safe way of fathoming out the various targets' identities and intentions.

However, such is the envisaged increased workload involved in processing and disseminating this barrage of incoming information, that the AWACS and J-STARS might soon have to rely increasingly on what is termed 'artificially intelligent fusion', with little scope for a man-in-the-loop to vet the system using human judgement. For example, the search for a system which can locate *Scud*-class transporter-erector launchers (TELs) and knock-out their missiles in a boost phase intercept (BPI) has been raging ever since Iraq employed its rockets indiscriminately during the Gulf War. In other words, a system which can intercept them immediately after launch before the weapons can arc down to disgorge multiple warheads containing a variety of nasty contents, such as chemicals and nuclear waste, which might merely be dispersed over a wider lethal area over friendly heads if successfully engaged by Patriot or Erint missile intercepts.

This obsession with what was then a relatively ineffectual military weapon (despite its political terror value) has since provided the spur to full-scale theatre missile defence exercises known as *Zealous Pursuit*, designed not only to defeat *Scud* and the Al Hussein and the similar Russian/CIS SS-21 but, arguably most threatening of all, the North Korean Nodong 1. In the insatiable quest to satisfy the BPI requirement, *Zealous Pursuit* combines J-STARS, AWACS, *Cobra Ball*, the earth-circling curios, and advanced strike jets such as the F-15E as the hard-hitting component. The fighter crew at the sharp end of the search-and-destroy process are to be vectored to the target as quickly as possible to launch a kinetic-kill vehicle (KKV) optimized for anti-ballistic work, before closing in to mop-up the rocket launch vehicle with smart bombs. The KKV is as yet an undefined weapon, presently at the Advanced Concept Technology Demonstrator (ACTD) phase, but likely to be based on a boosted version of an existing weapon capped with an exosphere third stage. Reaction time between detection of the rocket and the fighter crew launching the KKV would be in the order of under one minute!

Clearly, such an intercept would have to be largely managed by machines.

In the broader scheme of things, automation and increasing reliance on remote sensing is also entering the field of battle area interdiction (BAI), designed principally to knock out large second-echelon formations of enemy armour and pockets of artillery, and for deep interdiction way behind enemy lines. This will further remove the fighter pilot from the target discrimination process. The US, which leads the field, is working on a series of exotic *Talon* programmes, whereby target data derived from sensing satellites, J-STARS and even Elint platforms is disseminated to the strike forces while *en route* to the target. The bizarre new cornucopia of stand-off air-to-ground 'super smart' weapons and their submunitions (aired more fully later in the book) will make increasing use of such data. Thus, a series of target signature templates – based on SAR or high-frequency millimetre wave (MMW) radar, laser-radar (ladar), or infrared or E-O imagery – can be conveyed directly to the attacking aircraft alongside updated coordinates. This can be done by means of a satellite relay link and fed directly into their weapons' seekers to assist with precise target lock-on during the terminal phase of weapon flight.

The new weapons' inherent stand-off capability is made possible by new hybrid inertial global positioning system (GPS) Navstar guidance which will take them to the target vicinity prior to the programmed terminal guidance taking over. It implies that the pilots dropping them will not be obliged in any way to scrutinize the target in detail prior to weapons release. The attacking crews will simply call-up the appropriate stores stations, programme the weapons to fly to selected coordinates conveyed alongside the envisaged target templates, and then lob 'em and leave. This is indeed super smart technology in its own right. It is not without potential problems, however. What if, for example, a convoy picked up by J-STARS or satellite and passed on for attack turns out not to be a string of trucks conveying war *matériel* to the front line, but busloads of refugees, nuns and orphans!? That might be an extreme example of erroneous targeting, but in the fog of war it is sadly becoming all too possible.

Target hand-off technology is also being rapidly assimilated into the world of CAS, permitting fast-moving strike jets to lay down a barrage of fire blind, based purely on coordinates fed into their weapons-aiming computers in coded messages via a radio link. Pilots equipped with such devices as an automatic target hand off system (ATHS) receiver will be able to simply 'pickle' their weapons loads when the pointers on their head-up displays (HUDs) instruct them to do so, without recourse to examining (if at all visible) what lies beneath the HUD's aiming cursor. Blue-on-blue casualties occurred in the Gulf War even when passive 'friendly flags' such as infrared reflectors were employed. It poses the simple question: does excessive reliance upon automation result in an expectancy that the targets concerned have been adequately vetted? In the field of CAS, where friendly and enemy troops might easily be intermixed, the need to identify who is who becomes paramount. The perilous profession of Forward Air Controller (FAC) target-spotting remains equally valid today.

All the new developments are exciting, but a healthy gestation period, during which time operational procedures with extra built-in fail-safes can be established, seems to be essential if future tragedies are to be reduced to a minimum. The military has always taken a utilitarian stance with regard to friendly casualties (what is now widely termed fratricide), glumly accepting that a small percentage of losses may be an unavoidable by-product of prosecuting a successful air war. However, clear lines of responsibility have to be established, along with carefully understood Rules of Engagement (RoE) for different intensities of conflict. This is made essential by the increasing commitment to policing actions rather than all-out war, and the modern political and humanitarian dicta that 'all possible means must be taken to assiduously avoid civilian casualties' (euphemistically described as collateral damage).

At what point does a fighter pilot refuse to engage a target handed-down during the sortie, given that most of them are eager to do their job and blast the assigned target to bits? The outcome of the enquiry into the UN helicopter shootdown will be particularly illuminating in this respect.

In the Aftermath of the Storm

The remarkable F-117A Nighthawk stealth fighter also proved its mettle during the Gulf War. That peculiar polyhedron product from the famous Lockheed 'Skunk Works' represented the culmination of three years of intense flight-test work carried out under the *Have Blue* Experimental Stealth Tactical (XST) effort, followed by close-on a decade's worth of covert maturation. This hitherto stage-shy performer had peeped out from behind the curtains during late 1988 and made just a token cameo appearance over the Panama Canal Zone during Operation *Just Cause* the following December, before being thrust centre stage at the top of the billing for Operation *Desert Storm*. It took the fight direct to downtown Baghdad immediately after the city's

During the Gulf War, conventionally-armed cruise missiles were the first weapons to be fired in anger. Launched from ships and submarines, they woke up and exhausted the Iraqi defences in downtown Baghdad just before SEAD and stealth INT arrived on the scene. This use of land, sea and air combined was a key factor in the success of Desert Storm. *(McDonnell Douglas)*

defences had been subdued by a volley of tactical air-launched decoys (TALDs), conventionally armed Tomahawk cruise missiles, and barrages of HARMs. None of these was available during the Vietnam War, and the Iraqis probably quite justifiably considered some of them aircraft in their own right.

Using strictly complied-with times over target (TOT), deconflicted headings and heights, waves of the Bat Planes disgorged their 2,000 lb GBU-27A/B laser-homing smart bombs with astonishing precision, effectively severing the neck of the Iraqi Command & Control, Communications system during the first three nights of the offensive. This quickly left the forward-emplaced Iraqi ground forces stranded. Fearful of advancing and equally unable to retreat through the second-echelon enclaves of the die-hard Republican Guard, the front-line ranks comprising mostly reserves and conscripts quickly fragmented and

Another key ingredient in the success of Desert Storm *was modern satellite-netted communications. Here, chairman of the Joint Chief of Staffs, Colin Powell, speaks to President George Bush from Saudi Arabia. (US DoD)*

surrendered in droves once US Army aviation began the forward sweep for the Coalition ground advance. During separate attacks, the 42 F-117As committed to the theatre at Khamis Mushayt Air Base in Saudi Arabia similarly used their precision bombing capability to knock out key enemy chemical and biological warfare production and storage facilities, timing their bomb passes so that the rising sun would dissipate the various volatile agents. A similar raid during Week Two of the aerial campaign also knocked out a squadron of Tu-16 and Xian B-6D *Badger* bombers at Al Taqaddum that were being prepared for a chemical weapons attack.

Such delicate operations would not have been possible using stock fighters, even if equipped with commensurate smart systems. Only the cloak of stealth radar-attenuating technology provided the necessary freedom to acquire and bomb the targets so precisely, and with much-reduced support: the stealth strike packages mostly flew without escort protection. This was particularly well demonstrated during the series of attacks carried out against the Iraqi nuclear facility located just south of Baghdad. An initial daylight attack undertaken by 32 F-16C Fighting Falcons equipped with dumb bombs, backed by 16 MiGCAP and escort F-15 Eagles, four EF-111A Ravens and eight F-4G *Wild Weasels*, achieved very limited success. Eight F-117As (requiring one-sixth of the AAR tanking back-up put up for the bigger package) sent in to do the job properly under the cloak of darkness proved successful, knocking out three of the four reactors on the first night alone. They finished the job the following week. Remarkably, the F-117A Wing logged 1,271 combat sorties without even a hint of a scratch on the aircraft, despite having to contend with ferocious flak: more than 3,000 AAA pieces, backed by 60 SAM batteries, according to 415th TFS commander Lt-Col Ralph Getchell. Two thousand tons of smart bombs were expended, for a 95 per cent success rate.

However, for every technical wonder which performed beyond expectations, there existed some

Catch me if you can – the F-117A stealth fighter, known variously as the Nighthawk and Black Jet, was the most radical aircraft to see action in the Gulf War. It is actually quite a large machine, but is crewed by a solo aviator who uses the cover of night as well as stealth technology to hide his presence. The butterfly tail comprises two all-moving rudderons. (Lockheed)

unexpected shortfalls in other areas, and some surprises. For example, the easy-to-maintain multi-role F-16 (or swing-role fighter, as it was heralded at its Service debut back in 1979, and now a Free World mainstay type) inflicted surprisingly little damage. The daylight interdiction strike against the nuclear reactor, already described, was unsuccessful. This also was largely true of the CAS/BAI missions undertaken by the do-it-all F-16 'Electric Jet', despite some gallant and daring accomplishments in destroying enemy SAM and AAA complexes. Many strikes degenerated into every-man-for-himself harassment bombing sorties. At one stage, F-16 missions were ordered to close prior to 16:00L so that the dust and debris they left hanging over the battle zone would settle in time to permit the smart bombers to acquire and attack their targets accurately by night!

It was the vastly more expensive and sophisticated types which did the lion's share of the work, including aircraft which the Pentagon had hoped to retire in the aftermath of the collapse of the Warsaw Pact. Their

outstanding performance in the Gulf ensured that retirement was deferred. The 20-year-old F-111F was a case in point. This swing-wing jet, designed originally to carry out nuclear attacks in Europe, went on to serve almost exclusively as a smart attacker with targeting accuracies equal to or better than the much-lauded F-117A Nighthawk. It is being retained until new autonomous smart weapons, capable of being carried by fighters and bombers alike, are fielded at the end of the twentieth century. During *Desert Storm*, Col Tom Lennon's F-111Fs stationed at Taif comprised less than seven per cent of USAF air power committed to the theatre yet accounted for more than half of all targets confirmed as destroyed, a staggering 2,203 in all! The F-111F also was the sole machine in-theatre capable of dropping the giant 4,700 lb GBU-28 *Deep Throat* laser-guided penetrating bomb, the only weapon capable of taking the war directly to the Iraqi leaders in their deep subterranean bunkers.

Operations & Maintenance support costs for the aged Aardvarks (in common with the newer F-117A) remains in the order of three times those for the F-16, with costs likely to rise owing to increased age and contracted numbers. However, during the height of the recent swingeing US 'Bottom-Up' defence review, every four-star general polled by USAF boss Merrill A. McPeak (a former F-111 Wing boss) concurred that the F-111Fs had to be retained. Hopefully, the current *Pacer Strike* digital avionics update will make them cheaper to fly and even more capable. Its originally troubled airframe was later rectified, the fixes enabling General Dynamics (now part of Lockheed) to provide a 10,000-hour warranty, which means at current utilization rates it will remain structurally sound through to the year 2010.

Australia, the only other operator of this previously much-maligned machine, has recently acquired surplus American examples and fully intends to keep its F-111C/Gs flying until they become worn-out, face-lifted in the Avionics Updated Program (AUP). Unfortunately, west of the production plant at Komsomolsk-na-Amur in Russia, which is busy producing the Russian equivalent for the 1990s and beyond, the Su-34, there is no replacement in sight. The USAF has already taken delivery of its full quota of rather different F-15E

Eagle dual-role fighters (DRFs). Eclipsed by the success of the F-117A, the F-111F, one of the outstanding performers during *Desert Storm*, will soon fade away virtually unnoticed without a suitable successor.

Perhaps the most glaring shortfall during *Desert Storm* was theatre reconnaissance, essential for pre-strike and post-strike BDA and localized theatre intelligence-gathering. Owing to the paucity of traditional image-gathering reconnaissance jets engaged in combat duties in the Gulf, excessive reliance was placed upon satellites such as the KH-11/13 series, which often found their targets obscured by cloud, while the Lacrosse radar-mapping versions were not always available to map ground targets, creating what the commanders described as episodic coverage. The absence of adequate timely photo-reconnaissance a week or so into the air war resulted in pinpoint strikes against hastily chosen targets, and the assignment of an inordinate number of reconnaissance sorties to radar and optical sweeps in search of the elusive TELs, as soon as the *Scud* and derivative Al Hussein missiles entered the fray.

As the air war progressed, it became increasingly

The 494th FS form a squadron 'Victory-V' in front of one their swing-wing steeds. The F-111F accounted for only seven per cent of the force but knocked out over 60 per cent of the targets during Desert Storm! *The 66* Pave Tack *aircraft were stationed at Taif near Mecca, in Saudi Arabia. This one carries a typical combat fit of two GBU-24A/B bunker-busting Paveway III LLLGBs, plus a pair of 'winder AAMs for self-defence. (Craig Brown)*

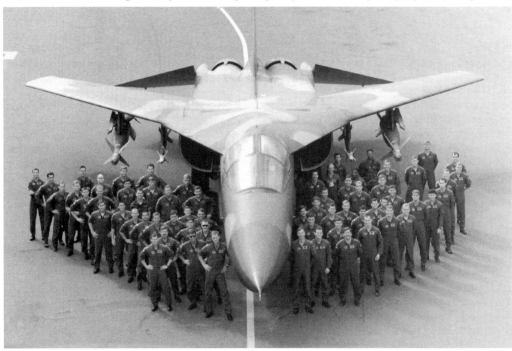

apparent that too many otherwise perfectly executed strikes were being carried out against relatively worthless targets. For example, the existing sideways-looking and forward-looking infrared (SLIR and FLIR) sensor technology available to the Tornado GR.1As and F-15E DRFs respectively, were unable to differentiate between *Scud* TELs and articulated lorries driven out to the desert at night as decoys. Relying on satellites in their lofty orbits to locate and distinguish between genuine Command & Control bunkers and civilian air raid shelters proved equally problematic. Similarly, many hardened aircraft shelters and dug-in tanks were struck repeatedly, long after they had ceased to pose a threat.

Photo-recce jets employing a combination of infrared and camera sensors, fused with signals-receiving equipment, could have painted a much clearer picture. However, there were not enough of them and, somewhat ironically, those that were able to produce such quality intelligence had not yet been adequately netted into the Riyadh Command & Control distribution system – the so-called Black Cell. This was because they were drawn from second-line forces such as the US Air National Guard, or were European in origin. Only 18 USAF and a dozen US Navy jets were involved in full-time recce duties, leaving token forces of RAF Jaguar GR.1As and Armèe de l'Air Mirage F.1CRs (the latter quite sensibly being prohibited from operations for several days owing to the possibility of them being mistaken for Iraqi Mirage F1.EQs) to bridge the gap. The untimely withdrawal of the USAF's glamour machine, the Mach 3 hotshot Lockheed SR-71A Blackbird or 'Habu' only eight months prior to the Iraqi incursion into Kuwait, was most keenly felt.

Intelligence garnered by the slow, high-wheeling Lockheed U-2R was prodigious but quite rightly tended to focus on Republican Guard positions to help the ground forces plan their pincer attacks, and not to produce target area imagery for the deep strike crews. Even Gen 'Stormin'' Norman Schwarzkopf acknowledged that *Desert Storm* represented one of the few occasions when pilots were tasked to fly combat missions without fresh photos of their targets, some of the imagery being 36 hours old and potentially well past its use-by date. 'It was a void all of us felt,' he later acquiesced. Moves are afoot under numerous *Talon* and *Constant Source* initiatives being managed by the USAF Space Warfare Center at Colorado Springs to disseminate useful target data to the battle area commanders and strike Wings in a more timely manner, but the means by which the images and other data are collected is still excessively dependant on remote sensors.

The shortfall in tactical theatre reconnaissance

The US is building a series of HAE UAVs for work in high-threat areas, including the Tier 2-Plus and Tier 3-Minus. Back in the early 1970s, similar work was undertaken on the less successful Compass Cope programme, which was eventually killed in favour of a new U-2R spyplane production run. The antipathy felt towards UAVs (formerly remotely piloted vehicles) has subsided a great deal, and the Tier efforts will make a really big splash in the years to come. (TRA)

capability was to have been addressed by the Martin-Marietta Advanced Tactical Airborne Reconnaissance System (ATARS), to be fielded on several American 'Teenage' fighters (specially reconfigured F-16R and F/A-18D-RC variants) and medium-range Teledyne Ryan Aeronautical Model 234 unmanned aerial vehicles (UAVs). It was to have included facilities for live and recorded imagery derived from E-O cameras and infrared sensors, which could be in-flight edited by a back-seat flyer or console operator at a ground terminal, and data-linked to interested parties. However, problems with the ATARS (mostly relating to image blurring and hiccupping) resulted in its recent cancellation as a package, although work on the individual sensors continues. The only comparable technology presently operational comprises the RAF's recce-Tornado GR.1As. However, these are in relatively short supply, and might not be made available to supplement the dwindling number of American tactical reconnaissance jets in a future conflict.

To a certain extent, concerns about the shortfall in conventional tactical recce aircraft are 'emotional as much as factual' as pointed out by USAF Deputy Chief Lt Gen Buster Glosson, formerly in charge of targeting during the Gulf War, and based on outdated thinking. The dedicated reconnaissance jet may be a thing of the past. The solutions appear to rest in newer and better onboard aircraft sensors based on improved versions of the F-15/16's low-altitude navigation/targeting infrared for night (LANTIRN) and the Tornado GR.1's thermal imaging and laser designator (TIALD, discussed later in the book). These are designed primarily to assist with smart bomb deliveries but nonetheless serve as superb BDA recce sensors in their own right. There is also an acknowledgement that high-altitude, long-endurance (HAE) UAVs nowadays offer a creditable alternative to the chisel-nosed recce jets of yesteryear.

The US is toying with a Tier 2-Plus HAE UAV effort, designed to stay aloft for up to 24 hours at a stretch at heights of up to 65,000 ft, and map up to 1,900 point targets daily using SAR radar plus E-O and infrared imagery, and convey this material in near real-time via satellite link, precisely to meet BDA needs. Ten are being built. Concurrent work on Tier 3-Minus, a stealthy UAV honed to penetrate hostile defences and map the enemy's electronic order of battle (EOB), is also moving from the electronic drawing boards to the hardware stage of development. Together, these should fulfil the round-the-clock, all-weather tactical reconnaissance roles that were until recently flown by select RF-4C Phantom IIs equipped with 1970s-vintage devices. The intrinsic hazards of these missions makes HAE UAVs ideally suited to the task.

However, these eyes-in-the-sky developments do not diminish the overall need for much-improved autonomous target acquisition sensor technology – to be used for air-to-air and air-to-ground attack – which will permit the fighter crews to make judgements about target validity based on top-quality imagery and radar maps derived from their own sensor-cueing, as a fail-safe. Whether or not to press the firing trigger, once cleared to do so, is a decision that must rest in their hands.

In reviewing some of the technology which won the war in the Gulf, and some of the trends that are taking place in its aftermath, it is becoming clear that a great deal of ambivalence exists towards modern technology. Few would question that it provides a vital ingredient to success, but neither is it a panacea: ultimately, it is the aviators who win or lose the day, and retaining the initiative of the man-in-the-loop is vital.

The next air battle, which in all likelihood will be a truly multi-national affair crossing even more delicate political borders than those confronted in the Gulf War, and quite possibly against a more technologically advanced foe than Iraq, will be one where human solutions will be as important as the technological ones. In a large conflict, the extra variables generated by increased numbers tends sooner or later to cause confusion, and confusion in turn tends to degrade technology very rapidly indeed.

One or Two Heads in the Cockpit?

Extending beyond remote off-board sensing and hand-me-down instructions, but not entirely unrelated, is the unresolved and still very controversial issue regarding crew composition: one or two flyers in the fighter cockpit, which works best? No other single point of contention gets more aviation analysts red-faced and hot under the collar, or is inclined to generate quite such stony-faced silence on the part of the actual aviators engaged in the job of combat flying, because of the increasingly political slant of the debate. The argument has raged at least since the introduction of the F-4 Phantom II in the early-1960s. Logically, if some of the aforementioned problems with hand-me-down targeting are to be avoided, then two-in-the-tub is preferred; one crewman can concentrate on flying the aircraft, the other on communications, target acquisition and tracking, electronic warfare, damage assessment and a host of tasks which all too readily saturate the workload of the solo flyer, and sometimes overwhelm him.

However, it is not quite so clear-cut as that. The expense of crewing fighters with two people is prohibitive in this era of shrinking defence budgets, both in terms of the costs of training and maintaining sufficient cadres of personnel, and in terms of design and weight penalties on the aircraft (twin-seaters are usually more expensive and suffer a 2–5 per cent loss in overall performance, and are vastly more expensive to design and build when preserving stealth characteristics is paramount). Furthermore, several single-seaters, on the face of things, acquitted themselves admirably during the Gulf War. The stealthy F-117A, rests in a class of its own, but the obsolescing Anglo-French SEPECAT Jaguar and the Dassault Mirage F.1CR did well. So did the GAU-8/A Avenger gun-toting Fairchild A/OA-10A 'Warthog' (slow and ugly, but well hung, as the saying goes!) which has not yet been stuffed with so many new gadgets so as to become troublesome to its pilots.

The more detailed analyses that have emerged since the Gulf War are equally clouded. Certainly, the F-16 (in its 'then' configuration, minus AMRAAMs or LANTIRN targeting/navigation sensor pod capability) came out badly, and accidents relating to pilot g-induced loss of consciousness (G-LOC) long ago gave rise to the derogatory nickname Lawn Dart for this machine. The little Texan has since proved it can live up to the job, and in style, however.

At approximately 11:00L on 27 December 1992, a 363rd FW Viper (one of the F-16's more flattering nicknames) on a *Southern Watch* patrol bagged an Iraqi MiG-25 *Foxbat* operating 20 miles deep into the Southern no-fly zone, using an AIM-120 AMRAAM of the class normally reserved for bigger, more sophisticated fighters such as the F-15 Eagle, F-14 Tomcat and Panavia Tornado. This was the first combat use of the missile. Then, at 05:45 GMT on 28 February 1994, while flying near Mostar, Bosnia, in support of Operation *Deny Flight*, and having received clearance to shoot from the Vicenza-based Combined Air Operations Command Center (CAOCC) via an E-3 Sentry AWACS, an F-16 from the 526th FS destroyed a Serb G-4 Super Galeb with an AMRAAM too. Notably, the missile-firing was preceded by visual confirmation of the target as hostile (it was sighted as one of six Super Galebs pulling-up from a bomb pass against a Moslem munitions facility that murky afternoon), and even a radio warning – sound doctrine for anything less than all-out war. The initial shoot was rapidly followed by two more kills against further fleeing Super Galebs by the same pilot, this time using AIM-9 Sidewinder short-range AAMs, before another F-16 from a second Flight engaged and brought down a fourth G-4. This successful intercept marked the first air combat action performed in the 44-year history of NATO.

More significantly, perhaps, it was the first time a Viper had been used in a scenario which hitherto remained strictly within the bailiwick of more sophisticated fighters: a stand-off kill with a radar-homing missile, followed by a close-in mopping-up with short-ranged heat missiles. Not surprisingly, the F-16 is now seldom irreverently referred to as the Lawn Dart and, in its latest Lockheed-Fort Worth production formats, provides an essential ingredient at the front rather than the rear of any modern fighter gorilla package. Its unchanged need to engage at short-to-medium ranges makes it the great air-to-air fist of diplomacy, and it can be argued that in accomplishing its recent exploits it might have relegated the heavyweights to use only in all-out war. This in turn raises the question whether the USAF needs 400 or more $100m+ fourth-generation stealthy Lockheed-Boeing F-22A Rapiers, when a smaller number, used selectively as silver bullets during the opening phase of an air war to counter the latest Russian-designed hardware, would probably suffice to meet the US DoD's latest win-hold-win concept (winning one regional conflict while holding the enemy at bay in another, and this having been accomplished, winning the second).

Indeed, the development of the F-16 serves as an excellent illustration of how single-seat bantamweight fighter technology has progressed over the past two decades. It is far removed from the primarily visual meteorological conditions (VMC) Lightweight Fighter (LWF) that spawned it, pushed forward by USAF Gen Brown who insisted on a 'low-cost, swing-role companion' to supplement his expensive dedicated air superiority F-15A Eagle. Indeed, many of the early-production F-16s which followed this LWF philosophy through the first succession of manufacturer's Blocks are being put out to pasture or have been consigned to second-line duties as hacks.

The original LWF airframe was subjected to unexpected loads when the USAF and its foreign military sales (FMS) clients began to hang heavy bombloads and missiles onto the type, and then proceeded to 'bend' it. The strenuous dynamic loads have resulted in numerous cracks deep in the structure. Higher than expected utilization rates resulting from its routine 90 per cent mission capable rate (MCR) – or availability, to coin the traditional term – have merely accelerated this process. It is important to note that the 9 g tolerance widely toted upon the F-16's introduction was originally based on a less-than-full fuel load and just two AIM-9 Sidewinder AAMs suspended on its wing-tips. It is simply wearing out more quickly than expected on a calendar year basis. At least these early examples are making way for follow-on batches of the newer, re-engined and beefed-up F-16 production Blocks which feature advanced communications, improved radar and facilities for more sophisticated weapons, alongside structural re-engineering commensurate to the task.

Similarly, the design that lost out to the YF-16 in the LWF fly-off, the Northrop YF-17 Cobra, was later adapted by McDonnell-Douglas for strenuous US Navy/Marine Corps service as the F/A-18 Hornet. This much heavier and predominantly single-seat all-rounder is presently being stretched into the longer-legged, even heavier, all-weather interdiction F/A-18E/F variant, proving its growth potential (although some would argue the E/F is in fact an altogether brand-new aircraft). With the addition of HOTAS, wide-angle HUDs capable of handling FLIR imagery, and excellent navigation and ballistics computers, the one-man jet concept has been vindicated. However, the LWF concept, which provided the original impetus for the F-16 and F/A-18, has not.

There is a definable trend towards bigger and more expensive single-seaters in the medium-weight class (35,000 lb, all-up). A mere 10 per cent or so of production is given over to twin-seaters to be used primarily as Operational Conversion Unit (OCU) trainers and Standardization & Evaluation (Stan/Eval) pilot checkride aircraft, which are employed principally to help pilots transition to these high-workload, and far from disposable machines. This 90:10 ratio will also be the pattern for the new range of fighters of Western European origin, such as the Eurofighter 2000, Saab JAS 39 Gripen and Dassault Rafale. The philosophy also holds true for the heavier high-performance tactical fighters such as the Lockheed F-22A Rapier and Sukhoi Su-35. Both are in full scale engineering development, and destined to be built primarily as single-stick machines with a modicum of twin-seaters incorporated into the production runs. The twin-seaters are intended to help build confidence in newcomers, most of whom will be young and very fit in order to take advantage of the extraordinary abilities of these machines, and thus by definition relatively inexperienced.

The increasing weight and complexity of modern fighter design appear to have effectively signalled the death-knell of the dedicated twin-seater which, for all its merits, is sadly becoming a thing of the past. F-14D Tomcat production has now ended, and Tornado F.3 and F-15E DRF production (in its definitive export F-15I/XP configuration) will fizzle out before the turn of the new century. As fighter procurement now seems firmly rooted in concurrent single-seater and twin-seater production, the crew debate can be thrown wide-open once again.

The following reasoning remains contentious, but many now quite rightly argue that the better path

would be to procure a healthier percentage of twin-seaters and reduce the solo-stick composition to a ratio something more akin to a 70:30. This would allow for more growth and specialized taskings, especially when avionics need to be adapted to meet unexpected contingencies; their interactive displays would ably permit the twin-seater to be flown by just one crewman *à la* the single-seater, if necessary, in lower-intensity scenarios where the extra pair of hands and eyes are not essential. Hence tandem seating as opposed to side-by-side, so that the pilot's grandstand view is not impaired when flying solo.

It can be argued that modern flight-training simulators are so good that newly qualified fighter pilots should be able to graduate straight to the soloing slot of high-performance fighters. Such is the realism of the displays and enveloping graphics seen through the windshield (and even a blown canopy), despite the lack of flight dynamics such as *g*-forces (though stall-shuddering and stick feedback forces are well-demonstrated), that many question the validity of producing even a token quantity of twin-sticked subvariants. If this mentality persists, then advanced simulators may well put the final nails in the coffin of the twin-seat fighter, and sooner rather than later owing to the rapid growth in increased-capacity, reduced-volume, very high-speed computer processors.

Latter-day *Wild Weasel* and reconnaissance crews flying the dwindling number of remaining F-4G and RF-4C Phantom IIs (none of which were manufactured as single-seaters at any time during the 5,195-aircraft production run of this pedigree) are unanimous in voicing their concerns over this issue. Within the US Services, the SEAD and reconnaissance missions are not being reassigned to suitably equipped twin-seater trainers adapted to the task, but to later F-15A and F-16C production, using podded technology. The RAF, Luftwaffe and Aeronautica Militare Italiane, which continue to

Simulators have progressed a great deal over the past two decades, thanks to advances in computer technology. Previously used for procedural function training only, they now can simulate a complete combat mission – bar the physiological and psychological strains associated with flying the real thing. The McDonnell Douglas Modular Aircrew Simulation System is a simple plug-in device that can emulate the characteristics of a number of fighters, including the Eagle and Hornet. Here, a Hornet pilot and his wingman are chasing two Shenyang F-7s (Chinese MiG-21s), with 'Gun' selected in nose-level, banking flight in a modest 2 g manoeuvre. (McDonnell-Douglas)

progressively field yet more specialized subvariants of the Tornado to fulfil these tasks, appear to have a better grasp of the need for twin-seaters in these most demanding roles – although it is questionable whether twin-seater models of the Eurofighter 2000 will be acquired as replacements.

Preserving an Institution

Particular angst is being felt in some circles because of the inevitable erosion in the navigation cadres which make up the extra crewman, and the institutional knowledge that goes along with them. In the case of the *Wild Weasels*, this knowledge and expertise has taken decades to mature. The question being posed is what happens when the do-it-all systems are jammed or go awry? It's the oft-quoted calculator syndrome: have microchips replaced the need to grasp mental arithmetic?

The Luftwaffe experience in the aftermath of the collapse of the Nazi regime and the Service's very gradual post-World War II return to normality as an effective fighting force and incorporation into NATO, was that the re-establishment of skills across the board proved to be a long and very painful process. It took the Luftwaffe nigh on two decades and considerable quantities of Deutschmarks to re-establish their cadres of middle-ranking experienced ground crews alone, during which time crashes seemed an all too regular occurrence. Sadly, bits from hundreds of Republic F-84 Thunderstreaks and Lockheed F-104 Starfighters litter the German countryside, mute testimony to the painful process of having to climb the learning curve all over again. And all of that despite quality crew training conducted in ideal conditions in the US. Years from now, attempting to relearn the back-seat institution might prove not only costly but equally impossible, particularly in the specialized fields of EW, given the relentless expansion of ever more mind-boggling technology sweeping modern air arms.

It has been claimed that a mere decade's worth of exclusive reliance on a pilots-only air force will cause the deep pool of navigators' experience that has been honed over the last 60 years to evaporate completely. If this holds true, what of the future? Will there exist droves of pilots pondering why there are no longer any whiz-kids who can sift out all the bugs from a maturing navigation computer, which all the engineers with their seemingly incomprehensible 'geek talk' and hundreds of diagrams fail to explain during induction lectures a million words long, let alone in a few meaningful sentences!? Recreating such a pool of knowledge would take years, and cost a great deal in human and financial terms. The time has come for navigators to shout and

for their hard-won skills to be properly assessed!

Ironically, the war in Vietnam underlined the need for dedicated back-seat specialists such as Weapons System Officers and Electronic Warfare Officers (wizzos and EWOs), and their trade had been honed to perfection when the Gulf War broke out. However, their contribution was grossly and deliberately underplayed in an effort to exaggerate single-seat fighter prowess.

The battle-hardened Israeli Heyl Ha'Avir have long since known the wisdom of operating mixed swarms, tailored as expediency and operational requirements dictate, while retaining as big a baseline of expertise as is possible. Virtually their entire twin-seater F-16D stock has been adapted to the all-weather Brakeet (Thunderbolt) mission, which has taken advantage of a surplus of experienced F-4 Kurnass (Sledgehammer) navigators (with training and pilot checkrides being only an ancillary function of these twin-seat fighters). Yet the service continues to acquire further copies of the F-16C Netz single-seater as this is cheaper and just as effective to operate by day, and has superior performance in the air-to-air arena. It is a healthy, well-adjusted attitude, unfettered by petty intra-Service politics and rivalries which have until very recently plagued some other air arms rather than spurred them to greater things. A similar mix of F-15I twin-seat strikers (21 on order) will be delivered during 1997, to work alongside the Service's air superiority F-15A-D Baz models. The F-15I will be incorporated into the fleet at about the same time that the last pool of elderly (for fighter crews) F-4 Kurnass navigators would otherwise be hanging up their spurs in exchange for permanent desk duties or a civilian job. The F-15I's introduction has been timed to build upon operational knowledge in the back-seat department before that role fades into anecdotal legend in the officers' bars.

The USAF, in the light of Israeli doctrine and its own experience during *Desert Storm*, is gradually coming around to this way of thinking. It has already begun to form ready-to-fight intervention Wings comprising a gaggle of types, as pioneered by the 7440th Combat Wing under Operation *Proven Force* during the Gulf War. This was a unique organization that prosecuted the air war in the North as a cohesive force flying from the one base, Incirlik, in Turkey. This goes beyond the basic *Linebacker II* era strike package concept by incorporating multi-engined ground-loving old bastards (GLOBs) such as AAR tankers and even long-range bombers, all under one roof.

One such experimental Superwing is the 366th Wing stationed at Mountain Home AFB, Idaho. Within the context of the mutually supportive, self-contained strike force, it is being evolved as three various-sized packages. Excluding tankers, optional bomber input, and specially seconded EW support, these comprise: 'A' with 14 singles and six twins; 'B' with 24 singles and 10 twins; and 'C', with 30 singles and a minimum of a dozen twins. With regard to the crew composition debate, this doctrine does in fact merge single-seaters and twin-seaters as fully fledged operational partners in something akin to a 70:30 mix. It is already beginning to have an impact on even the relatively impenetrable predominantly single-seater Wings containing only one type of aircraft. This had been a pattern that remained strong during the USAF's first 45 years of operations, until *Desert Storm* created new ideas. For example, the 48th 'Statue of Liberty' Wing at RAF Lakenheath, Suffolk and the 3rd FW at Elmendorf, Alaska, both now constitute complementary squadrons of F-15E interdictors alongside F-15C/D air superiority models of the Eagle, where direct comparisons can be made. Hopefully, the experiment will prove to be successful, and break down the crew debate to a position where a more sensible appraisal can be made, before all the wizzos and EWOs are pensioned off.

Overall, it seems that a healthier balance between single-seaters and twin-seaters is the best route forward. The single-seaters maintain the edge in performance and reduced operating costs. The twin-seaters maintain the institutional knowledge and assist with more specialized tasks such as deep strike, SEAD, and reconnaissance by night or inclement weather, especially against a heavily defended target where a competent navigator is a far better bet than a stack of cold-blooded microchips (which, as many pilots acquiesce, possess no innate desire to survive). Specialized equipment could be strapped on as required, be it radar 'sniffers', recce sensors or specialized targeting aids, and operated using standard avionics architecture common to both single-seater and twin-seater models of the aircraft which would be able to accommodate the same array of sensors and weapons. Using common design features which can support modular podded or internally carried hardware, minor changes of software, along with some pre-take-off calibration of specific antennae and optics (all conducted during the normal ground turnaround refuelling and rearming cycles), would be all that is required to adapt a machine on the flight-line to any number of tasks. However, this concept is another generation away. At the present time, different mission requirements are being met by different aircraft, or adaptations of a family.

While not modular in the hardware sense, the Russian Sukhoi Bureau has come very close to producing an array of types from its baseline T-10.

There is the vanilla Su-27 *Flanker* air superiority fighter and Su-27UB twin-seat trainer stablemate (with full operational capability). The Su-27P single-seater and Su-30 (formerly the Su-27PU) twin-seater are optimized for strategic interception duties and embody extensive data-links for intercommunication and long-range missile guidance. The Su-30M is the basic fighter with added provisions for ground attack. The Su-33 (formerly Su-27K) is the navalized version. The side-by-side seat Su-34 is an advanced strike model (formerly Su-27IB). Probably far from being the definitive version is the canard, digital avionics-equipped Su-35! SEAD radar-smashing, plus Elint and E-O reconnaissance versions are also being evolved, all from a common set of blueprints, and pushed aggressively by Mikhail Simonov, Sukhoi's general designer.

There is nothing comparable in the West. What is particularly commendable is that these diverse

RUSSIAN DESIGNATIONS

B	Bombardirovtchik	strike-bomber
IB	Istrebeite	fighter-bomber
K	Korabelniy	seafaring (carrierborne)
P	Perekhvatchik	interceptor
M	Modifatsirovanji	modified or updated
R	Razvedchik	reconnaissance
UB	Uchybno Boyevoy	twin-seat combat trainer

Individual model names may be added to these, for example MiG-25RB-K for a *Foxbat* reconnaissance-strike, configuration/model K, which does not imply carrier compatibility! NATO code-names, such as *Fulcrum* for the MiG-29, often translate into quite exotic Russian equivalents, in this instance Tochka Opori or Pivot Point, which CIS pilots sometimes adopt as nicknames, as they have in this example.

high-performance machines can be operated using the bare minimum of ground support equipment and a core set of war-readiness spares kits, making mixing-and-matching relatively straightforward.

Whatever the technical and moral dilemmas facing planners and engineers, and the continuing debate regarding these in the aftermath of war in the Gulf, flying and maintaining any modern fighter at an operational level in wartime or peacetime tempo begins with the ground crews' morning shift, and the aviators' 'show time' in their squadron building. The flying starts there.

Chapter Two

LAUNCH

Aircrew show time at their squadron complex is usually posted on the noticeboard the day before the flight, allowing the aviators to undertake necessary preparations. For example, an early launch (07:00L) probably means turning up at 05:00L or earlier in the morning, and a 12-hour alcohol-free period prior to flying is usually mandated. During peacetime, apart from occasional deployments, sortie-surge exercises and Operational Readiness Inspections (ORIs), most bases operate something akin to a normal working day, with two lots of launches and recoveries comprising two Flights of four jets apiece. This means crews may actually fly as little as 180 hours annually, or 15 hours a month (probably the bare minimum required to maintain proficiency) or, given a standard sortie duration of 1.5–2 hours, about twice a week.

In between, they fill their time with ancillary duties as military officers, making up the hours in the simulator whenever possible (this being the primary means of practising emergency drills) and getting to grips with the basic cockpit switchology. Of course in combat, or during Alert, show time can be any time of the day or night.

Mission Preparation

The first stop is at the squadron's Duty Desk. This is a counter where the day's flying schedule is posted, and acts as a focal point for tracking the flying activities. A big board lists the crew, their assigned call-sign, their aircraft tail number, and scheduled take-off time (customarily shown in Zulu, or GMT). Clocks on the wall show Local time, GMT and, in the US, the different time zones. It is here that the crews later sign out for the aircraft, their signatures attesting that the flights will be conducted in accordance with all applicable rules and regulations.

The next stop is to pick up a classified document called the 'frag' (Fragmentary Order). This is published every day during wartime and for contingency work, and contains the directions and mission objectives for every aircraft participating in the day's operations. All aircraft are included – tankers, bombers, fighters of all types, etc – and the crews scans through this hefty document in order to find the particulars for their Flight (usually of four aircraft, though often split into pairs), such as IFF codes, weapons, mission objective, tanker aerial refuelling control points (ARCPs) and so on. During gorilla or strike package operations involving many aircraft in the unit, the crews then attend a 10-minute mass briefing, where they receive weather reports and the general theme of the operation. The Intelligence Officer then briefs them on the latest 'intel' and outlines the threats in their area of operation. Finally, the mission commander coordinates altitudes and times so as to deconflict the sorties. After adjournment, the detailed, individual mission planning begins.

For switch-on-and-fly MiGCAP fighters such as the F-15C Eagle, it might only take each Flight as little as another 20–30 minutes to plan their portion of the mission, as they will be heavily reliant on AWACS. For twin-seat SEAD jets like the F-4G, which also functions fairly fluidly over enemy territory in response to the exigencies of combat, it might not take much longer, as so much of the groundwork – loading priority target data into the jet's AN/APR-47 radar-searching computer, and similarly prebriefing target information into the radar-homing missiles – would have already been accomplished by specialists. The residual tasks of mission planning in this instance are split between the front-seaters and back-seaters.

The Flight Lead and other pilots work on the frag

items, the Line-Up Card and coordinate their aerial defensive tactics, plus rendezvous taskings with other players (pilots from other Flights taking part in the mission, whom they support). The Line-Up Card is a 4-inch x 7-inch card carried by each crewmember (often tucked into the flightsuit knee) which bears all the oft-used information for the Flight (call-sign, IFF codes, etc). Meanwhile, the Lead Electronics Warfare Officer (EWO) will work with the other EWOs on the actual flight-plans (the Form 70, which lists all the route points, headings, distances, etc), and prepare the data-transfer modules (DTMs) for the fighters' navigation computers.

For the fighter-bombers, particularly deep interdiction types such as the F-111F, F-117A and F-15E, the detailed flight-planning stage can actually take up to 2 hours to complete. Again, workload division is dependent on crew composition and the size of the Flights; for example, in the case of the twin-seat Aardvark and Eagle DRF, each aircraft is flown by a pilot (known as the Aircraft Commander, or AC), and navigated by a Weapons Systems Officer (WSO, or 'wizzo'). The Flight Lead AC is usually an experienced aviator qualified to do just that, with at least one previous fighter tour (a posting of two to three years at an operational base) behind him. The junior pilots in the Flight might comprise aviators straight out of two years' basic and advanced flight training, some of whom might still be learning the ropes at an OCU. Similarly, the senior navigator is often the most experienced in the Flight, and demonstrates to his fledglings precisely how things are done.

Each of these individuals is assigned a task – and there are many. Notices to Airmen (NOTAMs) have to be checked first so that, for example, the Flight avoids ploughing into glider contestants scheduled for a one-off meet somewhere deep in the Welsh countryside, or a fly-by for the Queen's birthday, or even crop-spraying activity. NOTAMs are updated based on the frag too, including its classified aspects, while most aircrews are fully aware of civil air traffic corridors.

Weather is checked extensively. Munitions are factored in. And, in routine training, at least one realistic target training (RTT) feature, such as a bridge, would be picked out, just to help practice target acquisition, even if the crews' primary tasking was to pound a practice range to bits. Generally, the pilots focus on the pure flying aspects – communications and related settings, and making sure everything and everyone is working together – while the navigators focus more on the low-level legs of the flight-plan, what ranges are open, and the details of the point-to-point flight-plan, comprised of a series of legs between waypoints.

In a combat situation, the target area and enemy EOB is the primary consideration. Headings and heights designed to maximize weapons effectiveness and minimize exposure to enemy defences are crucial, including making use of terrain to mask a low-level ingress, as are coordinates pertaining to tanker ARCPs (to keep them topped-up with fuel on the outbound and inbound legs), and bull's-eyes (focal points on the ground known to the crews but not to the enemy) from which a bearing and range can be provided for the purpose of providing or calling-up MiGCAP, SEAD or other support. Diversionary airfields also must be considered, in case of weather, combat damage or an in-flight emergency.

Until very recently, most strike crews would laboriously plot their flight-plans using old-fashioned maps, rulers and geometry instruments, using a slide-rule or calculator to work out fuel requirements. They would also rely on specialists from intel such as radar prediction artists. These would actually sketch out fuzzy pictures of ground returns and the target (or offset) that the crew should later see on the radarscopes, based on the heading, height and contours of the terrain, and any prominent features, to assist with in-flight interpretation of the raw, direct-view radar imagery. This procedure long predates modern SAR radars, which, by comparison, generate something akin to a constant-scale high-grain photo on the cockpit radarscope. Prediction would also be backed-up by a filing cabinet library stuffed with radarscope photography (RSP) shots gleaned during previous sorties, which served much the same purpose. A great bundle of sketches, RSP snapshots and map-cuttings would then be taken on board the aircraft by the navigator. These rudiments still have to be acquired by navigators during their initial training,

Mission-planning proper for strike crews begins with detailed scrutiny of maps – the 'bumpies'. 1:50,000 scale Ordnance Survey or equivalent are usually used, and Tornado 'nav' Robbie Stewart demonstrates the basics . . . (Andy Evans)

along with celestial navigation (the use of a sextant), dead reckoning and other fundamentals. However, at an operational level, the process has largely given way to computerization.

The first inroad made by computers was the introduction of the DTMs in the late 1970s. A battery-powered pocket-sized device, the DTM could be loaded with mission basics, fed into it one leg at a time using a primitive route-planning computer in the Operations Room – push-buttoning numbers. Loaded-up, it could then be plugged into the cockpit navigation computer, to feed in the intended flight-plan in under 20 seconds. It has been steadily improved over the years, in line with advances in microelectronics. Lear-Siegler (now LSI) led the field, initially with a 64-kilobyte (K) DTM used for the USAF's ARN-101(V) digital modular avionics system (DMAS-mod) F-4 Phantom II update. The latest Harris DTM cartridges can hold 32 megabytes of information – 500 times as much!

The second inroad was created by the RAF, which had long since enjoyed a relationship with inertial moving-map displays (of the type introduced aboard the radarless Harrier and Jaguar). The technology came to the fore with the Service debut of the Panavia Tornado GR.1 in the late 1970s, which introduced a combined radar and projected map display (CRPMD). It can show a moving-map laced with steering cursors, or a relatively good quality radar sweep trace. Switching between the two adds to SA. Additional multi-function display (MFD) CRTs can be called-up alongside this to provide clear, synthesized graphics depicting a plan view of the mission's waypoints, radar sweep limits and aircraft heading and distance in relation to the target. Much of this is made possible by a cassette preparation ground system (CPGS). Crews run an electronic cursor over the map table during flight-planning and click-in key waypoints. The CPGS automatically loads this data into a cassette tape, which can then be carried out to the flight-line and plugged into the cockpit, just like a DTM, to load the flight-plan in about 30 seconds. The CPGS will also carry data pertaining to the terrain, the enemy EOB, tanker 'tow lines', etc.

. . . which are then transferred to cassette tape using the Tornado's CPGS cursor. The cassette will subsequently be inserted into the Tornado's nav-and-attack system to tell the aircraft where to fly, hands-off, on a point-to-point basis. Other data points will include tanker 'tow lines' and radar offsets. American and French INT aviators do pretty much the same thing using more advanced computer-based flight-planning systems such as PALOMA and MSS/AFMSS. (Andy Evans)

The American philosophy has been to expand upon the DTM approach by introducing a new range of easily transported, giant suitcase-sized computer mission-modelling support systems (MSSs), most of them supplied by Harris and Lockheed-Sanders. These enable the entire flight-plan to be drafted in soft copy format on the screen, before it is transferred onto DTMs and discs for loading in the fighter cockpits. The follow-on Lockheed-Sanders Air Force MSS (AFMSS) is being adopted as near universal equipment, with only minor software changes to accommodate the various aircraft. These are capable of furnishing all the data and imagery required for the mission: flight-planning graphs (heights, fuel consumption), route-planning (maps for the various legs of the flight, and other important data points such as aerial refuelling tanker Initial and Control rendezvous coordinates and established bull's-eyes), threat penetration (showing an updated EOB, with the circles of influence of enemy radars), weapons delivery (optimum release points), and radar predictions based on digital stored terrain data. As is the case with the RAF's CPGS, it may also be used after the sortie to unload DTMs to assist with post-flight analysis and debriefing. And, if required, the AFMSS can be linked to a good-quality printer which will churn out the contents of a combat mission folder – a handy underarm reference.

Terrain information itself, although accessed simultaneously on AFMSSs and transferable onto regular DTMs, may also be carried aboard the aircraft in raw form separately from the mission cartridge. One such system is the Harris Stored Terrain Access and Retrieval System (STARS), comprising detailed contour maps held on magnetic disc. These discs are prepared by the US Defense Mapping Agency using constantly updated digital land mass files derived from satellite SAR and optical scans. It represents a giant leap forward in cockpit-projected moving-map displays, which previously were film-based and thus cumbersome and expensive to update and maintain in good working order.

One of the first aircraft to use STARS was the Lockheed F-117A Nighthawk, which for many years

has boasted a 240-megabyte magnetic disc drive which can cope with about 400 square miles of territory at a go. The drives used are tough, able to cope with the buffeting, vibration and g dynamics experienced by a modern fighter. Accessed, it provides a digitally reconstituted projected map which can be laced with target and threat data stored in the navigation computer. Laser discs, similar to music CDs, with improved storage capacity, are presently being introduced with magnetic storage capacity three times that of STARS; enough not just to cover the mission profile, but a fair chunk of Europe, the US or the Middle East!

The French Armeé de l'Air have adopted similar state-of-the-art flight-planning technology for use in the Dassault Mirage 2000N/D nuclear and conventional deep strike aircraft, known as the Preparation Automatisée Locale des Missions Aériennes (PALOMA). Six scales of map stored on hard disc (ranging between 1:50,000 and 1:5,000,000) can be called up on the screen, and overlaid with the enemy EOB, tanker tow lines, the forward line of troops (FLOT) and other pertinent data. Also in common with the AFMSS, PALOMA can generate 3-D views from any direction and height, which can be tweaked to show, for example, the extent of shadows cast by solar grazing angles throughout the day, to assist with picking the ideal time and headings for the use of E-O smart weapons over the target. Once plotted and okayed, the navigational data is downloaded into two DTMs the French call pods, the first containing the mission waypoints, and the second for the Mirage's terrain-referenced navigation (TRN) system.

Interestingly, both the French and the US are now using spot satellite imagery, code-named *Eagle Vision*. Images from this, taken over enemy territory, can be converted by computer into different views of the target that the crews (or advanced E-O sensors or weapons seekers) will actually see out of the cockpit when approaching it at a given height and heading. Again, these snapshots of the target are loaded into the DTMs for easy in-flight reference. The autonomy the digital computer revolution has lent crews in mission-planning – now quite rightly termed mission modelling – has been extraordinary.

About 15 minutes prior to the allotted completion of mission modelling, the Flight Lead will ask his troops to get ready for the final Flight Brief. All four or eight

Suiting-up follows the flight briefing, and a water survival undergarment, fire-resistant flightsuit, anti-g suit, helmet and a bunch of other paraphernalia. This RAF aviator is also demonstrating the cumbersome nuclear, biological, chemical facial gear. (RAF)

flyers then recongregate behind closed doors and spend another 30 minutes going over the details they have all worked out, covering all aspects of how the four jets (the usual composition of a Flight) will work together under various contingencies, including emergency procedures.

Flight Brief over, the next stop is Life Support or the squadron locker room, to be issued with, or to grab off the racks, personal equipment tailor-made to fit each aviator. Suiting up – donning flight gear – then follows, before crews step out to the aircraft. A number of life-saving accoutrements are added to the basic fire-resistant Nomex flightsuit. Where ejection may take place over cool water, crews first don a 'poopy' suit, a rubber-lined garment designed to keep the cold at bay. In the freezing waters of the North Sea, for example, an aviator might not last more than 30 seconds without this. Over this goes the flightsuit and a life preserver (and 'water wings' threaded through to the tops of the arms), which self-inflates to keep the aviator buoyant.

Also added, over the lower torso and upper legs, is a g-suit girdle. The role of the g-suit is vital in today's fighter cockpit in preserving an aviator's normal senses. By squeezing the lower body and thighs, it helps the heart keep the upper body and head well-supplied with oxygen-rejuvenating blood which otherwise has a tendency to drain into the legs during hard, sustained manoeuvres. The theoretical disadvantage of tall, thin pilots, because of the greater distance between heart and head, does not exist in practice, according to the aeromedical people at the

Institute of Aviation Medicine at RAE Farnborough. Work in the US has similarly revealed there is no significant difference in the *g* tolerance between male and female aviators. The relaxed tolerance of a seated, up-right individual is usually only about 4 *g*, a level sufficient to produce a 60 per cent loss of peripheral vision; i.e. the onset of tunnel vision. Acceleration above 5 *g* is likely to result in G-LOC – total black-out – without visual warning symptoms if the onset rate is high and sustained. Standard anti-*g* trousers can increase relaxed tolerance by 1–1.5 *g* and the tensing and straining of muscles can enable a staggering further 4 *g* to be tolerated, theoretically permitting a 12 *g* aircraft (such as the MiG-29 *Fulcrum*) to be piloted reasonably safely; but the straining manoeuvre is tiring and the risk of G-LOC is high if it is performed incorrectly.

Another trick pilots learn is to keep their heads up during air combat manoeuvres; HOTAS and HUD devices combined have been a boon in this respect, as have reclining seats (such as the ACES II installation in the F-16). 'Keep the heart thinking the head is high.' However, even in today's fighters, there remain some unpleasant side-effects of being squashed down in the seat. Rapid head movements during banking and turning can induce nausea, brought on by the Coriolis effect which disturbs the fluids in the head, or ear balance. Ruptured capillaries, a condition known as Petechiasis but more commonly as high-*g* measles, can also result, causing itching, bruising and skin discoloration on the backside and thighs.

The final piece of kit is the crash helmet, a device that has grown steadily lighter and more durable in an effort to reduce neck tissue damage during air combat 'rubber-necking', and possible whiplash, while at the same time preserving its bone dome protective characteristics. Only the incorporation of devices such as night-vision goggles (NVGs), which add a weighty attachment, have reversed this trend. The latest types, such as the US HPU-55, are individually form-fitted to prevent extraneous noise entering the earphones, and are customarily strapped in place after entering

Serious stuff. SR-71A 'Habu' aviators, who routinely flew at heights above 80,000 ft, were required to wear full-pressure David Clark spacesuits. These are mandatory for all flights above FL450. At such heights, the air is so thin that a flyer's blood would literally boil, creating possibly fatal gas embolisms in the bloodstream. (Lockheed)

the cockpit, when the visors are clamped down too. Visors are tinted for daytime flying, and clear for night-time operations.

They come with the all-essential mask. Connected, this serves as an intercom and provides a steady flow of oxygen, excellent at curing lingering hangovers or the 'blues', and vital at preserving adequate circulation at altitudes of above 25,000 ft (FL250). Crews are well aware of the risks of black-out associated with hypoxia (oxygen starvation to the brain). They are introduced to the symptoms in hyperbaric chambers, where, as the pressure drops, accomplishing even simple tasks (such as doing junior school-level maths) can become perplexing. Awareness stops and starts like a stopwatch in relation to the oxygen supply. Physochomotor and thought processes degrade rapidly, not dissimilar to the rapid onset of drunken bewilderment. Depending on height, without oxygen there exists only a few seconds' Time of useful consciousness (TUC) before the symptoms of light-headedness give way to complete black-out. Aviators are made aware of the TUCs at FL250, FL300, FL350 and FL400 by being obliged to remove their oxygen masks, or having the supply cut off and reinstated, in the chamber at the appropriate time. Those particularly prone to the symptoms at lower flight levels are precluded from flying (as are those prone to intoxicating hyperventilation).

In flight, loss of oxygen can only be corrected by a rapid descent to flight levels where ambient air pressure approaches normality. Small oxygen bottles are stowed in the cockpit for emergency use precisely for this reason, and on the sides of ejection seats. For operations above FL400, full pressure suits are mandatory. Popularized by the David Clark Company 'Gold Suits' worn by high-flying SR-71A and U-2R jet-jockeys and spacemen, these provide a complete seal to prevent the hideous symptoms associated with depressurization at altitude: caisson disease, or the bends. Depending on height, the latter symptoms range from severe itching to fatality, as nitrogen gas embolisms form in the bloodstream.

Aviators are introduced to all these hazards during academic sessions and sessions in the hyperbaric chamber, including proper use of an oxygen regulator (very high oxygen mixes help with g tolerance, but can wear out a flyer). They are also introduced to the three types of mask, comprising continuous flow (self-explanatory), diluter command (oxygen supplied when breathing in) and pressure demand (oxygen force-supplied, which requires deliberate exhalation). For high-flyers, mastering all of these techniques is essential for survival.

One final piece of equipment issued and carried

Ground crew prepare an F-111F Aardvark for an impending sortie in the eerie, dank darkness of a TAB-Vee HAS shelter. Each and every aircraft has its own shelter replete with engine 'huffer' (at right, shown with only the electrical lead connected to the aircraft). Blast doors open at the rear of the TAB-Vee to vent the tremendous thrust and gases created by the aircraft's two powerful P&W TF30-P-100 turbofan engines. (Author)

aboard for combat missions, other than the usual array of mission-specific clipboard and knee-pad flight-plan paraphernalia, is a pistol. US servicemen tote a .38-calibre gun, holstered in the survival vest, while Russians prefer the Makarov 9 mm automatic. (Rumours that some *Afghansti* brandished folded AK-47s during combat missions might also be true!) Hopefully, there is no need for these. But they are there just in case.

Stepping Out

Dressed for action, the crews step to their aircraft; the term 'stepping' is used because, encumbered by all the equipment, crews perform a kind of 'rodeo walk' to their machines. They may drive out or be bussed to their aircraft in a van, but when the aircraft are clustered together near the squadron building stepping is customary.

Having arrived at their assigned tail, the first job is to be greeted by the respective Dedicated Crew Chief (DCC) and his or her aides, those responsible for ensuring the fighter's state of readiness on the flight-line, and to review the 'forms' – the maintenance records. These provide a quick review of what (if any) minor maintenance tasks remain outstanding, and also the configuration of the aircraft if it is one of a batch which might or might not yet have undergone updates during Phased Maintenance Inspections (PMIs) or Depot-level tear-downs – the big IRAN (inspect and repair as necessary) refurbishments performed like clockwork every three or four years. There are usually several items pending, mostly minor.

RAF crews sign Form 700, declaring that the aircraft is fit for action. Ground crews on the flight line and in the support shops spend as much as 53 hours on maintenance for every single flight hour (53 MMH/FH). Pre-flight, the look-over, ensues. The pilot checks that the flying portions of the aircraft look healthy, that the tyres are not worn thin and that nothing obvious is wrong with the machine, while the navigator checks the weapons, making sure that they are bolted-on securely, and fuzes and safing wires are all in order. The crew then amble up the ladder and squeeze into the cockpit, a task which requires professional practice in many instances.

Strapping-in follows pre-flight. The crew clamber up the ladder and slide into the ejection seats, otherwise known as 'bang seats' because of the pyrotechnics which violently vault an aviator out of an abandoned fighter at the tug of a handle. Nowadays pilots are universal in acquiescing that the physiological risks associated with being hurled out of an aircraft in under half a second (0.45 sec at lower altitude) are infinitely preferable to being

Strapping-in, with the DCC looking thoughtfully over the proceedings, which is akin to 'putting the aircraft on'. (Andy Evans)

burnt in a fireball, or making a big hole in the ground! Work is currently proceeding towards even better self-righting seats capable of working reliably during inverted ejections at low-level. Nearing this goal, and arguably the best today are the latest range of Martin-Bakers (such as the MB Mk.16, derivatives of which are used in the Rafale and Eurofighter 2000, among others), and the Russian Zevzda K-36D. Wiry or tall frames are apt to suffer more spinal concussion, and nobody takes ejection lightly: it is always a last resort. Nonetheless it has to be initiated speedily and almost instinctively, especially at low-level, such is the split-second timing which divides life and death.

Strapping into a modern ejection seat, cinching-up the harnesses and securing cockpit lines actually takes several minutes, as there are numerous connections to make. Fighter crews engaging these cocooning straps, wires and hoses are said to 'put the fighter on'; 'getting in' does not quite adequately capture the procedure. In the case of the Martin-Baker seat (fairly typical), this includes two leg straps per leg, one above the ankle, the other above the knee; two seat-kit connections (one near each hip); a lap belt; two parachute Koch attachments; and finally, the oxygen hose, g-suit hose, and communications cord.

Only at this stage, with all working to order, does the Crew Chief pull the last of the seven ejection seat safing pins (conspicuous as they are attached to fluorescent Remove Before Flight tags), and drag away the boarding ladders. If any one of these straps or umbilical connections appears unsound, the whole sortie can be scrubbed. Attention to safety details prevail, for such equipment checks tend to save lives (not to mention valuable equipment). Quite simply, there is no room for cavalier attitudes towards vital life-preserving equipment.

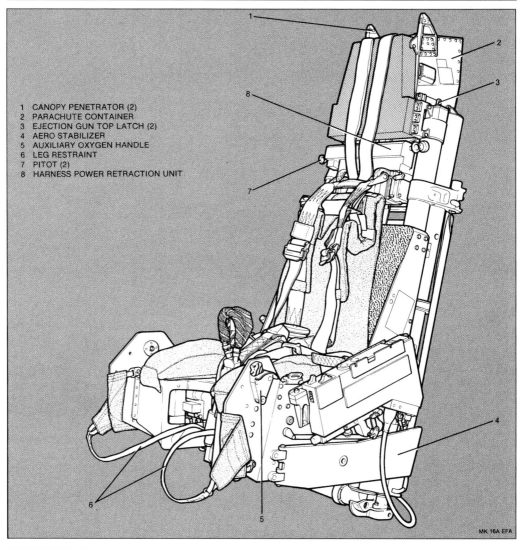

1 CANOPY PENETRATOR (2)
2 PARACHUTE CONTAINER
3 EJECTION GUN TOP LATCH (2)
4 AERO STABILIZER
5 AUXILIARY OXYGEN HANDLE
6 LEG RESTRAINT
7 PITOT (2)
8 HARNESS POWER RETRACTION UNIT

MK 16A EFA

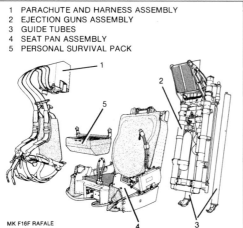

1 PARACHUTE AND HARNESS ASSEMBLY
2 EJECTION GUNS ASSEMBLY
3 GUIDE TUBES
4 SEAT PAN ASSEMBLY
5 PERSONAL SURVIVAL PACK

MK F16F RAFALE

Martin-Baker Mk 16 Ejection Seat: The lightweight Martin Baker Mk 16 ejection seat is the standard item for Eurofighter 2000 (Mk 16A) and Dassault Rafale (Mk 16F). The graphics are illuminating. (Martin Baker Company)

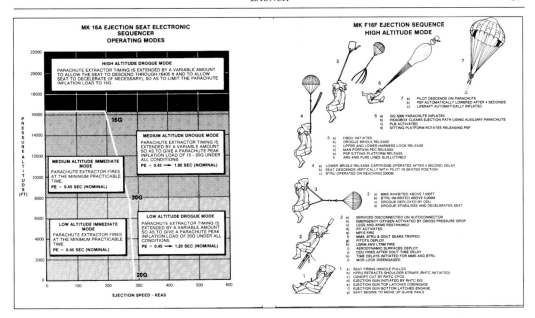

MK 16A EJECTION SEAT ELECTRONIC SEQUENCER OPERATING MODES

HIGH ALTITUDE DROGUE MODE
PARACHUTE EXTRACTOR TIMING IS EXTENDED BY A VARIABLE AMOUNT TO ALLOW THE SEAT TO DESCEND THROUGH 16405 ft AND TO ALLOW SEAT TO DECELERATE (IF NECESSARY), SO AS TO LIMIT THE PARACHUTE INFLATION LOAD TO 15G.

15G

MEDIUM ALTITUDE DROGUE MODE
PARACHUTE EXTRACTOR TIMING IS EXTENDED BY A VARIABLE AMOUNT SO AS TO GIVE A PARACHUTE PEAK INFLATION LOAD OF 15 - 20G UNDER ALL CONDITIONS.
PE = 0.45 → 1.90 SEC (NOMINAL)

MEDIUM ALTITUDE IMMEDIATE MODE
PARACHUTE EXTRACTOR FIRES AT THE MINIMUM PRACTICABLE TIME.
PE = 0.45 SEC (NOMINAL)

20G

LOW ALTITUDE IMMEDIATE MODE
PARACHUTE EXTRACTOR FIRES AT THE MINIMUM PRACTICABLE TIME.
PE = 0.45 SEC (NOMINAL)

LOW ALTITUDE DROGUE MODE
PARACHUTE EXTRACTOR TIMING IS EXTENDED BY A VARIABLE AMOUNT SO AS TO GIVE A PARACHUTE PEAK INFLATION LOAD OF 20G UNDER ALL CONDITIONS.
PE = 0.45 → 1.20 SEC (NOMINAL)

20G

PRESSURE ALTITUDE (FT) — EJECTION SPEED - KEAS

MK F16F EJECTION SEQUENCE HIGH ALTITUDE MODE

7 a) PILOT DESCENDS ON PARACHUTE
b) PSP AUTOMATICALLY LOWERED AFTER 4 SECONDS
c) LIFERAFT AUTOMATICALLY INFLATED

6 a) GQ 5000 PARACHUTE INFLATES
b) HEADBOX CLEARS EJECTION PATH USING AUXILIARY PARACHUTE
c) PLB ACTIVATED
d) SITTING PLATFORM ROTATES RELEASING PSP

5 a) HBDU INITIATED
b) DROGUE BRIDLE RELEASE
c) UPPER AND LOWER HARNESS LOCK RELEASE
d) MAN PORTION PEC RELEASE
e) PSP SITTING PLATFORM RELEASE
f) ARS AND PLRS LINES GUILLOTINED

4 a) LOWER BRIDLE RELEASE CARTRIDGE OPERATES AFTER 4 SECOND DELAY
b) SEAT DESCENDS VERTICALLY WITH PILOT IN SEATED POSITION
c) BTRU OPERATES ON REACHING 5000M

3 a) MMS INHIBITED ABOVE 7,500FT
b) BTRU INHIBITED ABOVE 5,000M
c) DROGUE DEPLOYED BY DDU
d) DROGUE STABILISES AND DECELERATES SEAT

2 a) SERVICES DISCONNECTED ON AUTOCONNECTOR
b) EMERGENCY OXYGEN ACTIVATED BY OBOGS PRESSURE DROP
c) LEGS AND ARMS RESTRAINED
d) IFF ACTIVATED
e) MPI'S FIRE
f) MMS, BTRU & DDUT SEARS TRIPPED
g) PITOTS DEPLOY
h) USRM AND LTRM FIRE
i) AERODYNAMIC SURFACES DEPLOY
j) DDU FIRES AFTER DDUT TIME DELAY
k) TIME DELAYS INITIATED FOR MMS AND BTRU
l) MOR LOCK DISENGAGED

1 a) SEAT FIRING HANDLE PULLED
b) HPRU RETRACTS SHOULDER STRAPS (RHTC INITIATED)
c) CANOPY CUT BY RHTC CPCS
d) EJECTION GUN INITIATED BY RHTC EGI
e) EJECTION GUN TOP LATCHES DISENGAGE
f) EJECTION GUN BOTTOM LATCHES ENGAGE
g) SEAT BEGINS TO MOVE UP GUIDE RAILS

Power On

Zulu Alert or quick reaction alert (QRA) interceptors must get airborne within 5–10 minutes (depending on their location and commitments) from the Klaxon call. Already warmed-up fighters undergoing a rapid between-missions turnaround with a fresh aircrew on board are equally quick. However, the starting-up of most jet fighters from cold is a time-consuming, almost laborious process which can consume as much as an hour, again designed with safety as the paramount consideration.

It begins with engine start. This can be accomplished by means of battery-fired cartridges (a violent, sooty and unpleasant way of getting things moving), but is typically conducted using a technique known as 'air on'. This is initiated by means of a trolley, such as the RAF's Houchin or the USAF's widespread A/MA 32A-60A 'huffer' (so-called because of the chugging diesel snores emitted at higher power settings), which can provide electrical power from its generator along with compressed air

fed through a reinforced hose, to get the engines turning over. Fighters of Russian origin use this technique too, though all feature forward-field operability. They have taken the logical step of introducing centreline fuel tanks with a built-in auxiliary power unit (APU), or engine-starter, which functions as a huffer to get the engines going during autonomous start-ups. Onboard heavily charged batteries take care of the electrical requirement.

The massive collection of turbojet or turbofan blades making up the initial stages of the engines need to overcome their state of inertia. Once spinning, even slowly, air is drawn in through the intakes and the first-stage fan blades begin to turn. The DCC will keep his eye on these and will signal to the pilot as soon as the discs, sharply defined in their motionless state, begin to assume a blurred, moving appearance. Before

Air-on. The reinforced pipe provides compressed air to the engines to facilitate engine start, turning the fan blades up to sufficient rpm before ignition, and the core of the engine starts burning fuel. Cross-bleed can be used in twin-engined aircraft, but it is customary to disconnect the 'huffer' pipe and reconnect it to the other engine, in turn. Here, the electrical lead has been disconnected as the engines are turning sufficiently to generate power and pressure to drive all the cockpit and hydraulic systems. (Tim P. Laming)

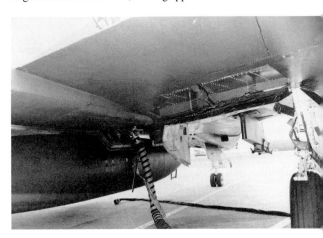

long, the whole front end of the tube of precision-engineered bearing-run discs begins to swirl at a sufficient pace for proper engine start to be initiated. Coaxed along by an electrical ignition at the pilot's initiation, usually by a push-button when engine rpm reaches 10 per cent, the relevant throttle is moved forward out of its cut-off position. (This rpm, and those featured in the ensuing account, are based on those used for the J79-GE/MTB-17 which powers the F-4G. These figures are fairly typical.) It is the latter-day equivalent of 'contact' from the piston-powered era of aviation.

Light-off takes place at around 15–20 per cent rpm. The ignition sequence, like a giant spark plug, gets some kerosene, introduced under pressure through nozzles which swirl and atomize the liquid into millions of minuscule droplets, burning in the compressor. This expands the air, which in turn drives the blades more speedily, draws in more air through the intakes, in turn creating more motion, and so on. Engine wind-up is slow because the whole powerplant is still relatively cool at this stage, and up to 98 per cent of the sucked-in air will simply provide a sheath around the core flame, preventing the casing from melting.

At 45 per cent rpm the external air is cut off, and the engine winds up to 65 per cent rpm: the idle setting. At this point the powerplant has reached an audible scream (created by excess energy dissipated in a shearing action at the edges of the nozzles, rather like a whistle). Ear protection is a must. The possibility of verbal exchanges between even ground crewmen has long since been blanketed out. Hand signals are used instead, while the DCC or Aircraft Captain managing the floor show talks to the aircrew via an intercom lead and headset, plugged into the side of the fighter. With the right (if twin-engined) powerplant merrily turning on idle, the pilot will scan the relevant instruments which display exhaust gas temperature (EGT), rpm, nozzle position, oil pressure, boost pumps and fuel flow, while the procedure is repeated all over again with the second engine. Cross-bleed is often used as a time-saving measure, avoiding the necessity of unplugging and reconnecting the huffer pipe.

If the pilot is relying on old-fashioned needles-and-dials, a feature still common to many current fighter types, engine discrepancies will now be much more apparent: the dials are customarily arrayed in two columns, with their respective needles working like synchronized dancers' limbs. As Gulf veteran 'Spike' Benyshek pointed out: 'In practice, the absolute readings are not examined so much as ensuring that both engines indicate the same. If they are different, then one of them is wrong!' Fighter cockpits relying virtually exclusively on MFDs present similar data in synthesized graphic form, 'with flashing lights and alarm bells' to inform the pilot if anything is patently wrong.

The latest digitally managed fighters also boast such features as full-authority digital electronic control system (FADECS) or digital electronic engine control system (DEECS), whereby fuel flow can be

EJ200 Engine: Cutaway of the EJ200 which powers the Eurofighter 2000. (Rolls-Royce)

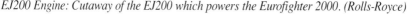

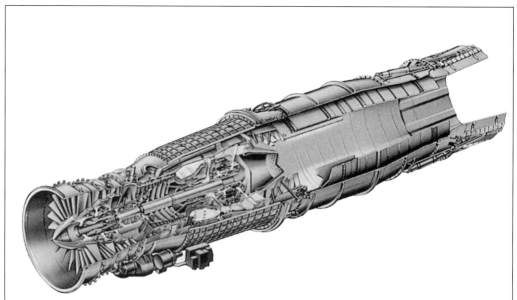

trimmed automatically for maximum efficiency, reducing the need to constantly toy with the throttle levers, which has a tendency to wear out the engines more quickly. DEECS and other generic devices such as Engine Monitoring System (EMS), also record engine performance in fine detail. This information can be downloaded by engine specialists for diagnosis after the aircraft returns from its sortie (or during ground-runs, if required), permitting them to fine-tune the powerplants and be forewarned of possible impending component failures. Older engines require the attention of a ground crewman's well-tuned ear to help isolate faults. Smell and hearing feature as strongly as visual cues, even through the barrier of ear protectors which actually tend to filter the noise down such that oddities (clanking, grinding, etc) become more apparent.

The big engines turn small generators mounted at the front of each engine, or attached to the side of the casing, capable of producing massive reserves of power. Second only to its high-pressure electro-mechanical hydraulic system, an aircraft's electrical system, fed around literally tens of miles' worth of voltage-regulated conduits, drive all the big power-guzzling electrical systems: radar, countermeasures, electro-hydraulics, and so forth. At this stage the huffer's ancillary electrical lead may be disconnected too, and the fighter becomes a free agent, with engines turning over nicely and the displays and key electronics warming up.

The engines also provide hydraulic power by pressurizing the whole flight control nervous system, and this accounts for the drooped posture of an inactive jet fighter. Compressed air piped from the engines is used also for cabin pressure, to inflate the crews' g-suit bladders during high dynamic flight loads, and (on board emerging designs such as Eurofighter 2000) to supply breathing air to the pilot, by means of a molecular sieve which furnishes oxygen with a purity of up to 95 per cent.

With hydraulics working, at the DCC's initiation the pilot flexes the bird's feathers, checking all the control surfaces are working satisfactorily: rudder, elevons, spoilers, flaps, slats and so on are all given a thorough workout, with the ground crew presiding at key vantage points. This includes normal control movements of the stick and rudder, verification of augmentation systems, normal flap and slat operation, and proper trim – establishing the controls near the normal neutral point, via a trim button on the control stick which can be teased up, down, left and right. By definition, loss of engine power customarily results in creeping loss of other control power, and this is why deadstick (engines out) emergency landings are such a hairy procedure.

Powerhouse of the koder fighter: its engines. Pilots' hearts start palpitating if these go awry in flight! The bullet fairings on these J79-GE-17s house the electrical generators which provide the aircraft's operational power – everything depends on them. (Ken Mackintosh)

Electronics check-out mostly falls within the navigator's job description. This is also conducted as part of the general Power On agenda. One of the first tasks is to align the inertial navigation set (INS), a crucial piece of equipment fitted to every self-respecting fighter. Older categories of INS, such as the Litton LN.12 used on most land-based F-4s, employ accelerometers and gyros which sense movement about the three axis (up/down, left/right and forwards). With the assistance of a navigation computer, they process these movements into meaningful information in the form of present position latitude/longitude coordinates which are constantly updated from the moment the aircraft's wheels began to turn. The displays generated by these Litton devices were known as 'windows' and presented the information on spinning counters, similar to a car's odometer. Gyro-compass alignment of these now obsolete systems with current position (the parking spot coordinates and its elevation) took up to 15 minutes on a cold day, and in-flight drift tended to be in the order of miles for every hour of flight-time, necessitating constant updates. They were also prone to in-flight 'dumping' (going awry), which necessitated in-flight realignment and updating, all over again.

Transistor number-crunching of the inputs provided by the electrical signals generated by the cogs and pulleys contained in the INS, a technology introduced in the late 1960s, witnessed the introduction of light-emitting diode (LED) digital displays, similar to those found on domestic radio-

By modern standards, an antiquated navigation display, using old-fashioned counters. In the 1960s such INS readouts were relatively cosmic. Compare this with . . . (Ferranti)

. . . the two MFDs and central CRT found in the cockpit of the F-117A stealth fighter. Note also the tiger-striped ejection seat handles and (at top right) one of the fold-down sunshades, which is held in place by Velcro! (Lockheed)

alarm clocks, but accuracy remained just as shaky until the advent of the solid-state ring-laser-gyro (RLG) INS a decade later, tied in with microchip number-crunching to compute the required information, which is now customarily displayed on an MFD in alphanumerics. Errors still are introduced, but system reliability in terms of both accuracy and mean time between failure (MTBF) is greatly improved. For example, F-15E crews praise their Honeywell RLGs highly: 'The thing is a rock. It aligns in 4 minutes, stays where it's supposed to in flight, then winds up with one knot or less of ground speed and within 100 ft of your parking place – every time.' At the time of writing, work on newer, even more sensitive digital quartz inertial (DQI) 'tuning fork' electrical gyros is underway. DQI INS systems will offer inexpensive throwaway technology (that is, if it goes wrong, it is cheaper to bin it rather than repair it), and in miniaturized forms these are also being developed for new smart weapons. It will take some time yet for this to percolate down into operational use.

To the uninitiated, it begs the question, why all this fuss over a system that can be prone to unreliability?! Updated, the INS is vital in helping to slave radar and E-O sensors to stored target or offset coordinates which are crucial for reasonably accurate blind or smart bombing. It is critical in assisting with navigation over vast expanses of nothingness such as ice-caps and oceans (or a truly black night), where there exist no visual identifying features to help follow the flight-plan even in conjunction with a moving or electronic map display, an all-weather eye such as radar, or night-time E-O sensors. It can be slaved to the navigation computer and an autopilot in some instances for virtually hands-off point-to-point flight, a vital asset in speedy low-level flight. And it is autonomous – i.e. it does not rely on outside sources, as do radio navigation aids, which are relatively easy for the enemy to jam. It thus serves to assist with surprise attack. Moreover, many modern fighters' air-to-air weapons and weapons-aiming systems are equally reliant on inertial reference inputs in order to work properly. INS can help narrow the area of choice or target parameters when identifying these with various sensors or weapons seekers – of crucial assistance in the time-compressed, exacting nature of military aviation, especially at low-level.

Navigation computers are also programmed by the

The back of the F-14 Tomcat is stuffed with circuit-breaker panels, fairly typical of a modern fighter and reflecting its enormous quantities of electrical systems. (Grumman)

back-seater during the Power On phase of pre-flight checks and preparations. At the top of the market, navigators use the DTMs, which stuff the brains of the navigation computers with all the pertinent mission data in a time span of 8–30 seconds. Such technology also features nowadays on relatively humble fighters, such as New Zealand's digitally updated A-4K Skyhawks. In intermediate technologies, such as the Lear-Siegler ARN-101(V) DMAS equipping the F-4G Advanced *Wild Weasel*, the DTM would provide only basics such as tanker ARCPs, information pertaining to established bull's-eyes, and the coordinates of diversionary airfields which might be called-up in the event of an emergency. In this instance, the specifics regarding the various legs of the mission must be tapped into the navigation keyboard one at a time, in sequence, correctly keyed with the proper prefix letters, 'D' (data point) or 'T' (turn point), such being crucial in the automatic activation of sensors on board reconnaissance jets, in particular.

In yet older analogue systems (the RAAF F-111C's pre-AUP Bomb-Nav-System being a prime example), navigation legs are entered one at a time, as the flight progresses, based on a checklist or computer print-out listing all the relevant information, carried into the cockpit by the navigator alongside his other flight paraphernalia. This can be a taxing task for single-seaters using commensurate technology, such as the A-7P flown by the Force Aérea Portuguesa. And much of this technology still is prevalent owing to the widespread market for refurbished hand-me-down fighters.

Diagnostics of the primary equipment, using built-in test (BIT) features, is also performed on such crucial equipment as the radar, or Big Eye, and E-O sensors, this being undertaken by the multi-fingered,

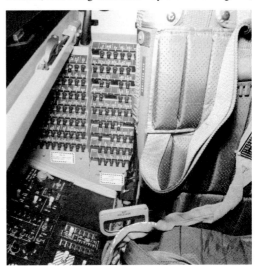

multi-toed wizzos. It may comprise simply checking the whole gamut of electrical circuits. On more modern, digital aircraft this often involves running a programme of checks; on older technology, actually switching through all the knob settings, one at a time, and ensuring that all is working satisfactorily, and *in extremis*, having a nose for the gear. Until very recently, before microchips came of age and valves and similar high-voltage, heavy-duty electronic components prevailed, many navigators ascertained the health of their equipment by smell! For example, a nauseous odour might indicate a short-circuit, or imminent failure of some component. Even today, equipment can be prone to overheating so has to be tweaked.

Such subtleties have largely been replaced by the computerized self-diagnostic MFD readouts common today, which even pilots in multi-crew types call-up and consign to the computers' 'bins' with surprising ease (such is the MTBF reliability of modern avionics, and the extent of their all-singing, all-dancing cautionary alerts). Most crews run through these checks in automaton fashion, as they are so well-rehearsed.

With regard to electrical current, in both ancient and modern systems, major electrical circuits are protected by copious banks of circuit-breakers. A power surge (such as that generated during powering-up) might cause some to pop (out), and normal service can be resumed by pressing them back in place again. If they keep popping, then something is genuinely wrong with the circuitry. This might result in a sortie

stand-down, or some head-scratching by ground crew followed by the insertion of a freshly serviced line-replaceable unit (LRU: a black box which can be readily uncoupled and replaced by a serviceable unit in only a few minutes).

With all the displays working as advertised, the BIT and other checklists complete, the Crew Chief gives the aircraft a final visual examination, mostly checking for obvious problems such as fuel or hydraulic leaks. Some of these leaks must be viewed in relative terms. All fighters (including stealth designs) feature numerous drain holes in their bellies to prevent an explosive build-up of fuel or hydraulic liquids, and it takes only a small amount to smear the underside of a modern jet fighter with their characteristic stains – ugly, but necessary.

Take-Off

During the last few minutes prior to taxi, the lead crewman will check-in the Flight on the radio. He will verify that the UHF radios are operable (and, if required, in the NATO-standard *Have Quick* jam-resistant mode, and also in the secure-voice mode, suitably cipher-scrambled). On an operational mission, the crew have a further 20 minutes of preparations ahead of them prior to actual take-off, despite some 45 minutes having elapsed since the crew originally stepped to their warbird. Then it is time for chocks away. A radio call to Ground Control provides the necessary permission.

Advancing the throttles beyond idle to push the jet

'Let's rock-and-roll!' An F-4G Wild Weasel *taxies out prior to take-off. At this stage the pilot will be 'stirring the pot' (stick) to flex all the control surfaces, ensuring that all is well. (Mike Dugre)*

out of its shelter or parking spot, waved out by the Crew Chief, the pilot employs his throttles to control speed and the rudder pedals to steer the machine, via its nosewheels. Thus, in this limited two-dimensional area of flying, 'driving' an aircraft requires a complete reversal of the psychomotor skills required to control speed and direction in a car. The stick, widely perceived to be the focus of play, actually only becomes useful during the take-off run. While taxiing, wagging *le manche* to and fro will merely cause the elevons to flip up and down like a whale's flipper. Side-to-side moments will cause a number of different things to happen, depending on the configuration of the aircraft. The independent elevons or tail slabs of a Teenage fighter such as an F-16 will waggle alternately, while a one-piece tail such as that employed on the F-4 will remain relatively stationary, but its left and right wing spoilers will pop-up alternately. In a delta configuration, such as that employed in the Mirage 2000 series, the trailing-edge flaps will flicker about. Canards, too, might flex a little on the latest designs, with the computer of the fly-by-wire (FBW) controls engaged.

Slapping or wagging or even stirring the stick and the corresponding motions serve the primary purpose of ensuring that the control surfaces are working satisfactorily. This is done only when various ground personnel are not near the aircraft, or if they are in strict control of the proceedings. Nevertheless, piloting instincts decree that gloved digits remain gently wrapped around the stick (or sidestick control

in some FBW types such as the F-16) whenever the machine is moving. Indeed, it's often possible to pick out a more jittery or impetuous 'knight of the air' during taxiing simply by the excessive movements of his steed's flight control surfaces caused by superfluous heavy-handed stick gyrations. If not, then it is probably a FBW system.

FBW controls are not linked to the flying surfaces directly via pulleys, cables, bobweights and power-assisted actuators, but through a computer which sends out appropriate electrical signals to the actuators commensurate with the flying mode (i.e. automatically sensing when an aircraft is taxiing, when heavy control inputs are needed, versus high-speed flight, when delicate inputs are required). These sometimes twitch of their own accord while an aircraft is in motion, adjusting proper trim automatically. Currently under replacement by lightweight fly-by-light fibre-optic technology, FBW is what makes essentially non-aerodynamic designs such as the Lockheed F-117A fly so stably, constantly retrimming the aircraft automatically. Without this, pilot-induced oscillations might all too easily set in as he fights to correct and then counter-correct various control motions, resulting in departure from controlled flight. Former 'Skunk Works' boss Ben Rich often joked that he could get the Statue of Liberty to fly coherently given sufficient thrust and a good FBW programme!

Interestingly enough, the MiG-29 *Fulcrum* is a fly-by-muscle machine, with all the pulleys and cables associated with fighters of yesteryear, aided only by

Everything is preened ready for the flyers by the DCC and his or her aides, including stores. Here, munitions personnel load and 'safe' a trio of iron bombs. (USAF)

power-assistance. No wonder its pilots are stocky! Actually, this is a great accolade to its inherently stable design. A modicum of transistor technology is at hand to deploy leading-edge slats automatically, and in the autopilot which can respond to the pilot engaging the so-called panic button: if he becomes disorientated, he simply pushes a button on the top-right of the stick and the big MiG automatically adopts a wings-level posture. The Su-27 *Flanker* features an almost identical system.

Still another quarter of an hour has to pass before take-off. The aircrew, in touch with one another over the intercom and running Before Take-off checklist items, progress to the Arming Area, otherwise known as Last Chance or Quick Chance. This is mandatory whenever weapons are being carried. Here, a pre-positioned team of ground crews (often the same DCC and crew which prepped the aircraft, and who have bussed out to the correct spot), pull the pins. These are more Remove Before Flight tags attached to bombs and other sundry stores, which permit them to be subsequently selected and fuzed from the cockpit. To arm many missiles and smart bombs, T-Keys (bearing similar fluorescent streamers) are twisted and removed to achieve the same purpose. From this moment on, use of the weapons is at the aircrew's discretion, and for this very reason the aircrew hold their hands in the air, or on canopy bows, to indicate

'No, I'm not going to flip a switch inadvertently which will cause a weapon to shoot off the rails into your face, or into the control tower'.

It is at this stage also that the final say – hence Last Chance – is communicated should any of the aircraft's systems prove visibly troublesome: for example, drop tanks gushing fuel, a weapon hanging precariously, or suspicious smoke emanating from the engine bay area. Engines are run-up (again) to thrust levels the brakes will tolerate to reconfirm nothing is likely to go bang because of mechanical problems deep in the aircraft's gizzards, or as a result of foreign object damage (FOD) debris ingested through the intakes. Most aerodromes are equipped with a fleet of taxiway and runway sweeper trucks to mitigate the FOD hazard (and to clear or brush away snow and ice). Modern fighters of Russian origin employing 'shark's gills' (and the F-117A Nighthawk, almost by default because of the need to preserve stealthy electrical continuity across the intakes) have built-in guards, and use secondary upper surface intake louvres and ports for taxiing. All part and parcel of rough-field performance.

Radar checks, working at higher power settings which might prove injurious to unwary bystanders, are also often wrung-out at this stage. Of course, a mission scrub might be caused by anything from a change in operational plans (aircraft are usually always

Prior to actual launch, the crews trundle along to the EOR for last-chance checks where the pins are pulled out and they await their scheduled take-off slot. Barometrics (altimeter) and frequencies are checked with the Tower, while Day-Glo-shirted ground crews check IFF systems with special hand-held devices. (Peter E. Davies)

recallable, even after take-off), or by the discovery of a tiny hole created by enemy flak or shrapnel in a key area which was previously overlooked. A great head-scratching session might then ensue, resulting in anything from mission stand-down to a wodge of very sticky electrical conducting tape being placed over the offending area, depending on the degree of damage.

Last Chance itself comprises a wide parking area capable of accommodating up to eight jets, all with assigned parking spots. This area is situated at both ends of the main runway and thus carries the unremarkable description 'end of runway' (EOR). Depending on prevailing wind factors, either EOR will be chosen for the day's operations – but never both. For this reason pilots grow accustomed to treating the same runway as two. Returning aircraft will land in the same direction as launches, partly to avoid the potential hazards of collision if traffic control is overloaded or if aircraft spacing is tight, but primarily to take advantage of headwinds which will reduce ground speeds both during take-off and landing, adding to true airspeed.

One final check performed prior to an operational mission is conducted by a ground crewman holding a black box similar in size to a camcorder. Pointing it at each aircraft in turn, the system interrogates their IFF squawk boxes and analyzes the responses, much as AWACS would do, ensuring that each aircraft can positively identify itself as friendly in its own peculiarly coded manner. Altimeter settings (barometrics) are also supplied by the tower and cranked in to ensure that altimeter instruments function accurately, along with various preset radio frequencies if this task has not been accomplished beforehand. Usually these are all keyed in as part of the power on communications, navigation, interrogation (CNI)) equipment preparations.

At the conclusion of the checks, the ground crews head back to their huts and hangars for a well-earned respite. Now, the Flight Lead – still the pilot in charge of proceedings, or senior AC amongst a cluster of two-man crews – holds up two fingers. This is not an insulting gesture. It signals everyone to go to Channel 2, the Air Traffic Control tower frequency. Tower coordinates their departure.

Capt Bruce Spike Benyshek, an F-4G pilot, takes up the procedure from the pilot's point of view, using *Southern Watch* talk, which engages the reader in the typically cryptic language of the fighter pilot, designed to reduce chatter on the airwaves to an absolute minimum.

'Tower, Bud[weiser] Six-One, in sequence, three-four left.'
'Bud, the wing three-one-zero at 12 knots, cleared for take-off.'
'Bud [acknowledging].'
As we line up on the runway, the lead EWO back-

Blurred by the heat of its own two afterburning engines, an F-4E from the Elliniki Polemiki Aeroporia begins its roll down the runway. (Author)

seater points at his canopy, and with the wingmen nodding ready, the rear canopies follow suit moments later from the signals of the Flight Lead. The line-up checks are quickly accomplished, and Lead looks at his wingman. Two nods his head as being ready for take-off. Lead twirls one hand in the air as a signal for 'run 'em up'. Both aircraft advance their throttles to achieve 85 per cent rpm on both engines. You must be careful not to go higher than this as the tyres may rotate on the wheel rims! The pilots make a quick scan of all the engine instruments [an ongoing process] and, all being well, we look at Two, who nods that all is well. With a salute, we look forward, engage nosewheel steering, release brakes, advance power to mil, pause, and select afterburner [or reheat: mil stands for military power, and is maximum power without afterburner]. Techniques vary slightly, but for us, the stick is held full-forward at brake release. This minimizes drag and maximizes the effectiveness of nosewheel steering should a tyre fail.

As we accelerate, we watch the airspeed indicator. 'Off the peg' is called as it comes to life, somewhere around 50 knots. 'Eighty' is called as the needle passes the first incremented mark on the instrument, followed quickly by 'One hundred'. At this speed, we will take off if we blow a tyre, so the nosewheel steering is released, and the stick comes full back. From brake release to 100 knots takes about 10 seconds. Even though the stick is full back, it takes another five or six seconds until the nose starts to rotate. In a combat configuration with missiles on board, this normally happens around 160 knots. As the nose starts to rise, we adjust the stick to hold the nose at 5–10 degrees nose-high. About five seconds, at 180–185 knots, [we are] airborne.

What used to be called minimum interval take-off (MITO) times are still used in war, customarily at 20-second spacings between aircraft rolling down the runway in a blaze of crimson-orange afterburner. Peacetime operations (with inert captive-carry munitions aboard, or for checkride or airshow purposes) are occasionally conducted in much more rapid succession, or in pairs in echelon, with Flight Lead positioned at left, usually something like an aircraft's length ahead and 10–12 ft wide of Two to

And up! An Armée de l'Air Mirage 2000N/D unsticks from Luxeuil, and soars into the sky. This machine is the French equivalent of the American F-15E Eagle DRF, optimized for air-to-air and INT work. (Katsuhiko Tokunaga via Dassault Aviation)

avoid inadvertent touching of wings during the speeding roller-coaster ride down the runway. However, the usual practice is for aircraft to line up in echelon in pairs, and then launch at 10–20-second intervals, before the next pair line up on the 'hammerhead' or 'piano keys' and pile on the thrust, one at a time, in their turn.

During Maximum Efforts, when a whole wing of fighters can be sortie-surge launched, it is possible to witness up to 60 fighter jets screaming off during a non-stop session lasting 40–50 minutes. It has to be seen to be believed! The reverberating blast generated by over 100 screaming, roaring engines (some in full blaze, some being run-up, others in intermediate taxi settings) is a truly awesome demonstration of air power. By contrast, in the cockpit there is usually a relatively eerie quiet. There is little noise apart from the background hum of the intercom on Cold Mike (permitting talk by a given crew to one another), the silence broken only by airspeed call-outs. It takes on a surrealistic *frisson* as peripheral vision becomes blurred with motion, signalling departure from the clutches of gravity.

Flying these machines requires a mind detached from the ground, but nevertheless well-focused. Actually, there is usually very little trim change required upon becoming airborne, though two or three clicks nose-down on the stick-mounted trim button 'will make it perfect' in non-FBW types. At about 50 ft at 200+ knots, the landing gear and flaps are retracted, and the focus is again on airspeed, hoping to get the gear locked prior to their speed limits – usually around the 250-knot mark. Fancy pilots will push the landing gear 'lollipop' handle 'up' whilst only a few feet from the runway, but in a combat-laden jet there are other things to worry about, and this might prove to be a reckless distraction. 'Gear up' is often a close, well-rehearsed thing, with the red lights going out at about 240 knots.

The next thing to focus on is the engines' afterburners. Throttles are usually retarded to Mil power around the time that speed has built up to

And with less thunder but equal aplomb, an F-117A takes to the skies over Tonopah, Nevada, tucking up its F-15-type undercarriage swiftly. The '9' on the runway is a 9,000 ft marker (which would read '7' on the other side, given a 16,000 ft-long runway). These markers help the pilots peg their speed against distance, although in twin-seaters the back-seater or right-hand seater would be calling out knots so that the pilot can keep his head up during rotation and unstick. (Lockheed photo by Denny Lombard & Eric Schulzinger)

300–350 knots. Otherwise, in afterburner, total fuel flow is a whopping 80,000–100,000 lb an hour! Considering most fighters will have already burnt up to a ton of fuel prior to take-off, remaining kerosene – say, 18,000 lb – could be exhausted in under a quarter of an hour!

Spike resumes his F-4G take-off.

We briefed the Flight to automatically change to Channel Three upon becoming airborne, thereby saving extraneous radio chatter.

'Director, Bud Six-One, airborne.'

'Roger, Bud, you are cleared on course, traffic your 11 o'clock, 6 miles, out of 5,000 for 3,500 [signalling other traffic on approach].'

'Bud, radar contact.'

We are climbing at 325 knots, with our power about 2–3 per cent less than military. This allows our wingman, Two, a power advantage so he may catch us. At low altitudes [under FL 150], the rate of climb is 4,000–6,000 ft per minute. The fuel flow is now about 7,000 lb per hour, per engine. As we wait for Two, we arm our chaff system, and check the status of missiles, radar and EW radar warning receiver (RWR). Today, all systems are functionally normally. If we had found a problem, we have various means of trouble-shooting to try and cure the fault. If it is not too serious, and can not be corrected, we will continue.

At this stage Lead awaits Two and usually a second section of two aircraft also, which are lagging a bit behind because of the take-off intervals.

Two now joins us, on our left, and about 20 ft out. We roll slightly to the right, and our EWO dispenses a single bundle of chaff. As Two sees the silvery wisp peel away in the airstream, they give us a nod of the head. Then he rolls slightly left, and we see the thin puff scooting away from the belly of his aircraft. With a nod of the head and a big thumbs-up from us, Two knows his chaff system is working normally. We wiggle the rudder, and 'kick him out' to 'route', a fluid position usually defined as up to 500 ft away from Lead. We are now passing 20,000 ft, *en route* to 24,000 ft. Our climb rate has dropped considerably, to about 1,000–1,500 ft per minute. The airspeed is still 325, but the fuel flow has dropped to about 6,000 lb per hour, per engine. We are approaching the limits of radar coverage for our airfield.

'Bud Six-One, no traffic, frequency change to tactical approved, have a nice day.'

'Bud, push Six.'

There are two ways of sending our Flight to a new frequency. If we had said 'Bud, go Six', we would expect the response: Two, and then he would change

frequency. The use of 'push' means no response is required, again, in keeping with our disdain for unnecessary radio chatter.

At this stage, the aircraft are cruising at near-optimum fuel efficiency. Most fighters settle around FL200–FL250 at 450 knots airspeed, accelerating only gradually on a cruise-climb profile. As is the case with many jet fighters, there is a marked change in performance when passing FL250–FL270. The aircraft are much more manoeuvrable and stable in the mid-twenties. Engine performance drops significantly in the upper twenties, and turn performance is thus degraded; the lower twenties often offer the right balance of high true airspeed and low fuel flow (for good endurance), while providing adequate indicated airspeed for manoeuvring. As Spike illustrates with his F-4G, the Phantom II has two characteristics which define its altitude and speed range.

The first is, it likes to cruise at .83 Mach. When the thrust from the engines is tapering off, and you haven't much to spare, the airplane will usually stop accelerating at .83 Mach. The other axiom is the airplane doesn't like to fly slower than 300 knots. As you may deduce, somewhere around 30,000 ft, .83 Mach and 300 knots indicated become one and the same! Obviously, the F-4 [and most modern fighters] can fly much higher and faster than this, but for extended missions, this presents a practical limit.

At this stage each of the F-4G's two J79-GE-17Fs would be down to 4,000–5,000 lb per hour, with true airspeed at around 480–500 knots.

The next item on the roster for all bar the F-111 (which goes aloft with up to 20 tons of fuel, offering prodigious range) is to replenish reserves, to ensure adequate fuel for the main thrust of the mission. This process, meeting with an AAR tanker at an established tow-line, is preceded by checking-in with AWACS, to confirm that the Flight is airborne, as fragged, and proceeding with their portion of the big mission as planned. AWACS can then keep tabs and swap updates from the Flight with picture calls – bearing in mind that, at the apex of a gorilla package of fighters, it will be the SEAD and MiGCAP fighters entering the fray first.

Tanking Top-ups

At about 100 miles from the refuelling track, the back-seat 'fightergators' will begin to search in earnest for the tanker on their radars, using an air-to-air B-Scan mode, though sometimes purely by means of a tactical aerial navigation (TACAN) direction-finding signal if

Priority one after take-off and prior to ingressing enemy airspace is to top-up the fuel reserves. An F-4 demonstrates the technique from the donor's perspective . . . (C. Lackman via Richard Ward)

. . . and from a buddy receiver's viewpoint, in this instance between two Intruders. Getting the 'basket' is not quite so easy as it looks. (US Navy)

they wish to be more discreet. The tanker will radiate its own beacon IFF code for which the receivers have been prebriefed in the frag, and the fighter will keep interrogating the various radar blips until one replies to the required mode. There is a standard means of confirming this, common to most air intercept sets employed: if the contact is carrying the right mode and code, the relevant radar return on the CRT screen will have two small horizontal lines, one above and one below. The only difference between the fighters is in acquisition range, and the quality of the actual return – a nondescript green blob in the case of an F-4's display, and a crisp little rectangle in the case of computer-processed synthetic displays available to newer types such as the updated Teenagers.

It is by means of IFF that AWACS and the advance elements identify each aircraft as coded in the frag. Of course, covert machines which would be plying their track to target at around the same time, simply correspond with AWACS using IFF squawks and trust

that low-observability keeps them out of trouble. Long before they near hostile airspace, all of their antennae are retracted, and the crews must rendezvous with AAR support, if necessary, using special codes.

At about 50 miles from the refuelling circuit, the fighters will adjust their altitude so they approach at least 1,000 ft above or below the 'go-juice donor'. This prevents a mid-air collision should anyone botch the rejoin or have a late visual on the GLOB. The tanker crew will maintain a steady altitude, on an oval track, roughly 40 miles long by 10 miles wide. Typical AAR plug-ins are in the low twenties. Again, this is because engine performance begins to suffer at higher altitudes, and much toying with the airspeed indicator is required to maintain a steady contact once plugged in. AAR top-ups have taken place as high as FL320, but it is extremely difficult for all concerned. Approaching 3 miles, the fighter crew 'push' to boom 'freq', that is, the boom operator's frequency. Slowing through 320 knots, the AAR probe is popped-out, or a

The other AAR method, which allows faster transfer of fuel and puts more of the onus on the donor, is boom refuelling. An F-117A demonstrates the 'on the Apple' technique in a ballet-like union with a giant KC-10A Extender. The polyhedron characteristics of the F-117A are most evident here. (Lockheed)

Tom 'T J' Johnson snapped this self-portrait while flying 'on the boom' in an Aardvark, which he entitled Cool Reflections. Interestingly, he went on to fly tankers not long afterwards, so has viewed things from both angles! (T. J. Johnson)

dorsal door is opened (usually using a switch near the throttle quadrant), and further speed is bled off as the big tanker and relatively petite fighter close ranks.

There are two principal forms of AAR here, as implied by the probe and door receiving mechanisms built into the fighters: drogue refuelling and boom refuelling. With drogue refuelling the fighter employs its probe which is flown into a hose trailing, shuttlecock-fashion, from the end of a big fuel pipe emanating from the rear or wing transfer pod of the tanker. With boom refuelling the fighter juxtaposes itself with the tanker with its dorsal door inviting penetration, and a specialist gas station attendant, using hand controls and fuel flow switches, flies a telescopic boom into the hole and tops up the tanks. Each has its merits. Probe-and-drogue, the more widely used technique, permits a whole gamut of aircraft (including buddy fighters, equipped with Douglas D.704 or equivalent pods) to replenish colleagues. Probe and drogue equipment is also easier to fit into transports on an *ad hoc* basis, as proved crucial during the Falklands War of 1982 when six RAF Hercules were hastily reconfigured to the C.1K configuration, in order to fulfil the AAR needs of the Ascension–Falklands supply express line. It also

allows for more scope for error, once plugged, as the receiver pushes into the hose which is usually – but ever so gradually – reeled back into its housing during the refuelling, according to probe pressure. However, aggressive poking can splinter a basket and result in an aborted refuelling, pending realignment on another drogue, if available.

Boom refuelling, on the other hand, permits more rapid transfer of fuel (and often at higher airspeeds) which, combined with the high-capacity reserves proffered by the KC-135 Stratotanker and KC-10 Extender, facilitates more time on-station and greater endurance. In theory, boom refuelling also places the bigger burden of the union on the tanker operator, alleviating stress when night or fatigue factors creep into the equation. However, it has its complications, and especially in vintage aircraft like the F-4 which have a marked tendency to wander. Spike Benyshek observes:

There are as many techniques [to AAR] as there are pilots. One of the difficulties lies in the canopy bow; for most pilots, it blocks the view of the 'director lights', which are mounted on the forward belly of the tanker, and give the pilot an indication of which way to manoeuvre to keep the boom centred in up-down and in-out. Some pilots raise their seat all the way up and look over the canopy bow; others drop their seat and look under it. Our technique is to use visual references for 'up' and 'down', leave the seat in the normal place, superimpose the canopy bow just below the boomer's station, and use the centre rear-view mirror to watch the boom and boom housing for a precise indication of in-out. We pull in directly, and are plugged-in in about 15 seconds.

Looking up, back-seaters (or right-hand seaters in the case of the F-111) call 'on the Apple', in reference to the orange ball painted on the boom. When the boom is extended the proper amount (based on the position of the fighter relative to the tanker), the 'Apple' will line up with the edge of the boom housing. The fuel-loading rate is about 2,000–2,500 lb per minute, resulting in 5–15 minutes on the boom, depending on the fighter's appetite. This can be very tiring for the pilot, owing to the concentration involved.

If we happen to be on the boom when the tanker is at the end of the track, power may be a problem if we are refuelling high and the tanker uses a steep, say, 20° bank angle. If the tanker uses 30° of bank, we will probably have to go to afterburner on one engine in order to hold position! You must remember that in Mil, we are essentially only at 65 per cent of our available power while the tanker has the luxury of being able to go to 100 per cent power without afterburner!

This can be taxing for the receivers, and fatigue really sets in during far-reaching deployments or long-endurance patrols when regular top-ups by night are routinely required. To offer flexibility, the USAF's KC-10A fleet is being fitted with Flight Refuelling Ltd's fully automatic Mk.32B AAR pods for three-point refuelling – a basket off each wing, and a boom from the rear – making it one of the most valuable tankers flying. This pod also equips the RAF's Tristar and VC10 tankers (the latter being the first to employ it), along with many tanker adaptations of the ubiquitous, rugged Boeing 707, and provides a very respectable fuel flow of up to 420 US gal per minute (2,800 lb per minute) per pod and an AAR envelope of 160–325 knots IAS. These high-volume systems only entered service during the 1980s, and put some oomph back into the basket technique. For example, even the venerable KA-6D Intruder tanker, top of the US Navy's carrierborne tanker force and capable of offering up to 350 US gal per minute (2,300 lb per minute) from its solitary hose, usually only offers 12,000 lb of 'giveaway' – and a maximum of 20,000 lb on shorter AAR tracks. No wonder it is one of the busiest aircraft on deck!

Tanks replenished, the fighter disconnects and lets its wingman take a drink. Although the frag specifies timing as virtually an absolute, time in country will be governed by the strikers' mission tasks and by fuel states overall. In American parlance, two fuel states will be briefed. The most important is Bingo fuel, which allows a fighter to return to the tanker or home base with an acceptable safety reserve. The other is Joker fuel, which is only slightly more than Bingo. If a fighter crew found themselves embroiled in combat against a fighter or SAM complex, upon reaching Joker, he should think about disengaging – 'so that he can be on his way home by Bingo fuel'. In general, Bingo is reached about an hour or so after leaving the tanker, or longer in the case of longer-legged jets. At that stage, they proceed back to the tanker for complete replenishment.

All is now set, to push (leave the first route point) preparatory to target ingress: things now are about to hot-up rapidly.

Chapter Three

AIR SUPERIORITY

Establishing air superiority both over and as far as possible beyond the FLOT is critical during the early stages of a conflict. It is a measure of the success of air power which is designed to reduce friendly losses to an absolute minimum, in the air and on the ground. Air superiority is a complex, protean thing – it has to be fought for, won, and held, yet the dynamics of it are constantly changing. Thus it represents a somewhat risky undertaking.

Most architects of modern air warfare concur that it comprises five prerequisites of more or less equal importance. The first is extensive knowledge of both the friendly and the opposing aerial Orders of Battle, the latter by means of AWACS real-time command, control, communications and intelligence (C3I). It has been argued that there has been a degree of over-reliance on this in recent years, but it is a vital coordinating asset. Between Britain, France, NATO and the US, some 50 E-3 Sentry AWACS – undoubtedly the best in the world at this job – remain available for operations at any given time.

Second is a sufficient number of well-equipped fighters ('well-equipped' being a variable defined by each scenario) honed exclusively towards air-to-air combat at the top end of the performance spectrum with which to rout the enemy aerial opposition at the earliest opportunity. Frightening them off with a few daring kills often works wonders. This is especially so if the inevitable enemy's elite 'sneak snipers' can be shot down and kept out of reach of E-3s and the other high-value aerial assets. With the best of the opposition wiped out, enemy morale tumbles. The third element is runway denial. As soon as the

enemy's air base facilities are rendered largely inoperative with boosted kinetic weapons a good proportion of the balance of enemy aerial power can be destroyed *in situ* on the taxiways, and in their revetments and shelters by follow-up interdictors.

The fourth is swarms of AAR tankers at established tow lines or ARCPs to keep friendly aircraft, particularly the vanguard, constantly replenished with fuel for long-duration patrols. And finally, though perhaps above all else, a well-coordinated SEAD spearhead, capable of neutralizing the enemy's EOB – the huge arrays of AAA, SAMs and ground control intercept (GCI) radars that provide

A Tornado F.3 with its spiky underbelly of Skyflash AAMs poised ready to put 'thorns' in the opposition. (BAe)

him with the key means by which to oppose air power. This is done with the subtle and highly skilled arts of soft kill EW (barrage jamming), decoys (by means of ground-launched and air-launched cruise missiles and drones, many of which pack a punch), and hard kill EW (knocking out everything from early warning dishes and masts to flak guns). Concurrently, stealth attack jets – a rather exotic additional element which only the USAF can muster – would be used alongside more conventionally armed cruise missiles. These would knock out the enemy's ground-based C3, including radio and TV networks that can keep ground forces informed of general instructions, and other lucrative but initially heavily defended targets.

Only with these mutually supportive advance parties working successfully together can the friendly airborne attack waves exist for very long, operating close to the FLOT to break the resolve of enemy ground forces, deep behind the lines to sever supply lines, and to smash their reserves. Nor friendly ground forces continue to function in any useful capacity or prepare their offensive action, with or without heliborne support. Air superiority thus represents the lifting moment which picks up the whole campaign by its bootlaces.

Situational Awareness: SEAD and Cappers

The crux of the issue remains to get in there early, and knock out the leading edge of the opponent: massive attrition *ab initio*. As SAM radars and enemy fighters pose the greatest initial threat, so 'first in, last out', as the Vietnam era motto decreed, are the SEAD forces and combat air patrollers (CAPs or Cappers). While this vanguard does operate with considerable autonomy which draws on their skill and initiative they, too, are inextricably intertwined. As Gulf F-4G *Wild Weasel* veteran Capt Spike Benyshek put it succinctly: 'There is a factor of mutual support between us and the Cappers, as we protect them from surface-to-air threats, while they protect us from air-to-air threats. Technically, we and they are both performing an air superiority mission – our actions allow the strikers/recces to move unimpeded, with impunity.'

This offensive action is designed to open up corridors into enemy territory which can subsequently be prized further apart, and begins along similar lines. Both Cappers and SEAD Flights will fill their tanks before entering hostile airspace, then adopt radio silence and go about their business in twins. Initially, up to 48 pairs of air superiority and radar-smashing fighters (based on Gulf War frags) will be thrusting forwards. Once the initial barrage is complete, a process that can endure for 48–72 hours using a succession of such large waves, tactics evolve into continuous patrols. Perhaps it is more accurate to modify the Vietnam era motto to 'first in – and remaining'!

En route to the 'push point' (the first route point or waypoint over enemy territory, usually planned for a precise pre-arranged time), the spearheads will first switch radio frequency to AWACS, and then arm their weapons. Some long-range weapons take time to warm-up adequately, while it is always a good idea to check through the various switch settings again, just in case a vital system indicates it is going to 'go ape' at a crucial moment in the thick of battle. AWACS is the great controlling agency which oversees proceedings from its lofty perch, and three or four such aircraft will be airborne at one time, covering various defined sectors. At this stage, these will be orbiting far away from the FLOT, but are nonetheless vital.

Periodically they will provide us with picture calls – a God's-eye view of aircraft activity in our area of concern. One may make the analogy that AWACS radar gives us the Big Picture, while a fighter's radar is like looking through a section of pipe. If they give us an initial picture, we concentrate our search in *that* area, and then take the appropriate action.

And it is worth bearing in mind that an air combat confrontation between opposing fighters, once vectored into position with engines blazing, might start at a closing speed of up to Mach 3 and guzzle up 45,000 ft of airspace in the vertical axis in under 1 minute! Speed, radar detection range, and knowledge of the opponent all feature strongly: different fighters have different strengths and weaknesses.

It can be argued that the major part of the skill of being a *successful* fighter pilot is the ability to force the opponent to fight on *your* terms using, say, superior radar or other sensors, especially before range closes to visual or eyeballing distances. AWACS can provide that edge, or suitable preparation for it, at least. The various missiles and radar modes (elaborated upon below) begin at a stand-off range of some 130 miles and close sometimes to virtually touching distances. It is important to bear in mind that

Previous page: *A fully-armed F-15C Eagle soars over Mount McKinley in Alaska, armed with Sparrow and Sidewinder AAMs. The Eagle was the first air superiority fighter to introduce HOTAS weapons/radar selection for air-to-air combat. (McAir)*

switching between these, and trusting that all is well, is often a time-compressed world where 'life or death, win, lose or draw, can all take place in under 5 minutes'. It is very difficult to relate these dynamics when lots of words stretch out time. Let the reader imagine that he is in a time-warped world and much of the aerial combat described in this chapter takes place in a matter of a few hundred seconds.

There are formation routines when leaving the push point. Common to both SEAD and Cappers is the overriding requirement to protect 'friendly tails', and not to go off on some wild-goose chase in pursuit of personal glory. The dangers inherent in these missions, and the accolades flowing from success, can sometimes prove irresistible, however. In terms of formation work, right up until the Vietnam War, the favoured tactic was for a Flight of four fighters to split into two and function as tightly knit pairs. The US Navy in Vietnam found this tactic too constraining, and evolved the Loose Deuce concept, which took advantage of the modern fighter's superior radar search ability, so that a pair of fighters could 'broomsweep' a much wider area and do so with much greater fuel efficiency. For fuel economy as well as tactical reasons, being spaced out is preferable to being welded.

Closely formating or trailing wingmen tend to burn up fuel much faster owing to all the minor throttle adjustments required to stay nudged close to their leader, even with today's DEECS and DAFECS trimming the engines automatically. The energy that can be rapidly created by the instantaneous thrust response available from today's top-of-the-line engines in 'slick' fighter airframes is truly awesome. The aircraft possess thrust to weight ratios well in excess of unity. Aircraft can even accelerate in a vertical climb, and reaccelerate to high transonic speeds in 15–30 seconds in an unloaded airframe with the throttle levers slammed forward from a virtual standstill following an aerodynamic braking manoeuvre. Thus, when these are combined with advanced and reliable digital radar and CNI avionics, much of the coordination between wingmen can be done out at the edge of visual range of one another.

The USAF, and many other air arms too, eventually adopted the US Navy's Loose Deuce formation. Of course, new names had to be conjured up, so as to preserve Service pride! In the USAF it was adopted as the Tactical Formation. As described to the author, the concept comes into play after the vanguard leave the push point.

JTIDS symbology assists the crew with that essential but intangible ingredient known as situational awareness. (Rockwell Collins)

Our wingman automatically moves out to Tactical, a position abreast of us and 1½–3 miles out. Usually, he will also stack high or low. That is, he will not be at the same altitude as us. In an aerial engagement, if you see one opponent, it is very easy to find his wingman if he is level with his leader – that is the tendency of the visual scan. However, if he stacks, the visual pick–up is much more difficult. The purpose of Tac Formation is to allow each aircraft to 'check six' behind the other aircraft for any approaching bandits or missiles, and have sufficient time to transmit a warning to his wingman. This is necessary as all aircraft have blind zones where they are vulnerable to undetected attack.

Such zones still account for 80 per cent of kills, a factor that has remained constant throughout the history of aerial combat.

Once at their assigned positions, the Cappers usually take up racetrack holding patterns 10 miles wide at optimum cruise heights in the mid-twenties. They use their look-up/look-down radar modes in concert with AWACS to establish BVR kill boxes to keep enemy fighters at bay from the strikers. In high-asset value combat air patrols (HavCAP) they take up positions further back to provide a protective umbrella over vulnerable machines like AWACS which will move forward towards the FLOT only after air superiority has been established. During *Desert Storm*, some of these HavCAP patrols lasted a staggering 6–9 hours

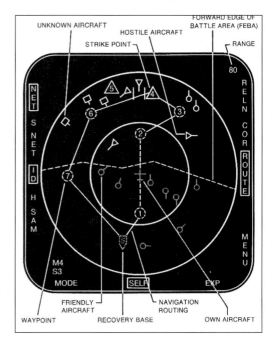

apiece, with multiple refuellings in-between.

Strike escorts, too, nowadays adopt more fluid formations, designed to maximize the use of their radar and E-O coverage while snaking or performing figure-of-eights around the main strike formations. SEAD jets adopt an even more fluid stance, generally working equally vigorously in the vertical axis. This is to minimize vulnerability and maximize the reach of their missiles in their cat-and-mouse duels with the enemy's ground defences. Escort *Wild Weasels* in the second tier often loft their rocket-powered radar-hunting weapons over the heads of the strike wave at launch heights of 25,000 ft or more, at a time when the latter are just beginning to 'wake up' the enemy.

So, cruising along in this manner is not such a leisurely activity as one might at first imagine. For a start, there may be the rumblings of 57 mm or 120 mm, high-altitude flak pounding the sky. Even lower-calibre, 37 mm AAA optically guided or aimed by 'wild-assed guess' can reach nearly 4 miles up into the air. If correctly fuzed to go off at the appropriate altitude, can be more than a nuisance. After all, the enemy gunners want to make a show of it too.

Amidst all this, and the enemy's deluge (initially, at least) of SAMs and fighters, there is the constant routine of getting updated picture calls from AWACS. These can be conveyed verbally using secure voice channels as in the case of a SEAD F-4G *Wild Weasel*. Alternatively, they are fed directly onto an MFD of one of the newer fighters fitted with a JTIDS terminal, such as equips a Multi-Stage Improvement Program (MSIP)-updated F-15A/C Eagle, or Tornado F.3 Capper. JTIDS is state-of-the-art. It exchanges sensor information, such as radar tracks, to compile a tactical picture that is shared by all users. The actual cockpit display provides a continuously updated, synthesized status report regarding the disposition of friendly and enemy aircraft. This is shown in plan-view from the receiver's perspective, and presented in colour-coded graphics.

Even routine turns in Tac Formation require some thought. As Capt Spike Benyshek reiterated.

It is not a simple matter of moving the stick at this point. Our wingman is [effectively] in formation, so when we turn, we are really turning the formation. One cannot just turn and expect one's wingman, 3 miles away, to be able to maintain his line-abreast position.

Let's examine the 'tac-turn'. We are heading north and our wingman is 2 miles on our right, at three o'clock. We want to turn left, so we make an exaggerated bank to the left (about 45°–60°), pause, and roll-out [wings-level]. At this point, our heading has changed only slightly. Our wingman, upon seeing this, goes into a 3 g turn to the left. We still continue straight ahead. When he reaches a position of about four-thirty or five o'clock, we start our turn to the left. If timed properly, we will roll out abeam him on the desired heading. Much practice has gone into these types of turns, beginning in pilot training, to allow us the ease of consistently achieving the proper formation on roll-out. It becomes apparent that the good Flight Lead must plan ahead for his turns, as it takes about 2 miles to accomplish.

Close-in formation-keeping is easier to the uninitiated, but the concept of going to battle in welded wing or finger four (as was practised by many air arms as routine, right up until the late 1970s) is very much a thing of the past. Once the force has crossed the FLOT and left the push point they are known to be in-country and are operating in their first period of 'vul time' (vulnerability). Real-time relay of the position of friendly fighters, furnished by data-links such as the JTIDS, is now coming to the fore. Obviously, in pitch-black conditions, JTIDS is the only realistic quiet form of communication. (Electro-luminescent strips, which glow on the aircraft's flanks and wing-tips, are only good for close-in formation-keeping and are of no help here.) Wingmen can go about their business and 'speak' to each other on their instruments, and use discreet visual cues such as a tail or wing waggle if there is good moonlight above the clouds. For the Cappers, these turns are virtually constant, as they maintain the various dog-legs of their holding positions.

Of particular concern during the initial stages of a rapidly joining conflict are enemy fighters swooping in fast and low using radar quiet intercept (RQI) techniques initially relying solely on passive RWRs to provide SA, to pincer-up far behind the Cappers to take out AWACS and their HavCAPs. Similar breakaway sniper elements from an enemy gorilla package, if it got off the ground in time, might also be closing range fast to swoop up and knock out the lead waves of Cappers and SEAD jets too. Therefore, checking six – using the RWR displays which provide 360° coverage, and looking behind, using both rubber-necking and the canopy bow's rear-view mirrors – forms part of the routine. This is in case the AWACSs are overwhelmed with their own problems and some of the enemy have successfully evaded radar detection by means of jamming. Coalition forces encountered remarkably little jamming during the Gulf War, and may have provided participating forces with a false sense of security.

Using such an electronic smokescreen, enemy fighters could well be lurking in the vicinity, employing RQI infrared search-and-track (IRST), such as the MiG-23's TP-23, or newer devices available to the MiG-29 and Su-27. These Russian-made IRSTs use reliable liquid nitrogen cooling. This is virtually inexhaustible, squirted into the sensor from a large Dewar or Thermos, to cool the sensor down to 77 K – only 77°C above Absolute Zero where all molecular activity ceases, or −196°C in ordinary language. With the sensor's system cooled, it can detect, at long-range, unusual contrasts in temperature about its forward upper hemispheric field of view (FoV), such as the hot engines or aerodynamically warmed airframe of a fighter or GLOB against the backdrop of the cool upper air. (Ambient air temperature cools with altitude until it reaches an internationally accepted average of −56.5°C at 36,090 ft, and then remains constant up to 65,617 ft before rising again at 0.3°C per 1,000 ft.) It can do this even though the aircraft might all have been shaded or hangared prior to take-off, and had their fuel pumped aboard from cold, subterranean holding tanks.

If the TP-23 IRST of the earlier-generation MiG-23 could obtain a positive lock-on against difficult (i.e. low-level) targets at slant-ranges of 15 miles, the follow-on devices can almost certainly track targets at significantly greater range in look-up mode. Their latest wide FoV heat-seeking missiles can be cued by IRST (as well as radar), with the quarry presented on the HUD, comparing favourably with the narrow FoV heat-seeking missiles of the West which rely exclusively on radar-sighting or visual-sighting to assist with lock-on. Aviators reliant on American hardware are becoming increasingly aware of the potency of their potential adversaries' IRSTs in this scenario (long since abandoned in their own fighters) and are beginning to reappraise their value.

Little ripples have now become big waves. Eurofighter 2000 is to incorporate the Italian FIAR Passive Infrared Airborne Tracking Equipment (PIRATE), which will work as both an IRST and use signal processing to furnish infrared images to boot. A similar electronic-based sensor array is under long-term development for the Lockheed F-22A Rapier. However, at present there are no Western fighters extant fitted with such a device, although some Blackworld (top secret) adaptations of existing American AAMs such as the Raytheon AIM-7R Sparrow III and AIM-9R Sidewinder employ non-pre-cooled passive IIR sensors. These are able to furnish a sketchy image of the target at BVR on the radarscope (which doubles as a head-down E-O screen to view the imagery when switched over from radar, to help identify the otherwise nondescript target symbol in a long-range intercept). In fact, it has been reported by two independent sources that such a Sparrow III adaptation bagged the first Iraqi aircraft claimed as

destroyed during the Gulf War: a MiG-29, brought down by a 33rd TFW F-15C Eagle, though only its pilot, Capt John K. Kelk, and those who worked with him, know for sure. However, such weapons still employ very limited FoVs which are heavily reliant on precise target vectors from AWACS and the fighter's onboard radar sensor, and so cannot be used to search and track like an IRST.

Apparently, the Pentagon is also now beginning to admit that at least two US aircraft participating in the Gulf War were *probably* destroyed by Iraqi MiG-29 *Fulcrum*s using a combination of that aircraft's unique IRST, helmet-mounted sight and the R-73 *Archer* heat-seeking AAM. Acknowledging this longer-range RQI capability has created something of a panic in the US, given the recent proliferation of the latest Russian-built fighters and missiles abroad. Both AWACS and the Cappers might have a tough time catching them in the net, in time, given the MiGs' penchant for pseudo-stealthy, passive intercept techniques.

As the SEAD and MiGCAP fighters will be the first to ingress hostile airspace with such a heavy burden of responsibility, nerves can run high. Fear is seldom debilitating to aviators screened to fly the truly high-performance fighters (though always present as a spur to performance). The weeding-out process undertaken during aircrew selection ensures this. The superb peacetime training and planning teaches the novices how to overcome it, slowly control it, and even mould it to their advantage, to give them an edge. This cannot be underestimated: boosting the adrenalin adds to SA, and developing an on-off tap works wonders. According to the flight surgeons, flight-line doctors who oversee crews' state of mental as well as physical health, it is the middle-of-the-road types who do the best, and learn the techniques gradually and resolutely. Highly strung individuals tend to teeter towards self-annihilation. Control freaks, who have no problems in mastering the human heart-palpitating, self-destructive instinct, are apt to behave recklessly without regard for teamwork, and often place their colleagues at risk. Highly strung or pathologically cool types are thus equally unsuited to flying modern high-performance aircraft and both categories are weeded out early on in the induction process.

If the carefully, and massively invested-in 'aviator jockeys get the "jitters", then it is time to "remount the horse and ride" and, if overly cautious, to dismount – forever'. Words of wisdom from an old Second World War instructor which remain equally valid today. Each machine on the flight-line costs tens of millions in taxpayers' money and can sometimes be irreplaceable, but the real consideration is that bad aviators can all too easily place their peers in jeopardy, and cost other aviators' lives needlessly – not to mention the mission objective.

All these thoughts trouble the commanders as the vanguard of their package pushes into enemy airspace to cut open a corridor through his defences in preparation for the main waves. If they fail, the whole operation can turn out to be a costly fiasco (and a major political embarrassment which can cost careers). During the Gulf War, one *Wild Weasel* commander became known as 'Zipper' because his anxiety developed into a nervous habit of toying with his flightsuit chest pockets. Most overcame such tremors by leading their flyers into battle.

Let us now get into the biting edge of the SEAD and air-to-air communities' massively different but equally demanding technology and tactics.

SAM-Busters

The SEAD mission dates back to the days when the opposition began taking pot-shots at aircraft. Aircraft would reply against machine-guns with machine-gun fire, *quid pro quo*. However, the concept of defeating ground defences as a specific mission only matured as late as the war in Vietnam. This was based on anti-radar missile (ARM) technology developed by the US Navy to counter the Soviet-supplied SAM-guiding radars they first confronted during the Cuban Crisis in late 1962. Three years later, seagoing American aviators flying with the 'Tonkin Gulf Yacht Club' against North Vietnam under the jurisdiction of US Navy Task Force 77 in the South China Sea had created a special package known as *Iron Hand* designed to knock out these SAM, AAA and GCI radars. The USAF knew it by the code-name *Wild Weasel*, developed a year later. This employed a succession of fighters specially adapted to the task.

Both services went about their missions using broadly similar technology, the crux of which was the Texas Instruments (TI) AGM-45 Shrike ARM. It could be lofted at arm's length, describing a big arc of 10–15 miles from the 45°–70° pull-up launch point, from which it descended on the target after reaching the apex of its flight. Alternatively, it could be pointed and shot directly at the offending dish within visual range of 1–2 miles, in a level or dive manoeuvre. Both tactics were accompanied by the radio call *Shotgun* so that wingmen would not mistake Shrike's rocket plume for an enemy SAM. As long as the enemy emitter continued to broadcast its tell-tale radar signals, Shrike would continue to home in. If the enemy radar shut down in a defensive mode, Shrike went ballistic: it lost guidance and simply shot along its existing trajectory. Either way, by destroying the

radar or obliging its operators to close down, the enemy lost guidance information for its AAA and SAMs and sufficient time was usually bought to enable the main strike waves to ingress and egress the area relatively unmolested.

Meanwhile the SEAD jets, in turn, closed in for the kill and demolished the AA complex, vans, dishes, SAM launchers and all, by lobbing barrel loads of 'pickled fruit' – one or more of many cluster bomb units (CBUs) containing Guavos, Oranges and Grapefruit. All of these represented various hideous modes of shredding gunners, radars and missiles with submunitions containing flechêttes, ball-bearings and high-explosive (HE). Iron fragmentation bombs, typically Mk 82 low-drag general purpose (LDGP) or Snakeye retarded fin 500-pounders, were also commonly employed (this class of bomb accounting for 90 per cent of the total tonnage dropped by the US Navy in South-East Asia). It was a dangerous and loathsome job, but one designed to 'protect butt' and, as such, commanded considerable respect from these flyers' peers.

Flak suppression was also conducted as part and parcel of this surprise package, located by looking out for muzzle flashes. This meant lobbing the metal straight on top of the enemy gunners' heads at close-quarters as further discouragement. *In extremis*, an M118 3,000 lb HE demolition bomb was used, fitted with a 3 ft pipe. Known as the 'Daisy Cutter', it caused the device to detonate just above ground-level and 'blow out eardrums half a mile distant'. Needless to say, accuracy with the M118 was not paramount! It was all fairly fancy stuff which combined fearsome weapons and clever tactics at the sharp end of aerial combat.

Initial target acquisition of an SA-2 *Dvina* SAM's *Fan Song*, or AAA *Fire Can* radar guidance system – the principal emitters encountered in South-East Asia – was based on Elint garnered by support aircraft and TF77 picket ships. This was suitably plotted on a map and was made available for flight-planning, when scrutinizing the EOB, or via in-flight warnings over the radio. However, the most vital real-time threat intelligence was derived from the SEAD fighters' own onboard RWR gear (known then as radar homing & warning system, or RHAWS).

RWR and related passive tracking equipment developed for *Iron Hand* was based around two principle types of 'sniffing' technology: interferometers and superheterodynes. Interferometers could pick up a signal within selected wavebands and determine its direction of arrival (DoA) and thus radar azimuth or bearing. Allied to these, superheterodynes mixed the incoming signals with a lower frequency to produce a beat, from which would be deduced pulse repetition frequency (PRF). Formerly known as pulse repetition rate or PRR, it is the pattern of pulses sent out by the enemy radar. The status or operating mode of the radar could be ascertained from this. Frequency within the radio frequency spectrum which would help identify the type of threat, and signal intensity which would provide a rough guess as to range, and also operating mode could also be determined.

From the cockpit perspective the multiple signals were processed to resonate in the receiving aviator's headset with warble sounds (something akin to a modern car alarm, but higher in pitch). Different radars were brought to the flyer's attention as different sorts of warbles – all very confusing to the untrained, and for this reason sometimes irritating or unnerving! Backing up the aural inputs was an RWR crystal video display, resembling a small dartboard on the main instrument panel, which furnished the threats as strobe lines poking in from the edges, as a means to help identify immediately the threat by azimuth. As the strobe sneaked inward (a strand of bright green light) it would pass various range increment circles, giving some clue as to the radar site's distance. Rectangular warning lamps mounted under the coaming would also light up to indicate imminent attack by an enemy AAA, fighter or SAM.

Twin-seaters had a second crewman dedicated to the task, such as an *Iron Hand* Naval Flight Officer (NFO) in the right-hand seat of an A-6B Intruder, or the EWO or 'Bear' in the back of a USAF F-105F/G *Thud Weasel*. They had access to more finely tuned receivers and a panoramic display. This flashed-up additional raw data relating to wave form and PRF which, with considerable training assisted the EW specialist in fathoming out the real threats, based upon the warbles, strobe lines and other data. The USAF, for example, ran a six-month EW course for 'new guys' that covered everything from EW theory through equipment functions and the development of hands-on kinesics of switching in mock battle.

In Vietnam, typical tactics called for the *Iron Hand* machines to fly in ahead of the strike waves at medium altitudes (FL180-220). When the enemy radars came on the air, they would take the jets down in a wild dive to 500 ft (below which SAMs usually could not function), prior to initiating their attack. The EWOs would then prick up their ears and exercise their hands and eyes using the various displays before commanding their pilots to perform a pop-up to 2,000–10,000 ft (depending on estimated range to the emitter) for a Shrike launch or bomb run. Against pre-planned targets using an established EOB to work

Wild Weaseling began in earnest with the introduction of adapted models of the F-105F/G Thunderchief, back in 1966. The type soldiered on in the SEAD role for 17 more years until the Dobbins-based, Georgia ANG relinquished their final 'Thuds'. (Lindsay Peacock)

An A-6B Iron Hand *Intruder is bombed-up on deck with Mk 82 500 lb bombs and the giant AGM-78B Standard ARM (still wearing its protective cap). (US Navy)*

The A-6B cockpit revealed. At left, the pilot has access to a repeater radar (below) and TV contact-analogue flight display – his 'highway in the sky' – which effectively relegated the traditional ADI and HSI to back-up duties. At right, the bombardier/navigator NFO or 'rad nav' enjoyed access to radar and copious BNS controls associated with DIANE. Note the little 'dartboard' screens at centre and far right which provided an immediate cue to enemy radar threats. This was state-of-the-art in 1972. (Grumman)

with, Shrikes would sometimes be lofted from low-to-medium level at great distance, a tactic espoused by US Navy A-6B NFOs. This enabled them to lob up to four Shrikes in a vertical fan pattern to cover a bigger footprint, before their colleagues followed-up the attack at close-quarters using Rockeye CBU canisters and iron bombs.

Beginning in 1968, the General Dynamics AGM-78A Standard ARM (known to Navy crews as STARM Mod.0) was introduced to combat. Initially, this worked in just the same manner as Shrike, except that it had an effective range of 30–35 miles. Passive angle tracking (PAT) methods soon followed with the introduction of a new gimballed missile seeker created with the AGM-78B Mod.1 *et seq*. It permitted the NFO or Bear to actually steer its broad-band ('I'm receptive to all threats') seeker about by means of a switch. Techniques were actually developed by academia at John Hopkins University, which helped devise the necessary computer programmes for the related avionics. Thus, the aircraft could give the impression that it was not tracking the enemy radar, while all the time STARM was locked-on. The missile would then change course after launch, to zap the emitter unexpectedly.

Additionally, two separate azimuth readings could be taken from the ARM's Maxson seeker which functioned much like a specialized RWR in its own right, and could be correlated with the SEAD aircraft's onboard equipment. This could then be used to triangulate the radar site's position. Flying along in a blasé fashion at 18,000 ft, two different DoAs could be read off on the correlator-receiver, permitting the SEAD jet to plot target position fairly precisely, which could subsequently be used for a more accurate ARM loft launch. It could also to help plot target position on the radar for a blind bomb pass – especially useful for night-time work. PAT/ARM, as these techniques were known, became available to A-6B Intruder crews during 1969. By this time *Iron Hand* had also evolved into a night-time task in support of interdiction (INT) strikes carried out along the Ho Chi Minh Trail on the Laos–Vietnam border. These were intended to knock out the heavily defended gaps at places like the Ban Karai and Mu Gia passes, through which much of the enemy's war *matériel* flowed to the guerrilla enclaves in the south.

The USAF continued to work mostly by day, and employed the coloured smoke given off by an erupting Standard ARM (their preferred appellation) to locate the site for the mopping-up attack with gravity weapons. This feature gave rise to the Israeli Heyl Ha'Avir, the sole export client for the AGM-78, nicknaming it the 'Purple Fist'. By the mid-1970s, every jet fighter in the US inventory had been wired up for Shrike, whilst a few specialist conversions continued to tote newer and even better models of STARM. These included follow-on SEAD aircraft such as the A-6E Intruder, F-105G *Thud Weasel*, and a newly evolved subvariant of the McDonnell Douglas F-4 Phantom II, described below.

'Hard kill EW' came of age during the Vietnam War. Along with smart weapons, it was one of the outstanding American technical achievements during that era, at a time when the conflict as a whole had deteriorated on a political level into a technical scrap. New devices could be wrung-out in combat trials in preparation for possible war in Europe. Overall, however, it helped to reduce losses to enemy radar-guided weaponry by over an order of magnitude, from a horrendous 1965 high in excess of 14 per cent to around 1 per cent by the time of the Linebacker offensives, seven years later. And this was despite the increased ferocity and sophistication of the defences.

The AGM-45A Shrike remains in use today, finely pretuned to some 13 different radar types as a cheap and cheerful means of getting the enemy to shut down his radars temporarily. STARM has long since been superseded by the broad-band TI AGM-88A HARM, and a veritable circus of new SEAD platforms crewed by a new generation of aviators. HARM is now in use on fighters ranging in size and complexity from the petite F-16C to the RAAF's bantamweight F-111C Aardvark bombers. Seven air arms from five nations employ it in their armouries. However, the basics of the equipment used draw heavily on experience in South-East Asia. Tentatively introduced to service in 1981 and first used in anger by the US Navy against Libya and Iran five years later, HARM may be employed in three primary modes.

First is pre-emptive, the Pre-Brief mode, used ahead of the strike waves, and based on operating frequencies preprogrammed into the weapon prior to take-off. This is a process conducted during ground handling, when the missile can be loaded with specifics of three different but usually closely arranged missile sites based on pre-combat Elint. These comprise primary, secondary and tertiary targets. Pre-Brief mode is used most often for lofting at stand-off ranges of up to 60 miles. It will then guide in azimuth to the first programmed threat, relying on the target to emit signals and identify itself in order for it to home in precisely. If that fails, it will then seek out the second target, then the third, before reverting automatically to target of opportunity (ToO) mode – the second option – and use its AN/AWG-25 passive seeker to lock-up unassisted on any radiation source known to be hostile. As a specific option, ToO is not particularly discriminatory, but can be employed 'down the throat' in the heat of exchange between opposing ground and air power, much like Shrike, or simply lobbed in the general direction of the enemy at range, in the hope it will do some harm. Finally, it may be employed intimately in the self-protect mode, when it is handed-off to a target precisely using a sophisticated SEAD jet's discreet radar sniffing apparatus for lofting or level launches. Here, the weapon will be in-flight programmed to go and turn onto a heading, and look for such a threat.

Arguably by far the most capable SEAD fighter employed in the Persian Gulf, and still operational in limited numbers today is the McDonnell Douglas F-4G *Advanced Wild Weasel V* – the fifth in this illustrious line. An examination of this aircraft's capabilities, and how it was employed in the Gulf War, best explains the HARM's capabilities and SEAD options, to the full.

The F-4G's AN/APR-47 *Weasel* Attack Signal Processor (WASP) represented the only credible, self-contained radar-hunting package available to the Coalition forces. This was updated from the late 1970s-vintage *Wild Weasel* V AN/APR-38 homing and warning computer (HAWC) under Phase One of the Performance Update Program (PUP) only a few years prior to *Desert Storm*. The HAWC (unfortunately the exact capabilities of the newer WASP remain strictly classified, although the original kit draws a good picture for comparison) was totally integrated with the AGM-78 Standard ARM, and follow-on AGM-88 HARM.

The F-4G's automated processors and interactive alphanumeric displays presented the threat data on three new displays dominating the back-seat EWO's 'wall of iron' or main instrument panel. Two of these comprised the panoramic and homing indicators, which provided such esoteric information as PRFs, frequencies, and so on. Pride of place was given over to a relatively huge plan position indicator (PPI). This was the equivalent of a giant RWR scope but completely digital, and furnished threats picked-up by the HAWC in simple alphanumerics on its giant concentrically ringed affair. These radars were prioritized on the PPI based on a preprogrammed threat library held in the HAWC – e.g. a '6' represented a Russian *Straight Flush* continuous wave tracking/illumination dish and allied trio of SA-6 SAMs. These were plotted exactly in terms of location and bearing on the screen, which also furnished precise range.

The display could be altered by simple switch settings to accommodate the 5, 10 or 15 most important threats at range increments extending out to 200 miles. The selection was up to the EWO, taking into account working ranges and the concentration of the enemy's defences. This permitted him to junk all

but the most serious threats if he was in danger of becoming overloaded amidst a multiplex of signals, and his own preferences or abilities in terms of task saturation. (There was a joke at one time that F-4G EWOs needed to take off their boots and use their toes in order to keep apace of the swift switchology.) One of these targets would be singled out by the computer as being the most dangerous and be highlighted by a triangular surround.

If the EWO objected to the computer's automatic choice, based on a cross-scan with the panoramic and homing indicators, and warbles fed through his earphones, he could override it. This he did by inching a diamond cursor across and over the preferred threat symbol, using a transducer switch (similar in all respects to a control stick trim button). Once the cursor was in place, he had effectively overridden the HAWC. This was where the EWO's sixth sense came into play. Hundreds of hours of practice on the Nellis, and USAFE Polygone ranges were used to help develop this art. Radar simulators based on captured Soviet equipment and specially fabricated substitutes provided the basis for EWOs to sort out a multitude of signals, reject decoys, and learn how to avoid SAM traps.

Whether the HAWC or EWO made the choice, with the cursor positioned all relevant target data would be 'handed off' to a HARM at a flick of a switch. The HARM received precise range and bearing, and radar characteristics via a navigational coupler interface (NCI) serving as an electronic interpreter to translate the HAWC language into missile language. The missile could then fired from the front or back seat at the press of the stick trigger button, after which it would remember where the target was located, and go about its business unaided from then on, impacting with a 125 lb blast-fragmentation warhead. This has since been modified with tungsten alloy cubes for added lethality; yet it only takes some of this shotgun-like blast to render a radar dish inoperative, while the kinetic energy from a direct HARM hit would destroy it utterly. The F-4G crew were then free to hand off a second target to another missile, and so on, if a third and fourth HARM were carried, until they ran out of weapons. Alternatively, they close in for the kill with cluster and iron bombs if these were being toted on that mission.

Interestingly, during the first 72 hours of *Desert Storm*, the F-4G crews carried out what was known as the SEAD Campaign. They flew almost exclusively with a centreline 'bag' (600 US gal fuel drop tank) and wall-to-wall HARMs comprising four suspended on individual launch rails under the wings. As it is understood by the author, the Sperry CP-1674 WASP system left the switchology unchanged from the

HAWC era, though by means of expanded computer capacity and new software the F-4Gs were able to acquire and analyse their potential targets five times more quickly. Anyone who has even a vague appreciation of the growth that took place in computer technology between 1977 and 1985 can readily appreciate the difference between the HAWC and WASP.

The 50 F-4Gs clustered together at Sheikh Isa AB, Bahrain under control of the 35th TFW(P), launched their first combat sorties on the opening night of the air war. They were preceded by BQM-174C *Scathe Mean Chukar* drones and US Navy/Brunswick ADM-141 TALDs which emulated waves of Coalition strike jets and woke up the Iraqi defences in time for the premier volley of pre-briefed HARMs which sought out many of them specifically. Literally dozens of Iraqi radar sites were knocked out within minutes of the opening offensive, to the F-4Gs' war cry Magnum. HARM flight was so rapid that EWOs would watch the threats disappear from the PPI shortly after launch. As veteran Spike Benyshek described it, from the pilot's position: 'At pickle [pressing the firing button], there is a resounding "clunk!" as the missile comes off the rail. Usually, the pilot's first view of the missile is when it is already 1,000 ft in front of the aircraft – this is a fast missile!'

Wave Two of the F-4Gs flew in trail behind the first batch of INT jets, and similarly launched HARMs in Pre-Brief mode over their colleagues' heads! Programming for the missiles was furnished by extensive pre-war Elint. Several hundred were lofted in gentle climbs during the opening hours of *Desert Storm*, timed so that the weapons started descending onto their preselected targets just as the strikers began to come within detection range of the Iraqi defences, which might be unimpressed by a second onslaught of decoys. Thinking they were just about to down some Coalition jets, the radar sites suddenly found themselves on the receiving end of a swarm of anti-radiation missiles!

During subsequent escort, the follow-up waves of HARM-brandishing F-4Gs patrolled sectors with the WASP receptive to enemy radar activity, then took them out using target data picked-up and prioritized by the WASP, and vetted by the EWO. The key factor here was to position the F-4G so that the HARM's high-speed flight characteristics permitted it to strike the target dish before a SAM was fired. If a SAM was being launched, the goal was to strike its tracking or illuminating radar during the mid-course phase of flight so that the enemy's weapon was rendered impotent in flight and would simply go ballistic; i.e. fly without guidance. This was an art which required considerable cool, as timing and target selection mattered a great deal. Interestingly, not one Coalition aircraft was lost to an enemy SAM while there were F-4Gs supporting them.

Brandishing small arms, the 35th TFW(P) pose for the camera in front of a pair of their F-4G Advanced Wild Weasels during the Gulf War, at Sheikh Isa AB, Bahrain. Elements deployed from California and USAFE. (Col Uke Uken)

Northrop BQM-174C Scathe Mean Chukar *drones were one device used to 'wake up' enemy defences during the Gulf War. This made the SEAD crews' job of identifying the sites and lobbing HARM missiles at them much less strenuous. (Northrop)*

Following the successful prosecution of the SEAD Campaign, when it was deemed that air superiority had been firmly established over the Kuwaiti Theatre of Operations (KTO) and most of Iraq, the 35th TFW(P) F-4G force switched from successive waves of a dozen aircraft apiece to what the crews described as 'Weasel Police' tactics. By this time the operating heights had escalated to the mid-to-upper twenties where only occasional SAMs and flak from 100mm AAA presented a hazard. Thus it was possible for a smaller number of aircraft to provide much broader area coverage, each toting only two HARMs and three bags of fuel. As Lt-Col 'Uke' Uken described it: 'Weasel Police missions typically tasked six F-4Gs, split into sections of two. Each would loiter in the target area for half an hour, with two jets inbound and two outboard for aerial refuelling replenishment. After 4–5 hours, another "six-ship" would take over.' The three F-4G squadrons committed to the conflict kept up this tempo throughout the air war, which endured until 3 March 1991, when hostilities were formally suspended.

Altogether, the F-4G crews launched some 1,300 HARMs, mostly newer AGM-88B models which could be programmed at the bases using fresh Elint data. These accounted for some 60 per cent of the total number of firings. The balance was largely employed by F-16Cs and F/A-18C Hornets in the lob-and-leave modes, assisting with the initial barrage, or providing covering fire for the F-4Gs which nuzzled in close to the targets to sniff out the sites individually for a greater probability of a kill. Radar sites confirmed as destroyed by the F-4G establishment amounted to some 250. The highest scores went to Capt Vinnie Quinn and his EWO Maj Ken Spaar, who fired 30 missiles and zapped 12 sites.

Remarkably, despite some close calls with major flak damage, the F-4G force suffered only one loss. On the night of 19 January 1991 Capts Tim Burke (pilot) and Juan Galindez (EWO) found themselves low on fuel (possibly following a 'lucky BB' or chance stray shot from an Iraqi AAA gun). After several attempted landings at King Khalid Military City, all aborted because of failed landing lights and dense fog at the final critical 400 ft, the engines finally ran dry and seized up. Both crewmen ejected – with Galindez parachuting down onto the main runway! Both aviators returned to duty 48 hours later.

Nine F-4Gs undergo 'hot pit' refuelling at Sheikh Isa. A string of supply trucks from Port Manoma kept the fuel bladders replenished. Long in the tooth, the F-4G did sterling service in the Gulf War. (Col Uke Uken)

Capt. Pat Pence sends his love to Saddam Hussein. Morale-boosting graffiti was commonly applied to weapons during the Gulf War. (Col Uke Uken)

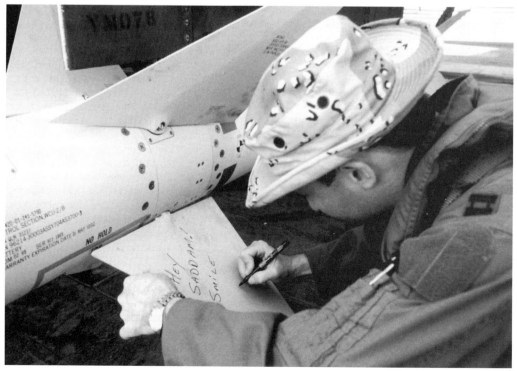

Vinnie Quinn (pictured in the cockpit) and his EWO Ken Spaar destroyed at least a dozen Iraqi radar sites during Desert Storm. *(Col Uke Uken)*

SEAD 2001

In all, 134 F-4Gs were converted from 'vanilla' Fiscal Year 1969 F-4E Phantom II stock under two separate batches. Today, 16 years down the road, only 48 F-4Gs (authorized) remain in service, split between two USAF squadrons. Recalled to duty just as plans were effected for their wholesale retirement, some of those now flying spent several weeks covered in protective Spraylat expanded plastic in the dusty desert Air Material & Reclamation Center (AMARC) at Davis-Monthan AFB, Arizona. However, since no new EWOs are being trained, all the officers are captains or higher-ranking and over 85 per cent are Gulf combat veterans. Curiously, the situation almost precisely mirrors that of 1973, shortly after the cessation of hostilities in South-East Asia, when only 44 of the F-4G's predecessor, the F-105G *Thud Weasel*, remained operational in two squadrons, and no genuine replacement was in sight.

It was Israel's Heyl Ha'Avir experience in the Yom Kippur War of October 1973 that convinced the Pentagon it needed the F-4G to begin with, owing to the horrendous Israeli losses inflicted by a post-Vietnam generation of Soviet-supplied anti-aircraft weapons. They seemed to be immune to contemporary self-protect ECM and some turned out to be invisible to existing RHAWS. Similar burning desires have been stoked with regard to the F-4G's replacement, this time based on its undoubted success in the Gulf War and the desperate need to replace the aged airframes. However, there is little impetus to create a follow-on dedicated twin-seater, and this has resulted in two parallel lower-key efforts: the interim F-16C-HTS (HARM Targeting System) and the longer-term F-15C-PDF (Precision Direction Finder).

The F-16C-HTS programme embraces 90 of the latest Production Block 50/52D 'Charlie' model, equipped with the AN/ASQ-213 HTS contained in a strap-on pod fitted to the right side of the nose – the so-called '*Weasel* in a can' capability. It entered service during the summer of 1994, expanding F-16 HARM modes to the full extent of the missile's operating envelope without having to rely on F-4G target calls. This had been the case previously when the little companions were used merely to lob missiles against lower-priority targets based on Pre-Brief threat data prioritized into the missile before take-off. Apparently, with HTS, 'and two thumb movements on the stick', a pilot can hand off a HARM against a freshly unveiled SAM site. However, Maj Kirk

Davidson, Idaho Air National Guard tactics officer is on record as claiming that HTS does not possess quite the flexibility of the F-4G's WASP. Its receivers are tuned to a narrower range of envisaged threats expected to be encountered on a given mission, and it is slower in analysing threat location, which might be critical at lower altitude.

Until the Gulf War, F-4G crews were trained to let down after the push point and conduct most of their mission's vul time at low-level, down to as little as 250–500 ft AGL. The two jets in each Flight would alternately use brief porpoising pop-up manoeuvres to acquire and periodically update their WASPs. The 'hi' altitudes that were commonly employed in the Gulf have effectively eroded this science, particularly in the single-seat community, whose pilots view themselves as air combat jockeys first, and radar 'dish-trashers' second. Nor is there a second crewman to analyse the threats in detail. As each foe operates his equipment a little differently and often changes tactics, the EWO is vital in being able to clarify what a computer cannot fully comprehend. It is the so-called sixth sense of these back-seaters, discussed earlier, which enables the F-4G to play its highly dangerous cat and mouse antics with the enemy. Moreover, as already outlined in the context of *Desert Storm* operations, current F-4G doctrine dictates that once the bulk of an enemy's EOB has effectively been neutralized by an initial barrage of HARMs, it is to use its sensitive equipment to operate close to the enemy. This is with

Already companions to the F-4G SEAD forces for some seven years, in the summer of 1994 selected F-16Cs began to receive the HTS, giving them an almost-as-good capability for medium-intensity combat. (Christian Gerard)

the intention of intimidating him into shutting down shop using intimate tactics with the missiles switched over to reaction modes. This permits the limited payload of HARM weapons to be held in reserve for possible use against a truly determined foe.

The single-seat F-16C-HTS might not be able to deal with such subtleties in the heat of battle and will have to go in for the kill every time a threat crops up. Realizing some of these limitations, the F-16C-HTS will thus be used first to supplement and learn its trade from the venerable F-4Gs, pending introduction of the more capable F-15C-PDF gear. This assumes that the dress rehearsals with that project meet all director's milestones, and the effort survives numerous fiscal contractions being imposed by its producers in the Pentagon, who seem to be seeking a gradually less lavish production.

F-16C-HTS and the new F-15C-PDF (some 100 of which will be adapted from aging single-seat Eagle stock at the turn of the century) will also make greater use of off-board Elint data gleaned by faraway giants such as the RC-135V/W *Rivet Joint*. This will help them get into good firing positions prior to switching over to the HTS and PDF systems. However, it has been pointed out that platforms like *Rivet Joint* do not get close enough to the targets to conduct raid assessment in near real-time. What might at first

appear to be a single threat may actually comprise two or more mobile SAM launchers clustered near each other. Repeated volleys of HARMs would have to be launched to ensure adequate SEADing *if* the F-16C's onboard HTS managed to pick this up in time before it was hacked down.

The fundamental rule of Weaseling is that the aircraft needs to be positioned 'where your missile time of flight is equal to or less than that of the SAM', not simply out at the edge of the SAM's lethal envelope, at 50 miles or more. The F-15C-PDF will use interferometric triangulation techniques for full 360° coverage similar to the F-4G (based on equipment in competitive development by Hughes and Litton/TRW) for close-in low-level and stand-off higher-altitude radar-smashing. It will be optimized to assist with HARM launches. But the reliance again on a single-seater, instead of the preferred choice of adapting the twin-seat, SAR radar-toting F-15E, may result in a grossly overtaxed pilot, and a commensurate loss of all the subtleties in searching, locating and analysing radar threats currently available to the twin-seat F-4G.

By contrast, in the aftermath of *Desert Storm*, Europe is pressing ahead with new EWO training efforts and dedicated SEAD technologies. Research and development currently far outstrips that being

A development Tornado GR.1 displays an unlikely load of seven ALARMs; in combat, the 'ALARMists' carried three such missiles on the centreline stations, the wings being burdened by giant 'Hindenberg' fuel tanks and the usual fit of BOZ-107 bulk chaff-dispensing and Sky Shadow ECM (as seen here on the outboard wing stations). (BAe Dynamics)

conducted by the US. Thus, the European equivalents based on the swing-wing Panavia Tornado will be in the same league as the WASP *Weasel* once they fully mature operationally. These are stock GR.1s with air-launched ARMs (ALARMs), an RAF and Saudi Arabian speciality relying on a hefty strap-on BAe Dynamics/GEC-Marconi missile, and Tornado Electronic Combat-Reconnaissance (ECR) aircraft, of which 51 are currently entering service with the Luftwaffe and Aeronautica Militare Italiane.

ALARM is self-contained for HARM-style pre-brief mode shooting. However, this is at the expense of the kind of detailed target discrimination described earlier, because of the lack of specialized sniffing gear on board the vanilla Tornado GR.1. If the F-4G WASP can be likened to a weasel with a big nose and an equally big bite, then the Tornado is mostly bite. Nevertheless, its greatest asset lies with the ALARM's pseudo-stealthy mode, whereby the missile soars up to 70,000 ft before para-descending at a comparatively leisurely pace. The moment a potential target starts radiating, the missile dumps its chute, ignites a

second-stage rocket motor, then charges into the radar. A similar nuisance capability was to have been furnished to the new American SEAD jets by the Northrop AGM-136 Tacit Rainbow, based on a cruise missile design which could offer 90 minutes' loiter time. However, this foundered, leaving ALARM as the only game in town. In the Gulf War, Sqn Ldr

Tornado 'ALARMists' from the RAF's No. 20 Squadron established their worth, firing 121 missiles and knocking out a couple of dozen sites. They kept heads-down. (RAF)

McAlpine's No. 20 Sqn ALARMists flew nine specially equipped Tornadoes and unleashed 121 rounds against Iraqi defences. It proved it worked.

Tornado ECR is fitted with a TI/Deutschland GmbH Emitter Location System (ELS) tailored to work with HARM. This enables it to use the missile to its maximum potential, while Litton-Litef Operational Data Interface (ODIN) link equipment provides a microwave relay of critical threat information to suitably equipped friendly aircraft – including AWACS – by means of JTIDS. This is similar in function to the Improved Data Modem (IDM) links equipping the F-16C-HTS. It allows them to join the fray and accurately deposit area weapons and iron bombs, even though they lack sharp emitter sniffing apparatus of their own. This is one area where the venerable F-4G falls down, because of a shortfall of funds to update it with suitable equipment: the relaying of critical target data to friendly aircraft it is supporting must be done verbally, over the radio, albeit scrambled. Phase Two of the F-4G PUP, which was to have updated the WASP with a new directional receiver group (DRG) and an IDM target relay system, was shelved some years ago, owing to the expected retirement of the aircraft and some technical problems. Quite sensibly, if retirement is impending, all updates not directly related to safety for that particular aircraft type are binned.

Moreover, target data picked up by the Tornado ECR's ELS is broad in frequency coverage *à la* F-4G, but by means of a modern channelized receiver as was intended with the latter's DRG update. This avoids the pitfalls found in wide-band and narrow-band receivers used previously to ensure a high probability of intercept of all pertinent ground signals. (Wide-band receivers tend to suffer from poor selectivity owing to their broad reception capabilities. Narrow-band receivers tend to suffer from limited coverage owing to their inherent selectiveness.) These are then compared with those stored in the threat library. The resulting threats are promptly displayed in typical Tornado, readily-digestible God's-eye-view graphics on the cockpit Combined Electronic Display & Map (CEDAM). Alphanumeric symbols are used to denote the type, status and location of each of the radars, which in turn is circumscribed by its known lethal radius of action. The Tornado's flight track is superimposed on that.

It is very much an EWO's aircraft. All of this relatively cosmic technology enables the back-seater to hand off targets to HARM, relay the threats to friendly fighters it is escorting as a pathfinder, and skirt around the emitters' periphery to tease them into going off the air, The back-seater can even record the Elint on airborne videotape recorder (AVTR),

alongside IIR reconnaissance data of the site if the crew dare to venture sufficiently close. ELS has been completely integrated with the Tornado's mission computer, cockpit displays, HARMs and control unit, and even ECM self-protect systems. Piloting cues are simultaneously furnished on the HUD for genuine head-up attack and evasion in all weathers. The aircraft might well be flown from the back seat using hands-off terrain-following radar (TFR) and autopilot based on the sequence of turn points held in the computer flight-plan, relegating the pilot to play with the throttles, and 'pole-pushing' on those rare occasions when his manual intervention is required.

With the F-4G all but bowing out, the F-16C-HTS providing only a '60 per cent replacement capability' in a high-intensity major regional conflict (MRC), and the F-15C-PDF a long way off yet, it is hardly surprising to discover that overseas air arms with a pressing requirement to update their defence-suppression forces have become interested in Tornado ECR. This is despite the cost and logistical burden of operating a small quantity of a sophisticated, specialized fighter.

Other measures are being evolved to defeat enemy radars and allied SAM complexes, but strictly for use by US forces owing to the classified nature of the various systems. Again, these have the goal of devolving the responsibility for SEAD across available air power. Diode-pumped, high-energy lasers could be installed in existing interdictors' navigation/targeting pods, such as the F-15E's LANTIRN, to damage the binary alloy detector array coatings of the optics in E-O tracking systems, and possibly to temporarily blind flak gunners too. Lasers could be tuned to the green part of the spectrum in which the human eye is most sensitive. Used in concert with the F-15C-PDF, a missile approach warning system (MAWS), flash indicators and a FLIR sensor for cueing, the laser could dazzle an optically-based anti-aircraft system long enough, or permanently degrade its capabilities, for it to be knocked-out with laser-guided smart bombs or missiles at much closer ranges at relative leisure. It is envisaged that two Eagles would work together on SEAD assignments, drawn from the new Composite Wings: an F-15C-PDF with HARM missiles, and a laser-toting F-15E lugging smart weapons on a 'locate, dazzle and smash' assignment.

These initiatives are important because they are aimed at filling the blind spot common to current SEAD aircraft. They have an inability to search and destroy passive anti-aircraft defences when relying on optical tracking (TV, IR or even old-fashioned telescopic viewfinders) as a primary or back-up mode of guidance. This is especially so when the longer-ranged SAM sites' radars are switched off in an effort to avoid detection. While intimidating radar units into shutting down is often sufficient to let friendly strike and escort aircraft slip under the main curtain unharmed, it is desirable to locate these sites and destroy them as soon as is practicable. However, these new systems are unlikely to become an operational reality much before the turn of the century.

With a demolition derby in mind, new smart weapons are also entering the arena with special applications for the opening phases of an aerial offensive: the SEAD Campaign. Relying on pre-strike and real-time target data gleaned by the Tier 2-Plus/3-Minus HAE UAVs, a hefty percentage of the enemy's defences would be destroyed using weapons programmed with target signature templates instead of radar-homing techniques. The templates will comprise the known SAR, MMW, infrared or ladar signatures of an adversary's emitters, which could be programmed into the weapons either prior to take-off, or conveyed over secure IDM or other data-links whilst the fighters are preparing to ingress enemy airspace. Following release, the weapons will fly to target by means of mid-course guidance such as a hybrid inertial-GPS autopilot before switching on their terminal guidance sensors which will permit them to home in on a target that matches the target template held in the memory. A barrage of these would be used in the opening day of any future conflict against fixed targets.

Based on current thinking, first to go in would be the Joint Air-to-Surface Stand-off Missile (JASSM). This is a design based on air-launched cruise missile technology and the aborted Tacit Rainbow effort. It would be launched at ranges of over 100 miles to demolish long-range SAM complexes such as the SA-5 *Gammon* and SA-10 *Grumble* using the explosive power of a unitary 1,000 lb warhead, or by scattering a commensurate payload of special submunitions. Once these have been peeled off, a second wave of devices comprising the Joint Stand-off Weapon (JSOW) would be launched from about 40 miles. It is a surprise package canister which may also be configured with one of a host of submunitions. It would be used to obliterate threats such as the SA-4 *Ganef* and SA-11 *Gadfly*. This would leave the Joint Direct Attack Munition (JDAM), mostly based on the Mk 84, 2,000 lb iron bomb, to polish off weapons like the SA-6 *Gainful* and Euromissile Roland at ranges of under 12 miles. Close-in anti-aircraft systems, such as Rapier, would be taken care of by helicopter gunships and Special Operations Squads, which will use nap-of-the-earth tactics to ingress enemy airspace. They will clear a swathe free of AAA and optically-aimed missiles, as was performed in the Gulf using a deadly combination of MH-53J *Pave Low IIIE* 'Super Jolly' pathfinders and AH-64A Apache gunships.

They are all going well in development. Accuracy with the stand-off devices, honed to knock out high-value fixed targets, will be in the order of under 10 ft. This is more than adequate to hack the SEAD Campaign job given that each of the HE unitary warheads has a lethal blast zone covering a couple of acres, while the half ton of submunitions available to weapons such as JSOW will be able to cover an effective footprint of a half a square mile. And it looks as if they will indeed work, owing to the massive investment being undertaken in super smart munitions in the US.

Of course, existing ARMs would supplement these, creating a veritable barrage of weapons of mind-boggling diversity.

Further refined AGM-88C HARM development, backed by a silent hard kill (SHARK) template-based ARM proposal, are also in progress to improve the chances of knocking out fixed bi-static threats (those using two or more widely displaced transmitters, receivers and guidance links). They would also knock out mobile threats, and defeat frequency-hopping radars. These are becoming tougher to detect, owing to the amount of signal-processing involved in accurately locating them. The new panoply of munitions will considerably ease the strain on the new generation of single-seat American SEADers. In derivative format packing other types of warhead, they will permit the main strike waves to carry out stand-off attacks against airfields and concentrations of armour with equal efficiency.

However, in the context of establishing air superiority, these new devices are all honed towards the SEAD Campaign phase of the air war. Once the ground war starts and the enemy begins redeploying his forces closer to friendly ground formations, the possibility of Blue-on-Blue fratricide is all too possible. At this stage, subtlety becomes paramount: the ability to locate, sift through and analyse the ground threats and their intentions is a job only an on-the-spot EWO-in-the-loop can perform. Without aircraft like the F-4G WASP and Tornado ECR to hand, one major element in the foundations could give way, and the whole air campaign come tumbling down.

Clean Air Act

The 'gallant heroes' flying the Cappers seldom actually have a free hand either. They are just as constrained as their strike peers, and must exercise considerable fire control. The public have a misconception of this as the Cappers are seen to be the real vanguard whether operating offensively or defensively. Much of this has to do with the glamorous machines they fly, at the forefront of air power, armed to the teeth with an array of exclusively air-to-air weapons, furnishing MiGCAP, HavCAP and escort strike in an offensive or pre-emptive posture. Many of these designs are also employed as interceptors, offering sector defence at 5–10 minutes' notice.

From their higher altitude dog-legs or holding circuits, the Cappers cruise at high subsonic speed (mil power), maintaining a vigil for, or deliberately hunting out trade. For greater range or endurance, aircraft achieve a good high subsonic cruise climb speed and hold it at Mach 0.8–0.9 tops. This is long before compressibility drag rise becomes excessive (i.e. usually before they reach the so-called sound barrier). Aerodynamic efficiency only comes into play again at speeds in excess of Mach 2.0 (twice the speed of sound) when the distance covered by a quick dash offsets supersonic drag penalties. It is thus far more productive to stay within the subsonic speed regime. It maximizes time on station between AAR replenishment, and minimizes unwanted emissions which otherwise exclaim 'I'm here, come and get me'. These are the inevitable by-products of high-speed flight. It increases the size of the Doppler shift in the returns received by the enemy's air intercept radars, making the shifts easier than usual to measure and pick out at longer range. Moreover, with afterburner engaged (customary at such speeds), more shorter wavelength (microns – millionths of a metre) IR radiation is generated. This is where systems like IRST and heat-seeking weapons operate at maximum efficiency.

Height provides the potential energy for rapid speed build-up by diving and pouncing on prey without being a handicap in tracking fleeting low-level targets, whose relative movement can be picked out against the backdrop of the terrain beneath using pulse-Doppler (PD) radar techniques (explained later). Height also extends the useful range of AAMs as much as two-fold.

These advantages, offered by subsonic cruise at medium-plus heights, provide that critical edge across the board. Only dedicated interceptors, or 'stock' fighters working supersonically in a short-legged defensive posture, employ fast zooming tactics, and then purely for reasons of necessity. Cappers also get constant picture calls from AWACS.

They fly weapons systems of mind-boggling performance compared with the fighters of yesteryear. At the top end of the performance chart, today's knights of the air ride cocooned in a twin-engined metal steed weighing some 20 tons and offering some 170,000 thrust horsepower with reheat. This enables them to carry aloft up to half a ton of sky-searching radar avionics stuffed in the nose, plus an average of eight AAMs of various types honed towards long-range, medium-range and short-range aerial combat. These are backed by a Gatling gun or cannon in the 20–30 mm calibre range with up to 600 rounds of ammunition.

The massively expensive fighters at the fingertips of today's aviators have an amazingly short operational life, even though the straight-from-the-factory warranted fatigue lives of modern fighters are in the order of 4,000 and 8,000 flying hours (F-16 and F-15, respectively). This compares with the nominal 1,000-hour fatigue life of an F-4, and the 300-hour life of early jet fighters like the MiG-15. 'Beef-ups' and Aircraft Structural Integrity Program (ASIP) efforts can quite dramatically extend their lives which are consumed at an average rate of 250 hours annually. All the same, fighter obsolescence is measured in years rather than decades, even with expensive modifications aimed at keeping the equipment viable. Maximizing their potential while they still remain at the top of the league thus requires the pilots to fly and push their equipment and themselves to the limits. That way, they become thoroughly attuned or at one with the aircraft's performance, and their own individual limits. It is an oft-quoted remark but fighter aircraft are only as good as the pilots who fly them.

Going through the switching motions, especially the clusters of buttons on HOTAS stick and throttles common to modern air superiority fighters like the F-15 Eagle, requires considerable practice. Learning the kinesics, and the relative interaction between the aircraft in a Flight, has been likened to playing a musical instrument to quartet standard while reading a complex score, while being subjected to stupefying g forces in a world where instinctive understanding of three dimensions is crucial. Positive make an aviator's limbs heavy, and simple movements exhausting; negative g causes sickening flotation. Extensive familiarization with the hardware during the dynamics of actual flight in peacetime training is thus paramount. 'Get to know the tune.'

No simulator or part-task trainer, no matter how good, can convey either the psychological joy or the fear in mastering a top-performance fighter. Nor can it convey the physiological strains which can upset switchology that has been well-rehearsed in a motionless machine. Thus modern fighters, despite their high acquisition cost and complexity, should be treated as expendable. Training altitude parameters can be expanded with experience, and speed commensurately. However, blanket safety measures are too inhibitive, unless tailored and only vetted for abuse. As most tacticians acknowledge, numbers

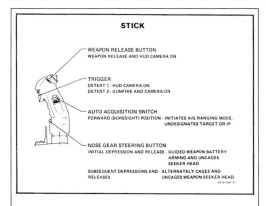

STICK

WEAPON RELEASE BUTTON
WEAPON RELEASE AND HUD CAMERA ON

TRIGGER
DETENT 1 - HUD CAMERA ON
DETENT 2 - GUNFIRE AND CAMERA ON

AUTO ACQUISITION SWITCH
FORWARD (BORESIGHT) POSITION - INITIATES A/G RANGING MODE,
UNDESIGNATES TARGET OR IP

NOSE GEAR STEERING BUTTON
INITIAL DEPRESSION AND RELEASE - GUIDED WEAPON BATTERY
ARMING AND UNCAGES
SEEKER HEAD
SUBSEQUENT DEPRESSIONS AND - ALTERNATELY CAGES AND
RELEASES   UNCAGES WEAPON SEEKER HEAD

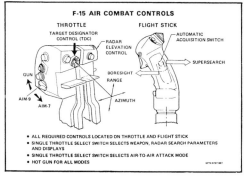

F-15 AIR COMBAT CONTROLS

THROTTLE   FLIGHT STICK

TARGET DESIGNATOR
CONTROL (TDC)   AUTOMATIC
                RADAR   ACQUISITION SWITCH
                ELEVATION
                CONTROL
                                    SUPERSEARCH
GUN   BORESIGHT
                 RANGE
AIM-9
    AIM-7   AZIMUTH

• ALL REQUIRED CONTROLS LOCATED ON THROTTLE AND FLIGHT STICK
• SINGLE THROTTLE SELECT SWITCH SELECTS WEAPON, RADAR SEARCH PARAMETERS
  AND DISPLAYS
• SINGLE THROTTLE SELECT SWITCH SELECTS AIR-TO-AIR ATTACK MODE
• HOT GUN FOR ALL MODES

count only in war, and then quality airmanship and effective teamwork matter a great deal more. This is true of INT, too, where ultra-low-level work comes into play.

Establishing air superiority over the target area (or the whole front) means maintaining a vigil in the broadest sense of the word. Pundits often use the terms 'bogey' and 'bandit' fairly loosely. In reality a bogey is an unidentified potential target and a bandit one that is confirmed as hostile, and for which authorization has been given to shoot it down. Moving out from the push in Tac or Loose Deuce requires both Cappers in the Flight to have functioning radars, irrespective of AWACS or GCI support. It acts as a fail-safe. Once vectored onto their targets (estimated range, bearing and height are provided) the Cappers switch their radar to the appropriate acquisition mode and set up the switches for a BVR missile kill using radar-guided missiles: Fox One.

At this stage it is useful to get to grips with the various radar modes available to today's fighters, and how these are used to assist with missile attack. Essentially, radars send out pulses in the radio frequency part of the electromagnetic spectrum – usually in the 8–14 GHz range (NATO I/J wavebands, way above normal radio-listening bands). These travel

HOTAS – hands on throttle and stick – switching was experimented with during the Vietnam War and reached fruition with the introduction of the F-15A Eagle in November 1974. The Eagle pilot's controls are illustrated here. (McDonnell Douglas)

at the speed of light. This frequency range offers the best compromise. It is not too high so that the pulses suffer from excessive signal absorption by the atmosphere, and yet it is sufficiently high to generate adequate gain (the output/input power ratio) to produce a finely-controlled radar beam without unwanted big sidelobes. Sidelobes can give away the fighter's presence on enemy RWRs without contributing anything to its own detection capability. Some of these signals will bounce back from any object that interrupts the beam, albeit significantly weakened by distance and the reflective properties of the quarry. The radar's antenna picks up the reflected signal and it is processed by the receiver to determine target range, bearing, and relative altitude and velocity.

The way this is done has grown increasingly complex since the advent of the Travelling Wave Tube and the digital number-crunching fire control intercept computer. Fundamentally, three PRF ranges are used by all the best air-to-air radars: low PRF, medium PRF and high PRF. Low PRF sends out the pulses at sufficient intervals so that each pulse has enough time to travel out to the target, be reflected, and return to the radar before the next pulse is transmitted. This permits precise ranging. It is the traditional way of doing things, known as pulse or monopulse mode, at 100 or so pulses per second. It tends to generate massive ground clutter when working in 'look-down', which has a tendency to swamp the radarscope and hide the targets. However, owing to the simple signal processing required and thus the minimal signal loss during processing, it is still the quickest and most discreet method. Thus it is still the favoured mode for look-up at long range, where it can offer 33 per cent more detection range.

High PRF is most commonly associated with PD radar modes, first introduced to operations by the AN/AWG-10 radar of the F-4J Phantom II. By transmitting stable and coherent signals (which are known to be phase-related) at rates up to a staggering 10,000 pulses per second, the radar is able to measure the Doppler shift in the signals reflected by the target. The Doppler shift is the apparent change in frequency of a signal caused by the relative motion between the target and the radar. As a target approaches more reflected signals per second reach the radar's antenna but as it recedes fewer signals per second reach it. Thus, target motion creates a tiny shift in frequency which the radar can acquire and discriminate from ground returns and other reflections. Much electronic filtering is necessary, using banks of black box circuits.

However, high PRF PD modes are poor at providing target distance, and are virtually useless in beam (side-on) attacks where there is relatively little Doppler shift. For this reason, lower frequency modulation (FM) is often added to the signal, or two simultaneous, closely-spaced frequencies are transmitted to help determine target range and to help detect beam attacks. But this is at the expense of reduced detection range again because of the complex processing required of the returning signals. Even very high-speed integrated circuits have to 'think hard'.

If the concept still seems perplexing, imagine standing on top of a skyscraper in a busy city during the rush-hour. Look-up low PRF is thus akin to watching an aircraft drift across the sky above you, which you can see a long way off. Look-down high PRF is similar to watching the crowds of people below. A roller-skater is easily picked out because of his relative movement, just like a fighter would be against the backdrop of the terrain beneath it, but focusing range is necessarily much closer.

Medium PRF, common to most modern radars featuring high and low PRF modes as optional settings, uses software-controlled digital signal processors to filter the Doppler signals. These can be automatically adjusted to match the changeable wave form being transmitted – in terms of pulse rate and actual frequency. It is thus more flexible than high PRF, able to look down, reject clutter, and match quickly-changing target speeds. But, signal processing losses remain high, reducing maximum detection range. However, this offers the best compromise for medium-range aerial combat. It is the cornerstone of fighters like the F-15, the first to add this capability with its Hughes AN/APG-63 medium PRF-focused PD radar in 1974. Its predecessors employed on tactical operations tended to compromise a great deal, employing so-called multi-mode radars which were not ideal for any of their given tasks. Microprocessing technology is largely responsible for changing all that, and delivering truly capable multi-mode radars.

If all this seems gobbledegook, then bear in mind that pilots are frequently none the wiser. It is important to stress here that PRF modes are no longer selected *per se*. Rather, each fighter's radar offers a number of long-range intercept (LRI) and medium-close air combat manoeuvring (ACM) modes, selected on a knob or via HOTAS switching. The aviators know which works best at such-and-such an altitude in such-and-such an attack scenario with such-and-such a weapon (as will become apparent when discussing various air intercept missiles) in their particular aircraft. Knobs and buttons are even available to tune the radar to front, beam and stern attack, taking the physics out of the switchology. Indeed, the air-to-air modes all carry their own range of proprietary acronyms on the selection dial or HOTAS switch settings, as part of the product.

Modern high-cost fighters, delivered fresh and spanking new from the factory over maybe a 20-year production cycle, all come with their updated instruction manuals, akin to new domestic equipment. Much of this will reflect product improvements, negotiated with the manufacturers alongside new blocks or production batches, incorporating various updates stipulated by higher authority using contractor-furnished or government-furnished equipment (CFE or GFE). It is an ongoing, often leap-frog process, conducted during PDM (the equivalent of custom rebuilds), or during Phase-Maintenance inspections on base (akin to a car's Ministry of Transport certificate). So, even looking at ostensibly identical machines on the flight-line and formating in the sky, some will have modes not available to others. Selective redistribution of freshly serviced machines will be attempted whenever possible to keep a squadron as homogenous as possible.

To make matters just a little more complicated, the radar scan patterns, particularly when conducting head-down LRI air combat in a big twin-seater, are frequently tinkered with! For example, the F-14A Tomcat's Hughes AN/AWG-9 radar system can search laterally in narrow or wide pie-slice or fan-scan sweeps (at 10°, 20°, 40° or 65° either side of the centreline) out to various selected ranges (which are defined by radar mode, but also selectable in range increments at 5, 10, 20, 50, 100 and 200 nm in terms of the synthesized radar display furnished in the cockpit), and in 1, 2, 4 or 8 'bars' in elevation (or vertical sections). Thus, it takes something like 13 seconds for the Tomcat's radar to traverse a sector of sky a full 130° wide and eight bars in elevation, compared with only one-quarter of a second for a 20° scan one bar high. Without the benefit of AWACS, it is common to search in a wide scan, then narrow it down for more precise target information once the enemy has been detected. With AWACS helping to reduce the search parameters, smaller, long-ranged scans can be used from the beginning, such as the Tomcat's Pulse-Search mode which is effective against fighter-sized targets out beyond 114 miles. All of this LRI stuff is accomplished head-down, with the back-seater's brow peering into the radarscope tube, while his hands adjust the relevant knobs.

Moreover, manual antenna slewing can also be accomplished to assist with target detection, using the

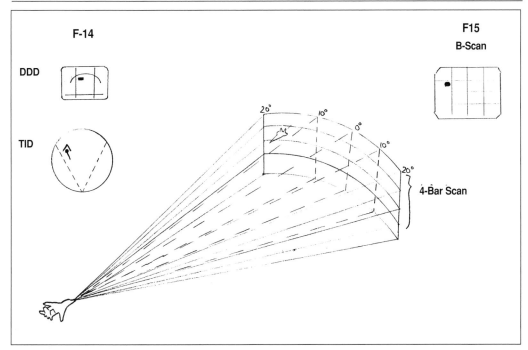

The F-14 Tomcat's track-while-scan radar mode is illustrated in the 40° four-bar scan pattern, along with the resultant radar displays furnished on the detail data display (DDD) and tactical information display (TID). Note how the TID provides a God's-eye view of things; for comparison, a B-scan radar display is also shown, such as is commonly used in aircraft like the F-15 Eagle.

navigator's radar tracking handle or sidestick control to move the dish axis left or right of the centreline. This expands the scope of the sweep left or right, respectively. The existing scan may also be shifted up or down – tilted – by means of a vernier control (thumbwheel) on the controller stick. In most instances, when conducting LRI against enemy fighters out at maximum missile range in a crewed fighter, automatic and manual modes are employed together, along with careful aircraft banking and turning, to ensure the enemy does not slip through the net. In the Tomcat, the NFO will select the basic scan pattern and mode, move the radar-searching zone about with judicious use of the hand control if the target is proving troublesome, leaving the system to automatically acquire and track anything that comes within its Big Eye. The target is then interrogated and, if hostile, shot down. At such ranges – i.e. BVR or non-visual – it is very much the NFO's show.

In the tactical scenario, there is probably no better fighter in the world for LRI work than our working example, the F-14 Tomcat. Its greatest assets are the radar and weapons systems supplied by Hughes. The AN/AWG-9 (or follow-on AN/APG-71) working in PD track-while-scan (TWS) mode, combined with the definitive solid-state AIM-54C/C-Plus Phoenix long-

range AAM (which obviated the need for liquid cooling of its extensive electronics). Up to six of them can be carried on a given mission. Typically only two are carried, allowing the extra hardpoints to be turned over to ACM-orientated shorter-ranged missiles. In TWS mode, the Tomcat can track 24 fighter-sized targets simultaneously out to ranges of around 103 miles, and bombers like the Tu-142 *Bear* at 230 miles. Radar data in TWS needs to be updated every two seconds, which means using either an 80° wide, two-bar scan, or a 40°, four-bar scan. Either will enable the AN/AWG-9 computer to store look angles, range, and closure rate for each contact in a separate track file, for possible hand off to an individual Phoenix missile, while all the time searching for fresh targets.

Target information is presented in both cockpits, though it is the back-seat NFO who really takes care of the proceedings, using his superior displays and systems management skills. He talks his pilot onto new headings or heights (the basics of which are also duplicated on the pole-pusher's instruments and HUD). The two primary displays used by the radar-scanning, back-seat NFO, surrounded by knobs and push-buttons, are a 10-inch radarscope known as the tactical information display (TID), and a much smaller tube above it, designated the detail data display

A VF-32 F-14A Tomcat displays a full load of six Phoenix missiles, and purposeful swept-back wings. This fit would be used for Fleet defence in times of extreme urgency, but a normal load (much of which might be brought back to the carrier) would include two Phoenix, two Sparrow or AMRAAM, and two or four 'winders. (Hughes)

(DDD). Once some trade has been acquired by the radar, the DDD shows a selected contact's relative bearing and velocity by means of a rectangular blip on a two-axis grid. The TID presents the targets in a computer-generated, synthetic, clutter-free God's-eye-view format featuring a large 'V' which denotes the radar scan limits from the nose. This can be displayed with the vertex at the bottom, or geostabilized with true North at the top of the screen. This air-to-air display is unique in the fighter community, reflecting the Tomcat's long-ranging whiskers and claws.

Individual contacts are presented as little tadpole-like symbols within the 'V', the direction of their tails denoting relative heading. Target altitude, range, heading and ground speed are presented in alphanumeric digits alongside these. IFF interrogation sorts them out into their various categories, and assigns them a little hat: an inverted 'u' means that the target remains unidentified, while an inverted 'v' denotes that it is hostile. Some of this IFF data may have been data-linked to the Tomcat by the E-2C Hawkeye carrierborne AWACS, which uses its screwtop antenna to track and interrogate targets out to much longer range. The Tomcat uses an AN/ASW-27 two-way data-link so that it can exchange information with the Hawkeye, and with its parent aircraft-carrier

or a picket ship.

The tadpole conveys other vital data via its beaded tail, the length of which helps to indicate computed time to being in range (maximum Phoenix missile launch range), optimum range (when the target symbol starts flashing), and minimum range. Up to six such targets are prioritized by the AN/AWG-9 based on a greatest threat basis. Each, in order of priority, can be handed off to a separate Phoenix missile using data held in the relevant track file. These missiles can be unleashed in rapid succession (by means of a big red push-button on the NFO's left knee-side weapons control panel) in a multi-shot attack against closing fighter-sized bandits scooting over the tree-tops or soaring as high as 103,500 ft at distances as great as 60 miles. One-shot or two-shot launch ranges from high altitude, say FL500, against lower, unmanoeuvrable targets in a forward-quarter attack are significantly greater, at around 125 miles, with the Phoenix covering a distance of around 85 miles.

It is important to appreciate that in front-quarter encounters the target is travelling towards our working example, the Tomcat, at a combined closing speed of between Mach 1.5–3.0, and thus the actual distance travelled by the missile is much less than the distance at launch. This is why discussing the limits of missile

The back-seat 'office' of the Tomcat, showing the two radar screens – above, the little rectangular DDD used to show target velocity, and below the big TID which provides a God's-eye view of things. (Grumman)

range, or even fighter performance, often is something of a nonsense, as it varies with altitude, relative heights, closing rates and a host of other variables including weather. Demanding specific data by asking such questions as 'what's it's top speed?' or 'how far can it go?' is a bit like asking how long is a piece of string. It varies considerably! A stern attack would narrow the attack ranges significantly, as the Phoenix would have to chase the target, although it would have more time to think about closing angles.

Time sharing is used during such multiple Phoenix launches, drawing on up to six of the AN/AWG-9's 19 transmission channels. In this manner, the radar provides mid-course steering instructions to the missiles in semi-active radar homing (SARH) mode until their own active radar sensors lock-on at closer ranges. That is, the missiles fly to the radar-'painted' targets on time-share at a burn-out speed of Mach 3.8 until their own miniature radars acquire their individually-assigned quarries and guide to them, autonomously. At this juncture, somewhere just beyond the midway point of missile flight, the Tomcat crew is at liberty to 'knock it off', and turn away

before the aircraft possibly comes within range of the enemy's typically shorter-ranged AAMs. Alternatively, the crew can press home their attack against other bandits using other radar modes and armament (described later). Meanwhile, the Phoenix AAMs continue to guide to the targets individually, all the way up to detonation. The impressive 132 lb fragmentation warhead is set off using a proximity fuze that rings the missile casing, or on direct impact. It is a formidable weapon system with a remarkable reach.

The only comparable fighter packing anything like the Tomcat's Hughes weapons system is the Voiska Protivovoz Dushnoy Oborini (PVO, or air defence force) MiG-31 *Foxhound* of the Commonwealth of Independent States (CIS). It is a massive twin-seater derived from the MiG-25 *Foxbat* but stuffed with much more modern technology and pushed aloft by a pair of DAFECS-monitored Soloviev, Perm D-30F6 engines rated at 34,170 lb static thrust each in afterburner, pushing the machine up to a red-line of Mach 2.8. This is a few hundred knots faster than even the GE-F110-powered F-14D, which introduced the

A slightly low-contrast, but nonetheless interesting view of a Tomcat letting loose a Phoenix AAM. The definitive AIM-54C-Plus is no longer in production and stocks will continue to dwindle. As with medium/short-range AAM technology, has the US given away its long-established lead to Russia and France? Probably. It is the allied AN/AWG-9 and follow-on AN/APG-71 radars which help the Tomcat still to reign supreme. (Hughes)

Replete with a radome-mounted TCS, which can be slaved to the radar to help with BVR identification of unknown contacts, or to monitor them at arm's reach, this Tomcat carries a typical (and strictly subsonic) load of AAMs and drop tanks. (Raytheon)

new GE-F110 powerplants as a means of finally giving the Tomcat 'some genuine push, without the hiccups and anaemia associated with its predecessor the TF30'. Produced at Gorky (now Nizhny Novograd) since 1979, and delivered to the PVO from 1983, a staggering 350 *Foxhounds* remain in CIS service covering the particularly vulnerable northern and Pacific sectors, backed by aged *Foxbats* which remain relatively abundant.

The *Foxhound* was the first fighter in the world to enter operational service with an electronically-scanned radar array, the SBI-16 Zaslon (NATO code-name *Flash Dance*), which has no moving parts. Its dish comprises a large active array of elements arranged in 24 rows which create a big beam which is controlled by passive phase-shifters. These shape and point the beam, as required, according to azimuth, vertical scan and ranging requirements. This system offers a number of advantages. The fixed dish allows the full fuselage diameter to be used for the antenna array, increasing the range of the radar through its bigger size (real aperture). The beam can be steered faster – virtually instantaneously – and more accurately through an arc of 240°, while controlled beam-shaping reduces unwanted sidelobes, thus giving it a low probability of intercept (LPI) by enemy RWR.

Figures in the public domain indicate that it can detect a target with a 16 sq m (172 sq ft) Radar cross-section (RCS) – something B-52-sized – at a search range of 186 miles. It can track up to 10 of them at 167 miles, by which time the bandits would have been prioritized down to four and handed off to belly-launched R-33 (AA-9 *Amos*) AAMs. These are akin in most respects to the Tomcat's Phoenix armament. Fire-control solutions are handled by the BTsVM(S) mission computer which generates the back-seater's radar symbology, prioritizes the threats (which can be overridden, of course, just as in the Tomcat), and hands-off instructions to the missiles, along with steering and firing solutions on the pilot's HUD and repeater scope. In fact, the system shares much in common with the Tomcat in terms of switchology and missile capability (albeit that missile reliability is not factored in here, and this is a major but unquantifiable consideration when discussing the system's prowess).

What makes the *Foxhound* so formidable is that up to four aircraft at a time can work in harmony, 'pushbrooming' with their quartet of Zaslons a sector up to 560 miles wide, the aircraft being spaced laterally at 124 miles. Working in this fashion, the four-ship or *Zveno* acts as mutual mini-AWACS, employing all four *Foxhounds'* man-in-the-loop avionics to interact and provide the Big Picture. This is simultaneously shared by all four aircraft automatically by means of an APD-518 data-link exchange system, furnishing solutions for the pursuit and coordination between the Flight (which may also be tied-in with GCI AK-RLDN data-link, too). In the cooperative mode, anything chancing to stray within a 620-mile-wide sector from tree-top up to 100,000 ft is likely to get zapped by one of the Zveno's 16 R-33 missiles, with little worry of overkill.

The *Foxhound* probably represents the world's best – and certainly the hottest – area defence fighter, but it lacks the mobility available to the globally-mobile, seafaring Tomcats, and is reserved strictly for strategic air defence. Some of the technology developed for the *Foxhound* is finding a new home on the carrier-borne Su-33 *Flanker*, while the MiG-31M and Su-35 Zhuravlik interceptors are being evolved with newer digital avionics and reliable long-range AAMs fitted with boosters for added reach. The latest, the KS-172, will offer a 250-mile range and attain hypersonic burn-out speed generated by ramjets to catch an AWACS or Hawkeye unawares. It is a frightening series of developments which, in a medium/high-intensity MRC (postulated in the Chinese region of influence around troublesome North Korea), might pull the rug out from under a *Desert Storm*-style Western-led coalition force, in much the same way that the Aerospatiale AM.39 Exocet anti-ship missile caused the jitters in the South Atlantic in 1982. In exchange for hard Western currency, much of Eastern Europe's best military technology is being sold to China and Iran. Unfortunately there do not appear to exist the political and moral constraints that prevent most Western companies exporting such war *matériel*, nor the available funds to create follow-on systems in the aftermath of the Cold War which fuelled the Tomcat-Phoenix weapons system.

For the bulk of the fighter force, things begin to hot-up at closing ranges well within 60 miles, when medium-range AAMs can be warmed-up ready for action. This is where the US also enjoys a clear lead for the moment, relying on the aged but constantly revisited Raytheon AIM-7 Sparrow III, now operational in M, P and R variants; and the newer Hughes (second source Raytheon) AIM-120A AMRAAM. Both of these enjoy a useful working range, when launched at altitude, of up to 40 miles (though this diminishes appreciably when launch height is reduced), while AMRAAM is more intelligent, and ups the kill probability (pK) appreciably. F-15 Eagle and Tornado F.3 Cappers will be working in medium PRF, LRI modes at cruise altitude, while some selected companions will be flying low using look-up to virtually exosphere heights. All will be constantly switching between various scan-patterns (not all HOTAS), and receiving their picture calls too.

It is valid here to discuss the principal radar presentation offered to most air superiority fighters. Unlike the Tomcat's rather unique TID display, which is strategic in nature, most modern fighters will only derive a God's-eye view via JTIDS, as a series of simplified SA snapshots conveyed to them over the airwaves. Their own radars, when working in the air-to-air mode, will present the returns in B-scan format. As explained to the author, B-scan 'turns the pie-slice-shaped picture into a square-shaped picture'. That is, if one imagines the radar scan working horizontally and vertically as a kind of rectangular funnel, sweeping from side-to-side in azimuth and scanning up and down in selectable 'bars' of elevation, then instead of getting a seemingly see-through plan-view of the funnel, as is the case with the Tomcat's TID, one is really looking through its small end. On the radarscope, the vertex of the display is thus spread out across the scope, to provide relative target bearing, while the vertical axis corresponds to height, divided

into increments according to the number of bars used in the elevation scan pattern, to provide relative target altitude. Usually, on HOTAS jets, bar scan and azimuth tracking are pre-adjusted so that when a particular LRI or ACM mode is selected, the scan pattern for that mode is initiated virtually automatically.

In older fighters like the F-4, the B-scan radar imagery is raw or direct, and potential targets will all appear as fairly nondescript blobs, with only IFF lines above and below (which indicate that the return is friendly) providing any degree of what is understood today as a graphic presentation. Until the advent of machines like the F-15 Eagle, locking-on to the target within the radar search sweep was completely manual. There was no automatic acquisition in those days. The lock-on procedure was likened to placing a torch beam on a frightened fly in a blacked-out room! Doctrine called for selecting two AIM-7 missile stations, which would be fired one at a time. Assuming it tracked as planned, the 1969-vintage AIM-7E-2 Sparrow III was capable of snap shooting onto a different heading or altitude, pulling instantaneous 6 g turns to catch its

The great exemplar of radar and heat weapons (and often lacking a gun altogether) during the 1960s and 1970s was the F-4 Phantom II, which used speed in hit-and-run intercept tactics. Much loved by all who flew her, the ultimate 'Phighter' machine remains in service with the air forces of Egypt, Germany, Greece, Iran, Israel, Japan, South Korea and Turkey – and Spain if one includes the reconnaissance-only variants. Successes like this are record-breaking in every sense. (RAF)

Whoosh! An AIM-7M Sparrow, a great Iraqi jet-feller, is unshackled and ignited beneath an F-15A Eagle from the Eglin, Florida-based Combat Echo *squadron.* Combat Echo *used to provide direct feedback to crews at operational units, giving them the rundown on updates, and correcting any hardware or software deficiencies they confronted on a day-to-day basis. (Raytheon)*

quarry, before setting off its 66 lb blast-fragmentation warhead containing over 2,500 steel fragments. Obviously, a punch from this Mach 3 weapon – which, like Phoenix, could be delivered into the rear, flank or nose of the adversary – blew the opponent apart. A proximity-fuzed detonation within what is known as lethal distance would also cause considerable mischief, fatally crippling the opponent's fighter.

Several advances followed just as hostilities were drawing to a close in South-East Asia. First, in 1975, came the solid-state AIM-7F Sparrow III, with an extended-range rocket motor (virtually doubling maximum range to 62 miles), and a warhead beefed up to 88 lb. Microminiaturization of the guidance system, and some rearranging of the sections, made this possible. This was further developed into the monopulse SARH seeker-equipped British XJ521 Skyflash, Italian Selenia Aspide 1A and American Raytheon AIM-7M, all with warm-up times reduced to under five seconds, and offering massively increased resistance to enemy jamming. Minimum range was also compressed to under half a mile, making it a useful ACM weapon too. This, and the follow-on AIM-7P (which offers preprogramming

features to help acquire targets with small radar signatures, such as cruise missiles), formed the mainstay medium-range AAM of *Desert Storm*.

However, arguably the biggest advances came with the medium PRF PD radar such as the Eagle's Hughes AN/APG-63 (and newer AN/APG-70), the introduction of fully-fledged auto-acquisition of targets, and the lethal combination of these with HOTAS switching and a comprehensive HUD. Targets automatically acquired and tracked by radar using the new LRI and ACM modes were presented on a clutter-free B-scan radar display (rotated so as to compensate for aircraft roll attitude relative to the targets), in a much easier to digest format. As one pilot put it, 'the computer cuts out all the crap; it synthesizes the raw radar returns into neat little target symbols'.

The HUD and HOTAS meant that the pilot could focus his vision out of the windshield, and take only minor peeks at the radar display. The whole radar intercept, including search, lock-on and missile firing parameters, could be conducted in a head-up fashion, with HUD cursors and alphanumerics replacing the old ASE circle and dot (which were also presented on the HUD, during the crossover in technology). Target

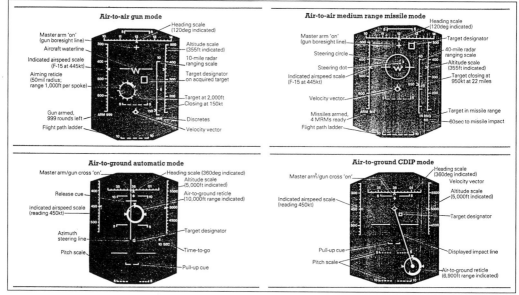

The F-15A's HUD modes are displayed, illustrating what a boon they are to pilot situational awareness. Today's pilots take them for granted. (McDonnell Douglas)

position was projected on the combining glass, along with range, closing speed and a host of other useful information. This was especially useful for air combat work in the single-seaters, when there existed no time in which to fiddle about with sidestick controls in a head-down manner in the heat of aerial battle. Bandits could be knocked out of the sky with the flick of a few switches on the throttle and stick.

Owing to the broader launch parameters of the new Sparrow III AAMs, this came particularly good in the ACM environment, as range shortened and the enemy closed to within eyeballing distances. It was here that the new short-ranged radar lock-on modes came into play, when the pilots of even the bigger twin-seaters would assume virtually complete responsibility for the engagement, relegating their back-seaters to watching the rear-view mirrors and monitoring the RWR scope. For example, in our old friend the AN/AWG-9-equipped F-14 Tomcat, three ACM modes could be activated by the pilot.

The first is pilot rapid lock-on (PLM), using a 2.3° radar pencil beam boresighted with the aiming 'pipper' in the HUD. When the pilot places this on target, lock-on follows and a Sparrow III can be squeezed off rapidly and let loose for the kill. Second, the Tomcat driver can select vertical scan lock-on (VSL), raised for high, or dipped for low search, covering a sector of sky above, through and below the HUD aiming area. This is particularly useful against turning targets with the Tomcat following suit in a roll. Alternatively, he might employ pilot-aided lock-on

(PAL), which provides a 40°, one-bar scan, to acquire a target at a similar altitude, but off-axis. Failing all three, if the pilot goofs the NFO can use manual rapid lock-on (MRL), which works much like PAL except that the NFO has to manually acquire the target in the beam using the sidestick control, in the 'frightened fly' supersearch mode.

What is significant is that *all* of these modes feature fully automatic lock-on out to ranges of 6 miles, so that all that is required is to place the target within the beam. During *Desert Storm*, much use was made of similar LRI and ACM auto-acquisition modes by Hughes radar-toting F-15C Eagle and F/A-18A Hornet jet-jockeys. The air-to-air kill to loss ratio rose from 2:1 of the Vietnam era to a dramatic 25:1, representing a veritable turkey shoot. Honing specialist crews with top-of-the-line weaponry, as opposed to committing a do-it-all fighter to combat, obviously played a big part. But the combination of AWACS, reliable radar-guided AAMs, HOTAS, HUD and medium PRF PD radar honed to the air-to-air role was significant.

Interestingly, at the start of hostilities, Sparrow III was on the verge of replacement by the follow-on AIM-120A AMRAAM, some of which found their way to the Gulf for fitment to F-15C Eagles of the 33rd TFW. But they were too late to see any action. The AIM-120A has since proved its mettle in ACM combat over fragmented Yugoslavia. It was a long time in the coming. Maj Jim Rotramel, USAF Ret.:

[AMRAAM is] an extremely controversial weapon. It

OPERATION *DESERT STORM* KILLS – AGAINST JET FIGHTERS
(all pilots USAF unless otherwise noted)

Missile (running total fired)	Shooter	Pilot	Kill
17 January 1991			
AIM-7R (1)	F-15C/33rd TFW	Capt John K. Kelk	MiG-29
AIM-7M (1/2)	F-15C/33rd TFW	Capt Robert E. Graete	2 x Mirage F1.EQ
AIM-7M (3)	F-15C/1st TFW	Capt Stephen W. Ta	Mirage F1.EQ
AIM-9M (1)	F/A-18C/VFA-81	Lt Cdr Mark I.	F-7A (MiG-21)
AIM-7M (4)	F/A-18C/VFA-81	Lt Nicholas Mongillo	F-7A (MiG-21)
AIM-7M (5)	F-15C/33rd TFW	Capt Charles J. Magill (USMC)	MiG-29
AIM-7M (6)	F-15C/33rd TFW	Capt Rory R. Draeger	MiG-29
AIM-7M (7)	F-15C/33rd TFW	Capt Lawrence E. Pitts	MiG-25
AIM-7M (8)	F-15C/33rd TFW	Capt Richard C. Tollini	MiG-25
19 January 1991			
AIM-7M (9)	F-15C/33rd TFW	Capt Craig W. Underhill	MiG-29
AIM-7M (10)	F-15C/36th TFW	Capt David S. Prather	Mirage F1.EQ
AIM-7M (11)	F-15C/32nd TFG	Lt David G. Sveden	Mirage F1.EQ
24 January 1991			
AIM-9P (1/2)	F-15C/13 Sqn	Capt Ayehid Salah al-Shmrani (RSAF)	2 x Mirage F1.EQ
26 January 1991			
AIM-7M (12)	F-15C/33rd TFW	Capt Rory R. Draeger	MiG-23
AIM-7M (13)	F-15C/33rd TFW	Capt Anthony E. Schiavi	MiG-23
AIM-7M (14)	F-15C/33rd TFW	Capt Cesar A. Rodriguez*	MiG-23
27 January 1991			
AIM-9M (2/3)	F-15C/36th TFW	Capt Jay T. Denney	2 x MiG-23
AIM-7M (15/16)	F-15C/36th TFW	Capt Benjamin D. Powell	MiG-23 & Mirage F1.EQ
29 January 1991			
AIM-7M (17)	F-15C/36th TFW	Capt Donald S. Watrous	MiG-23
AIM-7M (18)	F-15C/33rd TFW	Capt David G. Rose	MiG-23
6 February 1991			
AIM-9M (4/5)	F-15C/36th TFW	Capt Thomas N. Dietz	2 x MiG-21
AIM-9M (6/7)	F-15C/36th TFW	Lt Robert W. Hehemann	2 x Su-25
AIM-7M (19/20)	F-15C/33rd TFW	Capt Anthony R. Murphy	2 x Su-22
AIM-7M (21/22)	F-15C/33rd TFW	Col Rick N. Parsons	2 x Su-22

* Second kill, his first being a MiG-29 accredited to him which flew into the ground.
This table also excludes a Mirage F1.EQ drawn into the ground by an EF-111A Raven, an Il-76 *Candid* shot down with an AIM-7M on 2 February, and seven helicopters downed: two by A-10As using the GAU-8/A Avenger gun, one by an F-14A using an AIM-9M, three by F-15Cs with AIM-7Ms, and another destroyed by a laser-guided bomb while hovering.

has had a long and difficult gestation, [but] emerging is a missile far more lethal than the one it replaces. AMRAAM's most important improvement is the incorporation of an active radar seeker. Although done before with the AIM-54 Phoenix, putting this feature into a Sparrow-sized airframe is a significant achievement. It allows the launching aircraft to simultaneously engage several targets and manoeuvre

out of the fight before the missiles hit their targets. The Sparrow, by comparison, requires the launching aircraft to maintain radar contact with a single target until the missile hits it. The disadvantage of this was dramatically demonstrated during the famous AIMVAL/ACEVAL tests during the mid-1970s. In one engagement, which became known as The Towering Inferno, four F-15s engaged four F-5s with

simulated AIM-7s. Before they were all 'shot down' by the Sparrows, the F-5s were able to launch simulated AIM-9 [short-ranged heat-seeking missiles, described later] which 'destroyed' all the F-15s. AMRAAM would have allowed a single F-15 to target all four F-5s before withdrawing beyond the range of their AIM-9s.

'The other main area of emphasis with AMRAAM has been reliability and maintainability. Sparrow was infamous during the Vietnam War for its unreliability. Getting this feature right has been one of the main reasons it has taken so long to get the AIM-120 into production. Virtually all other areas of performance have been improved over the AIM-7 as well, including reducing motor smoke, increasing speed and range, improving warhead fuzing and lethality, and better electronic counter-countermeasures [ECCM]. Because it only weighs about 350 lb, it can be rail-launched from stations previously associated only with AIM-9 Sidewinders. This was done during the Gulf War. Unfortunately, by the time the aircraft software was set up to allow carriage of AIM-7s, -9s and -120s, the Iraqi Air Force was hiding in their shelters or fleeing to Iran and there was no opportunity to actually use the new missile in combat.

The main reliability problem actually related to problems with stores vibration in the low wing-loaded Eagle. Low wing-loading is an asset in ACM as it gives the pilot greater control authority, but it is disadvantageous in that it tends to massively increase buffeting and resultant shake at low-level where the air is much denser. It is interesting to note that the first two kills chalked up with AMRAAM have both gone to the F-16. However, AMRAAM will eventually replace the Sparrow throughout the US fighter inventory, as well as those of many allied overseas air forces. In this manner, it is expanding medium-range AAM capability on board existing heavyweights such as the Tornado F.3, F-14 Tomcat and F-15A/C Eagle. It is also offering such a capability to hitherto short-range-only types like the F-16 Fighting Falcon, and Blue Vixen-equipped Sea Harrier F/A.2 (one of the most recent customers).

In practice, with the target locked-on on radar, AMRAAM may be fired in a number of different modes, using the handed-off target data from the aircraft's missile control computer which gets it thinking where the target should be. At longer range for LRI use, the missile is continually updated with

AIM-120 AMRAAM – the killing machine. This is a fire-and-forget medium-range AAM, and an area in aerial combat in which the US and select overseas clients enjoy a clear lead. (Hughes)

fresh target position information while in flight (much like Phoenix), until its active radar takes over for the final stage of the intercept, freeing the launch fighter to break off. Alternatively, if the engagement proves overly difficult, the launch pilot can simply let it go without mid-course updates and trust its active seeker to work unaided. Finally, at much shorter ranges, lock-on of its active seeker can be accomplished prior to launch, for both a good pK and immediate evasive manoeuvres.

Previous page: *The most successful air-to-air fighter of Desert Storm was the F-15C Eagle, which accounted for 29 enemy aircraft, mostly with AIM-7M Sparrows. Those from the USAF's 33rd TFW, one of which is seen vaulting into the sky following its MSIP updates, accounted for no fewer than 16 of the kills. (McDonnell Douglas)*

Three RAF Tornado F.3 squadrons are represented in this formation. The F.3 serves with air forces of Britain and Saudi Arabia, and is shortly to join ranks with that of Italy, where it will use the indigenous Selinia Aspide AAM. (BAe)

France's Armée de l' Air operates Mirage 2000Cs equipped with Matra Super 530D (Sparrow equivalent) and Magic (Sidewinder equivalent) missiles. However, weapons like the MICA (AMRAAM equivalent) will make it formidable, especially if exported to Third World air arms which are greedy for French know-how. (Dassault Aviation)

Sustained turns of up to 28 g have been demonstrated, while in an exercise conducted during September 1993, USN/USMC F/A-18C Hornets fired 29 against target drones and achieved a 96 per cent success rate! Improved Operational Flight Programs for the fighters' computers are being constantly updated to maximize every minor improvement that comes with the latest production batch of AMRAAM. There is nothing comparable to it in service today, though trailing not far behind are the Russian RVV-AE R-77 (AA-12) 'Amraamski', and the French Matra MICA, which will provide dangerous competition within the next few years. For its own part, the US is adding stealth capability to the AMRAAM under Project *Have Dash 2*, as it evolves for covert air-to-air strikes, and eventual use aboard the F-22A Rapier.

When air combat has joined into a close-quarters

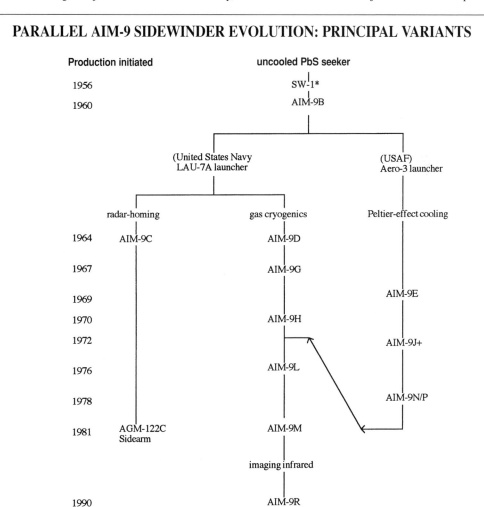

PARALLEL AIM-9 SIDEWINDER EVOLUTION: PRINCIPAL VARIANTS

Production initiated

uncooled PbS seeker

1956	SW-1*	
1960	AIM-9B	

(United States Navy LAU-7A launcher) · (USAF) Aero-3 launcher

	radar-homing	gas cryogenics	Peltier-effect cooling
1964	AIM-9C	AIM-9D	
1967		AIM-9G	
1969			AIM-9E
1970		AIM-9H	
1972			AIM-9J+
1976		AIM-9L	
1978			AIM-9N/P
1981	AGM-122C Sidearm	AIM-9M	

imaging infrared

1990	AIM-9R
1993	AIM-9X Boa/Box Office
1994	AIM-9X HALM

* Known to the US Navy as the AAM-N-7A, and to the USAF as the GAR-8A
+ The AIM-9J evolved into numerous subvariants, including the J-1 through J-4, N through N-3 and subsequently the P through P-3 series, all fundamentally similar but employing improved fuzing and other minor refinements

'No damn Ruskie with Archer *is gonna get the better of me!' A Hornet demonstrates the full heat load of six 'winders. As well as wholesale service with the US Navy and Marines, the F/A-18 is also currently operational with Australia, Canada, Kuwait and Spain, with Finland, Malaysia and Switzerland soon to follow suit. (McDonnell Douglas)*

visual-ranged scrap, pilots will more likely than not eschew Sparrow III and AMRAAM (or their equivalents such as Skyflash) and HOTAS-switch over to heat-seeking missiles: Fox 2.

Fox 2 equates exclusively with heat-seeking infrared AAMs, which traditionally rely on cryogenic cooling much like IRST, using either nitrogen or argon gas, or a Peltier effect thermocouple system (electrical cooling that works by passing a current through the junction between two metals or semiconductors of different conductivities, causing a drop in temperature). However, as described earlier, IIR versions such as the Raytheon AIM-9R *Pave Prism* are entering the fray. This is capable of furnishing sketchy images of the quarry when locked-on out at maximum range of 12 miles, to assist with target vetting. These are good at tracking the afterburning and mil power range of throttle settings. In the absence of a radar-slaved TCS, such as equips recently retro-fitted Tomcats, this capability is a boon. ACM radar modes may be employed to assist with target lock-on, slewing the missiles' seekers into the right sector of sky to assist with their passive lock-on process. But heat-seeking weapons are simply physically pointed in the right direction during the great air-to-air slicing chase or dogfight, as each fighter tries to gain advantage and slip into firing position.

During these so-called 'knife fights' or 'fur balls',

heat is exclusively HOTAS-selected. When the weapon's growl (newer versions chirp) is raised in pitch over the headphones, it has locked onto its quarry and may be let loose with a tug at the firing button. It is an excellent point-and-shoot weapon effective out to a realistic range of some 3–6 miles.

Probably the best known is the Sidewinder, conceived as Local Project 612 by US Naval Ordnance Test Station engineer William B. MacLean in his spare time at China Lake, California. He received a plaque from President Eisenhower for his efforts. The original Sidewinder consisted of only nine moving parts, and seven radio tubes! Forty years and 30 versions later, it still remains by far the most successful and deadly AAM in the US inventory. It has grown considerably in capability throughout its career. The original operational model, the joint-service AIM-9B, was equipped with an uncooled lead sulphide seeker and required the pilot to manoeuvre right behind the enemy's hot jetpipe – his six o'clock – at ranges of under 2 miles. Range and sensitivity were gradually expanded with the US Navy nitrogen-cooled 'Delta', followed shortly afterwards by the 'Golf' of 1967. This introduced Sidewinder expanded acquisition mode (SEAM), a feature which has stayed with the Navy derivatives ever since and uses fighter radar to expand look angle. In its current form, SEAM enables the Sidewinder to acquire targets within a 55°

Just in case you wanted a close-up view of the beefy Sidewinder (at right), here it is . . . (Raytheon)

. . . and in case you did not know what it is capable of doing, an AIM-9P obliges by taking-out a Pave Deuce PQM-102 Delta Dagger drone! (Ford Aerospace)

forward cone, and to continue to track them thereafter at up to 40° off boresight.

Seeker sensitivity was also sharpened over the years, as even when using SEAM the missile was effective only in the rear quadrants of the target. The all-aspect 'Lima' model, produced from 1976, turned it into a super weapon for its era, expanding lock-on coverage to any relative shooting aspect – even head-on. The true efficacy of this came to the attention of aviation analysts following the Gulf of Sidra incident in August 1981. A pair of hungry Tomcats from VF-41 operating from the USS *Nimitz* splashed a pair of Libyan Su-22 *Fitters* attempting to enforce Col Qaddafi's infamous Line of Death. It achieved worldwide attention during the Falklands War a year later, as the mainstay armament of Royal Navy Sea Harrier FRS.1s, which wreaked havoc on Argentine intruders attempting to cross the Total Exclusion Zone. Twenty-seven 'winders were fired, of which 24 achieved hits, destroying 19 enemy aircraft.

It was at this stage that the USAF abandoned Peltier effect electrical cooling (introduced on the AIM-9E and retained through to their 'November'/'Papa' models). It opted instead for the gas-cooled US Navy AIM-9L/M versions, but with argon gas systems self-contained within the missiles

(as opposed to nitrogen bottles housed in the launch rails). Nine years on, during the Gulf War, the somewhat aged orphidian beast accounted for no fewer than nine kills, and it remains a mainstay weapon in the armoury of the West.

However, even with SEAM, Sidewinder's FoV remains small. All-aspect or not, it still has to be pointed virtually right at the enemy, who must come within that forward-looking 55° cone of death for Sidewinder to lock-on. The weapon simply has reached a stasis in its development beyond which improvements are difficult to attain – although substantially redesigned versions are being evolved. Today, it appears that in the arena of close-quarters AAM missile combat, European and Israeli AAMs, and allied avionics developments, have overtaken the long-established lead held by the US.

Alamo and *Archer*

Because CIS fighters were dismissed for many years by Western analysts who mistakenly believed that the latest generation were not much in advance of their predecessors, development of American heat AAMs was conducted in a relatively laid-back fashion. Attention was focused instead on AMRAAM and

An F-16C assigned to the Eglin AFB-based Armament Development Center, lets loose one of the deadly new Box Office AIM-9X contenders – a Sidewinder with a totally new guidance and control system. This provides the only credible counter to the top-of-the-line Russian R-73 AAM. (Raytheon)

BVR weaponry. For nearly 16 years between *Linebacker II* and the collapse of the Berlin Wall, there was a prevailing faith in the West that it, and the US in particular, maintained an overwhelming technological superiority which would keep the West strides ahead for years to come. The MiG and Sukhoi OKB fighter bureaux were seen to be merely copying Western technology, and thus must be at least 10 years behind in development.

What the Soviets described as fourth-generation fighters, namely its MiG-29 *Fulcrum* and Su-27 *Flanker*, were thus viewed in the West to be no better than revised copy-cat versions of the LWF YF-17 Cobra and McDonnell Douglas F-15 Eagle, respectively. Such fighters were merely supposed to mirror the Cobra's wing leading-edge root extensions (LERXs) for high angle-of-attack (AoA, or Alpha) manoeuvres, blended wing-body aerodynamics and the twin-engined, twin-tailed philosophy embodied in Cobra, the F-15 and the US Navy's F-14 Tomcat. Neither of the newcomers was seen as much of an advance in terms of aerospace materials nor

propulsion technology over the MiG-21 Okurok ('Cigarette butt'; NATO code-name *Fishbed*). Nor were they perceived as any easier to master, owing to a lack of digital FBW flight control systems, than the sometimes dangerous MiG-23 'Crocodile' (NATO code-name *Flogger*). Nor were they thought any less frightening to fly than the MiG-25 'Flying Cocktail Lounge' (NATO code-name *Foxbat*), so-called because of the vast amounts of refined alcohol used in its volatile cooling and hydraulic systems, and injected into the intakes for added thrust on take-off (and sold diluted, on the black market, as cheap 'vodka'!).

However, the new MiG-29A Tochka Opori ('Balance Point', a literal translation of the NATO code-name *Fulcrum*), and the Su-27 Zhuravlik ('Crane', alluding to its long forebody, NATO code-named *Flanker*), represented giant leaps ahead. The leaps had been made possible by a good deal of parallel research work performed in the former USSR which in most instances lagged behind Western technology by only a modest margin, and in other areas secretly surpassed it.

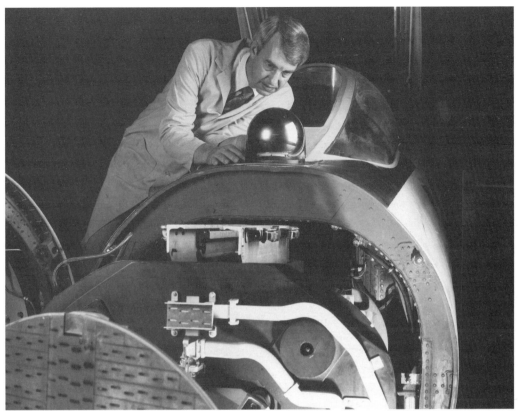

A regular sensor on board America's Century Series interceptors of the late 1950s and throughout the 1960s, the IRST was a remarkable back-up to radar. It fell from use along with retirement of the F-101 Voodoo, F-102 Delta Dagger and F-106 Delta Dart, and attempts to resuscitate it on the F-4D Phantom II (as depicted, alongside the F-15 Eagle's AN/APG-63 Medium PRF PD radar), failed. However, Europe knows better. IRST comes as standard on the MiG-29 Fulcrum and Su-27 Flanker, and an E-O version will shortly equip Eurofighter 2000. (Hughes)

These hefty but precision-engineered machines feature extensive use of aluminium-lithium alloys in their main wing-body blended structure, as well as graphite and carbon composites ('as strong as titanium but as light as cardboard', as the crews were briefed when the types were introduced to service). This gives them immense strength and incredible agility: the MiG-29 is stressed for 12 *g*! The powerplants are all new too, and are not updated Tumansky R-29 turbofans poached from the *Flogger* as was once widely believed. The MiG-29's Leningrad-Klimov (Isotov) RD-33 engines use a two-chamber bypass system to prevent overheating during sustained afterburner operation, pumping out 36,600 lb thrust with reheat. Based on an average combat fuel load of some 7,000 lb, this produces a thrust to weight ratio in the order of 1.35:1, and a sea-level climb rate, with missiles, in excess of 65,000 ft per minute.

Moreover, despite its lack of FBW flight controls,

former Soviet test pilots found it impossible to spin. From the outset, the MiG's traditional electro-hydraulic flight control system also proved easy to fix and offered immunity against the effects of a electromagnetic pulse (EMP) as generated by a nuclear explosion, and electromagnetic interference (EMI) which can sometimes be caused by strong electrical fields generated by radars and conventional weapons. Both are invisible enemies to delicate microprocessor-based avionics used in today's FBW systems.

The first of this new breed entered Soviet service during June 1985 with the two Voyenno-Vozdushniye Sily (VV-S) Guards Regiments at Kubinka, near Moscow, and Ros in the Ukraine. However, the third to form, the 176th Regiment at Ruslan (Mikha Tskhakaya) in Georgia were the first to be declared operationally ready, following a major ORI at Mary AB the following summer. Within five years no fewer

A study in grace and superlative aerodynamics, even if tempered by mass-production fabrication techniques: the Tochka Opori, alias the MiG-29 Fulcrum. *(Author)*

than nine more Regiments that had been using obsolescing MiG-23s were reformed with the new machines, relegating the MiG-23s to V-VS combat duties in Afghanistan. Meanwhile exports began to flourish. This amounts to some 750 for domestic use within the CIS (mostly used by Russia, with some 122 operated by the Ukraine), and 'several hundred' – at least 250 at the latest count – for export.

With the fragmentation of the USSR the production line slowed to a trickle, but exports continue and the slack of some 100 examples parked outside the factory during 1993 is gradually being taken up. Thus, this machine is being placed at the disposal of what were until very recently considered to be Third World air forces. Both Malaysia and South Yemen have since absorbed *Fulcrum*s into their arsenals, bolstering their capabilities considerably. The twin-seater remains in production, while an export MiG-33 FBW version is on offer to interested parties with uprated engines warranted to 2,000 hours,

overcoming earlier reliability problems.

The *Flanker*, too, represented a quantum leap in technology as well as performance. In particular, the Su-27's pair of Saturn-Lyulka AL-31F engines are rated at a combined total thrust of 55,125 lb, making it the hottest twin-engined operational fighter in the world in terms of raw thrust to weight performance. The engines of the Su-33 (formerly Su-27K), the navalized version, are 12–15 per cent more powerful yet. Most significantly, the powerplants can accumulate 2,000–2,500 tactical cycles (each representing the full range of metal-grinding throttle settings normally encountered in an average air combat sortie) between hot-section inspections. In contrast to this, in the West, the latest F100-PW-229 and GE F110-100 engines powering the Fighting Falcon and Eagle have been plagued by fourth-stage turbine blade cracks and turbine seal problems. These have caused engine failures after only 200 tactical cycles, and the loss of several aircraft.

'Hammer and nail' engine technology has in this instance been superseded by advanced materials technology akin to that available in North America: powder metallurgy. Atomized molten metal is super-frozen into powdery crystals, then bound together and tempered in moulds under intense heat and pressure. The technology was pioneered by Pratt & Whitney, along with ceramic-coated 'Gatorizing'. Powder

The Russian Knights' steed is the Su-27 Flanker, *known to many of its pilots as the Zhuravlik because of its crane-like forebody. Bigger than an F-15, it offers comparable performance, and its Su-35 derivative offers far superior statistics. USAF* Tac Brawler *computer simulations are creating angst! (Jim Rotramel)*

metallurgy offers incredible uniformity for highly stressed components such as engine turbine blades, which are twin heat-treated to produce a fine grain, massively strong bore and a coarser-grained rim optimized for greater tolerance to damage.

While Pratt & Whitney are ahead in the game, and are developing even more sophisticated metal matrix composites using carbon fibre reinforcement in a titanium matrix for engine parts for application to the F-22A Rapier's F119 powerplants, the technology is only just maturing. The latest Russian engines can suffer massive abuse by being speedily throttled up and down. Fast throttling was a feature previously unavailable to Eastern Bloc aircraft which required more gentle persuasion. Many early *Fulcrums* required new engines after only 1,400 flying hours, as well as regular overhauls at 250-hour intervals. Russian titanium forging for engine bay housings and airframe structural members has also long since surpassed contemporary Western technology. Moving engine production to specialist development factories appears to have paid off in terms of quality control too in recent years.

All of this has produced fighters equipped with powerplants offering phenomenal performance, yet with the durability that was seldom a hallmark of past, cruder design and fabrication methods. Traditional hydromechanical engine controls have similarly been replaced with a DEECS/FADECS-class system, controlling fuel flow and trim digitally. Supercruise (acceleration to supersonic speed and sustained supersonic flight without afterburner engaged) was just possible in the *Flanker* (given its massive fuel reserves). This was long before Lockheed's YF-22 and the competing Northrop-McDonnell Douglas YF-23 battled it out in the skies over California for Full-Scale Development Advanced Tactical Fighter contracts during 1990. But that the *Flanker* is far from the Mach 1.5–1.6 mil power maximum cruise climb class offered by the new American warplane, and the latest Mikoyan 'MiG 1.42' will lag behind a tad. Yet these concepts are flying off the computer-aided design/computer-aided manufacturing (CAD/CAM)) drawing boards and some are already reaching operational service. Surprisingly, nobody really took notice of the CIS hardware much before the pioneering production variants began to appear in large numbers, and then they mostly assumed that they were time-lag copies of the Hornet and Eagle.

The shock wave hit home when the Mikoyan, then subsequently the Sukhoi OKB, showed their wares off at Paris and Farnborough. The crowds were thrilled by amazing tail slides and Cobra manoeuvres which clearly demonstrated the new fighters' incredible agility, throat-choking engine relights at low-level,

and their massive stability at high-AoA. (AoA is usually measured as an index rather than in degrees. It reflects the angular difference between the wings relative to forward motion. The higher the AoA capability, the more forgiving and manoeuvrable is the fighter, it is argued.) The only Western fighters capable of hinting at such antics, apart from the much-delayed F-22A Rapier, are specialized research aircraft or heavily-modified Hornet stock. This gave rise to much balking about the validity of such Russian manoeuvres, probably rooted in not-invented-here petty jealousies.

In aerial combat, the nose-up Cobra and Pugachev's new Hook (similar, but conducted in the horizontal axis at 90° of bank while pulling 9 *g*!), in particular, can quickly nullify Doppler radar returns, causing AWACS and air intercept radars to hiccup. Although these antics massively burn up energy and thus may place the aircraft at a severe disadvantage in impending close-quarters air-to-air combat, in the LRI scenario in the counter-AWACS role, they might prove lethal. Of course, such a disadvantage does not necessarily follow. If both combatants have bled off a great deal of energy and are tumbling over each other, struggling for advantage in a horizontal or vertical spiralling barrel roll or scissors motions, the wide FoV of the Russian fighters' armaments can be brought to bear quickly and decisively in ACM, as we shall discuss shortly.

One tactic Russian pilots used to practise was that of approaching a simulated AWACS and its HavCAP protective Flight at high speed in a couple of closely-welded *Para* or two-ship Flights. Each wingman was placed 5 ft to the right and 70 ft behind his leader ('close enough to follow my visual signals but clear of my turbulent engine exhaust and wing vortices', as one former pilot described it). While still beyond the point where raid assessment signal processing techniques might be used by the defenders to resolve the two acquired tags into four aircraft, the two leaders signal a break the moment just after AWACS or a fighter PD radar lit up their coloured SPO-15 Beryoza RWR systems at full intensity. These then fling themselves out in Doppler-negating Split-S, Cobra or Hook antics, before diving down to low-level, building up energy reserves once more in the process.

Meanwhile the two decoys maintain their headings so as to keep the AWACS computers thinking all was in order, before they, too, 'knocked it off' and withdraw. This introduces some complacency into the minds of the AWACS operators. During these few precious seconds the two snipers close in for the kill at low-level. By the time the AWACS or its minions acquire them and before fighters can be vectored into a firing position, the two swooping snipers close, lock-on passively and launch up to four air-to-air rotordome-homing ARMs (believed to be aerial adaptations of the ramjet-powered Kh-31P ARM), or the first volley from up to a dozen KS.172 long-ranged AAMs. These go right through the defending HavCap, aimed straight at AWACS, kicking the proverbial wasp's nest and turning it into a frenzied but uncoordinated communications morass with Flights getting inadequate JTIDS picture calls.

Western pilots have become so dependant on AWACS that this scenario would cause them considerable confusion. It is important to note that Eastern European AAM missile technology – what the Russians refer to as rockets – includes much bizarre hardware optimized for specialist use by highly skilled sniper pilots, including devices designed to pick up the Doppler effect created by swirling helicopter rotor blades. Thus, they can take out low-level SEAD pathfinders, medium-altitude AWACS, and bombers too by means of home-on-jam techniques. AWACS-killing technology, in particular, is very sophisticated. It allows launch-and-leave at extreme range: 60 miles unassisted, and double that with boosters which offer massively increased burn-out speeds, making the rockets tough to intercept before they unleash their deadly cargoes.

The Su-35, successor to the Su-27 *Flanker* is equipped with canards, vectored-thrust engine nozzles, and digital avionics. It is a particularly fearsome machine. USAF *Tac Brawler* computer simulations have shown the Russian design to tie in radar capability and to be superior to the F-15 Eagle in all but a barely notable factor in flight performance. It is stated that the Eagle lags far behind in terms of short-range AAM capability and combat mission radius, which is only slightly better than the MiG-29C Gorbatov (or 'hunchback'). When the USAF simulated two Eagles escorting four INT bombers against eight defending Su-35s, the simulated Eagles were apparently 'trying to get out of the area with their last few remaining ounces of fuel and no missiles remaining, if they survived that long' when the nuclear-capable strikers were winding-up their work. Because of their relatively large RCS, the F-15s were obliged to shoot at BVR distances, at least two AMRAAMs being required to ensure a kill against their hefty opponents (bearing in mind that AMRAAM was designed originally to counter the more petite, single-engined MiG-23, and more volatile MiG-25).

The numbers in this simulation might seem weighted heavily in favour of the Russian hardware. However, given the Pentagon's stated need to be able to conduct win-hold-win combat in two simultaneous MRCs, and the wide demands placed on the F-15,

resources may well be stretched to the limit in any future conflict. This will be especially so when under the 'Bottom Up' Review the USAF inventory is cut from the existing force of 615 A-D models to 288 combat-ready aircraft. The mighty Su-35 is entering series production to supersede the Su-27 and is due to enter CIS service in early 1996, in favour of the MiG-33 with which it competed. (The Su-27 is presently largely confined to PVO duties, but is due to be redistributed to the V-VS and will be offered for export, with deliveries to China already in progress.)

In contrast, the pure fighter variants of the Eagle is no longer in production, even though the type boasts a 27-year fatigue life and enjoys an unprecedented 95:0 kill to loss ratio in the hands of Israeli, Saudi Arabian and USAF pilots. Only the tooling remains, for now. For this reason the USAF considers the stealthy Lockheed F-22A Rapier to be its top-priority fighter programme. However, it seems unlikely that it will replace its predecessor on more than a 3-for-1 basis, and that series production is not now to be initiated much before 2002. The Su-35 is thus likely to attain and hold the hallowed title of World's Best Air Superiority Fighter for the next decade. Given its new AAM missile armament too, including the BVR 'Amraamski', this realization is causing considerable angst in American fighter pilot circles.

In particular, the CIS have established noticeable headway in medium-range and short-range AAM capability, where the new MiGs and Sukhois have acquired a reputation for wily tactics. The ubiquitous Tochka Opori was the first to introduce the fourth-generation weaponry, comprising the Vympel R-27/AKU-470 (AA-10 *Alamo*, or Sparrow M equivalent) and R-73/AKU-72 (AA-11 *Archer*, Sidewinder X-plus equivalent). If these fighters can survive the first volleys of AMRAAMs by means of heavy jamming and trick manoeuvres, then the R-27 could inflict some damage and the R-73 exact merciless revenge.

What makes the latter so effective is that it can be slaved to the target by radar, IRST or the pilot's helmet-mounted sight or Schlem which is most devastating at close-quarters. The missiles already possess a massive inherent 30° FoV and can be slaved by the radar/IRST through an effective FoV of 180° at ranges of under 15 miles. With the pilot's Schlem it can be slaved through a staggering 210° at visual ranges, in virtually all aspects. Clearly, the R-73 is formidable when employed aggressively! Anything coming within those lethal zones is likely to be zapped by the weapon. It possesses extraordinary snap-shoot potential by means of nose canards, trailing-edge control trim tabs and a vectored rocket nozzle for extra agility. The pilot can conduct his attack without even

R-73 WIDE-ANGLE 'HEAT' AAM MISSILE

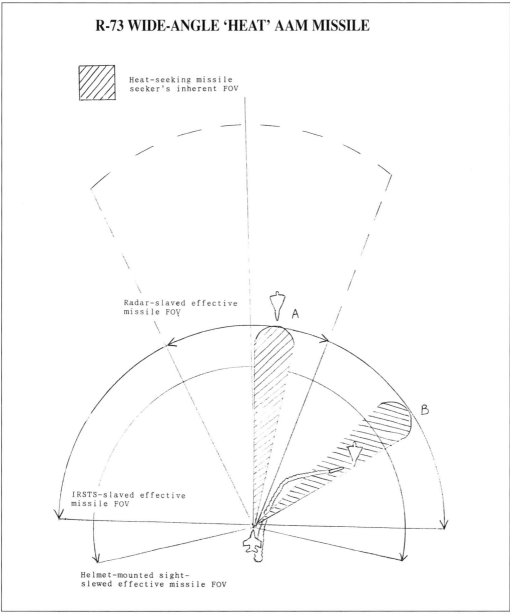

Heat-seeking missile seeker's inherent FOV

Radar-slaved effective missile FOV

A

B

IRSTS-slaved effective missile FOV

Helmet-mounted sight-slewed effective missile FOV

Employment of the Russian R-73 Wide FoV Heat-seeking Missile: The already substantial FoV of the R-73 heat-seeking missile (NATO code-name AA-11 Archer) can be slewed to target using radar, IRST and a helmet-mounted sight, permitting off-boresight lock-ons in the forward hemisphere. It is a formidable capability that has revolutionized short-range and medium-range air-to-air combat. Israel possesses a similar operational capability with the Python III AAM, and Eurofighter 2000 is to feature it with ASRAAM, slaved to radar, PIRATE IRST and a helmet-mounted sight. The US is experimenting with a similar capability as a sideline to the AIM-9X effort. Two separate heat attacks are illustrated. A A fairly untaxing, near-boresight radar-assisted lock-on is in progress of the type which currently represents the limits available to the Sidewinder AIM-9M Sidewinder Expanded Acquisition Mode. B A full off-boresight attack with the Vympel R-73 is underway, illustrating how the MiG-29 or Su-27 pilot need not point his aircraft at the target. Note, however, that the effective FoVs of the underwing missiles are partly obscured in the sideways-looking mode by obstructions such as pylons and drop-tanks.

having to point the nose of his aircraft at his enemy. Cockpit switching is slightly more complicated than that in contemporary Western HOTAS fighters, but only marginally so, and the latest MiG-33 and Su-35 cockpits have already provided suitable fixes. In the hands of a skilled pilot, this package is to be feared tremendously.

The AAM technology incorporated into fighters like the still-in-development Eurofighter 2000 is only just around the corner. It which would be a worthy adversary of the R-73, IRST and Schlem through the combination of BAe's AIM-132 advanced short-range AAM (ASRAAM), PIRATE and a Hughes-designed helmet-mounted sight of comparable ability. It is a combat scenario proven by Joust computer simulation. Israel's Hey'l Ha'Avir already possesses a similar capability on most of its fighters, made possible by the indigenous Rafale Python III AAM married to the Elbit Display & Sight Helmet (DASH). This is in the process of being exported to Romania and the Far East. The anxieties felt within the US Services at this apparent missile gap between their own forces and the Euopeans, Israelis and CIS has reached Congressional level. The Americans have two

options. First, to redevelop Sidewinder into a serious contender; or second, buy ASRAAMs or Python IIIs off-the-shelf from Britain or Israel. Each has its merits, but the cost-conscious US can only afford to tread one path seriously.

ASRAAM is a tail-steered missile employing a Hughes wide-angle IIR seeker gimballed for 180° cueing, which is maturing rapidly and will soon enter service aboard the RAF's fleet of Harrier GR.7s. The Deutsch Aerospace warhead is modest, but the seeker's focal plane array provides crisp enough images to enable the pilot to selectively pick out his quarry's cockpit, wing root or other vulnerable area. Primary cueing will be by means of the helmet sight and, once ASRAAM is locked on, the pilot will glimpse down into the cockpit to see the magnified target image generated by the weapon seeker and where it was poised to strike. When let off its leash in the traditional manner or in a longer-ranged helmet-directed shoot, its Mach 2 striking speed will pack enough kinetic energy to do serious mischief. The Python III is available now, and has been praised by many senior US military personnel (at least one of whom has evaluated the system against Aggressor

These two tail-steered weapons are AIM-132 ASRAAMs, an Anglo-American (BAe-Hughes) answer to the R-73 equipping CIS aircraft and their export equivalents. IOC is scheduled first aboard the RAF's Harrier GR.7 fleet, to be followed by the Cappers. (BAe Dynamics)

jets, and has conducted a successful drone shoot), but it is likely to be outclassed by ASRAAM and Sidewinder derivatives by the turn of the century.

For its own part, American industry is focusing on introducing the AIM-9X into service by the year 2002. The justification for further improving Sidewinder rather than starting from scratch or buying the BAe/Hughes ASRAAM is that it will take advantage of the massive stocks of existing missile bodies. Two concurrent developments have been taking shape since 1988 with this in mind. The first is the US Navy-sponsored Boa, with clipped 'winder-style steering canards and rear fins, currently in flight-test with the Kaiser Agile Eye 3 helmet sight aboard a brace of Nellis-based USAF Eagles, and US Navy Tomcats operating from NAS Patuxent River, Maryland.

The second is the USAF-sponsored 'Box Office' model, a tail-steered version designed for internal carriage aboard the F-22A, with half the drag and twice the g-manoeuvring capability of its forbears. This offers a 27–30 g turning capability in brief bursts, plus Mach 1.2–1.3 extra speed 'anywhere in the flyout'. This is very impressive given that even the original Sidewinder attained a burn-out speed of Mach 2.5 within 2.2 seconds of missile launch. 'Box Office'

is being flight-tested on an F-16C in conjunction with a Honeywell helmet-mounted sight, an advanced version of their 1970s-vintage AVG-8 visual target acquisition system (VTAS), originally designed to visually cue the F-4J Phantom II's radar to target for a Sparrow AIM-7E-2 shoot. Much of the test work remains classified, but it was reported that a test shot with 'Box Office' using the new Honeywell helmet to cue the Sidewinder was demonstrated successfully over the Gulf of Mexico during early 1994.

'Box Office' features a newly-developed Raytheon High Angle-of-Attack/Low Mach (HALM) seeker which passed 'within lethal distance' of an MQM-107 target drone turning away at 390 knots, 2 miles distant, 72° off boresight. The HALM 'Box Office' looks very promising indeed. The Raytheon seeker comprises a 13-element indium antimonide array, offering 2–3 times the range of the current AIM-9M Sidewinder, with 10 dedicated to tracking target hot spots, and the remaining three to spotting and rejecting IR decoys. The HALM adds two gimbals to the existing free gyro to permit fast, wide-angle target acquisition and tracking, allegedly effective out to 180° – i.e. the full-frontal hemisphere. The key advantage of this, in common with the

In a tight spot? Then use the six-shooter! The GE SUU-23/A gun pod can spit out 20 mm rounds at up to 6,000 spm. (Richard L. Ward)

European models, is that when employed in conjunction with a helmet sight the pilot's head rather than his jet does most of the physical manoeuvring. This eliminates the need for last second subtle jiggling of the fighter's nose during the critical phase of an engagement to compensate for any misalignment between the seeker and HUD-cueing pipper.

These advanced features effectively place the HALM 'Box Office' on par with the Russian R-73. Unlike its Eastern European counterpart, however, it is far from production. The R-73 has been available for nearly a decade and has been exported to numerous overseas clients, and is simply in the process of being refined further. And HALM may still lose out to ASRAAM during forthcoming comparative technical evaluations, during which cost and development schedules as well as raw performance will be measured.

Shooting Irons

A major knock-on effect of these new lethal short-ranged AAMs is that they have effectively relegated the gun, a long-standing fighter pilot's favourite, to a mere back-up function. More importantly perhaps,

some claim, they have reduced the need for super agility during aerial combat. A corkscrewing, slicing machine vying to get into firing position to let off a shower of lead is likely to be blasted out of the sky by an AAM long before it gets the chance to place its target squarely in the sights, some contend. This thinking echoes that of the late 1950s when it was thought that missiles had rendered guns completely obsolete. If pressed, most fighter pilots nowadays would choose an AAM in preference to a belly-holstered set of shooting irons. Yet many jet-jockeys would nevertheless feel naked without such a weapon as back-up, even in this era of super-reliable, allegedly unjammable AAMs cued by an array of sensors incorporating mind-boggling technology.

There are two principal types of gun honed for air-air combat. First there is the cannon, usually of a meaty 30 mm calibre, and essentially a big-calibre machine gun, chambering (sometimes from a revolver feed) and firing each round, then ejecting the spent case from the single-barrel breach. It has long been favoured for use on European fighters on both sides of the now-defunct Iron Curtain. It continues to be manufactured by a variety of specialists: Mauser makes the BK27 employed on the Tornado, Oerlikon

The Vulcan six-barrelled Gatling gun could be installed internally as well as in gun pods. In these instances rates of fire were often downrated to between 4,200 and 5,000 spm, to avoid undesirable propellant gas residue in the weapons bay – even the F-111 carried it for many years! (Frank B. Mormillo)

the KCA fitted to the Saab Viggen, and GIAT/DEFA the 552-554 series installed as standard items on the Mirage family. The GSh-301 30 mm cannon equips the MiG-29.

Its place in the US arsenal has long since been taken by General Electric Burlington's now classic electrically-driven M61A1 Vulcan Gatling gun. This was first developed in 1949 and has been installed on virtually every gun-equipped fighter built in the US since the early 1960s. The M61A1 uses marginally less devastating 20 mm calibre shells. This is offset by its ability to spew out a higher rate of fire by means of a sextet of constantly replenished spinning barrels, offering up to 7,200 shells per minute (spm), though typically a maximum of 5,000 or 6,000 spm. The maximum rate of fire of a typical cannon is 1,250 spm. The Gatling's weight of fire is such that a one-second burst pours out enough lead to show up on a radarscope! And it should be noted that neither single-barrelled cannons nor 'Gats' are habitually fired in bursts of more than 1–2 seconds' duration. This avoids overheating, a build-up of inadequately vented, potentially explosive residual propellant gas, and preserves ammunition.

Each of the two gun categories has its merits and drawbacks. In the case of the cannon, the real advantages are twofold. Firstly, the higher-calibre ammunition offers greater punch or 'throw' coupled with faster instantaneous rates of fire. On pressing the trigger, shells spit out of the muzzle in under one-twentieth of a second, whereas it may take a Gat a full four-tenths of a second to overcome inertia, spin up to speed and spit out shells at its preselected full rate of fire. Although these differences might at first appear negligible given the overall volume of fire involved, it is contended by several tacticians that it is only when the hunter crosses paths with his prey that his aim is the truest. And, given the short bursts customarily used in these incredibly brief, almost intuitive, aerial encounters, cannon therefore offer a much higher pK, especially when two or more of them are brought to bear at once. Arguments to the contrary usually draw comparisons between the latest models of the GE Gats versus obsolete guns such as the British Aden Mk IV and Ford/Pontiac M39, both of which were based on German Second World War designs, whereas modern cannon such as GSh-301 are incredibly lightweight and significantly more reliable.

To the Gat's credit, it has instantly selectable rates of fire (usually, 2,000, 4,000, 5,000 or 6,000 spm), and enjoys an enviable reliability record, with the Vulcan boasting an average stoppage rate of less than one shell in 10,000. Wear and tear is lower, too, and is divided between the six barrels. Each Vulcan is good for 30 years' service. It has also evolved into larger-calibre weapons such as the 25 mm GAU-12/A Equalizer equipping the AV-8B Harrier, and the mighty 30 mm GAU-8/A Avenger, centre-piece of the A-10A's arsenal, able to deliver depleted uranium slugs that can tear main battle tanks apart, let alone shred rotary-winged aircraft. Unequivocally, it has been the air-to-surface arena where the Gat has truly excelled itself.

Switching to 'Guns' is typically a HOTAS affair nowadays. Gone are the days when a pilot had to lean forwards, duck down and twist the knobs at what was often a crucial stage in an aerial pursuit or swirling air combat entanglement. When 'Guns' is commanded, the weapon comes on-line and the displays will all be reconfigured accordingly, including the HUD, which is the primary cue.

The aiming reference dot or pipper is not just an arbitrary point projected in the middle of the gunsight. Using inputs from the INS and central air data computer (CADC) which furnish such variables as aircraft velocity, attitude and altitude, and air density, the system computes the correct lead, so that the pipper corresponds to the point through which the shells will pass. At the same time, if it is up and running, upon selecting 'Guns' the radar will usually be 'caged' along the boresight of the aircraft, sending out a narrow range-finding search beam of invisible energy about the nose, which will be factored into the lead equation. As the target gets into the sights, the pipper will shift slightly to correct for external ballistics – the shells' trajectory out of the muzzle – if fired at that specific range, closure rate and aircraft attitude (which is constantly recomputed, of course). This enables the pilot to jiggle his jet into precisely the optimum firing position before pressing the trigger. As long as the system is up and running and the target is walked through the aiming pipper, the shells will strike true. Well, that's how it works in theory, anyhow!

In practise, things are rarely that easy because the enemy, if he knows he is being chased, will do his best to avoid becoming a kill marking painted on the flank of his adversary's aircraft. Evasive action will thus often be aggressive and determined, making hard work out of simply 'putting the target in the aiming pipper' as the brochures would have you believe. In all forms of flying, pilots need a natural ability to judge both distance to target and relative aircraft attitudes, virtually by instinct without recourse to instruments. This is especially so in fighters in the complex, vertigo-inducing three-dimensional air-to-air arena where up can suddenly become down, and the whole world seemingly starts gyrating outside the canopy. It is this quality which sets a good fighter pilot head and shoulders above even an average one.

Perhaps more than any other form of air-to-air combat, exchanging volleys of lead transforms flying from a science into an art. Good fighter jocks deviously corral their chosen quarry into optimum position with skilfully chosen moves and countermoves, so that they know roughly where the target should be at the climax of a given manoeuvre, how the pipper will shift when the target comes into the sight and is ranged, and when to fire. Firing is often slightly in advance of the aiming reference moving into the proper lead position, as such a pilot knows precisely what he is doing, and is not shooting wildly from the hip hoping for a lucky shot. In these instances the lead-computed pipper merely confirms his sound judgement, and a stream of bullets will already be traversing the sky when the target intersects it.

Even a 1.5-second burst guzzles up between 30 and 150 rounds at normal rates of fire, depleting the ammunition drum rapidly. You do not need a degree in mathematics to see that the 940-round drum contained in the F-15 Eagle, for example, offers a total of 9.4 seconds of fire in the high setting – good for five such bursts. However, it only takes a mere handful of these shells, exiting the muzzle at a velocity of some 3,400 ft per second, to tear away the target's wing or cut the fuselage in two.

The great air-slicing tactics used at close-quarters for most gun kills enter the realms of energy manoeuvring: using existing speed, height and engine thrust and understanding how these are interrelated and how they can be used to maximum advantage in various scenarios. This forms the nub of such intense courses as the Fighter Weapons School and Top Gun. It is an intense learning curve which combines cunning with a thorough working knowledge of the performances of different fighters, their strengths and weaknesses. And most pilots or crews get the opportunity to train at such a level only once, if they are lucky. Live ammunition is routinely expended once or twice annually under much less demanding circumstances, on Armament Practice Camps and Weapons Training Deployments. Crews head out into a sunny sky with a loaded gun to poke a few holes in a trailing dart or gunnery banner under near optimum firing conditions.

It is surprising how few shells actually hit home. Getting 12 per cent hits is rated highly indeed even under these less than realistic circumstances against an unmanoeuvrable, undemanding target – and it's shocking how often the target-towers get hit! 'Guns tight' discipline in aerial combat is probably essential for all but the more honed, skilled jet jockeys, as many crews do no better than 3 per cent. In the Gulf War, the only reported gun kills were by a pair of A-10As using their GAU-8/A 30 mm Avengers. They blasted two helicopters (a BO 105 and an Mi-8 *Hip*) apart. Aerial gunnery is a demanding task.

Enter the 'trainable' gun. The goal here is to take some of the guesswork out of the equation by tying the weapon to a snap-shooting computer. This utilizes a number of variables provided by the CADC, and extras such as conventional or laser radar ranging, to help track targets through a limited arc of movement. According to one USAF Major well-known for his knowledge of weapons developments, 'Some impressive work with "trainable" guns was done under the *Fire Fly* programme, during which time the test force blew a manoeuvring F-86 [Sabre drone] out of the air with a mere four rounds! The effort then suddenly went "black"!'

Certainly, the Russian fighters already employ laser-ranging in lieu of radar to help compute lead, and the MiG-29's designer Mikhail Waldenburg is on record as stating that he would have halved the size of the *Fulcrum*'s ammunition drum had he known how accurate the gun was! The GSh-301 is noted for its lightness but does not offer trainability, just an exceptionally well-harmonized lead cue on the gunsight. However, some of the best features of the American *Fire Fly* effort are being redirected into the ATF effort, for even the stealthy F-22A Rapier will feature a Gat behind a flush-skinned cat flap. The weapon has a proud heritage and a bright future.

TARGET INGRESS

Ingressing enemy airspace close on the heels of the Cappers and SEAD jets are the strike waves. They are supported by further 'police escorts' on an as-required and as-available basis, rostered by the individual Flights' frags contained in the master Air Tasking Order operations plan.

Amongst the strikers, there are three basic overland assignments, in the main performed by separate, dedicated units: close air support (CAS), battle area interdiction (BAI), and interdiction (INT). CAS focuses on the forward edge of the battle area (FEBA) or FLOT, the latter acronym being more in vogue nowadays. Battle area interdiction (BAI) operates just behind the FLOT where the enemy often combines his ground forces into attacking or defensive formations. Interdiction (INT), way behind enemy lines, is usually strategic in nature. It aims to cut off the supply lines of communication (LoCs), and destroy high-value fixed targets such as POLs, electrical and chemical plants, and the enemy's general capacity to wage war.

Traditionally, strike flyers were classed as bomber pilots; today, they mostly fly dedicated attack or swing-role aircraft possessing fighter performance and compromised only by heavy, drag-inducing ordnance – the bomb and missile load. Ultimately, the advance SEAD and Cappers are in the sky purely to aid these striking elements and to deny the enemy a similar capability. Even from their lofty platforms they can only reach so far, or venture so close down to the terrain.

Mud Moving

The function of the CAS mission is simple: to lay down a barrage of fire on selected coordinates in support of friendly troops engaged with enemy ground forces (TIC – troops in contact), at the behest of the Army. Indeed, the lines of jurisdiction over CAS-dedicated fighter aircraft have become increasingly blurred over the years. In the US the Army and Air Force are even beginning to merge resources under the guise of new Combat Wings tasked exclusively with CAS and the support of Special Operations Forces, with regular Army units to follow. It is a long overdue move combining flak-killing helicopters with CAS and anti-armour fixed-wing jets – as proved so successful during the Joint Attack Weapons System (JAWS) manoeuvres of the late 1970s, and so potent during *Desert Storm* where AH-64A Apache gunships took the heat off the Coalition fixed-wing flak suppression SEAD tasking. This, in turn, freed the CAS jets to work their assigned targets relatively unimpeded. Both Services benefited enormously.

The goal of the CAS pilot remains unchanged from its embryonic development during the closing stages of the First World War: to inflict as much damage as possible on the enemy while simultaneously keeping heads down. This is achieved with what can only be described as highly mobile, quick-reaction airborne artillery. CAS permits friendly forces to consolidate their positions or perform various tactical manoeuvres, including flanking movements, advances through heavily fortified positions, or even a timely withdrawal in a crisis. Knowledge of where the enemy and the friendly forces are located is thus crucial. Then add the fast-moving aspect of this air power: not only for the obvious reason of wishing to avoid dropping ordnance directly on the heads of the friendlies (an event now termed euphemistically as Blue-on-Blue, or more clinically as fratricide), but also to lay down the fire so that the main body of the shrapnel from the ordnance will cause them no mischief. This is where the FAC, ground or airborne, comes in, and is the key reason why the CAS and FAC missions are so inextricably intertwined.

Within the NATO framework, liaison extends to assigning selected fighter pilots for short tours of duty with the ground troops, so that they gain a better understanding of the needs of the infantryman on the ground. This originated in the USAF in December 1976 under the *Blue Flag* banner. By the same token, ground forces come to understand better the complexities and limitations of the fast-moving fighters supporting them. This permits them to evolve mutually supportive tactics which overcome the inevitable paradox: for the fighter pilot speed is life whereas for the Army commander or Special Forces squad, slower equates with greater accuracy. Obviously, compromises are needed.

The airborne FAC's traditional job is to orbit perilously in the vicinity of the FLOT and to relay suitable attack instructions to the CAS fighter crews over the radio. Usually, he is out of reach of enemy small-arms fire but inevitably within range of heavier-calibre AA fire and portable heat-seeking weapons. Along with magnetic heading from a common visual identification point (VIP), such as a topographical feature known to the FAC and CAS pilots, other vital

information will also be conveyed. This will include target distance (customarily in metres, or tenths of a nautical mile, depending on the degree of accuracy required, and the available information), its elevation above sea level, and possibly other data such as Universal Transverse Mercator (UTM). Even hyperbolic long-range airborne radio navigation (LORAN) coordinates may be provided. These are supplied in lieu of the copious flight-planned software programmes taken aloft in the BAI and INT jets, which work relatively autonomously.

By convention, ground forces call in an airborne FAC who, in turn, directs the strike jets. However, there are exceptions. Special Forces such as US Navy SEALS or the British Special Air Service (SAS) troopers are trained to liaise directly with the jets, as demonstrated on numerous recent actions – the Falklands War, the invasion of Grenada, Operation *Desert Storm* and, more recently, during the Serbian siege of Gorazde in Bosnia, where two SAS FACs lost their lives. Increasing use is being made of command and control agencies which convey requests for support up and down the communications lines.

In its latest, most sophisticated guise, the target data is conveyed by radio link direct to the CAS jets' computers by means of the Rockwell-Collins CP-1516/ASQ ATHS. Aircraft currently being equipped

With the introduction of the OA/A-10A Warthog came this massive shell-loading machine, which handles the aircraft GAU-8/A Avenger's linkless-feed 30 mm HE and API ammunition. (ANG)

with these receivers include early-model F-16A Fighting Falcons retro-fitted under the Operational Capability Upgrade programme. ATHS furnishes the target data in a brief coded burst, which in turn can be assimilated by the jet's onboard fire control computers to present target position on the instruments and HUD. The FAC and CAS aircraft need not even talk to one another!

A broader effort is underway to install IDMs. These are capable of receiving target data from Army ground stations, satellites and other strike and FAC aircraft using existing UHF/VHF radio receivers, for the benefit of more up-to-date target coordinates and improved pilot situational awareness (SA). This is one of the biggest but least publicized upgrades sweeping the Western fighter-bomber community. It is suffering from its fair share of teething troubles. Without a FAC on the spot to verify that coordinates and other vital information are correct, excess automation might lead to more Blue-on-Blue incidents, especially when ground engagements become more intense and the fog of war descends over the FLOT. The FAC, with boots in the mud or near rudder pedals close to the action, remains a vital resource, and as such must be maintained.

Because of the intrinsic hazards involved in the FAC mission in relaying strike coordinates verbally or purely electronically, the piston-powered FAC machines of yesteryear have long since given way to Fast-FAC fighter types such as the Fairchild OA-10A Thunderbolt II. At the time of writing, some 412 Thunderbolts continue to serve with the USAF, split roughly down the middle on dedicated CAS and FAC assignments. The Warthog, as the aircraft is affectionately referred to by its crews, was purpose-built for the job. It incorporates a mighty GAU-8/A 30 mm Avenger Gatling gun backed up by underwing bombs, FFAR rockets and TV-guided and IIR-guided AGM-65 Maverick air-to-ground missiles (AGMs). Any one of these is capable of puncturing unwary, threatening armour or AA systems.

However, even the Warthog is growing increasingly vulnerable in today's high-threat battle arena. Despite its armour-plating and redundant flight control systems which makes it capable of sustaining heavy battle damage, the jet can barely muster more than 320 knots and is limited to 3 *g* manoeuvres. This is ideal for precision FAC and CAS work but obliges the pilot to remain exposed to enemy ground fire for long periods.

During the course of *Desert Storm*, the 194 assigned Warthogs flew 8,500 sorties, destroying

Born in grey, later smothered in 'European One' greens and charcoal grey, 15 years on, the Warthog is readopting a grey scheme. The type recently has seen extensive action in both the Gulf and over war-torn Bosnia. (Peter E. Davies)

1,000 tanks, 1,200 artillery pieces and 2,000 other vehicles. High-wheeling, high-speed F-16s lobbing their Mk 84 2,000 lb bombs from altitude did little more than harass the enemy. The tank-mashing 30 mm Avenger Gatling gun spews armour-piercing and incendiary rounds at 4,200 spm – 70 of the 2 lb shells per second – which cover 4,000 feet in 1.2 seconds. By fishtailing the aircraft's rudders a pilot could spray an entire convoy in a flank attack, though the 12,000 lb of torque generated by the gun would bleed 5–6 knots off the already limited airspeed in 1.5 seconds.

The other key weapon was the ubiquitous Hughes AGM-65 Maverick AGM, with Warthogs accounting for over 90 per cent of the 5,300 such weapons expended during the war. This versatile, subsonic launch-and-leave missile has a maximum realistic aerodynamic launch range of 9 miles in bright, clear-weather conditions. In practise launches are conducted well within that limit and, once selected, often require a relatively hazardous period of 15–20 seconds of wings-level flight to set-up for launch. As used by the

A/OA-10A, it comes in two E-O versions: the daytime AGM-65A/B television-guided model, and the night-time AGM-65D/G IIR version which can see through smoke and haze as well.

In most single-seat fighters, the pilot simply rolls onto the target with the weapon's E-O sensor activated and boresighted with the gunsight. Thus by manoeuvring to place the target in the aiming HUD pipper (which is caged for AGMs), the missile seeker should be looking right at the target. This can be confirmed by looking down at a cockpit-mounted TV screen which will show the target squarely underneath the aiming cross-hairs in the middle of the screen. The pilot then presses the firing trigger and the missile shoots off its Teflon-coated rail towards the target, enabling him to pull up and away and out of danger. The kinetic energy generated by Maverick is often sufficient in itself to demolish a tank or bunker in a direct hit, compensating for its rather modest 125 lb shaped-charge warhead. The later 'Golf' model (alongside the USN/USMC models) employs a bigger

Rolling in on a practice target over the Eglin ranges, an F-4E prepares to lock-on with its AGM-65B Maverick missile. (Hughes)

300 lb blast-penetration warhead. Multiple launches against troublesome targets are also possible, using a 'quick draw' capability which slaves one or more back-up missiles to the first's lock-on point. Stocks are being augmented to make good Gulf War expenditure.

Nevertheless, the classified 6,000-page *American Gulf War Air Power Survey* prepared after the cessation of hostilities in 1991 pointed to the necessity of upgrading the Warthogs if they and the Fast-FAC mission were to remain viable through the turn of the century. Two initiatives have been spawned: the Low-Altitude Safety and Targeting Enhancement (LASTE) programme; and measures aimed at reducing the aircraft's heat and radar signature to lend it a modicum of stealth.

As the old saying goes, it is not possible to make a silk purse out of sow's ear; nor a super-stealthy dedicated Fast-FAC and CAS machine out of an aging Warthog. But given that the airframes have an estimated fatigue life (at current utilization rates) which extends until the year 2030, little needs to be spent to get value for money even if they are retired long before then. Signature-reduction measures include a new paint job, with the possible use of top secret radar-absorbent polyaniline coatings containing microscopic cyanate whiskers. A top coat of this paint could absorb at least 10 dB of radio frequency energy per square metre, enough to nearly halve the range at which the aircraft can be acquired on radar. This will permit it to operate closer to its intended target. Shrouds for the engines are also being evaluated, to reduce the vulnerability to shoulder-launched and vehicle-launched heat-seeking weapons which present a particularly unpleasant threat to CAS and Fast-FAC fighters.

The LASTE initiative, aimed more at the avionics suite, comprises several components. A ground proximity warning system and new radar altimeter are being fitted for added flight safety. Provisions are being made for the installation of NVGs so that the Warthog can begin to move further into the realm of darkness. BAe Terprom (described later) may also be added soon. LASTE also introduces a continuously computed impact point (CCIP) ballistics computer which doubles gun accuracy.

Pilots can confidently hit targets using the Avenger's depleted uranium armour-piercing slugs at slant-ranges of 2 miles, or cut-in close with rockets and phosphorus to target-mark for their colleagues and some of the faster movers. Combined with sweeping

scissors and wagon-wheel attack tactics, with constant changes of heading and dive angle to 'clear six' and keep the enemy gunners guessing as much as possible, the Warthog remains a formidable machine. It is fast enough to be accurate, yet not so fast as to be a potential menace to those it supports! Updated, it represents a superb compromise to the CAS fighter paradox.

Similar survivability updates were effected to the CIS counterpart, the Su-25 *Frogfoot* as a direct result of combat experience in Afghanistan. Twenty-three of these aircraft were lost during nine years of operations, several of them to man-portable Redeye and Stinger SAMs supplied to the mujahedin by the US. Overall, the *Frogfoot* apparently proved vulnerable when one of its two R-195 engines was hit, as the fire would quickly burn through the lower fuselage to the other engine. However, a relatively simple fix, which added steel panels 5 ft long and 0.5 in thick between the engine nacelles and fuselage, backed by a new Freon fire-extinguishing system, effectively cured the problem. Flare capacity was also increased to 256 cartridges – apparently sufficient to respond to eight separate attacks by numerous heat-seeking missiles – and the casualties abruptly ceased. The two losses incurred by the Al Quwwat al-Jawwiya al-Iraqiya on 6 February 1991 were felled by

Try dogfighting with that on your head! NVGs are not as cumbersome as they appear, but do only offer 'through the tube' vision to this RAF Harrier GR.7 night-attack CAS pilot. (Andy Evans)

F-15Cs volleying AIM-9M Sidewinders. But the aircraft were in the process of escaping to Iran with two other aircraft and distracting pyrotechnics may not have been loaded. Moreover, it is believed that none of these featured the Afghan *modifatsirovanji*.

Frogfoot also acquired a long-range navigation and weapons computer based on Tropik (Russian LORAN) matched to an improved optical sight linked to a laser rangefinder. Owing to the tiny wavelengths used with lasers, this provides extremely accurate slant-range information in lieu of radar to assist with semi-automatic CCIP bomb release. Along with the 1-inch-thick all-welded titanium cockpit tub, these survivability improvements account for a hefty 7.5 per cent of the aircraft's standard take-off weight of 32,100 lb. Twin-seat Su-25UB models exist for conversion training and Fast-FAC work, and are proving their mettle.

As an aside, the V-VS also employed MiG-23 and MiG-27 fighters in the CAS and COIN roles in the Afghan War, hitherto reserved for older Su-17 *Fitter* 'Warwagons' and the newer *Frogfoot*. Remarkably, in what proved eventually to be a successful Stinger-evading manoeuvre, *Floggers* would perform Il-2 Sturmovik-type high-angle releases (in this instance also below 5,000 ft AGL!) with their 1,000 lb cluster bombs or blast-fragmentation weapons, while building up airspeed to critical limits. On the pickle, they would then pull-up in horrendous 6–7 g gyrations, with the throttles cut back to idle (so as to reduce their vulnerability to shoulder-launched missiles, which would otherwise lock onto a glowing afterburner) during the ensuing 60° pull-up, riding purely on kinetic energy until the sixth sense (or airspeed indicator) indicated 'stage two'. Popping nearly every orifice of its flare cartridge dispensers in a frenzied display of pyrotechnics, the crews then rolled their wings inverted again, building-up airspeed during a nose-over descent (now at some distance from the target), finally recovering wings-level and nosing out in afterburner as low as 300 feet AGL! Quite how the pilots accomplished this without killing themselves in large numbers remains a closely guarded V-VS secret. Apparently, it was an unofficial option reserved for Class One pilots with a will to survive, or a penchant for madness.

Not surprisingly, the tactic had been rejected at its inception, though the characteristic kruu-mmps of their 500 kg fragmentation bomb impacts preceding the noise of the jet (which was transonic) remained a hallmark of their dive-bombing attacks for the last few years of the war. Only cluster and fragmentation bombs were employed, along with fuel-air explosives (FAEs). Apparently, it was a case of being killed (by the ground during the dive-bombing run, or

mujahedin if ejection was an option if hit), or surviving for another day. Many pilots probably kept their eyes closed during the bomb pass, knowing when to pull-up without reference to the instruments, and opened them again only after they had completed the hairy pull-up.

Perfecting Pippers

At this stage it is useful to examine the bombing and strafing systems employed in the close support mission, and how the technology has evolved. In many respects, the actual tactics employed date back to the days when RAF Typhoons and Tempests dived down from the stacked echelons of aircraft circling above the clouds, or zoomed in at low altitude, to knock out panzers with rockets and bombs. All that has changed significantly are the weapons at the crews' disposal, and the technology in the cockpit which has gradually taken much of the guesswork and luck out of getting ordnance smack on target.

From a CAS standpoint, there are two fundamental methods of attack: strafing and bombing in dives, or near-level laydown attacks at low altitude. High-angle, high-altitude dive-bombing may also be used (as was practised by some *Afghansti* on anti-bandit COIN strikes), but the release heights above the terrain (necessary to avoid ploughing into the ground in a fast jet) seldom provide the sharp target discrimination required, particularly in the thick of the smoke hanging around the FLOT, when friendly and enemy forces are in close proximity. Hitting the enemy behind the FLOT where there is less scope for confusion – BAI – is an altogether different mission, which customarily relies on a degree of mission-planning akin to INT.

CAS bombing is much more of an *ad hoc* affair, based on the pressing requirements of battle. Crews tend to just familiarize themselves with the working sector and draw up a rota to keep enough air power aloft to meet the Army's needs. Previously, navigation was thus traditionally rudimentary, and usually revolved around timing with a stopwatch and a fixed groundspeed (usually rounded off at 60-knot increments for ease of use, such as 420 knots in a Harrier GR.3) to judge time and distance to target. For example, initiating the stopwatch over the prominent VIP known to be 3.5 nm from the target at a bearing of 090°, meant turning East towards it at 420 knots groundspeed, and the pilot would reach it when the clock read 30 seconds. (Mental arithmetic works best if you round things up, so the pilot would probably instinctively think of this arithmetical problem as 420 knots ÷ 60 seconds = 7 nm/minute, and thus 3.5 nm = 30 seconds to the target.) He would then factor-in the delivery profile of his bombs or rockets, and let them loose using depressed sight-line (DSL) techniques, described presently. Before the advent of computers, this often required quick mental arithmetic in the cockpit.

In emergencies, CAS planning might simply comprise jumping into a bombed-up, gassed-up jet, setting radio frequencies and heading off from an Alert 'hot pad' at 5 minutes' notice to deposit their weapons on FAC-directed targets unknown to them until a couple of minutes into the flight. To use the description oft quoted by the 'flying grunts': 'It was boredom punctuated by moments of sheer terror, in turn punctuated by moments of math.'

The term 'bombing' is a slight misnomer owing to the cornucopia of weapons used nowadays. These not only embrace cannon, rockets, and iron bombs (steel fragmentation bombs containing tritonal explosive) but also a more grisly range of weapons that includes napalm and fuel-air explosives. For low-level work, iron bombs utilize steel airbrakes or 'ballute' canvas air-braking devices to retard the weapons so that the attacker does not get caught in the blast of its own ordnance during straight-and-level or low-angle deliveries. Napalm B canisters erupt in a ball of suffocating flame. FAE munitions spread large clouds of atomized liquid explosive (such as propane or ethylene oxide) over a wide area, which is then detonated. A wide variety of tactical munitions

dispensers (TMDs), each packed with purpose-designed cluster bomblets are also available.

The purpose of all this weaponry is to spread as much firepower as possible over a large area to disrupt, destroy and demoralize enemy ground forces, without having to resort to overkill. Western European models of TDM include the British Hunting Engineering BL755 and French Thomson Brandt Armaments BLG-66 Belouga optimized for high-speed low-level delivery. The US has created huge families of weapons offering broader delivery parameters, from as low as 250 ft, up to a staggering 40,000 ft. When released from this height a wind corrected munitions dispenser kit flies the bomb to the desired mean point of impact using inertial-GPS coordinates handed off by the attacking aircraft just prior to weapons release. These would only be used by BAI or INT jets, or CAS machines possessing extraordinarily accurate nav-attack systems in high base curvilinear attacks. Submunitions-dispensing takes place at a pre-determined altitude over the target, depending on the fuze settings and the submunitions carried.

The newest and most devastating of these are built around the SUU-64/B and -65/B TMDs, and comprise the combined effects munition (CEM), Gator, and the sensor fuzed weapon (SFW). Each works differently. The CEMs are so designed that on hitting a soft target they simply blow up like a grenade, but on contact

---

PRINCIPAL CLUSTER BOMB UNITS

Designation	Canister	Submunitions
Mk 20 Rockeye Mod 2	Mk 7	247 M118 anti-tank
CBU-49B/B	SUU-30	217 BLU-61/B fragmentation
CBU-52B/B	SUU-30	254 BLU-61/B fragmentation
CBU-55A/B	SUU-49	3 BLU-73/B FAE
CBU-58B/B	SUU-30	650 BLU-63/B fragmentation
CBU-59/B	Mk 7	717 BLU-77/B APAM
CBU-71A/B	SUU-30	650 BLU-68/B incendiary
CBU-72B/B	SUU-49 Mod	3 BLU-73/B FAE
CBU-78/B Gator	Mk 7	29 BLU-91/B anti-personnel mines
		38 BLU-92/B Gator anti-tank mines
CBU-87/B CEM	SUU-65	214 BLU-97/B CEM
CBU-89/B Gator	SUU-64	72 BLU-91/B anti-personnel mines
		24 BLU-92/B Gator anti-tank mines
CBU-97 SFW	SUU-64	10 BLU-108 Skeet anti-armour

APAM anti-personnel/*matériel*
CEM combined effects munitions
FAE fuel-air explosive
SFW sensor-fuzed weapon (autonomous)

with a hard target, such as a tank hull, the core of the miniature warhead forms a shaped charge to blast through the thick metal. Each CBU-87/B is packed with 214 BLU-97/B CEM submunitions which strike on a hit or miss basis instantly. The Gators are anti-tank mines which arm on reaching the ground and are then set off by magnetically or tripwire whiskers when the enemy stumble into them, and are thus used as area denial devices. Each CBU-89/B is stuffed with 72 BLU-91/B anti-personnel mines and 24 BLU-92/B Gators.

The Textron SFW is the most advanced. The SUU-64/B TMD contains 10 BLU-108/B submunitions, each fitted with four Skeet warheads. After release, the 'Bloos' para-descend over the target using a vortex ring parachute which generates a swirling motion. This enables the Skeets to scan a spiral sector of the ground during their descent. Skeet uses passive infrared sensing technology to search for targets. The instant it locates a tank or armoured vehicle beneath it (such target signatures are held in the Skeet's memory), the warhead fires a shaped charge directly at the target, which is sufficient to blast through tank hulls and cause all sorts of other mischief. Newer brilliant anti-tank (BAT) munitions, dispensed from a

variety of delivery canisters, will combine acoustic as well as dual-infrared sensors to seek out their quarry.

Target ingress – setting up each aircraft for the attack pass – typically begins in one of two ways. The fighters may peel off from cruise altitude and nose straight down onto the target in a roller-coaster dive, using the initial point (IP) like an imaginary maypole to swing onto the required heading. Alternatively, the aircraft may ingress at low-level and perform a belly-wrenching pop-up, vaulting up from 200 ft to several thousand feet AGL, the height varying with the desired dive-angle to be used during the attack. Target acquisition is effected by banking 90° and turning on a wing-tip, or by rolling completely inverted at the apex of the pop, before rolling wings-level and diving down on the desired target heading. In both instances, the aircraft in the attack Flight will vary their headings to keep the enemy gunners guessing and provide adequate spacing between splashes (bomb drops on each pass), so that the wingmen avoid the harrowing procedure of flying into the debris kicked-up by their colleagues' ordnance! Spacings of half a minute or more are not uncommon.

In more evolved teamwork, two aircraft in a CAS

Turning in formation. Before reaching the target the Flight of four will split into individual elements, each with their own heading and TOT, so as to maximize surprise. (McAir)

And bombs away . . . in a 45° 'down the chute' bomb run (although the camera angle belies this). This was the meat-and-potatoes of attack jets prior to the introduction of computer-assisted CCIP which took much of the guesswork out of the operation. (Mike Turner)

section will often use complementary ordnance on each pass. For example one Warthog, *Frogfoot* or Harrier will come in just above the tree-tops and fire 25 mm or 30 mm cannon high-explosive incendiary (HEI) and armour-piercing (AP) shells, alternately pushing the left and right rudder pedals to yaw the beast and spray a fan of fire about the CCIP aim point. This keeps the heads of the enemy down while the

second aircraft arcs up and noses over to volley a couple of anti-armour Mavericks, or a canister of 68 mm rockets. Both may deposit CBUs before breaking away to freedom.

In South-East Asia, when the jets were often tasked with CAS in low-threat areas considered to be milk runs, multiple passes were a matter of routine. While far more hazardous, multiple passes were and

Zooming over Loch Ness in Scotland. A LCOSS was about as advanced as things got prior to the introduction of the true HUD. This incorporated lead – pitch correction – for shooting rockets or guns, and dropping bombs, and incorporated roll indices and a radar-ranging analogue bar which wound counter-clockwise. (Dick Brown)

still are exercised in high-threat areas when crews are providing bombing in support of Combat Search & Rescue (CSAR) forces, keeping the enemy at bay so that a downed colleague can be snatched away to safety. To reiterate a common thread: such *ésprit de corps* is vital to unit morale.

Further refinement of visual attack accuracy came with the advent of the raster-scan HUD linked to a digital ballistics computer, first introduced in the LTV A-7D/E Corsair II in 1971: the revolutionary GEC Avionics HUD and IBM TC-2 '4π' computer. The A-7 was dedicated to CAS and CSAR, and introduced the CCIP method of uncanned visual bombing. This was used against unplanned targets of opportunity. It relied on the fighter's ballistics computer knowing the forward throw or ballistic characteristics of the chosen weapon, selected on a window on the WCP alongside store stations and Master Arm prior to making the bomb pass.

On more modern fighters this is accomplished using the buttons on an MFD periphery, selected alongside stores station, fuze options – nose or tail or both – and release options, such as singles, pairs or salvo. Now, as then, the computer then correlates the relevant ballistics data with aircraft speed, dive angle and height AGL and continuously recomputes the projected impact point or bomb splash point ahead.

This is presented as an aiming reticle on the pilot's HUD: the bombs will fall there if he presses the bomb release button now. Hence, on the A-7's HUD, and most modern heads-up devices which followed on its heels, the pilot is presented with a bomb fall line corresponding to the aircraft's velocity vector (where it is actually heading) with a short crossbar or circle indicating the CCIP ground impact point for an immediately released weapon.

The aircraft is flown so that the target tracks down the aiming line until overlaid by the CCIP reticle, at which point the pilot pickles the bombs, and they should tumble smack on target. Good CCIP ballistics computers uncan the procedure by compensating for all delivery angles and airspeeds, and the nature of the terrain, whether it is rugged or sloping (which would cause them to fall long or short). The latter variable is computer-corrected by comparing aircraft height versus target elevation, which can be furnished by a FAC, looked-up on a map and cranked into the system or, for greater accuracy, determined using trigonometry and slant-ranging sensors such as radar or laser. Good CCIP computers can also take into account the subtle aerodynamic nuances between weapons (for example, American 2.75 in FFARs versus higher-velocity Canadian CRV-7 rockets, or the tumbling or spinning properties of the Rockeye Mk 7

During a Greek VIP visit to HMS Ark Royal *in October 1978 No. 892 Sqn demonstrated its wares, including this Phantom FG.1 volleying rockets. (HMS* Ark Royal *via Richard L. Ward)*

MANUAL AND CCIP VISUAL ATTACK

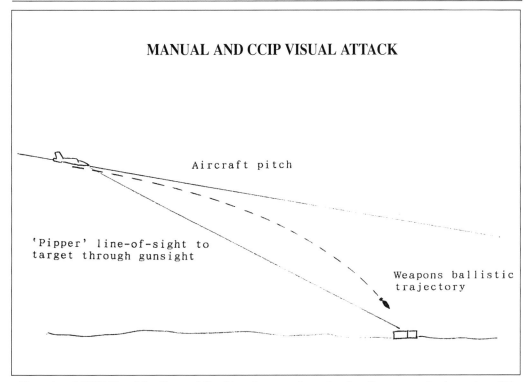

Aircraft pitch

'Pipper' line-of-sight to
target through gunsight

Weapons ballistic
trajectory

Manual and CCIP Visual Strafing and Bombing: In manual attacks, the pilot presets the depression of the gunsight/HUD aiming-reference – the 'pipper' – to correspond to a set airspeed, dive-angle and ordnance type (looked up in charts) so that the aircraft is properly pitched at the moment of weapons release, in turn conducted at a set altitude. As long as the target is in the pipper and the other parameters have been met, the bombs, cannon shells or rockets should hit the target.

In automatic CCIP attacks, the computer will constantly adjust pipper position for the given airspeed, dive-angle and height automatically, this corresponding to the continuously computed impact point – where the ordnance will hit – if released then. The pilot simply flies the pipper 'through' the target and presses the weapons 'pickle' button when the two intersect. He is free to adjust airspeed, dive-angle, altitude and so on throughout the attack manoeuvre; i.e. the attack procedure is 'uncanned'. All he has to do is to select ordnance type, which tells the ballistics computer what trajectory the weapons will follow.

class versus the SUU-64 canister). Back in 1971 when the vintage A-7's Operational Flight Program entered service, it held the data for all of the approximately 100 types of weapons the aircraft was qualified to carry, while the CCIP computer recomputed the impact point 25 times per second. Modern computers do it a whole lot faster still.

The technology was further refined with the General Dynamics (now Lockheed) F-16A Fighting Falcon, which incorporated a newer digital bomb-nav-system (BNS) with the Westinghouse AN/APG-66(V) multi-mode radar and hybrid stroke/raster GEC Avionics HUD. This entered service during January 1979 and proved massively popular with USAF and the many overseas pilots who got to grips with it. The CCIP circular error probability (CEP) was in the order of 7 mils or better. In effect, one mil equates to a 1-foot

CEP at 1,000 ft, so that, for example, when releasing dumb bombs from 8,000 ft, pilots could expect to lob their bombs within 60 ft of the aim point. Of course, wind and height factors degrade effectiveness (it is no good merely dropping slugs or lead pellets on the enemy's head, however precisely when his armour could be punctured at closer ranges), so the useful parameters of the weapons must still be taken into account – say, 2 miles maximum range for a 30 mm *Pave Claw* Gatling gun.

In the context of CAS, the F-16 came equipped with avionics tailored for both CCIP and dive toss. The latter worked in much the same manner as it did on the F-4, using radar slant-range, but allied to a much-improved INS, navigation and ballistics computers which handled the trigonometric and ballistic calculations much more accurately. Thus,

Over 5,000 units of the Westinghouse AN/APG-66(V) multi-mode radar and its derivatives have been manufactured since 1978, primarily for use on board the F-16 Fighting Falcon. It offers CCIP, CCRP, dive-toss, air-to-air and sea-search modes. (Westinghouse)

even 'F***ing New Guys' (FNGs) could produce visual-bombing CEPs of around 100 ft from ordnance release heights of up to 6,000 ft AGL, while 'Old Heads' achieved a 'shack' on just about every pass. HUD symbology was much more comprehensive too, aiding SA in an environment where the pilot might have to switch over to air-to-air combat or back again at the flick of a couple of HOTAS switches.

Before leaving the subject, mention must be made of the other options open to CAS jets. The FAC, or TICs themselves, can illuminate the target with a small laser gun. Passive laser receivers fitted to the attackers' noses, such as the Martin Marietta AN/AAS-35 *Pave Penny* equipping the A/OA-10A, then provide target range and bearing on the HUD and solutions for a CCIP attack.

The system was first used during the Vietnam War, code-named *Pave Sword*. It was linked to a pair of F-4D Phantom IIs' gyro-driven Horizontal Situation Display (HSD) and Attitude Director Indicator (ADI) flight instruments, whereby these compass and attitude instruments dominating the pilot's instrument panel would provide target bearing and the correct dive-angle cues for weapons release. This could then be performed pseudo-blind with visual corrections if the target was clear. *Pave Penny*, and similar marked

target receivers equipping such types as the Harrier GR.3 and Jaguar GR.1, simply automated the procedure and linked the steering and release cues directly to the HUD. The added advantage of this approach is that it places the responsibility for target acquisition and lasing squarely back in the hands of the TICs, FACs and Special Forces, who have the option of furnishing a spot for LGBs to home onto.

However, for the most part, the CAS mission relies on less technologically exotic weaponry combined with the tried and trusted method of visually acquiring the IP and target, prior to making the attack run, with the enemy squarely in the fighter's sights.

BAI

The fundamental difference between CAS and BAI is that the latter is usually conducted against pre-planned target coordinates some distance behind the FLOT. Kill boxes may be established to knock out troop concentrations and armour with CEMs and SFWs, or using individually guided LGBs to 'plink' the targets. BAI is where the ability to read a radarscope and update the inertial platform begins to enter the strike arena – a by-product of becoming increasingly 'alone' or detached, as the support peels off, heading back to

An F-16C LANTIRN sits on the ramp awaiting its next sortie. LANTIRN is fully integrated with the aircraft's radar and weapons systems for wide-angle raster-scan HUD and HOTAS air-to-ground work. The F-16's clamshell canopy hood provides superb all-round visibility by day too, although the task saturation in the cockpit takes some getting used to. (Martin-Marietta)

the tankers. This is compounded by the range factors involved and the unfamiliarity of the target area, let alone the target itself, which decree extra vigilance in navigation. Crews are heading into the unknown. And then there are the attack modes that go along with these ostensibly more treacherous assignments.

For example, for use against pre-planned targets, the F-16 features a continuously computed release point (CCRP) mode. This gives the one-man fighter a typical radar-assisted blind bombing CEP of 140 ft 'at normal release heights', and CEPs comparable to those achieved with CCIP when last-minute visual adjustments are made during the actual bomb pass. Such adjustments are made using the HUD-aiming pipper for making corrections. This feature requires some explanation.

CCRP works much like the old F-4's Freeze-Displayed Impact mode. Here, it is customary to employ a radar-significant offset aiming point (OAP). This is a feature at a known range and bearing to the pre-planned target, readily recognizable on radar, such as a bend in a river, tall building or distinct hill. Targets themselves are usually very difficult to pick out on the

'jizzle band' or radar sweep which is often likened to a smear from a paint brush in terms of what the pilot sees on the radarscope. Following a brief pop-up (when a radar map would be generated quickly, and frozen as the F-4 reverted to RQ attack), all the WSO had to do was inch the cross-hairs into place using thumbwheel cursor controls and then stab the 'freeze' button. In the case of the F-16, these coordinates were and still are usually called-up automatically from the navigation computer, based on the OAP and target coordinates fed into the system's guts (via DTM before take-off, or in flight by manual insertion, or IDM link).

Having established that the cross-hairs are over the OAP, the target-insert button is then pressed, and the system compares OAP and target coordinates, and automatically slides the cross-hairs into place over the often indistinct target return. The target will then continue to be tracked by the inertial cross-hairs, based on corrections from the INS which does this by constantly comparing present position with stored target position. Meanwhile the HUD furnishes comprehensive steering cues and a projected target marker. The pilot then presses and holds the pickle button down (giving consent to the system to release bombs when it is ready), and flies the aircraft so that the heading, projected target and bomb release markers intersect on the HUD. Initiating his pull-up as range to target closes, and ejecting chaff, flares or both and doing whatever else is deemed necessary to negate enemy ground defences (short of wandering way off the target path), bomb release ensues automatically. This happens when the computers judge that all the correct parameters to put the ordnance smack on target have been met. Of course, radar and an OAP may be used in this fashion simply to help line-up on the target prior to a visual bomb run.

If the target is recognizable out of the windshield through the murk in front of the HUD, and lies a bit off the spot marked by the projected target position cursor, the pilot can release the pickle button and correct target position in the aiming reticle. He then presses the button again. This effectively refines the equation to offer strike accuracies akin to CCIP. Again, actual weapons release is totally automatic and self-compensating. It is a good, flexible system.

When the F-16 was introduced, the twin-seat school of thought argued that, even with all the automation, the soloing F-16 fighter pilot would surely be unable to make all the fine-tuning

adjustments required. Two-man crews were used to coping with such adjustments. the pilot focused on flying the jet while the wizzo handled the radar and navigation systems. However, the F-16's genuinely all-electric performance was a generation ahead of many of its twin-seat service contemporaries. For example, only the small numbers of LORAN ARN-92 and DMAS-mod ARN-101(V) conversions from the F-4D/E possessed accurate target storage and call-up facilities. The AN/APG-66 radar of the F-16 introduced much clearer radar pictures to boot, made available by Doppler beam-sharpening (effectively squinting the radar ground images into clearer pictures), and turfing out a lot of rubbish from the display. In other words, it was essential to have two men in the F-4 to overcome that system's inherent outmoded technology.

The automation in the F-16 ensures that the pilot can cope very well. However in high-intensity combat scenarios this is not necessarily the case. For example, on an INT tasking, INS drift can become problematic over a longer radius of action. Fatigue and a host of distractions can prevent the F-16 pilot from adequately updating the inertial platform, or perhaps even setting all the switches correctly to ensure good targeting. On the other hand, BAI/INT jets, using much stored information, four hands and two heads, are not necessarily trouble-free in this scenario either. Constant rehearsing of the various switch settings during less exacting circumstances such as peacetime training are vital to mission success in the heat of battle.

F-16 daylight bombing in the Gulf was disappointing because of the high altitudes used, and lack of smart PGM terminal guidance such as laser-homing or TV-homing. When employing such high base curvilinear attacks with dumb bombs, it becomes crucial to keep the INS and radar properly tuned-in to the target. There is little scope for error. However, the F-16 is a very capable aircraft 'down in the weeds'. At the Nellis-run *Gunsmoke '93* bombing competition held during the third week of October, F-16 units took the first four places for bombing accuracy (and seven

Cruising along to the target, the pilot will have extinguished most cockpit lighting (which might produce weird goldfish bowl reflections on the curvaceous canopy hood) and will be focusing on the MFDs and HUD. Here, the F-16C LANTIRN is furnishing a real-world FLIR image on the wide-angle HUD (navigation pod), while the two MFDs are flashing-up targeting pod FLIR (left) and a Doppler-sharpened, frozen radar ground-map (right), permitting the pilot to navigate and attack under the cloak of darkness. (Martin-Marietta) out of the top 10), along with eight competition awards including those for Dive-Bombing and Low-Angle Bombing, Navigation-Attack and Top Gun. This *Gunsmoke* was stricter than past events too. No more than two pilots, 10 maintainers and one munitions-loading specialist in each 50-member fighter team were permitted to be competition veterans. Crews were not allowed to prepare for the event more than 60 days prior to their arrival at Nellis. And none of their standard training requirements were allowed to be put to one side in favour of competition preparations. The next *Gunsmoke* will introduce AGMs, LGBs and some night-time taskings too, making it even more 'sporty' and exacting.

The F-16 Viper actually excels at short-legged interdiction taskings, given the chance. For this reason, further automation and improved navigation systems have long since been viewed as paramount in updating the aircraft's capabilities, to make it a true F-4 replacement for all-weather, round-the-clock BAI assignments. In particular, the need to hug the terrain contours still remains an important survivability factor. Only after air superiority has been established can the attackers step-up to higher altitudes, as shown so successfully during the Gulf War. Several systems have been fielded, aimed specifically at enhancing the F-16 pilot's SA in this demanding role.

Perhaps the single biggest stride forward has come with the fielding of LANTIRN, which has successfully graduated the Viper for low-level and night-time work. Martin Marietta's LANTIRN comprises two pods: an AN/AAQ-13 navigation pod and an AN/AAQ-14 targeting pod. The AN/AAQ-13 navigation pod is fitted with forward-looking radar (FLR) and FLIR sensors employed primarily to enhance SA during low-level flight. The AN/AAQ-14 targeting pod is fitted with a slewable dual zoom-setting FLIR boresighted to a laser transmitter/receiver. This is used mainly to acquire, track and designate targets for destruction by LGBs and to determine slant-range to an acquired target. It also functions as a boresight correlator – 'look where I'm looking' – hand-off system to point AGM-65D/G Maverick IIR seekers which guide to a pre-selected contrast point in the image, not to a hot-spot as is the case with heat AAMs.

Under a $2.9 billion contract awarded to the manufacturers in 1985, the USAF alone have acquired 561 of the LANTIRN navigation pods and 506 of the targeting versions. They can be employed independently or in unison on both Block 40 versions of the F-16C, and all production examples of the F-15E DRF. LANTIRN achieved IOC on the F-15E during August 1990, and was used extensively during *Desert Storm* INT operations. Unfortunately it was not available in sufficient quantities in time to equip F-16C units, which were thus obliged to rely exclusively on CCIP and CCRP bombing techniques using iron and cluster bombs. However, it is now finally in service with select USAF and Turk Hava Kuvvetleri F-16Cs, six years later than planned, but boosting the F-16's capabilities considerably. It is on the order books for the air forces of South Korea, Greece, Saudi Arabia, Israel, Egypt and Bahrain.

In practice, LANTIRN's navigation pod is used by night to project a FLIR image onto the wide-angle holographic HUD which 'overlays the real world outside'. As explained earlier in the context of IRST, all bodies at temperatures above absolute zero radiate electromagnetic energy; various sensors are merely optimized to pick up a band or sector within each part of the spectrum (ranging from radio frequency, through infrared, to visible light and beyond). With FLIR, energy from the longer-wavelength infrared spectrum is collected and a thermal image generated by rearranging the signal from the detector to form a spatial analogue of the original scene. That is, the FLIR sees hot-on-cold or cold-on-hot contrast and generates a TV-like image of the outside world in the cockpit. In the case of the F-16C HUD, what the pilot sees is a precise FLIR correlation with what actually exists outside in front of the canopy, providing an other-worldly experience.

For an expanded perspective beyond normal HUD viewing limits, the pilot can HOTAS-select snap-looks left or right 11° from the centre. This gives him a broader view of things. The HUD flight path marker changes from a solid to dashed line format when snapping left or right to remind him that he is not looking straight ahead and may slam into some terrain if not careful. Interestingly, as is the case with most aircraft employing FLIR sensors, the image can be presented as either 'white hot' (akin to a negative image), or as a positive 'black hot' image, both green and white rather than black and white, which is easier on the eyes. Each pilot has his preference. Both formats offer remarkably crisp images, vastly superior to anything available from 'bottle-bottomed' NVGs which are akin to looking through a tube in terms of the perspective offered.

During boresight alignment checks with the bigger LANTIRN targeting FLIR (performed at the EOR, prior to take-off), things like the base's placards can be read even half a mile distant. It is a far cry from the blotchy imagery generated by pioneering infrared systems tested in Vietnam by the US Navy's A-6C trails, roads, interdiction multi-sensor (TRIM) Intruder. This could acquire its aircraft-carrier as a blob at 50 miles, but had enormous difficulty differentiating objects at short ranges for attack purposes. Although fundamentally the same in operation, E-O sensors have come a long way over the past 25 years, opening up the night and thus removing the traditional cloak of darkness previously enjoyed by most ground units and targets.

In flight, the LANTIRN navigation pod's FLIR imagery is fused with normal HUD symbology. This provides pull-up and nose-over cues at heights preset between 100 ft and 1,000 ft AGL, based on radar terrain-warning information furnished by the FLR. These are backed up by aural 'pull-up, pull-up' warnings, and 'terrain' flashes on the HUD. There are also left or right arrows which indicate 'it's not a good idea to turn left (right); you will slam into terrain you can't see if you do'.

Pilots usually fly following the TFR 'box' which, used in conjunction with the steering flight path marker (based on the loaded flight plan), acts as their guide dog through mountain passes, over ridge lines, and between rolling hills. TFR cues can be preset for hard, medium and soft rides, depending on how good the pilot's reflexes are, and how much g he feels comfortable with. Hard will attempt to keep him glued to the profile of the terrain below and generate the sickening sensation of zero g or weightlessness during nose-overs. Soft provides plenty of warning lead-time for gentler pull-ups and nose-overs, tends to create considerable ballooning over ridges, making life easier in theory but exposing the aircraft to the enemy's defences for prolonged periods. Of course, the ride selection is linked to the FBW software so as to provide commensurate responses from the stick, with hard offering greater control authority for the same sidestick control pressure, because of the harder manoeuvres entailed. Most pilots will switch between modes depending on the severity of the AA threats and the need for surprise.

LANTIRN manual TFR indicators remain in use at all times when switched on, and it is important to emphasize that the system is manual – the pilot follows the cues and the elaborate warnings. There is as yet no automated hands-off TFR capability. This is standard on the big INT types such as the Tornado IDS and F-111F, which are often obliged to bull their way through the defences below the radar screen, perilously close to the hard terrain beneath them.

For actual attack during pops and medium-level let-downs, the LANTIRN targeting pod's FLIR comes into play on one of the pilot's two MFDs. For example, during a night-time blind attack, one will be used for the F-16C's newer AN/APG-68(V) radar, and the other for FLIR. Having obtained a radar snapshot and called up the OAP, and target coordinates, and with the cross-hairs sliding over from the readily recognizable OAP to the usually indistinct target, the slewable FLIR is activated and slaved automatically to the same point. This provides a white hot or black hot image of the target area. (Radar, which is a longer-range sensor, is customarily used first, although as the MFDs are integrated with each other, and the INS and HUD, any one may be used to cue or update the other.)

Closing to within 15 and 5 miles of the target (depending on conditions), the pilot zooms in using the narrower FLIR FoV setting. The aiming cross-hairs on the FLIR display should be pretty much overlaying the target. Refinement of the cross-hairs position is effected using HOTAS transducer switches ('coolie hat', trim-type control buttons) – bearing in mind that radar cursors are shifted over the sharpened ground map, while FLIR cross-hairs are stationary in the middle of the display and the imagery is slewed about underneath. If the INS is working properly and is not 'out of whack' (drifting because of inadequate in-flight updates), there is usually little need for such refining. In practice, the pilot will have periodically updated the inertial system using the HUD navigation FLIR and by 'overflight' over a series of prominent features along the navigation track. This updates present position automatically at the push of a button.

The radar, INS, HUD and LANTIRN are completely harmonized. Thus, with the target precisely centred under the LANTIRN FLIR cross-hairs, and the pickle button on the sidestick pressed and held down to commit the BNS to attack, the pilot follows the 'fly to' pointers on the HUD while toying with altitude and airspeed to his heart's delight. Meanwhile, the INS maintains LANTIRN lock-on and furnishes time-to-target. The ballistics computer continually recomputes automatic weapons release based on slant-ranging derived from LANTIRN's laser transmitter/receiver. This is used in lieu of radar, which might be switched off, or over to an air-to-air mode in case the pilot needs to adopt a defensive posture.

All the while, the pilot may not even have a glimpse of the actual target beneath or ahead, except for the surreal stand-off FLIR image of it.

Of course, this procedure might just be used again to help line-up on the target prior to making a conventional CCIP attack. In this case, the navigation pod's FLIR imagery presented on the HUD would be the primary means of target acquisition, perhaps assisted by lights on the ground, a bright moon, or some other visual cues. By the same token, when working in the forward-acquire mode, the HUD can be used to slew the LANTIRN targeting pod FLIR in lieu of radar, and the laser squirted to furnish slant-ranging data for bomb ballistics.

There are multiple options to cater for just about every contingency, while the system may be made to work with PGMs too. For example, if IIR Mavericks are on board, their seekers can be boresight-correlated with the FLIR using the superior quality imagery of LANTIRN to acquire the target before unleashing each missile on a one-way trip to a tank, parked aircraft, SAM site or whatever. The targeting pod laser might also be squirted to provide a laser spot to guide a Paveway LGB during a 'mini-toss' manoeuvre (described later). Or radar might be slaved to the FLIR to help acquire a radar-insignificant target, such as a SAM site camouflaged by radar-absorbent stealth netting, to help compute bomb release in a 'laser out' (defunct) situation. Integration is total, permitting attacks to be pressed home in the face of systems going redundant. And if all is working satisfactorily, the options can be perplexing

As F-16 pilots take pains to point out, learning the synergistic skills of the expanded HOTAS switchology offered by LANTIRN (a process known as 'playing the piccolo') takes months of intense

practice over the ranges. Once accomplished, pilots endure the frustration of being able to acquire a firm lock on their targets at ranges of around 10 miles, way beyond the reach of their existing weapons. Without doubt, LANTIRN has shifted the little one-man fighter into the realm of precision night attack, but weapons capability lags a long way behind. Systems like JDAM and JSOW will be a boon when they become available, as will stand-off glide dispensers such as Matra's APACHE.

Concurrent with the USAF F-16C/D LANTIRN effort, the US Air Force Reserve's (AFRes) earlier-production fleet of some 125 F-16A/Bs are currently being updated with BAe Terprom software. This system is being added to avoid what is euphemistically described as controlled flight into terrain (CFIT) – crashing into the ground during low-level flight – a serious hazard in the absence of a good FLIR such as that available via LANTIRN.

The Terprom source code is being incorporated into the AFRes F-16A/Bs' 32-megabyte Fairchild

The ball-like device jutting out from this F-16B's glare shield is a Texas Instruments Falcon Eye, a compact FLIR slaved to pilot head movements which in turn projects the imagery onto helmet-mounted combiner glasses. This aircraft evaluated the package in concert with BAe's Terprom in this Reagan-era multi-tone green camouflage. The FLIRs are being evolved for retrofit to selected F-16A/Cs and OA/A-10As. (Texas Instruments)

The SEPECAT Jaguar uses passive and active lasers for marking and ranging purposes, as exemplified by this RAF example assigned to Gulf combat duties, complete with BL755 CBUs and overwing Sidewinder AAMs, a Phimat chaff dispenser (starboard outboard) and AN/ALQ-101(V) ECM pod (port outboard). The black nosewheel door formed part of a deceptive ventral canopy silhouette, designed to fox enemy fighters and ground gunners alike. The Jaguar did much better than everyone expected and was recently in action again against Serb armour in Bosnia, and on counter-air airfield strikes at Udbina in Serbian-held Croatia. (RAF)

DTM cartridges, capable of storing 400 nm² of digital terrain data at a go. During flight, the F-16A/Bs' radar altimeter is used to draw a cross-section of the terrain below, along the flight track. This is then compared with the 3-D Terprom database, to locate the aircraft's present position (using INS which helps narrow the area of choice and assists with heading information, and aircraft velocity). The Terprom software then looks ahead in the database of stored terrain, as if it had a contour map spread out in front and could draw a line depicting the aircraft's velocity vector (constantly adjusted, of course) to predict what ground lies ahead and to the sides, along with any previously charted major obstacles lying in the aircraft's path. Suitable terrain-avoiding 'fly to box' steering instructions are provided on the HUD (identical to those generated by the LANTIRN TFR software), along with the full gamut of pull-up cues and warnings, to permit safe terrain-clearing flight at heights of less than 1,000 ft above the terrain. When used in conjunction with NVGs, which offer a very limited FoV akin to tunnel vision but which can nonetheless be used to scan anywhere the pilot

chooses to look, operating heights can be stepped-down even lower, given cool nerves and considerable practice.

A wider-aperture FLIR, such as the TI helmet-slewed, glareshield-mounted Falcon Eye which turns in sympathy with pilot head movements and projects the resultant imagery on his visor, is a much better bet. A development F-16B has been testing Falcon Eye in conjunction with Terprom for some time. The combination offers the ideal long-term solution to updating older F-16A/Bs to the night/under-the-weather BAI format – if the money can be found.

Terprom offers other advantages beyond extending operations to around-the-clock. It may be employed also to automatically update the INS (with accuracies better than 300 ft, claim AFRes, even without the benefits of GPS Navstar inputs – described later). Also, as it is capable of plotting terrain elevation ahead of the F-16, it can help provide much more accurate solutions for CCIP attack, which is of special importance when attacking a target on sloping or ragged terrain. This could be performed using RQ techniques. At the time of writing, a decision is pending as to whether the system will be applied to the entire USAF F-16 and A/OA-10A inventory, with the Warthog also due to receive a back-up FLIR (again, the actual fit not having been settled yet).

Of course, Terprom cannot make allowances for previously uncharted obstacles not contained in the database (for example, old-fashioned barrage balloons and their tethers). However, such obstacles should become apparent if the pilot makes proper use of infrared or image-intensifying aids such as FLIR or NVG. Nevertheless, even when employed with cruder NVG technology, Terprom makes low-level target ingress possible at heights around 500 ft AGL or lower at speeds of 420–500 knots. The USAF reckon that the update will save the life of at least one pilot and two aircraft annually, given envisaged training requirements.

The regular-duty USAF Terprom package is being modelled with an automatic recovery feature

programmed into the automatic flight control system (AFCS, or autopilot). This would allow the jet to be taken up to a safe altitude in wings-level flight should the pilot become incapacitated due to G-LOC or hostile fire – or possibly disorientated by vertigo. This is not an uncommon occurrence when flying in fog and low cloud, or the blackest of nights. Under such circumstances a pilot can begin to lose faith in his HUD and ADI attitude references, and rapidly becomes out of touch with what is up and what is down, and ends up flying on a wing-tip or inverted. Such a fail-safe 'fly-up' was first introduced on the F-111's TFR, but such fits have always proved to be too costly, complex and cumbersome to be installed in smaller fighters. Moreover, unlike Terprom, they tend to advertise the attacker's presence because they radiate RF-spectrum energy ahead of the aircraft to map the terrain.

The automatic recovery system will engage to pull

Iron bombs still form part of the strike repertoire, and in high-speed low-level attacks the Snakeye-category retarded cruciform-finned bomb has given way to the 'ballute' – a balloon-cum-parachute para-braking device that avoids the attacker getting caught in the bomb blast. The RAF has used parachute-retarded bombs for years, but they only recently entered US service, used for the first time in anger during the April 1986 raid on Tripoli Airport inter alia. (Vought)

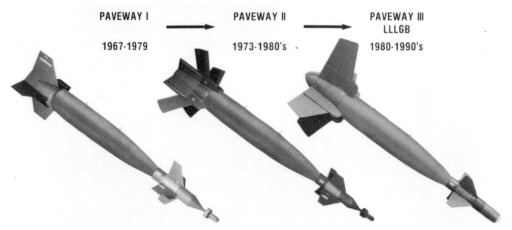

Paveway LGB evolution. The Paveway II offered greater glide range and counter-countermeasures capability via a laser code system. The LLLGB added yet more glide range, made possible by mid-course-assisted proportional guidance technology. (Texas Instruments)

the aircraft up and out of trouble and roll it wings-level even if the pilot is blithely unaware of the potential dangers being signalled in the form of alarm bells and flashing lights over the earphones and on the HUD. Presumably the system will be fine-tuned in the fullness of time to work with an auto-throttle system, to ensure that there is enough airspeed for a safe pull-up without fear of stalling the aircraft.

These many initiatives are turning the F-16 into a truly capable – and survivable – CAS/BAI machine with a great deal of potential. Lockheed is now offering them to the USAF, minus strap-ons and extras, for $20 million each. Given that the flyaway cost of the F-4 was $2.8 million in Fiscal Year 1969 money (without engines added), real cost considerations with inflation factored in make the F-16 a genuine bargain.

Lasing

In terms of the weapons technology used, BAI is not really a very different animal from CAS, but rather an extension of it. Bombs abound. Targets of opportunity necessitating a judicious drop of iron on them are equally abundant. Rear-echelon ground forces are often on the move, restaging, ferrying in supplies or formating into offensive patterns. Thus, BAI often involves a series of roaming strikes which require the use of point, lock and shoot missiles, or self-arming smart cluster submunitions like the SFW which can cover a broad footprint by picking out their own targets after being lobbed onto the enemy.

In the former category, probably the most well-known are the AGM-65 Maverick family. Less well-known is the French AS.30L *à guidage* laser, guided

to the target by Cilas ITAY-71 ATLIS 2 pods. These were used with considerable accuracy by Armée de l'Air Jaguar As which were part of the French Operation *Daguet* contribution to Coalition forces in the Gulf. Essentially, the pilot uses the pod's TV camera caged with the HUD so that when he puts the target in the aiming pipper the pod is looking at the

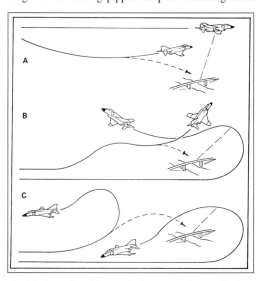

Buddy laser-bombing techniques require meticulous timing, but enable a small quantity of laser-equipped aircraft to guide a large number of otherwise dumb bombers. **A** *Bombing from a steep dive while designating from high altitude.* **B** *Low-altitude ingress, pop-up and shallow dive-bombing while the designator pops up to lase the target.* **C** *Loft bombing from low altitude as the designator pops up for lasing.*

AMERICAN DUMB & SMART BOMBS

Basic Iron bomb	Approximate weight (lb)	High-drag & Smart adaptations
Mk 82 slick	500	Snakeye with metal pop-open retard tail AIR with BSU-49 ballute retard tail GBU-12A/B Paveway I LGB, high/low-speed GBU-12B-D/B Paveway II LGB GBU-22/B Paveway III LLLGB
M117 vintage	750	M117R with metal pop-open retard tail KMU-342 with experimental Paveway LGB fit
Mk 83 slick	1,000	AIR with BSU-85 ballute retard tail GBU-16/B Paveway II LGB AGM-123A Skipper II rocket-assisted LGB
Mk 84 slick	2,000	AIR with BSU-50 ballute retard tail GBU-8/B Hobos EOGB I GBU-10/B or A/B Paveway I LGB, high/low-speed GBU-10C-E/B Paveway II LGB GBU-15[V]1/B EOGB, with wide-chord MXU-724 fins GBU-15[V]2/B EOGB, with short-chord MXU-787 fins GBU-24/B Paveway III LLLGB AGM-130 rocket-assisted GBU-15[V]2/B
BLU-109/B	2,000	GBU-10G-J/B Paveway II LGB GBU-24A/B Paveway III LLLGB GBU-27A/B Paveway III seeker, Paveway II tail GBU-15[V]32 EOGB, with short-chord MXU-787 fins AGM-130I rocket-assisted GBU-15I
M118 vintage	3,000	GBU-9/B Hobos EOGB I GBU-11A/B Paveway I LGB

target too. (Given the pressures of combat flying, the pilots only peek at the resultant TV display generated on the head-down cockpit CRT, and trust that the pod's head remains correctly aligned and the target image is indeed centred under the cross-hairs.) The ATLIS laser is then squirted to provide a laser spot from which is reflected a laser cone or 'basket' into which the AS.30Ls are launched. These then guide to the spot – the target – using semi-active laser (SAL) guidance. The system is akin to shooting a missile down a giant imaginary funnel, with the spot representing the orifice at the base, often no wider than 2–3 ft. Needless to say, it is hard to miss the target!

Sixty AS.30Ls were launched during BAI sorties against POL and ammunition dumps and other fixed sites dotted around Kuwait, with 80 per cent hitting smack-on, despite intense AA fire which must have created some target tracking distractions. Overall, the 28 Jaguar As flew 615 sorties, adding to the 618 BAI and recce missions flown by 12 RAF Tornado GR.1As. The SEPECAT 'Cat' was one of several unsung heroes whose success came as something of a surprise (given the age of the aircraft and the notoriously high pilot workload), and all the more so because the British and French models employ quite different avionics and weapons systems.

The RAF variant's Navigation and Weapons Aiming Sub-System (NAVWASS) relies exclusively on Ferranti INS and a projected map display, with a nose-mounted laser ranger for CCIP attack with gravity weapons, whereas the French versions rely

Some LGBs are boosted, such as the Emerson Electric Skipper II, two of which are seen departing this A-6E Intruder at some speed. The project was cancelled but stocks of the Shrike missile rocket section-boosted devices remain in the US Navy inventory. (Emerson Electric)

more on Dead Reckoning, assisted by the ATLIS 2 imaging pod to help guide AS.30Ls and LGBs. Neither are in the same league as the latest models of the F-16 LANTIRN by a long shot, but they remain excellent tools for daytime BAI – and reconnaissance, the *raison d'être* of the RAF's remaining operational recce unit, No. 41 Squadron. RAF Jaguars were most recently in action again on 22 September 1994, when they successfully zapped an unmanned Bosnian Serb T-55 tank near Sarajevo in response to an unprovoked rocket attack on a peacekeeping French/UN armoured personnel carrier. In that instance 1,000 lb bombs were used, followed by a strafing from an A-10A, without even a hint of a laser being involved. Interestingly, the only other SAL missile in widespread use is the unique AGM-65E model of the Maverick, employed primarily by the US Marine Corps' AV-8B Harrier IIs exclusively for CAS.

Most armed forces, when adding laser guidance to their BAI repertoire, actually rely on adaptations of iron bombs rather than dedicated missiles. These utilize strap-on SAL nose seekers attached via a special collar, and bolt-on rear-end tail 'groups' which feature pop-out fins to help stabilize the weapons and extend their free-fall range. The American Paveway II series, built around the Mk 82 500 lb, Mk 83 1,000 lb and Mk 84 2,000 lb series (which create the GBU-12, GBU-16 and GBU-10 formats, respectively), French Matra 2,000 lb LGBs, Israeli Aircraft Industries' Griffin and Guillotine models, and the British Portsmouth Aviation CPU-123/B 1,000 lb (based on the Paveway II), all use virtually identical SAL 'bang-bang' guidance. The bombs' steering fins are mechanically linked to the gimballed nose seeker, which thus flies them up and down the imaginary cone or basket – hence 'bang-bang' – until they reach the spot illuminated by a laser designator. The key difference here is that target designation is usually a more complex affair than that used with the point-and-shoot SAL missiles, owing to the bombs' more complex ballistics and slower flight-time.

From an altitude of 22,000 ft it can take one minute for the bomb to reach its target, during which time it can traverse several miles. At low altitude, they need to be tossed – thrown off the wing while the aircraft is conducting a 3–4 g pull-up or an arcing belly-up manoeuvre – so that they gain sufficient momentum to climb to a suitable height where the seeker can acquire the spot, and to reach their intended destination. This requires the target to be tracked by the laser designator through to bomb impact, albeit that the laser may only be squirted at it for the last 10 seconds or so of bomb flight (to avoid the SAL looking down too soon and causing the bomb to fall short of the target).

This goal can be accomplished in one of three ways. Special Forces operating behind enemy lines with a portable laser designator cued by a telescopic sight to mark the target is one way. Alternatively, one of two means of airborne lasing can be employed: buddy lasing, whereby one aircraft squirts a laser at the target to enable the other aircraft to drop LGBs into the basket, and autonomous lasing when the same aircraft performs both tasks when operating as an independent striker.

The airborne techniques had their genesis in the Vietnam War. They were used with considerable success by Pave Light (buddy only) and Pave Knife

(buddy or autonomous) laser-equipped USAF F-4D Phantom IIs and by USN A-6A *Pave Knife* and A-6C TRIM Intruders specially adapted to the task during 1972. These pioneers used TI Paveway I LGBs which had fixed high-speed (short) or low-speed (long) format fins. The various laser designators were boresighted with TV or light-amplifying Low Light-Level TV sensors which were cued to the target by the F-4D wizzo or A-6A/C NFO using a tracking handle to steer the sensor. Alternatively, a simple telescopic eyepiece was used in the case of *Pave Light*, which required the pilot to enter a relatively vulnerable pylon turn about the target. Bomb release could be effected from heights as great as 18,000–22,000 ft.

The weapons repeatedly demonstrated CEPs in the order of 10 ft with remarkably few going astray. The follow-on 1975-vintage Paveway II LGB added pop-out tail fins for greater glide range. Coupled with a new and superior panoply of laser designators, including *Pave Spike* and the A-6E's target recognition attack multi-sensor (TRAM), flexibility and accuracy increased. Laser coding allowed multiple bombs to be guided by two or more

This is what the F-111 is all about: with its wings swept fully back to near the 72° lock-out position it can slice through the sound barrier with ease; for landing, it can ease the wings forward to 16°, and deploy leading-edge and trailing-edge flaps. In cruise, lock-outs of 26°–44° sweep are most commonly used, these not overriding spoiler authority (these pop-up, lift-killing devices are being used in lieu of ailerons on many high-performance aircraft, as they can do their job with a quick 'flicker'). (T. J. Johnson)

designators to their intended targets. This coding also rendered them relatively immune to enemy laser jamming (using a laser transmitter decoy to lead the bombs astray). The four-digit laser code is entered into the bomb during ground-handling, and into the designator aircraft's appropriate cockpit console (for example, on the right-hand console in the case of the old F-4D).

Paveway IIs were used in anger for the first time during the Falklands War when RAF Harrier GR.3s dropped CPU-123/Bs on Argentine artillery positions designated by ground forces. Initially, they met with mixed success owing to the South Atlantic winter murk and the ground troops' general tendency to squirt the laser too soon which caused the bombs to fall short of the spot. It took several bomb runs for them to get the hang of it, something not encountered in the Gulf when the USMC employed laser-guided Maverick AGMs because these weapons' rocket motors provided sufficient momentum to compensate for this.

As a footnote on this subject, RAF Tornado GR.1s and Buccaneer S.2Bs both employed Paveway II CPU-123/Bs during the Gulf War too, guiding them to the target using TIALD and *Pave Spike*, respectively. They only rarely encountered problems with bombs falling wide or short. The navigators aiming the laser via boresighted TV and FLIR camera sensors knew how to hold off until only a few seconds prior to impact, and proved adept at switching the laser between targets to guide the bombs onto separate spots if required. Altitude helped, giving more leeway with which to work the targets.

As a rule of thumb, SAL missiles are better for CAS work, and free-fall LGBs better for BAI and INT work. However, airborne buddy lasing requires considerable coordination and thus can become excruciatingly complex in all but low-threat scenarios. Precisely for these reasons, buddy tactics have mostly given way to autonomous lasing and bombing. This is where the proportionally guided Paveway III comes into play, and we are now entering the realm of INT: Big league strike.

Deep Strike

Interdiction is conducted almost exclusively against high-value fixed targets deep behind the FLOT, such as enemy command & control installations, airfields and factories. The chief objectives are to cut off the enemy's command and support infrastructures from the troops at the front, and generally to diminish his ability to wage war. It includes operations like the acclaimed 'Dam Busters' and Ploesti oil refinery strikes of the Second World War, and strikes by stealth

fighters during the Gulf War, which sent bombs straight down ventilator shafts of critical C^3I facilities, taking the war directly to the Iraqi military leadership.

INT operations tend to sever diplomatic links (or forces the issue), unlike differences resulting from air-to-air skirmishes or retaliatory tit-for-tat strikes near a border or on the FLOT, which might be easily patched-up around a conference table with relatively little long-term repercussion. INT, on the other hand, customarily involves a systematic dismantling of the enemy's rear-echelon military infrastructure, nowadays almost exclusively by means of air-delivered PGMs, or smart bombs as they are more commonly known – and, in extreme cases, involves the use of thermonuclear weapons. Deep strike worked during *Desert Storm* because it was initiated with full fury at the very beginning of the campaign, rather than on a piecemeal, escalating basis. After all, why commit the best aerial assets, including armadas of sophisticated SEAD and CAP aircraft and their crews, unless full use is to be made of them?

INT is a hard profession, and has soldiers to match. Invariably, the types who fly these aircraft tend to be better educated and offer greater maturity than their AAM-volleying compatriots. They have to be. Not only are there enemy fighters to contend with, but also the full array of ferocious flak and SAMs, all while managing complex avionics and weapons systems – and all that on top of the grim prospect of internment (or worse) if downed. However, the technology and tactics used are really just a more elaborate, longer-legged version of those employed for BAI. They are distinguished, primarily, by the bigger radius of action offered by INT aircraft, and the more expensive, sophisticated weapons they lug under-wing or in their bomb bays. As veteran USAF commander Col Tony Sobol put it: 'You're not going to use a $50 million [INT] airplane to strafe the roads!'

This rule of thumb has few exceptions. For example, well into the late 1980s, USAF contingency plans called for the comparatively technologically obsolete but nevertheless long-ranging F-111E Aardvarks to be fragged deep into potential enemy territory. On the other hand, conspicuously high-tech F-16C/Ds, packing highly reliable all-solid-state avionics and featuring HOTAS, the GEC-Marconi wide-angle holographic HUD capable of flashing-up LANTIRN FLIR imagery, and in some cases (on a trials basis) even synthesized 3-D terrain contour graphics based on STARS, remained strictly relegated to CAS/BAI. Its 'legs' were simply too short and it lacked the 'press on' rapport routinely developed in the bigger twin-seat fighter.

The bantamweight bombers, which the crews concerned prefer to class as strike jets, were the real heroes of *Desert Storm*. At the leading edge are the F-111F Aardvark, F-15E Strike Eagle DRF, and Europe's Tornado IDS. The extraordinary F-117A stealth fighter is in a class of its own, using radically different technology and tactics. And from the former Soviet Union one can count the Su-24 *Fencer* and newer strike derivatives of the Su-27 *Flanker*. France's Mirage 2000N/D and IVP also qualify. They all share one common denominator: they offer prodigious range and endurance, often working autonomously with a bare minimum of support, together with a panoply of weapons configurations. And this is despite the expense and logistical complexities of pre-positioning these aircraft within reach of key trouble spots. In the space of a few days a single Tornado IDS, flown by several crews, might be tasked to execute a host of different missions: smart bombing with CPU-123/B LGBs; runway denial with boosted kinetic weapons such as JP233; SEAD with ALARM or HARM; reconnaissance; and even anti-shipping with Kormoran or Sea Eagle missiles! This is what truly sets them apart.

Even a renowned low-fuel burner such as the A-7 can only manage a 500 nm radius of action (assuming 10 minutes on station with a dozen bombs). But an F-111F can amble deep into enemy territory over twice that radius of action before reaching Joker fuel, and with double the warload – and yet still be able to conduct well over one-third of its mission time in sneaky, low-level flight on a med-lo-lo-med profile, 'down in the weeds' and kicking-up dust in the bottoms of valleys, day or night, 'in the weather'.

Squeezing commensurate performance out of a smaller machine like the A-7 or a 'bagged-up' F-16 would severely cut down on range or payload, or place it high in the sky where SAMs could use it for target practice. The much-vaunted F/A-18C Hornet, which packs a hefty load of air-to-air and air-to-ground ordnance and offers CCIP, blind and E-O-assisted weapons delivery, ends up flying on fumes very rapidly without tanker support. And AAR GLOBS are not going to oblige by venturing deep into enemy airspace, even with air superiority having been established and with Mk.32B pods fitted, except in dire emergencies or on an especially critical or sensitive mission. It comes as no surprise that, with the US Navy's A-6E Intruder scheduled for complete phase-out by 1999, and its KA-6D tanker derivatives alongside, the Hornet is being hastily stretched with increased fuel and stores capability precisely to fulfil this requirement.

The strike jets should also be differentiated from

The venerable B-52 still soldiers on today, and 94 of the turbofan-powered 'Hotel' model will continue in this capacity for years to come, toting only conventional weapons such as the AGM-142 Have Nap Popeye slung under this 'Golf' model BUFF. The weapons use data-linking for LOAL targeting. (Martin-Marietta)

their giant multi-engined jet and turboprop bomber counterparts, despite them sharing much in the way of nav-attack technology. Those are a luxury afforded by only very wealthy nations. The argument that they remain a vital peacekeeping tool of diplomacy is gaining credence in both the US and Russia, despite the defrosting of the Cold War. So the roles of the heavyweights within the new isolationist era are being steadily expanded into conventional warfare as a hedge against premature retirement.

Despite severe economic problems, Russia is in the throes of negotiating a buy-back of 42 bombers adopted by the Ukraine during the break-up of the USSR, giant swing-wing Tupolev Tu-160 *Blackjacks* among them. The Pentagon shares similar sentiments. It feels strongly that its own force of over 140 heavyweights will continue to form a lynchpin in its deep strike air power – including its B-52H Stratofortresses, and vastly newer compatriots in the shape of the Rockwell B-1B Lancer and Northrop Grumman B-2A Spirit. Some contend that the billion-dollar B-2A is too expensive an asset to commit to anything less than thermonuclear warfare and money should not be wasted adapting it to carry conventional munitions, while the B-52 is a much-loved but superannuated machine.

The youngest B-52 was rolled out of Boeing's plant in June 1962, and the design is '. . . very much 1940s with jet pods added'. Only with constant updates to its offensive/defensive kit has the Big Ugly Fat Fella (BUFF) remained viable. Nevertheless, it remains an excellent platform for stand-off munitions and can pack a hefty load of iron bombs for what is sometimes termed 'close battle' tasks. These were jobs it handled admirably over the jungles of South Vietnam and Cambodia during thousands of *Arc Light* area carpet-bombing missions conducted against suspected enemy enclaves. The feat was repeated during Operation *Desert Storm* 25 years later, but in a more conventional fashion against a clearly deployed foe in open warfare. B-52Gs rained down bombs on entrenched Republican Guard positions in north-west Kuwait, breaking their resolve.

With the updated Lancers and brand-new Spirit (an 'insect-sized' radar cross-section) entering the conventional bombing repertory, the US will soon possess the capability to drop vast tonnages of smart bombs around-the-clock, anywhere in the world: JDAMs, JSOWs and wind-corrected, inertial guided high-altitude iron bombs, capable of knocking-out SAM sites and tank divisions in one fell swoop. The prevailing philosophy is that these heavyweights can be held in abeyance at domestic bases, some of them operated by Reservists, and placed on alert in times of tension. They would then be dispatched on long-range, high-altitude bombing missions to wherever their talents are deemed to be most in demand, helping to win-hold-win two MRCs that might be flaring up on opposite sides of the world.

Critics claim that on a fundamental human level, there are physiological factors to consider. The two-man and four-man crews manning the Spirit and Lancer, respectively, might be called upon to traverse 10,000 miles or more to the target area with the only human amenities comprising a coffee thermos and 'piddle pack'. The crews of a twin-seat tactical interdictor, on the other hand, could set off 10 hours later, and be back home after a much shorter jaunt, long before the already utterly exhausted B-1B or B-2 crew were barely halfway home. Only the aged BUFF offers any real opportunity for crews to stretch their legs, and to pee into a chemical toilet rather than a sponge-filled plastic bag, with galley facilities to thwart dehydration on these long hauls. However, no permission is required from forward-based host nations to deploy or operate the heavyweights, and they can project a psychologically demoralizing blow to the enemy when he least expects it.

When employing newer technology, the bomber has demonstrated remarkable reach. During the opening phase of *Desert Storm*, seven B-52Gs launched 35 conventionally tipped cruise missiles against important targets dotted around Mosul in northern Iraq. They launched their weapons 50 miles from the Saudi Arabian border following a gruelling 34 hr 20 min non-stop mission from Barksdale AFB, Louisiana! The long-range bombing concept has been further demonstrated during a series of 'power projection' practice strikes direct from US bases. In late October 1994, under Operation *Vigilant Warrior*, a pair of Lancers from Ellsworth AFB, South Dakota, and a brace of BUFFs from Minot AFB, North Dakota, flew direct to the Udairi range 40 miles north-west of Kuwait City, where they dropped just under 28 tons of bombs on scrap tanks abandoned by Iraq during the close of the Gulf War. The journey there traversed 7,000 miles and took 16 hours.

These bombers provide sterling service, and will continue to do so well into the future using the newer launch-and-leave smart weapons, operating in a stand-off mode and at altitude. However, they remain entirely distinct from the traditional bailiwick of the theatre interdictor: deep strike missions conducted in the low-to-medium segment of sky (100 ft AGL through to 25,000 ft), flown from bases within 3–6 hours' flying time of their targets. Majestic though they doubtless are, the bombers are not numerous enough to undertake such complex

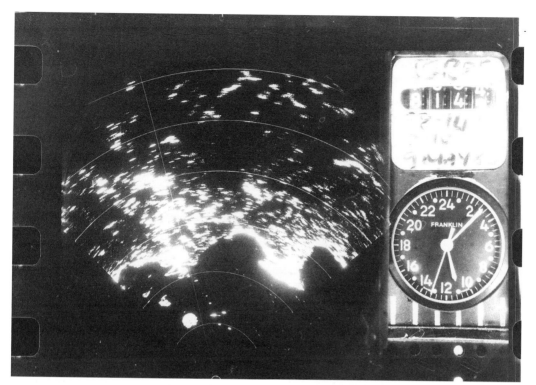

In the 'vanilla' models of the F-111 there exist two primary radar display modes: a wide, ground automatic sweep used for general navigation, and an expanded ground velocity stabilized version used for the attack run, with the target cross-hairs centred to assist with steering . . . (Both RSP shots courtesy of the RAAF)

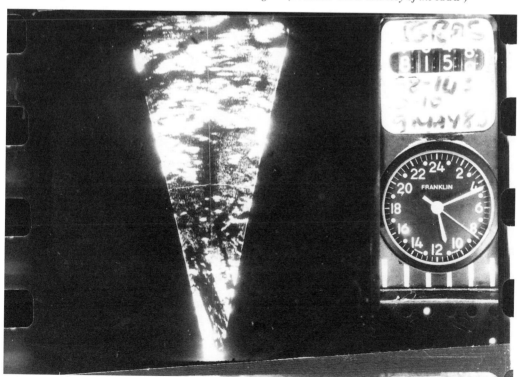

multiple strike taskings, where Tac INT can offer greater targeting discrimination and do the job at much lower cost.

Skimming the terrain

As is standard doctrine for fighters, strike-fighter crews join up after take-off and maintain their formation, albeit looser by night, coordinated by the customary calls from AWACS and other airborne command checking-in posts. They maintain the formation right up until they reach enemy airspace when the penetration or 'pen' portion of the mission profile begins. At this juncture, strict radio silence or 'comm-out' must be observed, and the aircraft begin a formation spread. What happens next depends on the perceived and actual risks – i.e. the intensity of the enemy's defences.

In a medium-intensity threat scenario, such as prevailed for the best part of Operation *Desert Storm*, the heavily laden strike jets will ingress at their optimum cruise heights in the 'high teens/low twenties'. (The revised *Maple Flag* exercise in Canada is based on *Desert Storm* experience.) They maintain these altitudes unless forced to take evasive action, ducking to lower altitudes only when passing through known pockets of SAM resistance or when it is advantageous to make full use of available radar-masking terrain to contribute to surprise. They also drop to lower altitudes when it is essential for the delivery of specific weapons. After the first few days of the Gulf campaign, many strike crews started flying just below their optimum cruise heights, then stepped up higher as the SEAD and Cappers gradually whittled away the remaining air defences. By the end of the first week most were flying at optimum heights with relative impunity, out of reach to all but heavy-calibre flak and a few stray missiles.

In marked contrast, in a high-intensity threat scenario, such as the central and northern European environment in which most of today's strike jets were designed to operate, things are very different indeed. Speed is life. So is anything that can help mask their presence: low-level terrain-hugging flight to stay below the enemy defences' radar horizon whenever possible, and to make the job of airborne fighter interceptors more taxing; night, to cloak them from optically aimed weapons; and weather, which degrades the enemy's defences more than the attackers' targeting accuracy when 'down in the weeds'. At a pre-determined time based on their meticulous plans, known as the low-level entry point (LLEP), they 'step down' and spread out into a gaggle or a trail formation. They will aim to maintain this right up until separation at the pre-briefed 'split point'

near the target complex, when TOTs, heights and headings are varied to maximize surprise and to overwhelm the defences.

In the case of the F-111F, the initial let-down at the LLEP is known as auto terrain-following descent (ATFD). It takes the aircraft down from cruise height to the initial 1,000 ft AGL set clearance plane (SCP) at a rate of 166 ft per second. It is an exhilarating, even frightening process for the uninitiated, and involves meticulous concentration, checking that all is working and responding properly. The key ingredients are the radars – all four of them! The latest configurations (the systems have undergone continuous minor updates, with changes to the designations used) are the AN/APQ-171 TFRs and AN/APQ-169 attack radar set (ARS), comprising an array of two bug-eyes and a dish located behind the pointed duckbill radome, and the AN/APN-167 low-altitude radar altimeter (LARA) mounted under the nose barrel.

First comes the extremely accurate and reliable Honeywell LARA, which looks down to serve as a fail-safe during ATFD and during terrain-hugging flight. This is especially useful over water or smooth terrain such as desert salt lakes where there are no terrain returns for the TFRs to digest. LARA is usually the first system to be kicked into operation and starts working at 5,000 ft AGL. It can measure height above the ground at angles of 20° of pitch and 45° of bank, and is set for 83 per cent. This means that if the TFRs are selected for the 1,000 ft AGL SCP, as during the initial ATFD, and the aircraft came within 830 ft of the ground, then LARA would automatically command an immediate 3 *g* pull-up, back to a safe altitude.

The Texas Instruments TFR scanners work in harmony with LARA, searching some 1,000 ft ahead of the aircraft in a 'ski-toe' pattern, probing ahead like invisible searchlights, constantly on the look-out for terrain. Ridges and even gentle hillocks will all produce noticeable returns. On receipt of such a return with the ATFD mode selected, the system generates suitable pitch commands to the autopilot to pull the aircraft up, then down, over the topography totally automatically. The TFR system checks itself at 0.7-second intervals and if it detects a failure will switch over to the back-up antenna. If the back-up is also suffering from a touch of the gremlins then the autopilot will again be commanded to initiate an immediate 3 *g* pull-up. It can function during rolling moments of up to 30°, looking into the turn.

Thus, once the crew is satisfied that all is working to order, they begin the process of stepping down further to six progressively lower terrain SCPs, automatically skimming the terrain. These begin at 1,000 ft and culminate as low as 200 ft AGL. Hard, medium and soft ride modes are available for ATFD.

These are selected on the centre console at the crew's discretion, while pilots may opt to fly even lower in the manual mode if they dare.

Former 'fightergator' Maj Jim Rotramel, USAF Ret., describes the descent to chimney heights: 'In a way, this is easier to do at night when concentration on monitoring the instruments allows a certain amount of detachment; during daylight one is confronted with the reality of the situation!' The high wing loading and self-adaptive flight control system of the Aardvark provides a glassy-smooth ride, 'so smooth that it almost seems like the earth is moving beneath the aircraft, rather than the other way around . . . an almost other-worldly experience of rocketing along'.

In the full moonlight at 200 ft at 9 miles per minute, it is awesome! Capt Tom 'TJ' Johnson recalled that 'from the exhilaration of bending the "Vark" through the valleys in Tac formation to the intense concentration of a night IFR/TFR [Instrument Flight Rules/TFR] radar laydown [attack], the F-111 was a total joy to fly. A "Vark" at Mach 1.2 at 50 ft is a sight that will water your eyes.' The shock wave kicks up a cliff of dust and crud in the aircraft's wake, making this form of flying science fiction!

In fact, even today, 30 years after its ancestor first took to the skies above Fort Worth in Texas, nobody really knows how fast the big Aardvark can go. Friction-generated heat on the lightweight windshield is the key limiting factor, and crews are furnished with a warning lamp and 300-second digital countdown in which to throttle back if the sensors become unhappy.

During the ATFD, or 'skiing' as it sometimes known, there is no room for complacency. Owing to Murphy's Law, the crew are provided with several key instruments to ensure that all is running to order, and the pilot keeps his right hand gently wrapped around the stick at all times, ready to step in. The critical instrument for the pilot is the E-scope. Deriving its information from the TFR, this presents an eerie, strobe-like profile of the terrain ahead known as the 'grass' along with a command or 'ride line' template. The idea is that the ride line stays above the grass, 'so as not to fly into "cumulo rocks"', as Col Terry Simpson put it succinctly. Additional pull-up and nose-over bars are presented on the head-up lead-computing sight and on the head-down ADI.

The wizzo plays a big part too, peering into the ARS radarscope hood or 'feeding trough'. This is the Big Eye used for tracking waypoints, OAPs and the target by night and in the weather. For normal navigation purposes, it presents a wide-scan, wind-corrected real-beam ground map known as a Ground Auto display. The rugged terrain ahead will show up clearly on this like luminescent green ink smudges, and if there's a noticeable radar shadow behind any of these – an area of darkness – then the Aardvark is heading straight into a big obstacle! The fightergator will provide suitable warning – 'I see terrain ahead which we should be climbing over soon' – and if the shadows persist as range closes he will in all likelihood shout and scream. As the aircraft noses up and the ARS starts to see over the top of the oncoming ridge, the shadow should disappear.

Over their headsets, the crew receive an aural indication system: beeps and boops which signal climb and descent, respectively, increasing in repetition rate commensurate with the rate of ascent or nosing-over. When vertical velocity is very rapid, the tone becomes virtually constant. Partial reheat, say, in Zone Three – the F-111F's TF30-P-100 turbofans offer five-stage augmented thrust – may be called upon to assist with the adventurous ascents in the face of precipitous terrain, so the pilot keeps his left hand near the throttles most of the time, too. The brochure statement 'Hands-Off' must thus be qualified.

Target ingress speed and variable-geometry wing-sweep (manually selected via a 'trombone lever' on the left canopy sill) is very much an individual affair, just like ride selection. Maximum sweep at 72° in hard ride mode glues the aircraft to the terrain profile but is a bit dicey and would require plenty of reheat during 3 g ATF ascents. These would almost instantly switch to a stomach-gyrating zero-g environment during nose-overs, with everything not battened down flying around the cockpit. Most crews aim for the 44° setting where the spoilers on the wing are still able to provide roll control. Another standard wing 'lock-out' is 54°, an excellent high-speed cruise setting which selected with 'medium' ride produces a maximum of 0.5 on the g meter.

Fuel consumption remains a concern, though less so with the Aardvark than on equivalents such as the Tornado IDS as it carries a fuel load equivalent to the all-up-weight (AUW) of a Jaguar GR.1A! Instead, Flights of Aardvarks roller-coast over the terrain close to the edge of the speed of sound: transonic. Fuel consumption rises dramatically when approaching the sound barrier, even with 'area rule' (so-called Coke bottle shapes, which make air rub on air instead of on metal, thus reducing drag; or shift the main drag wave aft). Noise – sonic booms laid down by the fore and aft shock waves generated by supersonic speeds, just like wakes from a boat – alerts the enemy's defences. And supersonic speeds at low-level leave too little a margin for safe recovery if the systems start malfunctioning. At least two Aardvark losses over Vietnam were put down to this problem. Half a second (or less) does not present adequate time in which to tug back on the stick and avoid laying down a string of wreckage a mile long.

Essentially, the Aardvark flies automatically from turnpoint to turnpoint all the way to the target and back home if necessary, based on the data points loaded into the navigation computer before take-off. Up to 1,000 of them were available prior to the *Pacer Strike* update, along with 20 sets of 100 sequence points. This is why it is often described as a 'hands-off system' (despite the reservations mentioned already). Of course, if a large radar shadow turns up on the ARS and there's a valley off to the left, or the pilot wishes to dart around a pocket of flak, there's no need to bulldoze over or through it. He will in all likelihood elect to press the autopilot hold switch on the stick and take the appropriate action. When the switch is released, the aircraft will automatically swing back on course to the next pre-planned turnpoint, resuming service as normal.

Oftentimes, it is the right-seater who is flying the aircraft in the horizontal plane. By entering a new destination or sequence interrupting the flight-plan he may command the aircraft, for example, to go from point 17 to point 23 and bypass the zig-zagging in between. All it takes is a few stabs of the finger on the navigation keyboard. He can fly it to a tanker IP/CP, to an alternative target, or to a diversionary base using these simple keyboard entry techniques. Meanwhile,

the pilot continues to monitor engines, fuel consumption and fuel remaining, and wing sweep, playing with the vertical axis when required to do so.

As can be seen, the F-111, like most INT types, is highly dependant on its INS and navigation computers functioning correctly in order to guide the crew to their target and back home. But some drift is inevitable. The F-111F's Mk IIB BNS is a hybrid which combines old-fashioned cogs and pulleys with newer transistor-based and chip-based avionics. So, the crew might wind up way off course if they blithely sit back without a care in the world, trusting that the computers are keeping everything in order. Thus, the wizzo constantly monitors things. He checks present position on the LED digital displays, banks of which are scattered over his portion of the main instrument panel. He cross-checks with the ARS. With his head in the feeding trough (more correctly termed the virtual image display or VID), he looks at prominent waypoints along the navigation track. He calls up OAPs alongside it. And with his hand on the 'goat turd' (radar tracking handle) located under the right canopy sill, he refines cross-hairs position.

Essentially, the radar can be tilted and tweaked for different range settings, to vary the radar perspective slightly and pick these features out more clearly, but they remain fairly nondescript at the best of times. The ARS is an old-fashioned real-beam ground-mapping system which requires considerable interpretative skills, so great use is made of the OAPs – up to two of them for each critical destination or turnpoint along the navigation track. When calling one up on the navigation panel by pressing one of two OAP buttons, the cross-hairs should slide straight over onto the appropriate radar-significant return in the display. If they are out of place, the INS has drifted. It can be updated by simply pressing the enable bar on the 'goat turd', and moving it about like a joystick to inch the cross-hairs into the right place.

The process may be repeated with another offset to increase accuracy, as this automatically updates the system, keeping the INS 'in whack'. This is critical. When the target insert button is pressed, the BNS computers are steering the aircraft along its intended

. . . and on the F-111F version the radarscope comprises part of the VID, which plays corresponding imagery from the aircraft's belly-mounted Pave Tack, *combining radar and FLIR which are integrated but can be used independently. Here, off the coast of Kuwait, the radar sweep is naturally looking ahead but the* Pave Tack *cue dot (to the bottom left of the cross-hairs) indicates that its FLIR is looking aft, and to port. (via Rick Stephens)*

track based on the inertial platform and stored coordinates. The present position and aircraft velocity data furnished by the inertial platform will be used subsequently for the bomb run. It has to be bang-on.

At this stage it is important to raise the subject of the Rockwell-Collins GPS Navstar, which has created something of a revolution in the world of navigation. Interestingly, the Aardvark was one of the first aircraft to receive the GPS update, initially applied to two dozen F-111Es in the Avionics Modernization Program. Along with new cockpit MFDs, databus, navigation computer and RLG gyros, the F-111Es were outfitted with Rockwell's AN/ARN-151(V) five-channel GPS Navstar receivers, manifested as a bump on the glare shield. GPS Navstar will shortly be

retrofitted to the combat fleet of F-111Fs as part of Rockwell's related F-111F *Pacer Strike* digital avionics update. The five-channel receiver is also being installed in the heavy bomber fleet, plus F-15E and F-117A interdictors.

Navstar, and the very similar CIS Glonass system, employ a constellation of 24 orbiting satellites some 11,000 miles above the Earth to enable a suitably equipped aircraft to get a fix. The constellation is monitored by ground stations which transmit position corrections, and time data based on a common standard GPS atomic clock. It is as sophisticated as it sounds, but using it is very straightforward.

The navigator first switches on the GPS receiver (initiates it) and enters an estimate of present position, velocity (aircraft speed) and time via its keyboard. The

GPS Navstar Operation: Several 'spheres of range' help determine aircraft position precisely, based on time and range to each satellite and elementary geometry. (Rockwell-Collins)

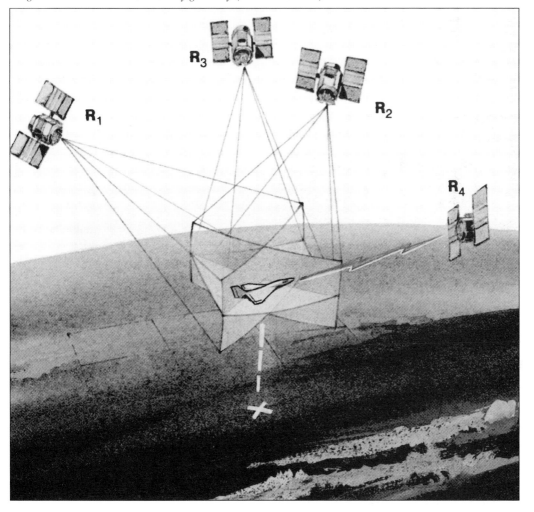

The RAAF operates 22 F/RF-111Cs from Amberley near Brisbane on swing-role recce-strike, under No. 1 and No. 6 Squadrons. They have recently been supplemented by 15 ex-USAF F-111Gs, which will act as a 'spare parts locker' for major portions of the airframe. (RAAF)

As seen through its rear-facing Pave Tack *turret, an F-111F from 'Lujac Flight' egresses at speed from Tripoli Airport on the night of 14 April 1986 as its bombload of Mk 82 'ballutes' tumbles onto the Il-76* Candid *transporters below. (US DoD)*

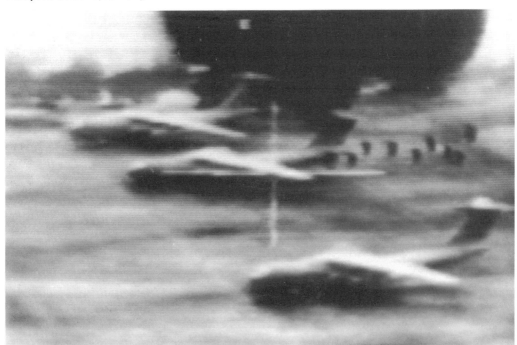

system then starts working automatically, locating and tracking suitable transmitting satellites. The time of receiving the coded time/location signal from the first is then multiplied by the speed of light to determine its sphere of range, R1. The process is more or less instantaneously repeated with two other satellites to determine their spheres of range, R2 and R3. By means of elementary geometry, the receiver can thus determine its precise position in terms of latitude and longitude, and altitude above mean sea-level (MSL). Range to a fourth satellite, 'R4', is used to correct any time difference between the receiver's quartz crystal clock and the GPS atomic clock time standard, giving the correct time to within one-millionth of a second to further fine-tune accuracy. Velocity is determined to the nearest one-tenth of a metre per second by counting the Doppler shift in the transmissions from the satellite (bearing in mind that the aircraft is effectively moving towards or away from the transmitters at any given time; most allege that the faster you go, the more accurate is GPS!).

The receiver is thus more or less instantly aligned and can then be switched to navigation mode within a few seconds. It will then continue to provide a continually updated present position accurate to within 16 m, day or night, rain or shine. It remains unaffected by sky waves or polar magnetism which can seriously degrade other, more primitive, ground-based forms of airborne radio navigation (ARN) aid. A figure-of-merit indicator tells the navigator how accurately the system is performing, with FM1 being the best.

With the constellation all but up-and-running, military P-decoder-equipped receivers are likely to enjoy virtually uninterrupted performance. The AN/ARN-151(V) system is able to sustain the punishment of high acoustic vibration with maximum reliability, and offers plenty of scope for rolling and pitching without causing the system to break lock. This was the bane of early ARN receivers such as the Vietnam-era *Pave Phantom* ARN-92 LORAN D 'Towel Rail', which enjoyed only limited coverage and a useful working range of only 200 miles. It was apt to break lock during aggressive manoeuvring or as a result of static noise discharges when hooking-up to a tanker.

Navstar goes beyond the basics of simply informing the crew where they are, their height above MSL and how fast they are going. It can be fused with a navigation computer to keep an INS continuously properly torqued and on track. Thus it can help drive moving maps based on film or disc, even provide steering cues and times to the next waypoint, IP or target on a HUD and integrated radar map display. This is especially good when fused with FLIR. Crews can thus conduct precision navigation and attack with only a bare minimum of active, radiating sensors, making them pseudo-stealthy. It was one of the unsung heroes of *Desert Storm* even before the Navstar constellation was completed, providing Special Forces with essential positional information in the murk of night in the middle of a featureless desert. It will have an even more revolutionary impact on INT air power.

Back to basics in our ingressing Aardvark, which is proceeding on course and on time to its target. With or without the benefit of Navstar, the navigator's primary focus of attention remains the giant protruding VID. This actually comprises two tubes, one above the other, located behind the same viewing trough. As range to target closes to within 20 miles, the wizzo will have already switched the radar on the big tube over to a narrower but sharper ground velocity stabilized mode. This centres the point of interest – the called-up target – in the top centre of the sector scan on the azimuth cross-hairs cursor, helping with target line-up, while the range bar cursor progresses down the pie-slice. In fact, the system can be linked to the autopilot to fly the aircraft to and over its target for an automatic blind bomb run, with the weapons automatically coming off the racks when the ballistics system judges all to be correct. But it is customary for the pilot to remain in full control and receive steering cues from his wizzo.

Long before the radar range cursor reaches the vertex the wizzo will have already unstowed the huge phallic Loral AN/AVQ-26 *Pave Tack* at the push of a couple of buttons between his knees. A big door in the Aardvark's belly then does a 180° turn, and the turret-ball of *Pave Tack* is unstowed. *Pave Tack* is a glorified version of the LANTIRN targeting pod, combining FLIR and a laser ranging/designating system, but in this instance mounted in the weapons bay to reduce drag while travelling to and from the target area. It is used exclusively by the surviving 78 F-111Fs, and the F-111Cs of the RAAF which shares some nine pods between 15 aircraft. The imagery from the big pod's window is initially presented on the navigator's smaller six-inch VID tube. As range to target closes to about 5 miles and *Pave Tack* assumes greater importance, the displays might be switched over with the FLIR taking up the bigger radar tube – actually a fairly modest nine-inch one, capped by a magnifying optic.

The FLIR sensor can be used in any of five different modes. Caged at boresight along the aircraft's velocity vector ('TFR Monitor' mode), the wizzo can simultaneously view the magnificent sensor imagery generated by this device in white hot or black hot viewing modes, and warn the pilot of terrain ahead. It works much like the FLIR in the LANTIRN too, for cueing by the pilot's gunsight (forward acquire, except that it projects no imagery there), or ARS and navigation computer (appropriately called the cue mode). It can even be slewed independently using the 'goat turd' in a couple of gyro-stabilized tracking modes designed to make manual sensor tracking easier (Snow Plow and left acquire) during navigation and more specialized forms of attack. As with LANTIRN, the purpose is to provide accurate target acquisition and tracking by night against non-radar-significant targets, using a wide and narrow FoV coupled to one of the target-tracking modes. Radar or laser ranging may be used subsequently to help the ballistics computer deposit dumb bombs accurately, or the laser can be squirted to guide LGBs.

Pave Tack first entered service during 1981 aboard the F-111Fs and was blooded during the April 1986 punitive strike against Libya, Operation *El Dorado Canyon*. It is the chief reason why the 20-year-old swinger remains in service today, despite recent

swingeing defence cuts which very nearly axed this force altogether. Ironically, much of the aircraft's space-age technology has proven to be its Achilles' heel, notably the ejection capsule which remains unique to this day. Despite neutron-radiographic, ultrasonic and X-ray testing which turn up any faults on an airframe during a 24-hour robotic inspection, the pyrotechnics of the ejection capsule dictate a lengthy PDM tear-down once every four years, using skilled personnel and expensive procedures. As it is easier to do any impending updates and undertake corrosion control measures at the same time, this is done at the same time. Thus, F-111Fs undergoing systems improvements such as AMP and *Pacer Strike* have been slated on the basis of this time-critical criterion alone, and have never been individually selected on a merit basis (e.g. lower airframe hours).

The RAAF, with their AUP have taken a longer-term attitude and have no desire to scrap their F/RF-111C fleet, which many see as pivotal to Australia's defence. They have even added ex-USAF examples to

An impressive line-up of stores, including 20 mm Gatling gun ammunition, iron bombs, smart bombs, Karinga CBUs and Harpoon anti-ship missiles. The RAAF's AUP F-111C is one of the most potent INT aircraft in service today. (RAAF)

It is possible to gauge the size of the GBU-15 E-O-guided glide bomb in this context. The F-111F carries an AXQ-14 data-link pod between its strakes with which to 'talk' to the bombs after release, for fine-adjustment to target lock-on prior to impact. These 1-ton bombs can be released at supersonic speeds to give an 8–12-mile glide range. They remain the best in the current free-fall smart bomb category. (Jim Rotramel)

bolster their force; and all this after having taken delivery of their *Peace Lamb* F-111Cs five years late to begin with, when confidence in the aircraft was shaky! The USAF, however, seem bent on ousting the F-111F and its stablemate the EF-111A Raven by the turn of the century, even though it will remain viable for another two decades. Many forget quite what a technological marvel it was, and still is. It introduced a huge number of firsts: augmented thrust (afterburning) turbofan engines qualified to operate at supersonic speeds at sea-level; swing-wings; a self-adaptive flight control system (forerunner of the modern FBW systems); the ejection capsule; and a host of the avionics already described, which were pioneering when they were introduced.

Back to basics. With TOT, time to 'bombs off' and a variety of other alphanumerics crowding out the periphery of the VID displays, the aircraft is set up for a blind radar-bombs pass. This is traditionally conducted at low-level using retarded weapons such as the cruciform steel-airbraked Mk 82SE Snakeye or

M117R, or the Mk 82 or Mk 84 ballute Air Inflatable Retard (AIR) bombs. Pop-ups to higher altitude may be used for 'slick' bombs or CBUs, which might also be tossed in a 3 *g* pull-up at a set range to target. Release of these weapons from their snug-fitting BRU-3s (low-drag MERs known as Bomb Release Units) is nearly always conducted using the automated ballistics system. It relies on velocity, plus radar-ranging inputs from the INS and ARS or laser-ranging input from *Pave Tack* for accurate targeting, though manual modes are available as back-up. All the pilot has to do is to press and hold down the pickle button to commit the Mk IIB BNS to attack. The wizzo will have already set up the switches on the WCP: ordnance ballistics (weapon type), and release mode.

In contrast to CAS jets, which might deposit a pair of bombs at a go during multiple passes or against separate targets of opportunity, INT is usually a first-pass-only-pass affair. It involves dumping everything off the BRUs against the one pre-planned target. This is where the intervalometer comes in: 'salvo' or 'train'

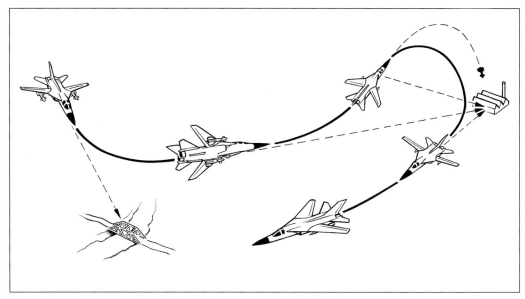

Pave Tack *'Mini-Toss'*: *A* Pave Tack *'mini-toss' bombing manoeuvre. The aircraft first identifies its initial point, then the target, on radar and FLIR to help compute weapons release in a 3-g pull-up manoeuvre. The aircraft then turns belly-up at about 135° of bank, lasing the target as it egresses to assist with LLLGB guidance during the terminal phase of bomb flight. Finally, the* Pave Tack *turret continues to track the target to record bomb damage assessment imagery.*

Autonomous Laser-Bombing: Autonomous laser-bombing – i.e. the same aircraft dropping and lasing – is the more common technique employed by INT attack aircraft, such as the Pave Tack *mini-toss. Note the refined trajectory of the Paveway III series, which employs proportional guidance, compared with the 'bang-bang' path taken by the earlier Paveway I and II series. The aircraft will track the target for much of the manoeuvre, but laser designation is confined approximately to the last 10 seconds of bomb flight.*

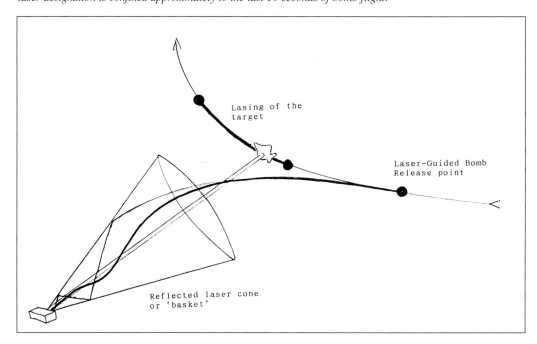

Twinkle-twinkle big F-111F Aardvark. Navigation lights and electro-luminescent formation strips would be turned off prior to the strike run. (Jim Rotramel)

must be selected on the WCP, along with interval. The former means the whole lot comes off in one great mass of iron; the latter means, as it implies, the bombs come off in a string to straddle the target.

This is of particular importance when attempting to drop a bridge or put lots of holes in a runway, either of which require bisecting the target at a cross-angle with weapons straddled. Aiming along a bridge or runway might result in the bombs landing adjacent to it, making big splashes or churning up the grassy knolls, thus rendering the mission ineffective. Intervalometer settings ensure suitable timing between the release of each bomb. With the intervalometer (set in milliseconds) pegged at 0.075, an Aardvark whooshing along at 480 knots at low-level will deposit its 'stick of iron' with a bomb spacing of some 60 ft. Given even a modest load of a dozen Mk 82 500 lb bombs alternating off each wing (so as to preserve stability in the roll axis, as the aircraft is quickly liberated from its cumbersome load), it can lay down a lethal blast zone measuring 1,000 ft by 500 ft, not counting the effects from shrapnel and terrain-focused concussion. That is the traditional way of conducting low-level INT.

However, in the Gulf War, the F-111Fs assigned to the 48th TFW(P) at Taif, Saudi Arabia mostly flew at medium altitudes and 'plinked' targets with PGMs, including targets of opportunity within prescribed killing zones, such as dug-in Republican Guard armour, and HAS at airfields. *Pave Tack* resolution was sufficiently good that wizzos could differentiate between dummy or previously knocked out targets and live ones. For example, the earthworks involved in digging in Iraqi armour stirred up the top-sand, making such points easily identifiable as they presented a slightly different FLIR signature from the surrounding terrain.

In many respects, the pride the crews continue to exude in the F-111 has as much to do with survivability as it has with the Aardvark's trail-blazing technical merits and superb bombing package. This is a morale-boosting feature matched only by the new stealth types. Nine of its contemporaries went down in Vietnam during the course of 4,060 crucially important combat missions which established the concept of autonomous low-level interdiction. A further casualty fell in the Libya strike (attributed to some hasty, last-minute change to mission planning imposed by a ham-fisted Marine Colonel, resulting in too many aircraft flying the same altitude and heading, a tactic never to be espoused). But there were no F-111F combat losses during the entirety of *Desert Storm*. The only damage was a tiny hole in the tail of one machine together with a nick in its windscreen, along with what appeared to be a shotgun-like dent in the intake trunking of another.

Its brutish airframe certainly helped: machine-milled aluminium and steel skins up to half an inch thick, wrapped around Ladish D6AC steel, cobalt-nickel-titanium and carbon-carbon stringers and frames. Few aircraft quite match the Aardvark's beefy skin-loaded construction. In all, the 86 F-111s (which include 22 'E' models assigned to Incirlik AB, Turkey) notched-up 2,830 *Desert Storm* combat sorties, during which time they dropped 60 per cent of the total tonnage of smart bombs expended by the USAF. This culminated in a remarkable balance sheet: over half of all targets confirmed as knocked-out, while representing a mere seven per cent of the force! As one former 'swinger' put it, 'Like the proverbial "Bad Girls", the "Varks" went everywhere and did everything' including the heavily defended sites dotted around downtown Baghdad. What precisely did they do to gain such accolades?

'Smart' bombing was their true forte, employing some tremendous hardware: the Texas Instruments GBU-24/B Paveway III low-level LGB (LLLGB), and the Rockwell International GBU-15 E-O-guided glide bomb. Both of these weapons, based on the Mk 84 blast/fragmentation or BLU-109/B penetrating one-ton warheads, moved the realm of smart bombing to a higher order of precision while simultaneously permitting greater stand-off launch ranges.

The LLLGB system differs from its predecessors in that it incorporates a solid-state seeker. This is electrically rather than mechanically linked to the forward steering canards, a weapon equivalent of FBW. The device flies using proportional guidance rather than bang-bang homing; that is, the weapon describes a smoother flight path to the laser spot and, given its much broader chord, pop-out tail fins, the weapon's range is virtually doubled (dependant on release height and speed). Moreover, inertial mid-course guidance permits it to be tossed at transonic speed at low-level, before it pops up to cruise height and descends in a smooth arc down the laser basket. Crews fly what is known as a mini-toss delivery, lobbing the bomb from low altitudes in a 3 g pull-up. The F-111F then goes belly-up in almost an inverted attitude, 135° from the horizon. This enables the wizzo to continue tracking the target with *Pave Tack*, and to squirt it with its laser during the terminal phase of bomb flight, as the Aardvark descends and arcs

away. Still sliding back towards the ground, the pilot recovers the aircraft wings-level, sometimes perilously close to the ground if there is a good deal of flak or SAMs to contend with. Indeed, the only Gulf War casualties were Capts Frederick 'Art' Reid and Tom 'T C' Caldwell, who crashed into a mountain during a *Desert Shield* practice GBU-24 mini-toss exercise during the early morning hours of 11 October 1990. Situational awareness is at a premium during bombing, too.

The weapon remains standard fare at the 'Swing-wing Inn' alongside earlier models of the Paveway series, and accounted for a good percentage of the total tonnage expended by the *Pave Tack*-toting 48th TFW(P) during their contribution to the so-called 'Baghdad Bash'. They dropped 2,542 quarter-ton, 2,052 1-ton and two 2-ton LGBs! Col Tom Lennon's 66 F-111Fs proved crucial to the outcome of the air war. Behind closed doors one very senior commander said: 'I want this target hit – give it to the F-111s.' The final tally was 2,203 targets obliterated. During an LGB attack on 28 January 1991, Capts Matt Young and Greg Chapman scored a direct hit on an ammunition storage area at Tallil AB, Iraq, resulting in the largest non-nuclear, man-made explosion ever detected by a missile warning satellite. Smoke rose to 30,000 ft and only one other aircraft in the attack was able to see through the quagmire to deliver its weapons! But the unit's *pièce de résistance* came on the final night of the war on 27 February, when Project *Deep Throat*, the ultimate LGB, was deployed in combat.

The background to *Deep Throat* bears some retelling, as it represents one of the most rapid weapons developments in the annals of modern air warfare. A Lockheed engineer hit upon the idea of encasing explosive in lengths of used gun barrel from US Army self-propelled howitzers. In December 1990, engineers at Eglin AFB, Florida, were told they had 10 weeks to develop and field the weapon (a process which customarily takes three and a half years!). According to the Project Manager Maj Dick Wright, the effort 'acquired added urgency . . . when members of the Air Staff at the Pentagon saw a graphic illustrating the shortcomings of existing bombs against hardened bunkers in the newspaper *USA Today*. It showed that none would get to the target, and that was pretty accurate!' On 25 January at the Army's Watervliet Arsenal, Technicians began to cut and machine 30 of the gun barrels before boring out an extra 2 inches. The modified barrels were air-freighted to Eglin AFB 22 days later, where they were stood in the ground and filled with molten tritonal explosive by a 'bucket brigade'. The bombs were then mated to a modified Paveway III guidance kit, to create the 4,700 lb GBU-28.

On the morning of 24 February at Tonopah Test Range, Nevada, an F-111F test-dropped the first bomb. It hit the target and penetrated deeper than 100 ft! On the afternoon of the 26th, a second weapon was fitted to a rocket-sled at Holloman AFB, New Mexico, and punched through 22 ft of reinforced concrete slabs before shooting a further half mile downrange! That same morning a pair of the weapons, still warm to the touch from the cooling tritonal, were loaded aboard a C-141B Starlifter and ferried to Taif in Saudi. Within 5½ hours of arrival they were strapped to a pair of 492nd TFS F-111Fs, bound for Iraq!

Lt-Col Dave White and his wizzo Capt Tom Himes, in the slot position of the two-ship Flight led by Lt-Col Ken Combs and his navigator Maj Jerry Hust, dropped their penetrator smack onto a command and control bunker at Al Taji airfield, just north of Baghdad. 'It was an unknown munition, we didn't have any delivery parameters and didn't know any of its characteristics,' recalled the crewmen, so 'the profile we flew was pretty much what we'd been flying all along'. To impart extra kinetic energy they executed a step-climb to a higher-than-normal LGB release altitude. Maj Hust recalled, 'What we were aiming for was basically a piece of dirt' beneath which sat the enemy bunker. The effect may have been decisive. As another USAF officer noted, 'Much like the atomic bombs which ended World War II, these bombs sent a clear message to the Iraqi leadership that they were personally at risk – in a matter of hours they accepted all United Nations Resolutions!' Today, the balance of 26 bombs remain on stand-by while series development and manufacture of purpose-built equivalents continue.

The other key smart bomb employed by INT F-111Fs was the GBU-15, which comes with two forms of guidance: a daytime TV DSU-27/B seeker or a night-time WGU-10/B IIR seeker. The latter is identical to those employed in the AGM-65 Maverick AGM. Making sure the target was lined-up in the seeker's cross-hairs was effected on the VID, which doubles for such E-Os. The big difference between this and Maverick, however, was that rather than using line-of-sight, lock-on-before-launch (LoS-LOBL) techniques, the system

The AGM-130 is a rocket-assisted GBU-15 which offers yet further range – around 15 miles from the release point. The real point of interest here, however, is the 16° wing sweep, locked fully-forwards, with the leading-edge and double-slotted flaps shown to good effect. Such complex moving surfaces have fallen out of favour in the US, where FBW and compound wing curvatures have become possible. (Rockwell)

was employed lock-on after launch (LOAL).

Tactics were profoundly different from Maverick too, as the weapon flew purely on kinetic energy imparted during a toss release, with the wizzo keeping track of events via a data-link. This conveyed E-O pictures of what the weapon's seeker saw all the way through to target impact. He corrected cross-hairs-on-target using a small toggle switch on the right-hand console, so that he could effectively fly the weapon to the target during the terminal phase of weapon flight. By contrast, as it uses no data-link, the imagery generated in the cockpit by the launch-and-leave Maverick goes blank as soon as the missile shoots off its rail. Data-linking was made possible by the Hughes AN/AXQ-14 and newer derivative, which was fitted to the 'ass-end' hardpoint of a select few F-111Fs. These carried their ECM pods on the outside of the stowed *Pave Tack* cradle, precluding its use on those missions.

However, it was not just a case of 'heading out' and lobbing these weapons willy-nilly. Costing 10 times as much as an LGB meant they were used judiciously by a few, select crews from the 493rd TFS. They had been practising with it for years. Training sorties tasked a pair of F-111Fs to the mission, with one aircraft (with data-link switched on) guiding its companion over the radio, while the other (with its captive bomb seeker activated) acted as the bomb and 'glided' to the target. The latter then broke-off as it got close to the ground, permitting the two crews to trade roles. In combat, with elements from the 493rd TFS in action, the GBU-15 was tossed at Mach 1.3 for a 10-

BENINA AIRFIELD
15 APR 86

DESTROYED F-27

DAMAGED MI-8/HIP

DESTROYED MI-8/HIP

mile glide range. Graphs existed to help crews plot the weapon's release point at specific speeds and heights AGL. It received worldwide fame following a feat of 27 January, when two GBU-15(V)-2/Bs (the IIR version) were used to destroy oil manifolds at the Al Almadi pumping station which were feeding an Iraqi-created oil-slick in the Persian Gulf. Range has since been extended by rigging the weapon with a rocket motor, to create the AGM-130 – now a mainstay PGM in the armoury of the F-15E Strike Eagle DRF, too.

But there are occasions where low-level flying in dangerous overflight is necessary, particularly for counter-air runway denial, using radar bombs or visual bombs (or a combination of the two, if the target is lit-up by lights or roving traffic). The idea is to tear up the enemy strips and keep his air power on the ground. It is a tough assignment because the target complexes are invariably huge and well-defended. In the vast expanses of desert offered to the Iraqis, they spared no expense in creating giant sprawling complexes. Talill airfield, for example, covers an area of some 9,000 acres – about twice the size of London Heathrow!

The one factor working in the attackers' favour is that the perimeter fences, runways and taxi tributaries are often distinct on ground-mapping radar (GMR, a term Tornado crewmen use for their ARS). This provides scope for target acquisition at very long range and the possibility of freezing the display early on in the attack. This way the actual bomb pass may be conducted RQ, with the radar in stand-by mode so that it does not give off tell-tale emissions. The ballistics system then need get its much-needed slant-range-to-target data only from laser and inertial sources. It is a trade-off.

The greatest successes of Operation *El Dorado Canyon* were the strikes against Tripoli Airport and Benina airfield, both of which were at the centre of civilian activity. A combination of radar and *Pave Tack* (or radar and TRAM in the case of the A-6E Intruders) was deemed essential for system redundancy and accuracy in first-pass-only-pass strikes. In fact, as many aviators have since admitted, the Libyan defences were fully aware of their presence and switching off the ARS would have contributed very little towards surprise. It is possible also that at least one crew neglected to turn off their navigation

The Tornado's answer to smart bombing requirements is the GEC-Marconi TIALD pod, two of which were used in the Gulf, carrying curious Viz *comic strip 'Fat Slag' characters daubed on them. The TIALD head is covered between sorties. (Author's collection)*

beacons too! On that occasion the airfields were struck using Mk 82 AIRs in a laydown attack – too soft a blow to do more than make a few shallow holes, but more than adequate to destroy two helicopters, four MiGs and three transports, not counting many more damaged beyond economic repair. The only really effective way to tear up runways, which was not the objective of that particular mission, is to use boosted kinetic energy weapons such as the one-shot-one-hole French Matra BLU-107/B Durandal, the British multiple submunition-dispensing Hunting Engineering JP233 or its German equivalent the MBB MW-1 stuffed with StaBo runway-cratering bomblets.

During the Gulf War, and for much of the time leading up to that within the context of NATO, the task of airfield INT thus fell mostly on the RAF's Tornado GR.1s. The Tornado IDS shares much in common with the F-111 series in that it is primed to bull its way deep behind the enemy's lines, and uses much common core technology, if not some outwardly similar characteristics too. In terms of avionics, the Tornado, with its CGPS flight-load system, true HUD, computer-synthesized CRPMD drawing on a Texas Instruments suite of TFR and GMR and offering a

The Vietnam-era equivalent of the 1980s' F-111F Pave Tack and the A-6E TRAM Intruder was the A-6C TRIM. Here, a TRIM Intruder sits in its revetment with its wings folded and sporting 20 Mk 82SE iron bombs and its giant TRIM cupola in view. There was no laser on this prior to 1972; instead, crews used the system's LLLTV and FLIR sensors simply to acquire non-radar-significant targets on the cockpit display, and slew radar to them to help DIANE compute bombs away . . . (Grumman)

. . . whereas during the Libya strike, A-6E TRAM Intruders employed radar, FLIR and laser. They successfully struck Benina Airfield, as attested by this BDA shot taken just over a day later by an SR-71A 'Habu'. (US DoD)

Left: *The Tornado's TIALD was used to guide Portsmouth Aviation CPU-123/B LGBs onto hardened enemy shelters during the Gulf War, as the logo on this one testifies! (Author's collection)*

Below: *TIALD cross-hairs on target, laser on; BANG! as a CPU-123/B strikes home true. (GEC-Marconi)*

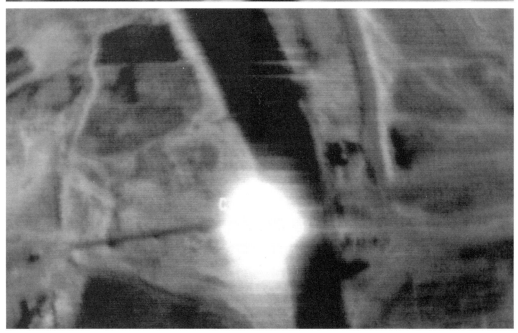

Ground crews load a giant JP233 anti-runway canister onto the belly of a Gulf War Tornado. (RAF)

A Tornado crew show off their high-speed, low-level capability. On the outboard pylons the machine carries a Sky Shadow ECM pod and a BOZ-107 bulk-chaff dispenser. Flare decoys are released via AN/ALE-40 dispensers bolted under the rear engine compartment. (Author)

radar freeze mode, a chin-mounted laser rangefinder/marked target receiver, and the option of a TIALD pod, currently lies somewhere in between the vanilla *Pave Tack* and *Pacer Strike* upgraded F-111F in the league table. However, it is slightly shorter on range, arguably bigger on flexibility and is younger. Moreover, it is now flying in significantly greater numbers – over eight times as many. The philosophy of nav-and-attack remains essentially the same too, except that the Tornado IDS has been honed for battle with a slightly different INT weapons kit. And the JP233, a giant 21.5-foot-long dispenser canister carried in pairs which attracted some controversy during the Gulf War, is what every runway-busting Tornado wears to war.

Operation *Granby*, the British contribution towards the Coalition build-up in the Gulf in the four months leading up to initiation of *Desert Storm*, witnessed the creation of three Tornado IDS detachments, each with a nominal strength of 15 desert pink GR.1s and 24 crews. For most of the war, the aircraft were fragged against airfields – the heavily defended Ubaydah bin Al Jarrah, Al Asad, Al Taqaddum and Shaibah. Initially low-level strikes with forged-case iron bombs and JP233s were used, but later graduated onto LGB attacks against HASs with CPU-123/Bs from cruise height.

The first series of attacks were the most hairy, all initiated down at sand-stirring heights in conjunction with radar. Following the split, the aircraft would take up their attack headings using the GMR to acquire and line up on the chosen target for a classic radar bombs delivery. A frozen radar map was often used for the last 5 miles or so to the release point, using the nose-mounted laser and inertial references to compute automatic bombs-away in a pseudo-stealthy mode. The crews had no FLIR (TIALD entering the war much later on, and primarily for laser bombing). Instead, they relied on the comprehensive HUD pointers and optional NVGs. Those hauling iron built up impressive speeds of up to 600 knots, before pulling up just prior to weapons release to loft their bombs for a couple of miles at the chosen target – in this instance a flak or radar site. Otherwise, such sites would be turning their attention towards the Tornadoes that would be shortly afterwards running the gauntlet with JP233s. It usually had the desired effect of keeping enemy heads down.

Meanwhile, the JP233-carrying Tornadoes, encumbered by their massive weapons, would be lining-up to cross paths with a preselected key point on a runway target. At 500 knots in maximum mil power, they went as low as 180–200 ft AGL. The JP233 then did its business on cue from the ballistics system, dispensing in a downwards-firing mode 30 57

lb SG357 runway-busting rocket-assisted concrete penetrators, together with 215 5.5 lb HB876 area-denial submunitions. These are designed to hamper any subsequent efforts to repair the torn-up strip. Wg Cdr Jerry Witts later described the JP233 ejection sequence as '. . . a pulsing glow from beneath the aircraft. Then, suddenly, two massive thumps as the empty canisters are jettisoned'. The unladen Tornado would then rapidly accelerate to 540–550 knots!

One hundred JP233s were expended in the first days of *Desert Storm*. With air superiority established, the strikes were no longer deemed vital, and the Tornadoes shifted all their energies towards higher-altitude laser bombing and *Scud*-hunting. Misinformed members of the Press preferred to think that JP233 attacks were halted because they put the Tornado crews at particular risk with little reward for their gruelling efforts, and that such missions had accounted for the eight Coalition Tornado losses during the first five days of combat. In fact, one of the losses was an Italian machine engaged on independent duties (bombing; one of only eight to make its target owing to inadequate AAR experience, obliging all but the lost crew to return-to-base owing to inadequate fuel reserves). Two were stricken due to 'operational causes', and of the five RAF combat losses, only one was actually downed during a JP233 sortie. The four other Tornado fighters were downed while performing bombing missions with 1,000 lb weapons, with six crew members ejecting and parachuting into captivity.

Overall, the RAF Tornado establishment flew 1,650 strike sorties, for a 0.36 per cent loss rate; nine times higher than the overall Coalition rate of 0.038 per cent during the grand tally of nearly 110,000 sorties. However, this was largely due to the particular derring-do of the Tornado aviators who were obliged to confront the enemy's flak where it was often least Elint-mappable and most intense, and where no protection could be afforded by the F-4G *Wild Weasels* against optically aimed SAMs. Neither do the cold-blooded statistics reflect the fact that these sorties were all deep strike, and do not include massive elements of rearward tankers or high-altitude patrols both of which distort the overall Coalition picture in terms of numbers of sorties. Shifting to medium altitudes ('hi' for strikers) after the first week did, however, enable them to work more closely with the SEAD and Cappers, and the losses fell sharply.

The sixth and final Tornado to tumble occurred near the end of the aerial campaign after a lossfree period of just over three weeks. The Tornado was involved in a mass buddy laser attack conducted by 12 aircraft over Al Taqaddum – seven other Tornadoes in concert with four Buccaneers. It was brought down on 14 February by a pair of SA-2 SAMs. (These were

A deadly duo, and scourge of the Royal Navy's South Atlantic Fleet during the Falklands War: the Dassault Super Etendard and the Aérospatiale AM.39 Exocet anti-ship missile. This Super Etendard also carries a centreline buddy refuelling pack, of the type used by Argentina when pairs of Super Etendards were tasked to strike British shipping – one to extend range, the other to lob the missile. (Dassault Aviation)

possibly Iraqi optical-guided instead of command-guided derivatives of the otherwise antiquated Russian *Dvina*, though operational models of *Fan Song* radar guidance remained at the time of writing, confirmed during an October 1994 USAF U-2R *Olive Branch* sortie.) The pilot escaped but the navigator Flt Lt Stephen Hicks went down with the aircraft.

All things considered, the Tornado crews did a fine job and the aircraft acquitted itself well, having been press-ganged into carrying out extraordinary duties.

However, despite improvements to low-level-delivered weapons such as Durandal, JP233 and the StaBo-stuffed MW-1, there are moves afoot to shift the mission into a stand-off mode. This is in keeping with the crews' ability to accurately identify their runway targets at a minimum range of 10–15 miles. A series of aborted US glide dispenser initiatives, such as the Brunswick low-altitude dispenser (LAD) and follow-on, Multi-national stand-off weapon (MSOW) have all fallen on stony ground. The exception which has applications in the dangerous anti-runway arena is France's Matra APACHE. Sqn Ldr Chris Bain, weapons employment course director at the Department of Air Warfare, reckons that APACHE will be a boon. The 2,429 lb weapon can carry a 1,012 lb payload up to 93 miles, using a combination of a

rocket motor, an inertial measurement unit and MMW nav-update system. With its envisaged 10 881 lb Kriss submunitions, it would make a genuine stand-off runway attack possible. Like the American JSSAM (which is suffering from development woes) it will offer a number of alternative warheads, including unitary ones (one big blast) and others designed to pick out and destroy armour, SAM sites, etc. Hunting Engineering's conventionally armed stand-off missile (CASOM) is also entering the equation in response to Air Staff Requirement 1236, but looks further away from fruition.

With or without stand-off devices, keeping the versatile Tornado IDS viable has been an on-going affair, adjusting to new requirements such as reconnaissance and electronic combat. For their own part, the RAF has been putting a lot of money into a mid-life update (MLU). The crux of this was to be the introduction of improved, sharpened radar software along with a new digital databus, making it more adaptable to ever more weapons technologies. GEC Sensors' thermal imaging common module (TICM II), and Spartan, a terrain-referenced navigation (TRN) system similar in concept to the BAe Terprom, intended to reduce reliance on radar emissions during the critical target run-in, were also to be added. The requirement was originally to be applied to 165 Tornadoes as part of the GR.4 MLU (some under a Batch 8 buy).

Terrain-referenced navigation systems all work along similar lines: by employing LARA to determine height AGL, and barometric pressure to determine height above MSL, it is possible to deduce both aircraft altitude and the elevation of the terrain below. These electronic notes are then compared with position data furnished by the INS or GPS Navstar and the carefully prepared contour maps or 'bumpies' stored on magnetic or laser disc on a digital database. It involves a cross-checking process that is repeated umpteen times per second. Spartan thus anticipates the terrain ahead of the aircraft along its velocity vector and commands the autopilot to pitch appropriately – just like a TFR radar, but without its tell-tell transmissions and give-away side-lobes.

The system was also to project synchronized 3-D terrain imagery alongside FLIR on the Tornado's HUD, outlining the edges of up-and-coming ridges for increased pilot SA. This would bypass the limited-vision 'through the cardboard tube' phenomenon associated with NVGs (which will probably gain greater acceptance in the absence of the more sophisticated equipment).

It would have been a remarkable package. However, on 4 May 1993 it was announced that Spartan and the TICM II FLIR would be omitted from the Tornado GR.4, mostly as a cost-cutting move. However, other aspects of the GR.4 MLU would be retained and applied to a select 80 Tornadoes.

Getting the Boat

Another area in which the Tornado IDS is beginning to find an increasing operational niche is the equally arduous task of anti-shipping missileer, a subject which cannot be ignored in the context of modern air power. Indeed, this has long been the province of US Naval aviation (as would be expected), but has also been steadily falling within the brief of several land-based 'squealers'.

Nobody can forget the harrowing images of HMS *Sheffield*, hit amidships during the Falklands War on 4 May 1982 by a sea-skimming AM39 Exocet launched from a Dassault-Breguet Super Etendard of the Comando de Aviacion Naval Argentina. The crippled destroyer took six days to sink, but its destruction sent shudders through the world's naval chiefs for the first time since Pearl Harbor. The largely unprotected MV *Atlantic Conveyor* represented a bigger, easier target during a separate attack on 27 May, and many men and much *matériel* went down with it.

NATO's Tornado forces, by dint of sheer numbers, have become the most adept land-based units at conventional anti-shipping tasks. Two Marineflieger wings were formed with Tornado IDSs toting Kormoran anti-ship missiles during the latter half of the 1980s (presently in the process of being absorbed by the Luftwaffe). More recently, the RAF has adapted 24 Tornado GR.1s to the GR.1B tasking, with BAe Sea Eagle missiles. Other land-based exemplars of this tasking include the RAAF's fleet of F/RF-111Cs, which are Harpoon-capable (amongst other tasks), Hey'l Ha'Avir Kurnass F-4Es which can use Gabriel IIIs, and Norway's F-16As equipped with Penguin anti-ship missiles. And exports of the strap-on Exocet flourished after the Falklands War, giving added punch to relatively obsolescent fighters such as the Mirage F1.EQs flown by Iraq.

These aircraft and their taskings should be differentiated from the heavyweights. They are designed exclusively for Coastal Defence and for interdicting surface vessels in key sea lanes at suitable choke-points in the Baltic, Mediterranean, Black Sea and straits in the Pacific. They are not designed for waging wars in mid-ocean. The transoceanic multi-engined machines such as Russia's AV-MF fleet of Tu-16 *Badger*, Tu-22 *Blinder*, Tu-22M *Backfire* and Tu-95/142 *Bear* carry belly-mounted stand-off missiles. These mostly comprise last-resort nuclear devices which fall into the category of weapons of Armageddon. In any case, the fleet is being gradually contracted. The US Navy, for its own part, is similarly focused on deep-water warfare which, in common with the Russian hardware, performs a mission altogether outside the domain of INT and its spin-off tactical air support, maritime operations (TASMO). Much of the Tac-INT class of anti-shipping is aimed at vessels ranging in size from fast patrol boats to radar picket ships; not mallet-blows between capital ships and their companions.

'Getting the boat', as the mission is often known to land-legged crews, is no piece of cake. Owing to the fact that the only radar-masking feature of the sea is the natural horizon, there is little choice but to skim within 1,000 ft of the surface where the usual radar horizon falls to a fraction under 40 nm (46 miles). This is the maximum trade-off point between popping-up to establish a brief radar contact on the ship and setting the switches in motion prior to the ship picking up the fighter's radar and lobbing a missile at it. It cuts both ways. Not surprisingly, most anti-ship missiles are optimized to work at these launch ranges or beyond, obliging the launch platform to venture closer only when absolutely necessary – for example, if a close-range radar map is required to help categorize the target and confirm it as hostile.

In fact, the radar horizon varies quite a bit owing to

The American Harpoon anti-ship missile evolved into the AGM-84E SLAM, the first conventional weapon to employ GPS guidance. It was used for the first time during Operation Desert Storm. *(McDonnell Douglas)*

local conditions. The ability of radar waves to bounce off the upper atmosphere and back down to the target, and then back to a sensitive radar such as those equipping the US Navy's *Aegis* Class destroyers, might come as a nasty surprise to an unsuspecting pilot. The ships' sophisticated ESM detection devices are surprisingly good at discerning an attacking fighter's different radar modes. So, for example, if it switched from a wide mapping mode to a narrower, expanded attack scan to build up a better picture of the convoy or individual vessel (where its radar would be beaconing across the ships that much more rapidly), then it is effectively announcing hostile intent. And the water is not a level playing field either. Tidal influences make the seas bend and stretch. Then there are the 'dense, lumpy bits' deep in the Earth's core which affect the water level dramatically. These can create continent-sized bowls and bulges which differ in depth (or height) by up to a staggering 750 ft or so in sometimes relatively local areas. These produce peculiarly longer or shorter horizons in certain places (hence use of the term mean sea level). Many more sophisticated Naval radars are finely tuned to cater for these contingencies, and have the advantage of look-up.

For the short-ranged aerial attacker, the qualities of vast expanses of water can provide some advantages. Even without SAR (or its sophisticated over-water inverted-SAR ship-classifying stablemate) stuffed behind the radome, the sea comes out black as black can be on the radarscope owing to the fact that its inherent flatness bounces radar waves away. Anything floating on it in all but rough conditions tends to reflect like a beacon. Many of today's fighter radars employ a specific sea search mode, which takes advantage of these characteristics, optimized towards detecting and tracking ship movements and to compensate for any choppiness. For example, the F-16's sea surface search has two submodes, SEA-1 and SEA-2. SEA-1 uses frequency agility to detect stationary and moving targets in sea conditions up to sea state 4. SEA-2, which employs a narrower Doppler notch, can locate moving targets in higher sea states (as well as provide a Moving Target Indicator capability against radar-significant land targets). Norwegian F-16 crews have become expert at this, matching the F-16A's APG-66 radar to the Penguin.

Switchology remains pretty much the same, irrespective of the fighter/missile combination. Once a target is acquired the radar map is then frozen if at all possible. The aircraft ducks back to an ocean-skimming posture, and the data – range, bearing and target speed – is then handed off to the missile. When the ready lamp or in range lamp shines, or an MFD broadcasts 'all systems go!', the weapon can be fired in the normal trigger-squeezing manner, leaving the launch aircraft to break away from its attack heading and take a vector for home.

Tactics are more complex. As is the case with SEAD, a tiered approach works best. Attacking a convoy would mean first peeling off the radar-missile umbrella provided by picket ships, using SEAD

An F-15E Eagle DRF prepares for launch on a cloudy April morning from RAF Lakenheath, Suffolk. The 48th FW operates two squadrons of F-15Es and a Capping F-15C outfit, all under one roof – an excellent move. (Author)

A quartet of F-15Es on the wing. The type's Hughes AN/APG-70 SAR radar offers a freeze-frame HRM mode and is unquestionably the best in its class worldwide. (McDonnell Douglas)

weapons retuned to defences such as ALARM, HARM or Shrike before closing-in with a second barrage of Exocet, Gabriel III, Harpoon, Kormoran, Penguin or Sea Eagle. A final thrust might then be made using conventional iron bombs. Even if the ships are not mortally damaged, the anti-ship missiles will prove to be more than a distracting nuisance as fires are dowsed and the captains concerned get to grips with possible evacuation procedures, just in case. The anti-ship missiles, however, have a fairly lethal track record. As already outlined, Exocet is just one in a vast armoury of such weapons produced by a number of different manufacturers, and not the only one to have witnessed action. The American

FOURTH-GENERATION STAND-OFF MUNITIONS

Short-range

Wind-Corrected Munition Dispenser (WCMD)
This American weapon employs a TMD such as the SUU-64/65 fitted with the wind-correcting guidance kit, for pin-point accuracy from high-altitude deliveries up to 40,000 ft. The warhead will comprise CEM, Gator, SFW, Bat and Skeet submunitions, or a non-destructive payload such as carbon-fibre wires (see JSOW below).

Joint (US Service) Direct Attack Munition (JDAM)
A free-fall weapon designed to replace SAL Paveways with hybrid GPS-aided inertial guidance, based on the Mk 80 bomb series and the BLU-109/B penetrating warhead. Will offer a 10–12-mile range with accuracy of 10 ft. IOC 1999.

Medium-range

Joint (US Service) Stand-Off Weapon (JSOW)
Designated AGM-154, this is an outgrowth of the US Navy's Advanced Interdiction Weapons System (AIWS). A brand-new dispenser-based device capable of carrying multiple types of payloads, e.g. a unitary warhead, cluster-category submunitions, or non-destructive payloads such as CSAR survival kit, chaff/active decoys, or carbon-fibre wires designed to fuse electrical grids and thus deny the enemy industrial power for up to two days at a time. Will use inertial-GPS Navstar hybrid guidance with optional autonomous template-based seeker technology for target acquisition for a range of up to 40 miles.

Long-range

APACHE
A subsonic, turbine-powered delivery dispenser being jointly produced by Matra of France and Deutsche Aerospace of Germany; due to achieve IOC in 1997. Uses all-weather terrain-skimming radar and GPS Navstar guidance during its 8-minute low-level flight to target after launch at low/medium altitude for a range of up to 86 miles. Currently equipped to carry 10 Kriss anti-runway submunitions, but has the growth potential for other payloads of up to 1,212 lb.

Arme de Precision Très Grande Portée (APTGP)
A long-range precision weapon concept being formulated by Matra of France, in one of two formats: a derivative of APACHE with a unitary warhead; and the Asura, a ramjet-powered device with a range of 215 miles derived from the ASMP-C nuclear missile. The Asura would climb to 65,000 ft and then dive onto its target, enhancing penetration of hardened targets.

Conventionally-Armed Stand-Off Missile (CASOM)
A concept defined by British Staff Requirement (Air) 1236. Designed to deliver a unitary warhead by means of a ramjet-powered missile capable of accelerating to Mach 3 for a range of 230 miles within 7 minutes of launch. APTGP (see above) may also fulfil this requirement.

Joint Air-to-Surface Stand-off Missile (JASSM)
Replaced the Tri-Service Stand-off Attack Missile (TSSAM) AGM-137, powered by turbofan and featuring stealth characteristics, Northrop's family is designed to deliver a 1,000 lb unitary or cluster payload out to a range of 180 miles. Template IIR guidance is being incorporated into the unitary warhead version.

McDonnell Douglas air-breathing, turbojet-powered AGM-84 Harpoon followed close on its heels, and has seen action against Libya and Iran with equally decisive results.

We close this digression into Naval warfare with Harpoon because this weapon has evolved further into a land-target striking weapon, the AGM-84E stand-off land attack missile (SLAM), setting us back on course with our main theme. SLAM has created a modestly priced covert attack weapon by incorporating GPS Navstar mid-course guidance – the first all-conventional weapon in the world to do so – by utilizing a mix of Harpoon inertial reference guidance with a two-channel GPS Navstar receiver. An AGM-65D Maverick IIR seeker is used for LOAL during the terminal phase of weapon flight, with the imagery and commands being relayed via an AWW-7/9 Walleye data-link pod (à la GBU-15/AXQ-14). The crew can steer the missile precisely to the target during the final phase of flight.

Seven SLAMs were used during the Gulf War, launched from the wings of A-6E TRAM Intruders, with data-link guidance being provided by A-7E Corsair IIs. Four hit their targets smack-on, some almost striking the identical spot: one of the pilots remarked, 'My eyes were like this big watching the second missile go into the first hole!' Two of the weapons struck the end of an Iraqi industrial complex, and during the second successful attack against an enemy Naval Headquarters building, target lock-on was achieved while the pilot was in the process of evading a SAM and coping with an illuminated master caution light on his instrument panel!

Measures are being undertaken to speed up the time it takes for the man-in-the-loop's weapons correction instructions to reach the missile and return its imagery. SLAM-ER (extended range) is also in the making, which adds new long-range glide wings for a 100 nm (115 miles) reach when launched at high altitude. This is a far cry from pioneering E-O weapons of the Vietnam-era such as Walleye and Hobos. These were strictly LOBL and were prone to all sorts of malfunctions. Many rightly argue that such long-ranging LOAL applications of the Maverick IIR seeker make far better use of the guidance technology. They argue that what CAS aircraft really need is a host of as-yet unconceptualized short-range weapons (along with improved rockets and guns), not more Maverick bodies with these seekers stuck on the front of them. Only in the realm of INT, by means of buddy bombing via data-link, does there exist the scope for refined target lock-on.

For most crews, however, it's back to bombing and other basics. And even if concepts such as Spartan TRN still are considered unsafe for manned INT right

now, other inroads are being made, most notably in the area of radar. This is far from being made redundant by infrared and reliable passive navigation aids. To reiterate: radar is an active sensor which needs to be used with discretion, but remains the Big Eye at all times. Deep into enemy territory, crews can get lost without it as they must work autonomously whenever possible; there is no AWACS to guide them.

Onboard radar, inertial and GPS Navstar references are thus essential prerequisites for a successful INT mission, linked by banks of black boxes to offer massive redundancy, and performing countless computer-processing operations. Key elements such as the satellite portions of GPS Navstar may be down for maintenance or fine-tuning, and onboard sensors and computers playing up at crucial times. And the deeper into enemy territory the aircraft venture, the more the flak, acoustic vibrations and inherent errors tend to degrade individual sensor accuracy, or simply cause them to break down. But working collectively they pull each other up by their bootlaces. However, 99 times out of 100 the Big Eye remains the crucial sensor, without which the mission might well have to be aborted. There is nothing else that offers the ability to look so far ahead – 40 miles or more out in front of the attacker.

Dual-rolers

The fundamental difference between the F-15E Strike Eagle DRF's Hughes AN/APG-70 radar and the models used in the Aardvark and its successors such as Tornado, solid-state though they have become, is the F-15E's SAR capability. Instead of presenting the wizzo with only a real-beam ground map, the traditional and often quite nondescript pie-slice sector scan full of distortion due to perspective, the F-15E's SAR, as its name implies, provides the option of a quality synthetic high-resolution map (HRM).

SAR uses the movement of the aircraft with respect to the target to create the impression that the antenna is larger than it really is (hence synthetic aperture), and all that needs to be done to create it is to fly at 10° or more offset from the area of interest. The radar then 'can get a good look to the side of it a bit'. Microprocessors then convert the returns into the HRM which features a more or less constant scale along and across track, with the baseline fairly well spread out, giving a true bird of prey's perspective, looking out and down in a plan view format. The end result is akin to a grainy photo presented in eerie green, which is easy to compare with the corresponding moving map (tactical situation display) projected on an adjacent MFD, making extremely light work of identifying waypoints, offsets and the target.

Stand-off weapons will be central to any future major aerial campaign. The Brunswick LAD depicted here has long since been abandoned, but the emerging range of INT weapons such as Have Slick *and JSOW are not exceedingly different either in concept or appearance. The shorter-winded JDAM more closely resembles a heavily-modified Paveway III LLLGB. (Brunswick)*

Maj Dick Brown, USAF Ret., who flew F-111Fs and spent some time on the F-15E programme, pointed out that you can 'pick out a 6 ft man dressed in tin foil at several miles'. Current crewmen reckon that the SAR HRM imagery is so good that, for example, at 40–50 miles away 'you could take a picture of your housing lot, then not only pick out your house, but tell if your car is in the driveway!'

The HRM is obtained by looking at the standard ground map return and picking out an area of interest using something akin to a cropped-shield shape as a reference cursor. The wizzo customarily does this using the right-hand tracking handle (the back-seat 'office' of the F-15E actually features two console-mounted multi-function slew sticks, making it easier for left-handers to operate, and simple for the ambidextrous). The tracking handles feature a transducer switch on top, the so-called 'coolie hat'. This looks and behaves much like a stick trim button, but acts more akin to a computer mouse in this instance. By pushing it in any given direction, the cursor will move about the radar display.

Once in place and selected (effected by pulling at the trigger Enable bar), the AN/APG-70 will concentrate its scan on that area for 3–6 seconds, building up the more detailed HRM map of the selected area and then flash it up in expanded format. This can be done as far as 160 nm (184 miles) to produce an 80 x 80 nm (92 x 92 miles) patch offering a resolution of 1,000 ft; or at ranges of 10 nm (11.5 miles) to produce a 0.67 x 0.67 nm (0.75 x 0.75 miles) patch offering a resolution of 10 ft! This is staggering finesse. Moreover, patch maps can be obtained while executing 4 *g* manoeuvres, and then frozen for the attack run. This can then be conducted wholly RQ. At the same time, the FLIR sensor in the LANTIRN targeting pod is slewed to that area, making it possible for the wizzo to zoom in rapidly, acquire the target and lase it for slant-range, a mini-toss with a Paveway III, or even just to squirt photons at it to dazzle the eyes of flak gunners. Specific targets can be picked out usually at ranges of around 20 miles on radar, permitting pseudo-stealthy attacks closer-in with smart weapons like the proportionally guided Paveways and even the GBU-15/AGM-130, which are released on cue. Seldom is there much need to use OAPs to help identify targets for straight-in attacks, whatever their merits for general navigation. Clearly,

The F-15E simulator, showing some of the cockpit MFDs in action. The pilot is using an E-scan terrain elevation warning display from LANTIRN, along with stores selection; the back-seat wizzo has (from left to right), tactical situation display, navigation FLIR and a frozen HRM SAR ground map, and a radar air-to-air B-scan in operation – very impressive stuff! Israel and Saudi Arabia are to operate the very similar F-15I and F-15S models of the aircraft, respectively. (McDonnell Douglas)

in company with its peers, the F-15E DRF anxiously awaits the operational debut of the new range of stand-off smart weapons and delivery canisters such as JASSM, JSOW and JDAM.

Of course, the F-15E's avionics are totally integrated for the purpose of delivering dumb iron bombs too, using radar, optronics and the inertial platform for fully automatic, totally uncanned blind weapons deliveries in loft, toss, dive, etc; and in conjunction with the HUD for air-to-ground radar-ranged (AGR) visual-aided CCIP bomb runs. A few HOTAS and back-seat switch changes and the whole format changes instantly from one preferred mode to another. All the while, the pilot is presented with comprehensive steering and target-cueing symbology, while the LANTIRN navigation pod can be used to its full effect, combining the best of many BAI and INT technologies already discussed. But woe betide any cavalier pilot who detaches himself from reality by failing to communicate with his back-seater: playing the piccolo (working the multifarious HOTAS switches studded all over the stick and side control handles) in both offices requires complete harmonization. The pilot and his wizzo must be in constant touch via a few choice phrases to coordinate their button-pushing.

A pair of EF-111A Ravens on RAF Upper Heyford's ramp in July 1992. The 42nd ECS contributed aircraft for Gulf War operations along with the 390th ECS, all of which flew under the latter's banner at Taif, Saudi Arabia. The aircraft have since been pooled under the 429th ECS at Cannon AFB, New Mexico. (Author)

A Raven on the wing over sinuous river mud flats. The aircraft flies on stand-off support, CAS, and primary support – deep strike – EW missions, safeguarding its colleagues from the worst ravages of enemy radars by using selective spot-noise jamming in lookthrough model. (USAFE)

The Raven's weapons bay was modified to house the 10 exciters which drive the jamming antennae located behind the underfuselage 'canoe' (out of sight here). The Raven is undergoing a SIP update which will expand jamming to 10 wavebands, ranging from early warning through to high-frequency terminal-threat systems in use by the latest SAMs. (Grumman)

Irrespective of whether the crew coordinate perfectly, computer processing enables each of them to demand information from the single multi-mode radar and the LANTIRN navigation pod's TFR, which are clever enough to channel data to the relevant interchangeable MFDs as demanded. The exception is the LANTIRN FLIR, which can only look in one direction at a time. By convention the pilot relies on the navigation pod's sensor and the back-seater on the targeting pod's. Each then have what they need. This eases coordination on long-range missions where everything has to be kept running smoothly between them all the time. In the single-seat F-16C cockpit, on the other hand, the pilot can do as he wishes but is apt to become overloaded with choice and can end up widely off the mark with his TOTs.

With regard to radar, the same is true to a certain extent. The pilot relies on the Elevation Scan furnished by the LANTIRN navigation pod to provide terrain-warning video (backed up by suitable pull-up and nose-over cues on the HUD, and a fail-safe fly-up system). The navigator uses the Big Eye for various ground-mapping modes and air-to-air B-Scan (fully processed into blips with relevant IFF bars, gladly bereft of ground clutter when looking down). These are presented on the MFDs and synthesized into steering and firing cues on the HUD, when called up on the up-front control panel. The opportunities are virtually limitless, providing a great deal of redundancy for visual bombs, radar bombs, optronic bombs and the redundant fail-safes.

Although the F-15E works on the premise that the 'pilot rows the boat and the wizzo shoots the ducks', the activation of one solitary switch, on the AC's decision, will reconfigure the aircraft completely for air-to-air combat. Radar and radar displays, ordnance stations, everything will suddenly switch over for immediate use. This is another feature which makes the F-15E so different from the F-111F and Tornado IDS. The now-retired F-111D did feature limited provisions in this department. And a similar philosophy is being embodied in the Russian Su-34, which features Aardvark-style side-by-side seating with the MFDs and lightly loaded wing of an Eagle-class fighter. The F-15E pilot can command this option and tell his radar-interpreting back-seater to 'get the bogey; forget the bombs, get the fighter'.

The downside is an agitated crew in a high-workload environment. This is principally because F-15E pilots do not yet perform the kind of hands-off terrain-skimming flight that is available to the Aardvark, Tornado IDS and the CIS counterpart, the Su-24 *Fencer*. Owing to the F-15E's much lighter wing-loading the crew can be tossed about in the cockpit a great deal, especially at low-level or in mountain turbulence. This can be particularly tough on the back-seater who might be performing delicate tracking movements and switching with his two hand controllers, taking the weight on his elbows while his head is down.

It is a delicate balance which most crews have to resolve on an individual basis, given that their strike objective is the paramount goal. Some prefer the inherent smoothness of the Aardvark and Tornado IDS at low-level (ground-skimming up to 1,000 ft AGL) and their most definite 'WSO union: shut up and drive' philosophy. Others prefer the rough-and-tumble of the F-15E which can readily take advantage of that low loading and manoeuvrability to transform the 'Mud Hen' (one of the F-15E's lesser-known nicknames) into a MiG-killer with the pilot firmly in control at most times – not that INT crews get to mix it up much in reality, owing to the great entourage of Cappers providing a protective umbrella.

Mixing INT and MiG-killing is usually bad news. The g loading tolerance of modern aircraft, along with their speed and climbing performance is severely hampered by heavy ordnance: far better to dump and run, or turn the fight around, rather than present a sitting target. So, while the Mud Hen can respond to enemy aerial opposition effectively, it must still first jettison its load of air-to-ground weapons – up to 24,500 lb of tangentially carried ordnance – in order to do so. And, alas, even the simplest of procedures, practised a zillion times during training sorties, can and probably will be forgotten in the heat of battle when the enemy is bringing flak and other lethal weaponry to bear. Focusing on one key task is often the route to success and survivability, even if a fighter possesses the brawn and the know-how to handle the dual-role mission. However, it seems to be the way forward.

Surviving the Gauntlet

Not surprisingly, assimilating all this switchology is a task which takes the best part of a year, even for more experienced flyers entering the F-15E programme. Most F-15Es require over 320 hours annually. Incoming crewmen need 20+ hours a month which compares favourably with many dedicated INT aviators. Given this requirement, the F-15E arrived on the scene barely in time for *Desert Storm*: the first operational Wing to form, the 4th TFW, began working-up from late 1989 and went into combat just over a year later.

Their chief accomplishments were the proving of the potency of LANTIRN and the SAR radar, and the type's massive growth potential as a missile launch platform for anti-*Scud* tasks. It also demonstrated its

Russia's counterpart to the Raven is the Su-24MR Fencer strike-recce, jamming and Elint platform. Unlike the Raven, this aircraft boasts provisions to carry a pair of R-60 rockets (AAMs). (Ka'Roly Gere via Ga'bor. Szekeres)

potential as a prospective leading component of future SEAD. But they actually spent the best part of their time dropping LGBs in much the same manner as the F-111Fs had been doing for years. And only after *Desert Storm* were they qualified to use some of the new smart weapons such as *Deep Throat* and the GBU-15/AGM-130.

If we are to refocus on the F-111, albeit briefly, then it is because of its vital ancillary role as support EW platform in the guise of the EF-111A Raven. This fights a seemingly silent but nevertheless vicious electromagnetic battle. While all the pounding and exchanges of missiles takes place, numerous EW support aircraft are lurking offstage to provide warning of enemy activity (an ancillary function of the AWACS and *Rivet Joint* sentinels) and what is termed soft kill SEAD or jamming. The 18 EF-111A Ravens assigned to Taif near Mecca proved crucial to the successful outcome of the 42-day-long air war against Iraq and Occupied Kuwait. Their sole armament comprised electrons fired at the speed of light – a mission the crews referred to as 'Rockin' Iraq' in deference to the electronic 'music' they played.

The heart of this ostensibly passive EW fighter is its 3 tons of receiver and jamming equipment, collectively referred to as the Grumman/Eaton AIL AN/ALQ-99E electronic jamming system (EJS). The receptive part of this, the system integrated receiver (SIR), is contained in the 'football' mounted on top of the fin. In concert with additional receivers built into the nose, the SIR sweeps through preselected frequencies in the A–J Bands (around 0.1 to 10.5 gigahertz), listening for potentially hostile radar emissions contained in its constantly reprogrammed computer threat library. With only minor intervention from the right-seat EWO, who can review the threats on a DDI, the system then responds with finely tuned spot-noise jamming. This is directed right at the relevant threat(s) by means of a bank of 10 steerable antennae driven by powerful 1,000 Watt exciters, contained behind a 'canoe' on the underside of the Raven. Engine-mounted 90 kW electrical generators ensure adequate power reserves for the job.

The system is carefully arranged so that it can work in look-through mode. The Raven can listen and jam simultaneously, with little risk of electromagnetic interference to itself, the *Wild Weasels*, or even Allied AWACSs and other friendlies, which might otherwise be swamped by all the noisy signals. This is made possible by using selective spot bursts, often of very short duration, carefully tuned to the operating frequencies of the enemy radars. The net product is to white out the enemy's radar screens or clog-up their automatic gain receivers (AGCs), making it virtually

impossible for them to acquire airborne targets. Air-to-air fighters also can be thus hindered in their attempts to acquire their trade.

The Raven flies three distinct missions, whereby enemy radars assume different priorities in the threat hierarchy. Stand-off is the relatively safe mission assignment. It involves two or three Ravens orbiting in racetrack patterns at up to 50 miles behind the FLOT at 15,000–20,000 ft with their wings spread-eagled at 16° for maximum cruise economy. They loiter for up to 4 hours at a stretch. Between them they put out a maximum jam footprint to generate an electronic smokescreen to obscure the position of strike packages ingressing and egressing enemy first tier defences, as well as to help conceal backstage AWACSs, GLOBs and other support machines.

Close-in tasks a solo jet or pair of Ravens close to the FLOT at more discreet altitudes of around 500 ft AGL, to support 'mud-movers' engaged in CAS or Special Operations work. The task is to shelter them from all but the E-O-guided devices and small-arms fire, which they must take care of themselves. It should be pointed out here that these tasks can also be performed by the USN/USMC Grumman EA-6B Prowler, a stretched, four-man version of the A-6 Intruder equipped with the EJS. It also specializes in communications-jamming (comjam) and covert ESM listening duties, often with a language expert sitting in one of the three Electronic Countermeasures Officer (ECMO) positions.

The American penchant for developing sophisticated EW machines has been matched only by the former USSR. Russia still boasts an impressive array of tactical jamming aircraft capable of conducting deep strike, including the still novel-looking Yak-28 *Brewer* (being phased out), Su-17UM-3K *Fitter*, and the Aardvark-look-alike the Su-24MR *Fencer F*. All may be outfitted with jamming and Elint pods. Very little is known about their true capabilities, but suffice it to say that the CIS is highly skilled in the art of EW jamming and has a clearly defined penchant for the esoteric. However, cruder avionics fabrication methods, which still lag behind the West, probably limit capabilities to blanket-noise jamming, without look-through as an option. In other words, they head straight into the thick of it radiating power in large bursts, possibly without regard to what effects it might have on their colleagues!

What makes the Raven unique is its third mission category, made possible by its earth-hugging transonic performance: primary. This frags between four and six crews on deep strike escort assignments way behind enemy lines. A pair of Ravens may precede, accompany or even trail behind a loosely knit strike package. They stay low in TFR mode and pop up to

500 ft or higher for brief bursts of radar-jamming activity to cover colleagues during the heat of a bombing run, or when a particular threat breaks out on the airwaves. It should be pointed out here that the spot-noise jamming undertaken by the Raven during stand-off and escort missions is mostly performed against early warning, height-finder and SAM acquisition radars working in the lower-frequency bands. Primary mission extends the tasking to the higher-band terminal guidance threats. These are tracking and illumination radars used to actually guide SAMs and flak to their targets. The mobility and frequency-agility of these devices makes it a tough assignment. Crews must learn how to work decisively in a time-compressed high-threat environment where EMI can all too easily become a problem. And enemy jamming (designed to swamp attack radars and even jam TFRs) and decoys (luring the Raven into a trap) pose a real threat.

Improvements to the EJS's software is virtually continuous. Hardware updates under the Systems Improvement Program (SIP) are being developed by Northrop Grumman. These are intended to massively improve its electronic jamming reflexes: an astonishing 100-fold increase in threat tracking with jamming response-time halved, keeping the Raven viable through to the year 2017 when the airframe's 8,000-hour fatigue life will be exhausted.

While retention is subject to the whims of higher authority (the Ravens might be axed alongside the F-111E AMP and F-111F force at the end of the decade), the sleek ghost machines remain crucial in supporting non-stealthy strike aircraft. These will continue to make up three-quarters of American air power, and a greater percentage of that of their allies whom the Ravens regularly support, well into the next century. But contrary to official propaganda, they are essential to stealth survivability too. There were many subtle tactics used during the Gulf War. Some of the F-117A Nighthawk's extraordinary survivability can be directly attributed to Ravens. They got Iraqi flak batteries to blaze away in the midst of jamming which the Iraqis believed was intended to mask Coalition strike machines – effectively causing the gunners to overheat their gun barrels with indiscriminate fire. In fact, it was timed a quarter of an hour prior to the Nighthawks' TOTs! By the time the guns had cooled down sufficiently to be fired again, the Nighthawks had long since dropped their bombs within strict 30-second 'gates' and had sped south-west!

Ultimately, however, the EF-111A force can only be spread so far in combat. With 30 of the 40 surviving airframes available for operations, only half of which can realistically be airborne at any one time, fighter crews need to exercise a good deal of self-reliance and use their own strap-on or internal ECM equipment in a crisis. By the time a missile is on its way, or a line of flak is being radar-walked to a fighter, reaction measures give no leeway to call up a Raven and cry for help!

Self-protect systems are truly multifarious, comprising the great circus parade of American ALQ (airborne countermeasures, special-purpose) hardware produced by ITT, Loral, Northrop, Sanders and Westinghouse, and their European equivalents which bear code-names such as *Barem, Barex, Rapport, Remora* and *Sky Shadow*. Backing them up are the expendables, chiefly chaff and flare ALE (airborne countermeasures, expendable) devices, but there are also some newer weird and wonderful throwaways. In describing how these systems negate the enemy's missiles and flak it is necessary to go back to basics.

While the first indication of imminent danger may comprise nasty flashes of AAA with tracer holding uncomfortably steady in a crew's peripheral vision, or the flicker of a rocket plume from a missile, the chances are that the RWR will light up first. We have already aired this device in the context of SEAD. To reiterate, most fighters are studded with spiral receivers which pick up radar activity in the 0.5–12 GHz frequency range. They process the threat signals into suitable alphanumerics on small dartboard-like crystal video displays located in the cockpit. Range and bearing is shown relative to the target aircraft (which is denoted by the centre or bull's-eye in the display) by the symbol's relative position. The type of threat is denoted by its annotation: '12' for an SA-12 *Gladiator* SAM, an inverted 'V' for an enemy fighter, 'A' for triple-A, and so on. If they start flashing, and the warble warning sounds over the earphones rise in intensity, then that radar type is guiding anti-aircraft weaponry. Time to 'get the pod, and hit the chaff/flares'.

There are some variations on the RWR theme. For example, the Russian MiG-23's Sirena 3-M and newer MiG-29's Beryoza SPO-15 RWRs work on concentric coloured lights. The outer row of yellow show priority threats by type, and the inner green ones their bearing. The L-150 Pastel derivative works in a similar fashion to the F-16C-HTS. It is able to cue ARMs as well as activate countermeasures. However, the philosophy remains the same: hit the countermeasures buttons! First, let us deal with the pods (or internal) radar ECM suite.

In common with many other systems aboard the aircraft, the ECM switchology has been simplified to 'on' and 'off' (with minor subtleties such as Mode A, Mode B, etc). In reality, the devices operate using a number of well-established theoretical techniques which can be roughly divided into noise jamming, and track-breaking (deception). Noise-jamming works much like that generated by the EF-111A Raven to fog enemy radar screens and overload AGCs, but is less selective and not so powerful. It is usually preset on the ground prior to take-off, although more sophisticated jammers can respond with signal noise tailored to the threat on the basis of signals received by the RWR (for example, the Westinghouse AN/ALQ-101(V)-10, which remains in use on board RAF Jaguars).

This technique usually works best when the aircraft is part of a formation. Several aircraft can white out a sector on the enemy radarscope (or its

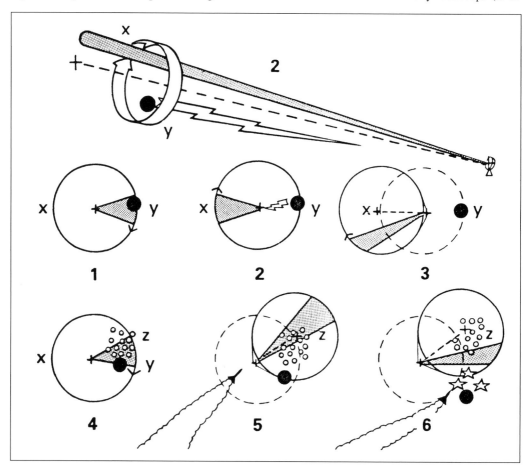

*Fooling a conical-scan radar and related SAMs, first with ECM. **1** The aircraft's receiving systems listen to and analyse the enemy radar emissions so that onboard ECM can subsequently respond with convincing fake echoes (i.e. the same frequency and pattern). **2** The ECM replies with modulated output. When the radar beam is off the aircraft at point X (as depicted) the pod sends out strong fake echoes, and when the beam is on or near the aircraft at point Y, weak or non-existent signals are transmitted by the ECM. This modulated output is repeated over several conical scans. **3** The radar dish now swings its axis over to scan the sky around point X, believing the aircraft to be there. It has now been 'walked off' the aircraft which will disappear from the radarscope. **4** Simultaneously, on receipt of a SAM launch warning chaff is released which blossoms into a distracting cloud at point Z aft of the aircraft. **5** The reflective cloud overdrives the enemy radar automatic gain control, and the dish now swings its axis over to scan the sky around point Z. Command-guided SAMs and radar-directed AAA are directed onto this spot, out of harm's reach, while semi-active radar-homing missiles will similarly be attracted to the radar-painted chaff cloud. Active and towed decoys could also be used with similar results. **6** As a final measure, flares are released. Infrared heat-seeking missiles (or radar-guided ones with terminal IR guidance) may not be fooled by the chaff or jamming pods, so a gaggle of strong-burning sources is used to lure them away*

AGC brains) or create a superblob on the display. Flak and SAMs usually then wind up off the mark, or pass at mid-point, between the aircraft. When used in this fashion, it is a perverse form of countermeasure as it first actually advertises the Flight's position, and then merely aims to make the job of tracking individual aircraft tough. By and large, this approach remains a switch-on-and-leave-on one which lacks the necessary frequency agility to cope with today's more sophisticated tracking radars. And the system breaks down completely when the aircraft depart from their canned formation spreads.

Far better are the track-breakers, which actually generate spoof targets or even cause the enemy radar to break lock altogether. Amongst these devices are the Northrop Grumman AN/ALQ-135 built into the F-15E Eagle DRF, and the F-4G *Wild Weasel*'s external Raytheon AN/ALQ-184 pod. This uses Rotmen lenses – fan-like transmitter arrays – which can direct the jamming power to increase effective radiated power (ERP) by an order of magnitude by electronically focusing the jamming at the chosen threat. Still, the actual signals need to be properly matched to be effective and the techniques used with deception jamming are complex. By and large, they fall into two distinct subcategories, which use frequency-modulated or amplitude-modulated techniques, with the ECM responding automatically when switched on. These systems can usually cope with up to 30 different wave forms spread out over two or three bands.

The first is Range Deception or the Transponder Mode. By taking in the enemy radar pulses, analysing them and then transmitting them back at the radar alongside the echoes, the enemy radar's AGC will more often than not lock on to the ECM signals, as these are stronger and clearer. Once the AGC has locked on to the ECM signals and has begun to ignore the true returns, 'all' that is required is to gradually introduce a time delay between receiving a radar pulse and transmitting back a spurious echo, and increase it. As time of return relates to aircraft range, the increasing delay in the echoes put out by the jammer causes the radar computer to believe that the aircraft is further away than it actually is, throwing SAM and AAA lead-firing angles off the quarry.

False azimuth and elevation data can be generated by getting the pod to reply out of phase. This is especially effective against conical-scan radars which use a narrow beam which quickly and repeatedly scans a tract of sky. Their echoes are strong when the beam hits the aircraft, and non-existent when it misses. So, as the whole radar dish turns towards the last known position of the aircraft, as indicated by the strongest echo, repeater mode signals, matching the radar's output but out of phase with it, can be used to throw it off whack. This works because the ECM signals copy the radar signals but are phased so that when the beam is off the aircraft the ECM transmits strong fake echoes, and when it hits the aircraft (the AGC already having locked-on to the jammer's signals), weak signals are dispatched. The whole radar dish then tends to swivel onto the point in the sky it was looking at when the strong fake returns were received, thus walking it off the target. Over a period of scans – a process conducted in a matter of seconds or less – the enemy guns should be shooting at clouds with SAMs fired off in the wrong direction in pursuit of elusive prey. More complex modulation techniques are required to defeat Doppler and coherent radars. Frequency modulation is used to give false closure rates and false ranges. Modern jamming number-crunching is often surprisingly good at the job.

However, the radar might not be fooled sufficiently to adequately misdirect a SAM which is using infrared terminal homing to catch its quarry. It is here that the chaff and flares come into play, released rapidly as individual cartridges through slots in the dispensers, most of which resemble ice-cube trays. Crews often preselect the rate of release – say, six flares every 2 seconds – or leave the system to work autonomously at full speed on hitting the 'go' knob.

Fundamentally, the chaff cartridges provide a radar-reflective cloud which obscures the target's position by swamping the hunter's radar with false returns. There are hundreds of strips of aluminium or metal-coated plastic ('tinsel') in each cartridge, precut to suitable dipole lengths (quarter wavelengths of most anticipated radar threats). This makes them far more convincing as fake echoes on radar. By simply churning out a sufficient quantity, it is likely that the radar will be fooled into thinking that at least part of the cloud is a target, and will break lock from the fighter. Bulk-chaff dispensers such as the Swedish Philips BOZ 100 series (as equips most Tornadoes) are especially good at this, owing to the sheer volume of chaff. Some American and Russian pods take this one stage further. They can sow a blanketing corridor on receiving suitable RWR inputs and cut the Swiss roll of suspended tinsel into suitable wavelengths as it is being dispensed. For the most part, these dispensers (e.g. the MB Associates AN/ALE-38) were produced in such small numbers that they are used chiefly for EW exercises and systems development, making sure weapons like AMRAAM possess adequate ECCM to function properly in the face of such adversity.

Flare cartridges are intrinsically more simple – electrically ignited magnesium. The magnesium burns with intense heat to distract heat-seeking weapons. However, in practice these do not always work adequately owing to the improved ECCM capabilities built into modern missiles. The Tracor AN/ALE-40 'square-shooter' flare module has become one of the best-selling EW strap-ons in the West. Many are even held in reserve for fitment during times of tension. Many were fitted onto Tornado F.3s at the onset of Operation *Granby* by teams at RAF St Athan. They worked round the clock to produce the bolt-on adaptors. Employing MJB-7 cartridges which were originally introduced on board USAF and Heyl Ha'Avir F-4s 20 years ago, the systems have become a little long in the tooth, and no longer provide full protection.

Their CIS counterparts, ejected from the equally ubiquitous ASO-2W dispenser fitted as standard to many MiGs, Sukhois and transports, still seem to be effective, however. On flight tests against former East German MiG-29s, many NATO aircraft found they could not get an AIM-9M Sidewinder lock in the face of such a fireworks display. During *Desert Storm*, many potential heat kills fell foul of the Russian flares owing to their faster temperature rise which made

them effective that much more rapidly. Conversely, AAM 'rockets' such as the R-73 *Archer* can see through Western flares quite easily. Eighty per cent of Coalition losses were due to IR-homing missiles which were not adequately put off course by the ubiquitous AN/ALE-40 and the US Navy AN/ALE-39 'round-hole' equivalent. The problem lies with the mostly downwards-and-sideways trajectory of their release patterns: it is no longer convincing. The broad but discriminating heat-seeking capabilities of missile seekers in Eastern European AAMs and SAMs easily ignore them. However, that does not mean they are useless – far from it. Timing the proper release of these expendables is the true key to making them function successfully.

Originally, automatic release was preferred. The pioneering F-111, harbinger of so many new technologies, used automatic release. Unfortunately, in those early days when the technology was still maturing, the system was apt to generate many false alarms, and consequently dumped pyrotechnics at the merest sight of the moon, sun or the hazy glaze of a

The unmistakable and bizarre shape of the multi-faceted F-117A Nighthawk stealth fighter. Inlets employ a mesh to diffuse radar waves – engines being a major source of unwanted radar reflections – while exotic and rare metal-based screens are similarly employed over the IRADS sensors and canopy glazing, to preserve electrical continuity. (Lockheed)

Bomb-loading in progress. The F-117A's mission mostly revolves around the use of penetrator BLU-109/B warheads which are adapted with LGB guidance, as with the all-up GBU-10G-J (depicted) or GBU-27A/B. These 1-ton bombs penetrate reinforced concrete before detonating. (Lockheed)

colleague's afterburners. In a high-intensity scenario, this meant exhausting stocks of expendables way too quickly, while the system's eagerness to pop off chaff and flares every time it saw a threat was apt to advertise the fighter's position. As many of the crews made clear, the automatic link was kept switched off most of the time. Consequently it was deleted by the mid-1980s. The technology is now being revived with altogether brand-new sensors known as missile approach warning systems (MAWS).

MAWS relies on ultraviolet detection techniques for much greater discrimination in acquiring missiles. Such may be used for simple alerts, prompting the crew into action, but is really finding a home when allied to directed infrared countermeasures (DIRCM) for altogether more satisfactory self-defence. DIRCM is actually a laser-based system. Perhaps the most successful to date is the US Naval Research Laboratory's *Fly's-Eye* sensor, gradually being reduced in size to a package occupying less than 1 ft³. Using YAG laser rods (of the type normally used in

smart laser designators) doped with holmiun and thulium, they created a high-powered emission at a wavelength of 2 microns that was not available before – ideal for burning the sensitive optics of heat-seeking weapons. The system is scheduled to be fielded after the turn of the century aboard new-generation stealth designs and the US Navy's fleet of F/A-18E/F Hornets and F-14A/D 'Bombcats'.

In the meantime, Tracor Aerospace has switched to its AN/ALE-47 chaff/flare dispenser, which will soon become a mainstay self-defense system. This automatically programmes the ejection based on inputs from the RWR and MAWS suites, enabling it to make smart decisions. Release is sequenced not only according to the threat but also in response to evasive manoeuvres made by the pilot when increased or reduced decoy-dumping might be beneficial. Fully automatic, semi-automatic and manual bypass modes are available, taking the guesswork out of timing a good charge of decoys while at the same time preserving the option of full intervention by the crew.

More significantly, the system is fully compatible with the latest range of active decoys such as Generation-X, which buzz around after release emulating the radar characteristics of the fighter, and towed flares which behave substantially more in keeping with a fighter aircraft to ward off missiles. Larger, active towed decoys are also being developed, such as the GEC-Marconi ARIEL, and Raytheon's ALE-50. The idea is to divert the enemy rockets and cause them to detonate at ranges beyond their lethal blast radius – which may be as large as 1,000 ft!

Tactics, of course, prevail as much as technology. Using terrain to mask the fighter's presence from radar during the infiltration and exfiltration legs of the mission helps, as does judicious use of radar which might be tracked using ground-based or air-based ESM and RWR devices. Other more wily tricks include the use of higher wing-sweep settings on the manual swingers such as the F-111F and MiG-27BN, which might give the false impression that they are going faster than they really are, and therefore would be hard game to catch. Unfortunately most, like the F-14 Tomcat, out of sheer necessity in the ACM environment, use mostly automatic sweep. Then there are the lethal forms of evasion: bomb in face (BIF). With a fighter on their tail at low-level, an attack crew could pickle off a retarded bomb such as a ballute or BL755 and blow their adversary to pieces. Even more sinister, during belly-out manoeuvres performed by the *Pave Tack* F-111C/F or IRADS F-117A, the YAG laser might be squirted in the face of an opponent, blinding him or his IRST.

Standard tactics, however, are more conventional. To execute what is known as a Threat Reaction Manoeuvre: turn and change course rapidly, and jink violently; if that does not shrug off the fighter, unload the aircraft in a negative *g* let-down (assisted by commanding extra wing-sweep from the screwjack drives in the case of an Aardvark or Tornado) while simultaneously piling on the thrust to build up airspeed rapidly to get the hell out of the enemy's clutches in maximum afterburner. Interestingly enough, the newly formed Air Combat Command have effectively disallowed any gun kills from the rear of the remaining fleet of B-52Hs – the only Western aircraft with a sting in their tail – by closing down the BUFF gunner programme. The six-barrelled rubber-cushioned waggler is being removed too. Yet the venerable antique bomber remains most vulnerable when it is egressing with its rear to the enemy's IRST, usually climbing into cooler air to give the crew some respite from the genuinely gruelling leg-wrestling and arm-wrestling contests the pilots endure with the manual flight controls.

Black Plane, Black Bombs

Of course, the whole issue becomes academic if the attacker is protected by the straightforward but ingenious concept of stealth: the science of rendering an aircraft virtually invisible to the enemy's defences. This is achieved with RAM and the elimination of radar-reflective electrical and surface discontinuities.

In common with all better breeds of INT aircraft, the famed F-117A Nighthawk stealth fighter has been

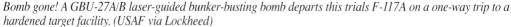

Bomb gone! A GBU-27A/B laser-guided bunker-busting bomb departs this trials F-117A on a one-way trip to a hardened target facility. (USAF via Lockheed)

Former stealth boss Tony Tolin's F-117A undergoes an inspection prior to its departure from Tonopah TRA, Nevada for the 1990 airshow circuit. The DCCs' use of breathing masks is puzzling – perhaps a spin-off from the RAM coatings? (Lockheed)

subjected to constant updates ever since it achieved IOC in August 1983. These have been usually conducted during IRAN or PDM cycles at Plant 42 under the scrutiny of Lockheed's Palmdale facility. First came the switch to metal-bottomed graphite reinforced thermoplastic fins following the loss of a 'flipper' during side-slip in a supersonic excursion (the pilot recovered safely).

Beginning in late 1987, not long after two 'Bat Planes' were lost during night-training operations , an Offensive Combat Improvement Program (OCIP) was initiated. This added an up-front control panel beneath the Kaiser HUD (a feature it shares in common with many Teenagers, providing ready access to those switch functions not always accessible via HOTAS). It also added two colour displays either side. This update was still in its early days at the outbreak of the Gulf War. It introduced Harris STARS terrain data stored on magnetic disc along with a drive to flash this up as an electronic moving map on either one of the new colour MFDs. The electronic map is laced with speed,

altitude and target heading plus relative position, to which could be cued the F-117A's automatic target-tracking Infrared Acquisition and Designation System (IRADS) made by Texas Instruments. This reduced pilot workload during the critical target acquisition and tracking phase of the attack. New auto-throttles which trimmed airspeed automatically to ensure good TOTs, were also added, aiding the pilot still further.

However, only seven of the 56 F-117As extant at the end of 1990 had been re-equipped with the OCIP updates. Owing to the sensitive nature of the new technology they were kept at home at Tonopah Test Range Airfield, along with a further seven machines in for deep maintenance or being held in reserve as trainers with the 417th TFS. So the total war party deployed to Khamis in Saudi Arabia comprised only 42 aircraft. Nevertheless, the F-117A deserved much of the glamour reputation it accrued during *Desert Storm*.

IRADS, the heart of the F-117A's offensive kit, comprises two wide-aperture infrared sensors akin in

The BDU-46/B white 'training shape' emulates in all but explosive thermonuclear destructiveness the characteristics of its operational sibling, the B83. Nearly half the weapon is taken up by a Kevlar para-braking parachute for laydown LADD/dual bomb timer deliveries. The smaller B61 has a more sinister, utterly pristine alumunium finish with a reddish-brown fibreglass tip. Stocks of these devices are being reduced as part of the Bush–Yeltsin accords signed in 1991. (USAF)

function to the single one used in *Pave Tack*. One is forward looking (known as the FLIR), the other downward looking (unimaginatively known as the DLIR). Both have wide FoV general scan, and narrow FoV target tracking zoom modes. Given the one-man cockpit, an extremely accurate INS was a prerequisite.

Lockheed, in the 'Skunk Works' tradition, bought, borrowed or scrounged the best they could, adopting the B-52G/H's SPN-GEANS inertial platform. This employs an electrostatically suspended gyro based on a spinning beryllium ball that comes within five-millionths of an inch of being perfectly round. Inertial movements converted into electrical signals provide phenomenal accuracy in terms of speed, up/down and left/right movement. Barring complete SPN-GEANS failure, which occurs every 400 hours of flight-time, it cues the IRADS very precisely indeed, and holds it in place for automatic lock on through the laser-squirting bomb run with only minor trim adjustments from the

pilot. It has to be this good in the absence of tell-tale ground-mapping radar (although LPI SAR HRM radar might be installed in the future).

Moreover, in the Gulf, target discrimination relied upon extraordinary skill, especially in built-up areas where individual buildings had to be picked out, using only satellite snaps and easily recognized initial and offset features as an aid. However, once the target had been found and locked into place, the IRADS/SPN-GEANS laser spot accuracy was in the order of 1–1.5 ft. It was this staggering accuracy in laser placement that made the Bat Plane such a success in the Gulf: 95 per cent of its bombs struck true.

Imagine riding the tip of a 25-ton velvet-black angular arrowhead with a target to strike, knowing that the FBW system is the only thing that stops your fighter from flat-spinning down into the flak. Such were some of the fears of the F-117A pilots going into combat for the first time with only inertial-guidance

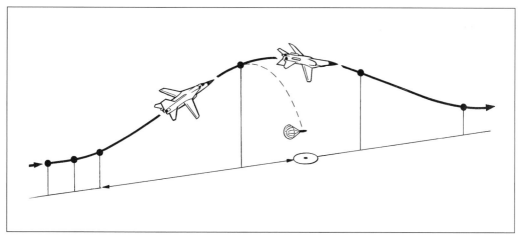

Nuclear Terminal Laydown Delivery: The LADD and dual-bomb timer profile used airspeeds well in excess of 550 knots (the absolute minimum), a 3–4 g pull-up and inverted dive back towards the ground to build up speed during the egress, immediately following weapons release. The B61 could be fused for an air or surface burst, and time-delayed if required.

aided infrared sensors to guide them, and an almost non-existent self-defence package (which might otherwise betray the aircraft's presence, owing to the radar-reflective lumps and bumps associated with these devices). Stealth itself deflects and absorbs the radar energy that directs SAMs and triple-A – but offers scant protection against heavy shells the way an A-10A's titanium 'bathtub' shroud might. During the initial phase of the Gulf War there were up to 9,000 artillery pieces of various calibres available to Iraq which could deal such a mortal blow.

The F-117A's structure mostly comprises aluminium alloys wrapped in radar-absorbent material (RAM), and so is just as prone as its non-stealthy stable-mates to pot-shots from a sharp-shooter. Night merely adds the welcome cloak of darkness. Stealth characteristics give it the ability to operate at cruise heights in excess of FL180, out of range of the lighter gunfire which in theory should pop off harmlessly below. Few flyers had any illusions. A golden BB (a lucky shot) might have caused considerable mischief, and sent an F-117A tumbling. In that event, while wondering 'Can I regain control, safe attitude, altitude and pull through?', and anticipating a thump in the saddle prior to ejection, the pilot would also have to be thinking about setting the self-destruct buttons to blow-up top secret portions of his aircraft into fragments.

During combat it was much more mundane. Two types of 'Bat Bomb' were employed, both bunker-busting LGBs built around the 2,000 lb *Have Void* BLU-109/B warhead: the GBU-10-Improved (GBU-10G-J/B), and the GBU-27A/B. The former employed

a Paveway II unit, while the GBU-27A/B had a Paveway III proportional guidance section which was specially clipped to fit the F-117A's bomb bay, and Paveway II tail groups. The latter common configuration allowed for a slightly quicker descent, adding momentum to the penetrating warhead. Three-quarters of this were strengthened steel and only one-quarter Tritonal explosive. It proved capable of punching through 12 ft of reinforced concrete at oblique strike angles of up to 60°. The LGBs guided to target under the IRADS cross-hairs in just the same fashion as the systems employed by the other laser bombers, except that the F-117As tended mostly to fly more shallow manoeuvres. This was possible because they were shielded by stealthy RAM coatings and the angular airframe which reflected what little radar energy that was not absorbed away from the enemy's terminal threat acquisition and tracking radars.

The 37th TFW(P) clocked up 1,271 sorties of 5.5 hours' average duration (around 7,000 combat hours in total) during *Desert Storm*. They initially focused on communications and headquarters facilities, then took out chemical weapons and nuclear test facilities, before being relegated to lesser-value targets such as LoCs (bridges), and airfield HASs as smart bomb-trucks.

It was the initial strikes, and the astonishing imagery generated by IRADS, which made the news footage on most TV reports as the air war unfolded. Sorties were launched beginning in the late afternoon around dusk, so that two or three waves could be put up each night. The 37th TFW(P) alone accounted for 31 per cent of all critical targets knocked out during

NATO NUCLEAR WEAPONS

Designation	AUW (lb)	Yield	Production	IOC	Training Shape Equivalent
B57 Mod 0-11	500–510	variable, 5–20 kilotons	1963–1970	1964	BDU-12/B
WE177	950	50 kilotons	classified	1966	conventional high-drag bombs
B61 Mod 0-82	718–765	variable, 10–500 kilotons	1967–1987	1968	BDU-38/B
B83	2,408	variable, 1–2 megatons	1981+	1984	BDU-46/B
W80 (AGM-86B ALCM)	3,200	200 kilotons	1979–1987	1981	unarmed ALCM

1. Being phased-out. Was also available as an air-delivered nuclear depth charge.
2. The weapons family features selectable yields in the 100-kiloton and 500-kiloton range, with a special low 10-kiloton option. Later Mod models comprise updates.

the first 24 hours of *Desert Storm*. Overall, the pilots averaged 21 sorties each, the F-117As 30 sorties each, with several aircraft logging well over the average. No losses were incurred throughout the entirety of *Desert Storm*, nor in subsequent combat actions at the time of writing, and the F-117A can still boast an unmatched safety record for a modern jet fighter.

Updates are continuing today. The latest Weapons System Improvement effort is replacing the cumbersome SPN-GEANS with a Honeywell H-423/E RLG, offering INS accuracy of less than 0.22 nm/hr drift. It is also receiving the flush F-22 GPS Navstar receiver, making it compatible with new smart bombs as well as providing a fail-safe and update in case of partial or total INS failure. An upgraded IRADS featuring bigger optics, probably based on mercury–cadmium telluride sensor technology, is also in progress. The exit slots of the famous platypus shrouds are receiving flame-damping improvements too, to improve aircraft survivability (so-called because the acoustic and infrared attenuating shrouds bear a remarkable similarity to the snout of their antipodean mammal namesake; exhaust from the pair of F404-GE-F1D2 turbofans is vented through these two ASTECH nickel alloy type 718 shrouds).

Capping it all, spray-on stealth coatings are constantly evolving. With their 20 dBm-2 signal reduction characteristics adding to an already astonishingly low RCS, they are capable of unsettling an enemy fighter pilot whose only sense of an F-117A's presence might be an unnerving aerodynamic disturbance as he flies past his elusive quarry and into its aerodynamic wake. In all likelihood, he would this put down to wind shear or some other meteorological phenomenon. And if he was flying an FBW type he wouldn't notice a thing. More than one F-15 pilot has confirmed, off the

record, flying past an F-117A in daylight without having received a hint of it on radar.

Much of the USAF F-117A stock will continue to be gradually improved in subtle ways. Before long, it will begin to tout bombloads externally for use after air superiority has been established. *Have Slick*, and stealthy RAM-coated derivatives of JDAM, JSOW and Shark are scheduled to be bolted to its zig-zag-tipped weapons-bay doors. Missiles do not form part of its repertoire.

There is another mostly unspoken-about weapon in the F-117A's arsenal: the B61 thermonuclear bomb. Up to two of these may be carried in the weapons bay (though one would suffice for most tasks, given its explosive power of a 'mere' 10 kilotons). Topping-out at Mach 0.9 at 20,000 ft, the pilot would be already cocooned behind hood flash-curtains. He may also be preparing to shut down some of the unhardened FBW systems to avoid the electromagnetic pulse generated by a nuclear explosion which might burn up some of the delicate microchips, ready to rely on partial hydromechanical controls. A worrying scenario. In fact, to everyone's relief, it is something which the F-117A will in all probability never have to perform. As the general thinking goes, first put forward by former chairman of the US Joint Chiefs of Staff, Gen Colin Powell: 'In anything short of a general war, or need for a nuclear retaliation, conventional precision-guided munitions are as capable at target destruction, and much less controversial.'

However, no self-respecting book on modern fighter technology would bypass the controversial nuclear issue, or the value of such weapons as a deterrent in a troubled world plagued by nuclear proliferation. Just about every high-performance military aircraft built since 1945 has the potential to deliver nuclear weapons. During the Cold War years, they flourished alongside the expanding air power, and not wholly coincidentally. What changed most over the years was the introduction of thermonuclear weapons offering much greater yields than their cruder atomic forebears. Thermonuclear weapons also added greater handling safety and reliability. Moreover, they had significantly more dynamic modes of delivery compared with the relatively straight-and-level attacks on Japan in 1945, in keeping with the burgeoning anti-aircraft radar threat.

By 1970, the low-angle drogue delivery (LADD) and its digital equivalent the dual bomb timer system were in vogue. They offered a number of delivery techniques in concert with full fuzing options (FUFO) introduced on later models of the B61, America's latest thermonuclear weapon. This provides optional yields of between 10 kilotons and 0.5 megatons (depending on its tactical or strategic application), amounting to between 0.5 and 25 times the power of the bombs dropped on Hiroshima and Nagasaki!

The weapon can be in-flight selected and armed for one of a number of deliveries, including slick and retarded laydown.

Slick delivery is free-fall from a lofting manoeuvre. This would typically entail a Half Cuban Eight or Idiot Loop 4 *g* pull-up at up to 70°–75° with the bomb being released at the apex of the climb before the attacker winged-over and ducked-out at full speed. Retarded laydown at 550 knots IAS minimum uses a telescope-activated Kevlar (formerly nylon) 17 ft-diameter parachute to ensure the attacker could get the hell out and evade the weapon's impending shock wave. The weapons can be set for air-burst, immediate-contact surface-burst (when dropped from altitude), and delayed surface-burst (when employing retarded laydown). Delivery is based on a nuclear IP on radar, at which point the clock starts counting down to automatic pickle, delivering the weapon over its intended target. The detonation modes cater for different targets. For example, a sprawling one such as an industrial complex would be best destroyed by an air-burst, whereas a hardened C^3 facility would require a pinpoint surface-burst. USAFE crews knew the B61 as the silver bullet ('like Coors Lite, it doesn't slow you down'). More jocular, vulgar trade

France's Armée de l'Air and Aéronavale both use nuclear-tipped missiles, such as this AMSP being carried by a Super Etendard, as part of their nuclear deterrent – the Force de Frappe. They are unique in employing such devices on ostensibly tactical fighter aircraft. (B. Thouanel via Dassault Aviation)

names for the mission included 'Warming the homes in Winter – Warsaw Pact Central Heating', or 'The Mushroom Squad' ('kept in the dark and fed on bullshit').

Much the same manoeuvres are applicable to the virtually identical British equivalent, the WE177. This and the standard Russian tactical thermonuclear devices were loosely based on the American B57, precursor to the B61, using either military liaison or espionage. Britain's WE177 offers a 50-kiloton yield and became operational during 1966. Some 100 remain in use for use aboard Tornadoes. However, the heady days of 'Alert' are long since over.

On both sides of the former Iron Curtain, the major threats are perceived to be the emerging Third World nuclear powers, such as North Korea, which may have fewer reservations about employing such weapons. Having said that, some right-wing Russians seeking a move back towards superpower status in the face a woefully troubled economy have not ruled out some aggressive sabre-rattling with their own weapons. Britain views its WE177 purely as hedge against possible nuclear brushfire wars threatening members of the Commonwealth, or lunatic aggression by 'nations unknown'.

France, which suffers less domestic ambivalence towards nuclear technology as a whole, is progressing towards longer-ranged stand-off missiles, possibly making it the only nation in Europe to be still chasing this technology. Currently, Armée de l'Air Mirage 2000N/D and IVP fighters fulfil this role, along with Aéronavale Super Etendards, employing the Aérospatiale Air Sol Moyenne Portée (ASMP). Tactics are classified. It is likely that the 186-mile range weapon, packing a solid-propellant booster to zoom it to altitude before a ramjet sustainer kicks in, is launched at low-to-medium heights and follows a trajectory carefully programmed into the missile prior to take-off. Mirage 2000N/Ds, in particular, with a sizeable terrain-referenced database on board their navigation computers, would also be able to launch the ASMP at precise coordinates and headings at extremely low-level. As back-up, the French still employ CEA AN-22 and AN-52 free-fall gravity bombs, though these are of greater use in demolishing submarines and shipping.

As France's quite substantial arsenal has not been factored into the NATO versus Warsaw Pact balance of power since President Charles De Gaulle took his country out of the 16-nation Western Alliance in 1966 (specifically so France could pursue a nuclear deterrent – the Force de Frappe – on a go-it-alone basis), the French continue to possess one of the most potent aerial nuclear arsenals. It is sandwiched west of Ukraine and east of the North American seaboard. US 'dual-key' B61s previously possessed by Germany, Italy and Turkey have been wound down as an adjunct to the Bush–Yeltsin accords, which continue under President Clinton. Hopefully, it is the end of an irksome era, one in which the world habitually held its breath every time a major international incident flared-up. But in its modern keyed-down level it remains part and parcel of most INT crews' briefings – just in case.

Chapter Five

RECOVERY

At this stage in our overall perspective of modern air power, the aircraft in one strike package will be completing their interwoven taskings and those in another will be preparing to repeat the whole process. If air power is to succeed, it must be relentless. Ironically, outbound fighter crews will probably have a more up-to-date picture of events from a cable or satellite news network long before word gets through on the grapevine. Such is the power of today's all-seeing, often obtrusive media.

Once the vul time specified in the frag is completed, the crews will prepare to depart enemy airspace. That is, having done the job – Capping, SEAD, bombing – and evaded all the major threats with a reasonably healthy aircraft, it is time to head back to base; in peacetime, the comfort of home in the literal sense; in wartime, back to a dormitory or tent, possibly without a drop of beer in sight if hosted by allies with Muslim sensibilities to respect.

Before crossing the border, with the aircraft now much lighter, their stores having been expended and weight of fuel down, typical cruising altitudes are in the upper twenties to low thirties if air superiority has been accomplished. The first task on the agenda is to re-form and check on aircraft and aircrew status, visually at this stage (communications are resumed only after crossing into friendly airspace), using an agreed join-up coordinate and time stipulated in the mission plan. Hopefully, everyone is present and correct. By night, radar and JTIDS, with some input from AWACS, are the primary references, followed perhaps by judicious glowing of afterburners by Flight Lead – or torching by an Aardvark – to help stray wingmen formate, like a mother duck squawking and wagging her rear. If it is a daytime mission, then the Flight usually rendezvous roughly as planned, but are dispersed. They see each other but don't talk. The Flight or Section Leaders will rock their wings, and the aircraft merge on visual references.

Spike Benyshek resumes the procedures from the front seat of his F-4G: 'As he comes on board, we give him a visual signal with thumb and forefinger that looks like a check mark. This is the comm-out signal for battle damage check.' This is not only a check for battle damage *per se*, including that self-inflicted by ordnance, but also is 'a chance to ensure no hydraulic leaks or missing panels, etc. as we prepare to land. The wingman manoeuvres up and down and underneath our aircraft, looking us over. As he does so, we examine him as well. Both satisfied, we give each other a thumbs-up.'

Resuming radio communications once over the border, first comes the ticking register with AWACS, which often will provide an update on the weather conditions back at base and possibly suggest a suitable diversion if it is deemed necessary. There might be fog

An Aussie Aardvark demonstrates the 'torching' technique, an airshow stopper which has some tactical applications – to help stray wingmen reformate at night, but primarily to burn off excess fuel prior to landing (especially in an emergency shortly after take-off). (Author)

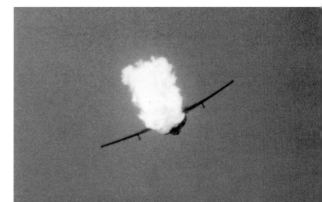

Hornet-four: a neat join-up in formation at the conclusion of their sortie. (Raytheon)

at the critical final stage of descent blanketing out even the runway lights. There might be a complex launch or recovery going on in response to an urgent or sensitive requirement, possibly even a rescue taking place with an airstrip covered in debris. Or the runway might have been torn to pieces by an enemy attack and is full of giant potholes. Many strikers replenish their virtually exhausted fuel reserves at this stage too, though the relatively free-ranging patrollers such as the Cappers and Weasel Police, which would have returned for top-ups every 2 hours or so during their vul time, should still possess adequate reserves – they would plan it this way. The strikers usually have fuel first and foremost on their minds. Top-ups are typically geared for just prior to entering, and just after exiting, enemy airspace at either end of their mission vul time.

What follows is usually a sequence of repeating BIT checks on the avionics and noting anything that is giving trouble. Crews might also reflect on the nearly empty chaff/flare dispensers, and the close misses. The Gulf War Tornado Dhahran Detachment alone, comprising 21 GR.1/1As, consumed 21,330 bundles

of chaff and sucked-in over two million kilograms of kerosene through their probes during multiple AAR rendezvous. It is such statistics which make modern air power so impressive.

'Still 150 miles away from base, we call the squadron and pass our maintenance codes: the condition of the aircraft which alerts Maintenance to any problems they will have to trouble-shoot.' These codes are vital when aircraft are scheduled to be relaunched again shortly after recovery for another mission with a fresh crew. Code One is an aircraft in perfect working order; Code Two, one which has a minor write-up that can often be corrected during integrated combat turnaround (ICT); while Code Three signifies a more serious problem which will require the aircraft to be pulled from the flight-line and wiped off the operations roster until it is fixed. The gravity of Codes Two and Three varies considerably with the type of aircraft. A modern fighter built with maintainability in mind through extensive use of LRUs, such as the F-16, can usually have a radar or other problem repaired *in situ* during the ICT process when the aircraft is fuelled and bombed-up in less than an hour, using the take-it-out-and-replace-it LRUs. An older jet like the F-4, or a more complex machine like the F-117A, would in all likelihood be towed away for specialist treatment in the hangars before it was deemed fit for duty. Russian Zveno and Para would provide similar reports to their ground troops, and trust that they might be turned around, personally, in a freshly serviced example. Russian philosophy is to keep going or quit, and not take things at a steady pace.

At this point the returning aircraft switch to Approach Control.

'Director, Bud Six-One, 100 miles out, flight level 3–2–0.'

'Bud, radar contact, descent pilot's discretion to 2,500 ft, altimeter 30.03.'

'Bud is out of 3–2–0 for 2,500, 30.03.'

We will usually begin our descent at 90–100 miles from home, and descend at 330–350 knots. Typical arrivals during the day will be to an overhead pattern [otherwise known as a visual circuit], with the Flight coming in twos or fours. If it is night, or the weather is

poor, we will remain together until a 15-mile final, then the wingman will 'drag' to allow about 5 miles separation between aircraft for a 'straight-in'.

The overhead pattern is normally entered from about 10 miles out. We approach the runway on centreline, at about 1,500 ft, 350 knots. At about 5 miles out, we rock the wings – the signal for Two to join to close, a position about 5 feet out and 3 feet lower than us, and for this runway, on our right (as it is a left-hand pattern). As we fly over the approach end of the runway, we look left to make sure the downwind leg is clear of air traffic. We look at Two, twirl a hand, and hold up five fingers. This is the signal for the break; the five fingers means five seconds spacing between aircraft in the break. Looking ahead again, we snap the stick over and roll into 60°–70° of bank, and pull. The 2 g break is a continuous turn to downwind, and slows us from our initial speed to one compatible for landing. About halfway through the turn, we make a slight power reduction, to about 85 per cent. Airspeed is slowing through 275 knots.

As we roll out on downwind, the airspeed is below 250 – the landing gear handle is pushed down, and the

A KA-6D Intruder tanker on final approach to its carrier, the USS John F. Kennedy – *that tiny object just visible through the left windshield! An ACLS, mirror landing aid and a Landing Signals Officer to wave the jet away if it is coming in too fast, short or long are the current safety measures used at sea. The technique of 'trapping' is really the subject of a separate book. Of special interest here is the pilot's TV artificial horizon display. The Intruder was the first to introduce such technology. (Grumman)*

flap switch is pushed down. The gear drops with a clunk – the nose usually locks first, in about 3 seconds, followed by the mains at about 6–7 seconds. The flaps are protected by a speed switch, and they usually do not begin to move until about 220–210 knots (even though they are certified to 250). We call out to the back-seater: 'Three down, out and down, anti-skid on, light out, good pressure, landing light.' We all increase power slightly to hold about 200 knots in this dirty configuration. 'Out and down' refers to the slats being out, the flaps being down. 'Anti-skid on, light out' means the switch is on and the associated warning light is not illuminated. 'Good pressure' means the Utility Hydraulic Pressure is holding steady.

If any of these items is awry, such as loss of utility hydraulics, then the pilot might be obliged to make a straight-in at high speed so as to maintain lift and stability and 'take a wire' – a BAK arresting cable or net strung across the runway. This becomes acute in variable-geometry aircraft such as the Tomcat and

Tornado which rely on full forward sweep and deployed leading-edge and double-slotted trailing-edge flaps for critical lift at normal landing speeds. A Tornado with its wings stuck back at 45° would have to come in at up to 220–230 knots.

Similar emergencies might be created by battle damage or a mid-air nudge, such as happened to Glen Perry and Ken 'Alley Cat' Alley during the Vietnam War. Having lost several feet off the wing of their F-111A, Perry headed for the emergency strip at Udorn, Thailand, squealing on the runway at a dramatic 240 knots (like finding then hitting a motorway at nearly 277 mph!). 'Lowering the tailhook after passing the approach-end BAK-12 arresting barrier, he didn't realize there was also a BAK-9 barrier at mid-field. He took out the BAK-9 and carried it all the way down to the departure-end BAK-12, which he caught successfully,' according to one of his colleagues. Most land-based fighters are equipped with a tailhook for precisely this contingency, even though they may never see sight of

Land-based jets also use a hook, during emergencies. An RF-4C 'Photo-Phantom' from the Edwards AFB-based Test Pilot School demonstrates just how, using an All-American Engineering mobile arrestor gear. These so-called BAKs and mobile arrestor systems are to be found at all good fighter bases. (William Bridges via AAE)

The more conventional approach, with rudder and nosewheel moving in unison. Note the differential tail slab movement being used to correct for crosswinds. (Peter E. Davies)

a carrier deck and the airframes are not stressed for 'traps' at sea.

Assuming all is going well with the overhead pattern approach . . .

We are approaching the 'perch point', which is the point from which we will start our continuous turn to final. When the runway threshold is 45° behind the wing-line, or 135° from the nose [of the Phantom], you are at the perch.

'Tower, Bud Six-One, base, gear down, stop on the left.'

'Bud, the wind 330 at 10, cleared to land runway 3–4 left.'

'Bud Six-One.'

At the perch, we roll to about 45°–60° of bank. Normal airspeed coming off the perch is 180–200 knots. Air Force aircraft have an aural tone system, which gives the pilot an indication of AoA through the pitch of a tone, modulated by pulses. One of the many uses of the headset. It is an excellent system, and allows the pilot to fly the correct airspeed without reference to his airspeed indicator. [Many US Navy aircraft, prior to the wholesale introduction of HUD pointers as back-up to the automatic carrier-landing system, had to rely on a tiny 'chevrons and donuts' indicator, and it is to this that Spike is alluding in extolling the virtues of the aural indicator.] This

permits us to concentrate our view on the runway.

About halfway through the turn, the bank angle starts to decrease, as we see we will be able to roll out on final without going wide ('overshooting', which means something else entirely to an RAF aviator [approaching 'long' and going around]). As the bank angle decreases, power is modulated as we slow to 'on-speed'. This airspeed will vary according to gross weight, but will always be 19.2 units AoA [in the slatted F-4]. The term 'units' does not refer to an angle; rather, it is an arbitrary calibration of the AoA indicator.

The F-4, despite its wobbly characteristics 'on the boom', behaves very well on approach; and the newer American Teenagers are even easier to land, assisted by FBW and other self-adjusting stability augmentation systems. The MiG-23 *Flogger*, however, can be a bear in the circuit when speeds are below 150 knots, and pilots who fly the type advocate 'clockwork, by-the-book, long approaches, airliner-style if at all possible'. Of course, the later American Teenagers and Russian twin-turbofan types are a breeze by comparison. Spike Benyshek again:

Now on about a half-mile final, we double-check the landing gear, and concentrate for the landing. The indicated airspeed will be in the vicinity of 170–180 knots [high, as a result of the head wind; true airspeed in, say, Northern Europe with a MiG-29 will be something like 140 knots across the piano keys in a flat approach; a semi-delta-winged F-117A, with only flaps to assist with slow-speed lift, will come in at around 165 knots, depending on headwinds.] We concentrate on a spot 500 ft down the runway from the threshold. This is our desired touchdown spot. Control of glide path and airspeed is similar to that in light aircraft: if the touchdown spot is drifting up in our windscreen, we will end up short. If it is going down in our windscreen, we will go long. Glide path is most easily controlled with power, while refinement of AoA is generally controlled with the stick, although the two are always interdependent. Down now to 10 ft above the runway, we flare, or raise the nose slightly to reduce our sink rate (or 'round-out').

Correcting for wind with the rudder booted in is not uncommon. Side-slip for big-tailed aircraft like the Tornado or EF-111A Raven might mean exercising a wing-low, rudder-correction technique using 'crab' (the nose pointing left or right of the approach path) at 10° or more, depending on the limits of the main gears. These contact the runway first and might cause severe headaches if a tyre blows.

Flame-Out Approach: A flame-out approach, also known as deadstick landing, is possible even in today's jets, but requires considerable cool. Most pilots would prefer to eject.

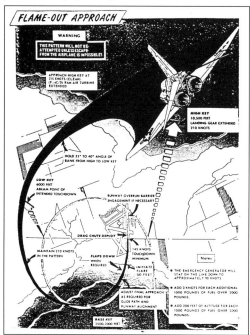

If we were to have performed a straight-in, we would have maintained 300 knots, and called for our wingman to drag at about 15 miles. He would go to idle and deploy his speed brake. As he slowed through 250, he would have configured with gear and flaps, and slowed to 180 knots. We, having maintained 300 knots until 10 miles, will end up 5 miles in front of Two. Now we can perform individual landings in conditions when visual separation is not possible, such as night or poor weather [or the emergency conditions described previously, requiring 'taking a cable'].

These speeds are not atypical of modern fighters as a whole, and there exist two universal techniques for touchdown, depending on the aircraft's pedigree. Aircraft with a Navy heritage can be slammed onto the runway in a no-flare landing, which instantaneously scrubs 10–20 knots of airspeed off the indicator. Even the F-111 can do this, using its misnamed giant Variable Terrain High-Flotation Landing Gear (using a pair of C-130 Hercules wheels) to cushion the blow. However, it can be unnecessarily abusive to less well-built aircraft or ones prone to hydraulic breakages. A good flare technique, on the other hand, permits the fighter to be placed back on *terra firma* more gently, and scores points from the ground troops. The RAF's venerable Buccaneer S.2, for example, which was fitted with a belly fuel tank holding 3,500 lb of fuel, would have split like a haemorrhaged gut and gushed volatile fuel everywhere had it attempted a Navy-style, no-flare on deck with this refit.

Since runway length is not usually a problem for non-seafaring folk (although F-117A pilots always demand a 2-mile runway for safety), most land-based pilots use the flared landing technique as routine. Flying gliders, albeit far removed from jet fighters, will explain why – thump!! Braking and slowing to taxi speeds, however, quickly becomes an issue. With minimal braking only and no other assistance, most fighters will guzzle up 7,000 ft of runway – though just over half that distance with heavy braking, which is not good for the undercarriage either. In some Latin American countries where spares have become a problem, the crews get reprimanded if they don't use flare techniques or as little braking as possible; they actually stop on the runway, to be towed away by tractor! They are similarly pre-positioned at the EOR for take-off. This cuts down wear-and-tear on the hydraulics and tyres, but engineers have added their various bags of tricks to ease this what is probably the most demanding of all tasks for a thoroughly exhausted flyer.

There are a number of devices used to reduce speed rapidly on touchdown, usually deployed using a lever or switch on the left forward console near the

A large drag chute is in evidence as this F-117A kills speed during the roundout. (USAF)

pilot's hip: the ring-slot drag chute, airbrakes or 'boards', and thrust reversing. The drag chute is standard fare for the F-4, hotter MiGs and F-117A, and employed by some F-16 operators who need it to correct for directional instability on icy runways. Airbrakes are of the type which pop out from the top and rear of the American Teenagers and latest Russian fighters as an aerodynamic brake. Thrust reversing, by use of deflector buckets which swing down and clamp shut behind the exhaust nozzles to redirect thrust forwards, is standard on the Tornado. All of these methods are remarkably efficient if the hydraulics are working as advertised, or in the case of the drag chutes, if they are properly packed.

Nosewheel steering, anti-skid and brakes become critical at this stage on wet runways. A phenomenon known as hydroplaning – skating uncontrollably on a wet or icy surface due to loss of grip – can happen on even grooved runways which minimize this problem. Just as prior to launch, the bulldozers and brushsweepers will have been busy, pushing away snow, ice, rain and hoovering up debris. They trundle

out to the apron and runway and repeat their antics with every subsequent movement. It is ongoing at snowy bases, like a series of toy trucks on display in a shop window at Christmas time, round and round the base all day. In aircraft featuring narrow-track (minimum distance between the main gears) and big fins, such as the F-104 Starfighter, there's usually a need for a good amount of corrective rudder too, to prevent 'weather-cocking'.

Having slowed down to taxi speed, the aircraft clear the main runway along an assigned tributary, allowing room for the next fighter to come in. 'Cleared' by Ground Control, the crew then amble along to de-arm at the departure end of the runway, where they dump the drag chute (if applicable) and do in reverse what they did prior to launch: safety pins are installed, and canopy hoods opened up. Made safe, the aircraft then proceed back to their parking positions or HASs, where the machines are shut down using a defined checklist, and pushed back in by a chugging diesel tractor.

Taxiing back to the hardstands, post-mission, with drag chutes billowing in their wake, a pair of F-4 crews open up the canopies and breathe the fresh air. However, there are copious shutdown procedures to follow before they alight from the cockpits. (Frank B. Mormillo)

In the case of the SR-71A Blackbird, shutdown procedures consume as much as 45 minutes. The inimitable shape of the beast still inspires wonder, 35 years after it first flew, and conjures up the description by the designer of the masterpiece, the late Clarence 'Kelly' Johnson: 'Like a snake swallowing three mice'. (Frank B. Mormillo)

A BDR trainer dangles from a crane. In wartime, BDR teams patch-up damaged aircraft and pluck or bulldoze wrecked ones off the runway. Obsolescent fighters provide the means for the 'metal-benders' to practice their skills without wreaking havoc on the expensive serviceable hardware! (Tim P. Laming)

As engine power is lost, so is hydraulic power, and each aircraft's flight controls resume their relaxed posture. In the case of twin-turbofan-engined machines like the F-14, F-15 and F-111, this can occur before the nozzles close up, leaving dilated the last one to be shut down, frozen in motion, like a giant pupil. Unplugged, the aircrew alight from the cockpit and swap notes with the ground crew once again, shake and slap hands, salute or exchange thumbs-up for any kills (which the DCC will proudly stencil-spray onto his or her aircraft), and note any discrepancies contained in the aircraft forms. These new write-ups can be a major nuisance, but tend to be repetitive on particular aircraft, and are often never fully resolved until IRAN refurbishment cycles crop up, and the beast is magically transformed into a seemingly factory-fresh example. The whole write-up cycle is then repeated: ground crews check through the manuals and fix what they can before the next launch, noting what they cannot fix because of lack of spares, 'an aircrew as opposed to a systems malfunction', or time. Depending on the urgency of the situation, time factors are negotiable.

Meanwhile, our intrepid aviators will have already reported back to their squadron building to log their flying time, and will be searching out a comfortable chair in the debrief room. Debrief might take only a few minutes, or may consume a couple of hours. In essence, it is designed to cover the mission – what went right, what went wrong, and what could have been done better. Cappers, SEAD and Raven crews, who spend more time studying academics on the latest threats during special briefings than agonizing during debriefs, may adjourn to the bar, canteen or bed only after 20–30 minutes of 'candid discussion'.

For the deep-strikers and 'recces', who have unloaded videotape of the AVTR/VCR targeting imagery as well as cockpit displays and, perhaps, banks of celluloid that are being processed 'wet' from the PI's cabin, not to mention radio recordings and downloaded DTMs or mission pods, may be about to recount their mission in excruciating detail – in peacetime, anyway. In combat, unless there are complex incidents to recount and sort out, the process is often simply a case of how adept an exhausted flyer is at tossing his now obsolescent mission folder into

Completing the mission may entail a milestone, and receiving a soaking! Here, Maj John Long is given a ceremonial hosing-down following his 3,000th flying hour in the F-111. Such bravado prevails throughout operational units (Dick Brown)

the bin at 10 paces; Vietnam veteran Tony Sobol jokingly gestured an over-the-shoulder movement when quizzed on this. Even during the *Linebacker II* era in South-East Asia, the enemy could have made much out of yesterday's paperwork, had they chosen to retrieve it. Modern systems like the MSS and PALOMA, and video recordings, keep a much tighter lid on it all, using encrypted material that is gobbledegook to the uninitiated – if they can hack into it – and quickly runs past its useful date.

Spike concludes his story:

It is now 7 or 8 hours after we first entered the squadron. It has been a long day, and we are physically drained. And our day may not be over yet. Every member of the squadron has an 'additional' duty, an office job besides our primary duty of flying. We may spend several more hours in the squadron accomplishing these duties until we finally go back to our quarters.

A couple of beers and a well-earned rest ('climbing up to 1 ft 6 in and levelling out' on a cot) are usually on the roster, along with light duty the next day, before the whole process starts up for them all over again.

For the DCC and his aides, the working cycle is resumed when the aircraft is returned, shut down and chocked. During the Gulf War, crews typically worked in 12-hour shifts (day or night). In the extreme heat of combat (in both senses of the word, as temperatures reached 49 °C in the midday sun), they might launch their machine twice per shift. This involved checking the aircraft thoroughly for any damage and personally attending to it or presiding over it as BDR teams patched up holes or pulled out dents, reviewing the flyers' maintenance write-up and fixing any problems with the multifarious systems. Then they refuelled and rearmed the aircraft ready for action. And all the while keeping an eye on the novices and ensuring they are doing their jobs satisfactorily.

In the extreme, during wartime or a sortie-surge exercise, this whole process can be squeezed into 45 minutes, using ICT techniques, whereby the aircraft is simultaneously checked, refuelled and rearmed, sometimes hot (i.e. with the engines running), before the whole launch procedure is repeated. During mass launches and recoveries, there is an all-pervasive air of energy. It is a profession for the young, and increasingly is becoming more so.

Chapter Six

FUTURE TECHNOLOGIES

How is future fighter technology shaping up? Super smart weapons, integrated cockpits and raw gains in engine/airframe performance are all having an impact, as is stealth or low observability. The greatest exemplar of the latter of these thrusting new developments within the fighter community is the Lockheed/Boeing F-22, tentatively titled the Rapier, which is destined to enter operational service at the beginning of the next century. A peek at this programme, originated as the Advanced Tactical Fighter (ATF), and also at the runner-up (the Northrop/McDonnell Douglas YF-23) in the effort, provides a clear insight into what every well-dressed fighter pilot will be strapping on a decade hence.

Advanced Tactical Fighters

Go-ahead for the F-22 came on 23 April 1991 when Team One ATF winners Lockheed-Boeing had cause to pop some champagne corks. The USAF's decision to proceed with the F-22 model of the ATF on that day came as both a financial blessing to the partners, and as a vindication of their aero-engineering and managerial skills. Low risk and low cost were cited as the key issues which swayed the decision in their favour. Initial plans called for a low-rate initial production anticipated to kick off in Fiscal Year 1998 (FY88) close on the heels of an intense, four-year FSD effort, peaking at 48 aircraft annually between FY2003 and FY2015, when the USAF should have taken delivery of a grand total of 648 aircraft worth $98 billion. However, in the light of recent budget cuts and major programme stretches, that schedule has been knocked back nearly four years and procurement already reduced to 442 aircraft, and possibly will be halved. Nevertheless, it still represents the fighter Sale of the Century as it represents one of the most

technologically advanced products to emerge from American industry at the start of the new millennium. What precisely is this new fighter concept?

The aesthetics of the runner-up YF-23 design captured the hearts of many. Nicknamed the 'Black Widow 2' by Northrop workers, the curvaceous YF-23 embodied such innovative features as Allison's patented Lamilloy photo-etched titanium transpiration exhaust ducts to massively reduce the infrared signature, and a wing-body blended airframe for all-aspect stealth. Many of these Northrop trademarks were pioneered on the B-2A Spirit. It exuded hallmarks of a Gerry Anderson creation. Pilots loved the look of it above all other factors. Why, then, was the F-23 proposal considered to be so high risk compared to the winning design, given that on aesthetic grounds, Lockheed's own F-104 Starfighter appeared to be from a comparatively more futuristic epoch than its winning design which was 30 years older?

Some of the reasons are more obvious than others, but most revolve around the simple fact that the future lies in technology beneath the skin of the fighter, in more ways than one. We are now delving back into computers and the micro-miniature hardware that make them work so magnificently. Within the context of the ATF fly-off, the YF-23's technological stablemate the B-2A rose in cost by an alarming factor. The 20 being manufactured (reduced from the originally intended 132) are being housed in luxurious $5 million hangars at Whiteman AFB, Missouri, where humidity, temperature and cleanliness are kept firmly under control and the aircraft preened at comparative leisure. All this is with the knowledge that most of them will take to the air only twice a month.

By contrast, the ATF is expected to be deployed in

The two competing ATFs, the Lockheed/Boeing YF-22 (which won the 1990–1991 Dem-Val) and the Northrop/McDonnell Douglas YF-23. The butterfly tail and low heat signature jet nozzles of the 'Black Widow 2' looked impressive, but the USAF preferred the 2-D vectoring nozzles and made-to-turn-and-burn characteristics of the YF-22. (Lockheed and McDonnell Douglas)

relatively large numbers at locations where the facilities and prevailing meteorological conditions can be austere, placing much more exacting demands on the aircraft – such as air defence alert in such far-flung locations as the icy vastness of Alaska and the steamy Gulf of Mexico. The marginally superior supercruise performance and all-aspect stealth allegedly possessed by the YF-23 Prototype Air Vehicles (PAVs) would be of questionable value if half the force remained chocked in their hangarettes awaiting specialized maintenance. The baby-smooth skin has to be capable of enduring the rigours of endless ICT turnarounds, and of pilots routinely attempting to break it during gut-wrenching aerial combat manoeuvres.

The Lockheed-led team clearly foresaw this, and drawing upon experience gleaned during the F-117A *Senior Trend* effort, took a more straightforward approach. The F-22 incorporates zig-zag signal-trapping edging (the so-called sawteeth or chevrons) in frequently articulated components such as canopy frames, key access panels, and undercarriage and weapons doors, ensuring that stealth integrity is maintained at all times, even when panels become slightly out of true as a result of rough treatment in the field. These are bigger than those found on the F - 117A to lower RCS further and add structural bracing. Similarly, bumps in the skin have been refaired. To top it all, Lockheed's Advanced Composites Center has perfected durable radar-absorbing electrochromic and thermalchromic coatings which, as well as massively reducing the F-22's radar signature, also eliminate some 60–70 per cent of infrared emissions in the 3–5 and 8–12 micron ranges. This makes the aircraft difficult to acquire by heat/IRST and FLIR sensors, respectively, when operating at up to 100 per cent mil power.

The technology is classified for obvious reasons and so some of the finer points remain conjectural. Essentially, however, the new coating is embedded with modified carbon molecules. The coating comprises a matrix of polyaniline filled with cyanate whiskers. The composite is formed into sheets or is available in liquid form. The material may also contain a high molecular weight polymer produced from such mysterious substances as red mercury, RM20. The composite can be bonded or sprayed onto the airframe – and the outside of new stealthy weapons too, which could be bolted onto the exterior to supplement the aircraft's Convair-style internal trapeze weapons fit. The whiskers effectively break-up radar waves already reduced in strength by the fourth power in relation to the distance from their point of emission, and converts them into heat which is quickly dissipated throughout the material. Perversely, the resultant heat actually improves

stealth! Such coatings can reduce reflected energy by a staggering 25 dBm^2, effectively wiping out all but one per cent of the incident energy. What is reflected, and then seldom right back at the radar source, is negligible. Moreover, some of the latest coatings can last for up to 50 hours' exposure to temperatures as high as 500°C, and are transparent, so can be used over passive E-O sensors (and even canopies) as well as over engine housings and nozzles, necessitating only periodic respraying.

Thicker portions of RAM are employed at wing roots and other 'problem areas' susceptible to massive reflections. Dielectric 'lossy' RAMs are one such type of material used for these applications. Electrical conductance changes with depth or thickness throughout the material; the impedance of the outside of the RAM closely matches that of free space, encouraging absorption, but as the radar wave passes through the material the changing dielectric properties causes the energy to be gradually dissipated throughout the material as a low-voltage which generates heat. These tailor-made pieces of RAM also serve to isolate various electronics which might interfere with one another, a problem known as EMI, discussed earlier in the book, to improve the performance of EW devices and reduce unwanted emissions such as sidelobes. The magnetic absorbers are much thinner, coming as sheets tuned to specific frequency ranges and consist of a high density of tiny particles of a magnetic material (such as special ferrites and graphites) blended into a non-conductive binding agent thickness of which corresponds to one-quarter the wavelength of the anticipated radar waves. This soaks-up and reflects the radar waves in phase so that they effectively cancel each other out!

Although still widely used in nooks and crannies, these latter have been superseded to a certain extent by the newer polymer spray-on coatings which are more expensive, but nonetheless lighter and much easier to apply. The earlier forms of magnetic RAM required extensive use of toxic binding agents to fix them in place over the airframes. Indeed, Lockheed's lead in applying RAM and polymer coatings was developed during the heyday of the F-117A *Senior Trend* programme, when the company was forced to abandon its use of wallpaper-like rolls of thin plastic 'lossy' RAM; these sheets possessed an alarming tendency to peel away in flight! Northrop Grumman developed similar coatings for the B-2A which were to be applied to their YF-23, but the fear existed that the exotic Black Widow 2 would be making far too many visits to the paint barn for relaminations and resprays.

Some pruning of the envisaged test fleet has taken place, and the final shape of the F-22 design will be frozen during the final design reviews in February 1995. Compared to the Dem-Val aircraft, the canopy has been moved forward and wing shape refined, and the tail area reduced. Beneath the stealthy paint job, the use of composites is extensive. These include advanced bismaleimide thermoset resin and reformable – and therefore easily repairable – thermoplastics, which will account for some 27 per cent of the structure. These improvements are aimed at bolstering both performance and the F-22's stealth attributes, particularly in its lower rear-quarters. (The balance of the structure comprises 33 per cent titanium, a mere 11 per cent aluminium, 5 per cent steel and 22 per cent miscellaneous or unspecified substances such as copper, silver, gold, fibreglass, plastic and ceramics).

Weight growth is being closely scrutinized. Changes to the structure to reduce RCS, such as reducing the number of drain holes in the belly of the machine from 200 to 44, add something like 150 lb and cost tens of millions to effect, despite extensive use of CAD/CAM techniques. To keep these hiccups in check, all departments report directly to the top, thus ensuring that the aircraft will not run into the terrible weight-cost spiral that plagued the US Navy's A-12 Avenger 2, causing its cancellation and ultimately removing long-range air power from the US Navy inventory.

As we mentioned in the opening paragraphs of this discussion, Lockheed/Boeing are aware that future technology is more than skin-deep. The US Air Force were thus reassured by the winning team's proposals for the avionics systems architecture. The USAF's *Pave Pillar* concept, aimed both at advancing the state of the art in avionics and visionics (displays) and at substantially reducing maintenance down times, revolves around the use of standard electronics module E-size (SEM-E) chipboards boxed-up as common integrated processors (CIPs). This array of electronics (the YF-22 PAVs each boasted 16 CIPs), which have replaced discreet black boxes installed in previous fighters, are intended to be mutually supportive, providing massive redundancy. Any one unit can handle mission, defensive or offensive data processing (all managed by databuses). This confines the use of dedicated items to the flight and mission sensors such as IRST and the multi-mode AN/APG-77 radar antenna. This is optimized for low probability of intercept on enemy RWRs, of course, via beam-shaping and the judicious use of RAM near the antenna array to negate unwanted sidelobes. 'I can see you but you can't see me' is the philosophy behind the ATF avionics package, currently being flight-tested on airliner-category platforms   which

can carry the hefty test equipment along with a gaggle of engineers to scrutinize the test data.

The versatile avionics will have far-reaching effects on the military maintenance organization, and systems integrators, Lockheed, seem to have struck a common chord with the Pentagon's desire to see this massively expensive system streamlined. As MTBF of the SEM-Es is in the order of 15,000 hours, line DCCs will simply pull out a defective unit and slot in a brand-new item fresh from the stores inventory, as they do now, but the difference is that they will bin the defective unit. There will be no intermediate-level or depot-level avionics shops wasting time with non-economic repairs. As outlined in the winning submission, during the course of FSD the F-22 will also gradually incorporate some smart-skin technology, using embedded microelectronics (including portions of the planned integrated electronic warfare suite (INEWS) and Integrated Communications/Navigation/Interrogation Avionics (ICNIA) suites, respectively, the core of which will in all likelihood outlive the airframe!

Building on current JTIDS, Milstar, integrated EW and targeting sensors, projected life-cycle operating costs for the stubby F-22 Rapier fighter (aircraft, crew training, the support infrastructure, maintenance, fuel and spares for a squadron's-worth of aircraft over a 20-year period) were estimated at just over $1 billion in 1990. This equates to approximately 60 per cent of the cost of operating a similarly sized eyrie of F-15 Eagles. That crops a staggering $600 million off the O & M budget per Wing over that time, or $30 million a year – enough to potentially finance a lot more much-needed flying. Easing the strain on the O & M budget is becoming an increasingly important issue as manufacturers strive to ease the 'ility' figures: maintainability, reliability and availability. Including spares, back-up maintenance, flight-gear, training for everyone involved in the support pyramid from the commander down to the runway patchers, it costs something like $18,000 per hour of flight-time to operate a modern fighter. The UK equivalent for this American figure is something like £12,000 per hour (although raw operating costs for the actual machine are really only a third of that).

Exact performance summaries of the competing ATF designs remain classified, but the data that has trickled into the public domain provides an excellent yardstick. We shall deal with that shortly. What is equally interesting is that the decision to move ahead with the Lockheed/Boeing proposal was virtually unanimous, with little in the way of the customary grinding of teeth that was typical of the head-to-head flyoffs of the 1960s and 1970s. The 54-month-long ATF Dem-Val, which culminated in the

August–December 1990 flight phase, was unique in another respect: both competing teams were given specific performance criteria to meet. They were also given the leeway in which to conduct their own exclusive demonstrations which would exemplify the virtues of their respective proposals for full-scale engineering and manufacturing development.

One-upmanship doubtless played a part in the demonstration sorties, but marks were awarded when the designs achieved or exceeded their respective performance proposals, even if one team lagged behind the other in a specific area. Very unorthodox. Lockheed/Boeing's submission scored on all counts during its 74 Dem-Val sorties, flown by company test pilots Dave Ferguson, Jon Beesley and Tom Morgenfield plus 'blue-suiter' Maj Mark Shackleford, and this fact was stressed in the 20,000-page document which outlined the team's FSD

proposals. It is perhaps more than interesting to note that Northrop/McDonnell Douglas' slinky YF-23s generated 24 fewer sorties and 26.6 fewer flying hours, resulting in a commensurately thinner document; not that its pilots let it down.

Supercruise

The winning contractors' position was also surely aided by the demonstrably successful launch of Sidewinder and AMRAAM missiles from N22YX, proving the all-essential offensive capability was in the bag. As a BAe Dynamics engineer involved in the British side of AMRAAM noted, most fighters tend to be given pet status by aerodynamicists first, pilots second, structures engineers third, and only then are weapons integration specialists given a look-in. This was certainly true of Lockheed's last fighter, the

The NF-15B S/MTD demonstrator was a key factor in Pratt & Whitney/United Technologies winning the ATF Sale of the Century engine contract, though some would argue that the GE variable-cycle YF120 engines offered more advanced technology. P & W simply had an excellent track record, and that counts for a great deal when cost is factored into the equation. (McDonnell Douglas)

F-104, but in the case of the ATF, equal emphasis was placed upon stealth, agility, speed and avionics/-weapons integration *ab initio*. To their detriment, Northrop/McDonnell Douglas' key cards comprised speed and stealth. Manoeuvrable the YF-23 most certainly was, with its low-slung butterfly tail and big wing, but it lacked vectoring nozzles which gave its competitor the crucial edge when set alongside the latest designs to emerge from Russia, such as the Su-35.

Experience in dealing with the USAF and knowing what it covets most played an equally big part in the concurrent engine win, which also pushes the boundaries of fighter performance. General Electric seemed to have the edge in technology with their YF120 powerplant when set alongside the competing Pratt & Whitney YF119, but lost to United Technologies who had been flying a highly reliable F100-PW-220 2-D nozzle in the NF-15B STOL/Maneuver Technology Demonstrator (S/MTD) for well over a year before the ATF demonstrators took to the skies. This helped to resolve a number of bugs inherent in the adoption of 20° vectoring nozzles in the higher performance PW5000 (father of the YF119), effectively clearing the path for a smooth Dem-Val and adding substance to their FSD proposals. The production version embodies advanced materials such as metal matrix composites (MMCs) composed chiefly of titanium reinforced with silicon carbide to give immense strength and stiffness so as to preserve flow patterns, maximizing thrust and fuel efficiency.

GE's more revolutionary variable-cycle alternative was considered just a little too radical (and suffered minor problems when some of its lines chaffed against aircraft test instrumentation, causing at least one sortie to be cut short). However, it was in many respects by far the more progressive of the two. The turbine's variable-cycle system enabled it to operate like a conventional turbojet at supersonic speed, while demonstrating the characteristics of a more fuel-efficient turbofan at subsonic cruise settings. The engine switches between the two functions by means of fan-bypass doors; the system is a core-driven fan engine in which the core drives a secondary fan that supercharges fan-bypass streams when maximum mil thrust is engaged. In essence, this means a turbojet-like quick pile on of thrust whenever needed coupled with the superb range characteristics associated with the turbofan. GE continues to work on the concept, which offers much hope for future development.

Since February 1993 its engineers have been working on a follow-on Joint Technology Demonstrator Engine (JTDE) incorporating new blade materials like MMCs to overcome the susceptibility of variable-cycle engine fans to twisting and flutter, which degrades performance. Other materials being developed for use in the new class of superfighter engines include organic matrix composite resins such as AFR700, a lightweight material for use in casings and vents, capable of withstanding temperatures of 371°C. Already, this is being applied to the engine trough trailing-edges of the F-117A, which are currently prone to charring.

Much to its credit, the 35,000 lb-class YF119 experienced no stalls or in-flight shutdowns during the gruelling 65 sorties and 153 hours it accumulated during the Dem-Val. Perhaps more to the point, it boasts 25 per cent fewer parts overall and 63 per cent fewer moving components than its competitor, partly thanks to advances in one-piece compressor discs and MMC materials technology. Thrust growth, to match the adventurous YF120 engine, is also planned. Walter N. Bylciw, Vice-President for the Pratt & Whitney effort, claimed during the Dem-Val that static tests have indicated that the definitive version will exceed USAF ATF requirements by at least 20 per cent. The long-term FSD will give the Corporation extra time in which to fine-tune their product.

Along with stealth and refined aerodynamics, the turbines form the crux of the F-22 effort. As mentioned earlier in the book in the context of Capping and INT, fighters seldom fly supersonically because of the excessive fuel consumption and noise generated by such high-speed antics. Within the limits of current turbofan engines, it is customary to 'unlight' the afterburners shortly after take-off and then adopt a maximum cruise climb profile, gradually building up more speed and height as more fuel is guzzled-up, as the fighter gradually becomes lighter. Fighter pilots want more, but it is not readily available without the use of reheat, even with turbine-busting developments in ceramics and MMCs, which are only now just reaching fruition.

There are sound military reasons for this. Afterburning does not tend to emit a more powerful IR signature than maximum mil power settings *per se*, but rather a stronger output in the 2–3 micron wavelength range, making them distinct. (Afterburning is more correctly termed 'augmented' thrust as it boosts power beyond 100 per cent of the maximum mil power when the throttles are yanked forwards beyond the military or dry thrust detent into new multi-zone settings to squirt additional fuel into the rear of the engine to superheat the air efflux.) Photo-conductive sensors such as those employed in IRST and heat-seeking weapons are especially good at detecting these wavelengths. Moreover, it guzzles-up fuel like it was going out of fashion, and at night those 'tiger-tailed' shock diamonds or orange-crimson flickers are an easy giveaway to ground gunners and marauding enemy air combat pilots.

Climbing the efficiency curve into new realms has now become far from an impossible goal based on only around-the-corner technology. By means of its new engine technology and gracious lines, the ATF concept introduces the notion of supercruise: the ability to attain supersonic cruise without having to resort to reheat. By employing excellent fuel burn to thrust ratios, by the time it reaches the push point, the fighter should be happily soaring through the skies supersonically and yet be virtually invisible to enemy radar and infrared sensors (while contrails, too, might be negated by the use of fuel additives such as chlorofluorosulphonic acid, during the early hours of a campaign). A gentle push from a burst of reheat would speed up the process, if called upon. Long before the new superfighter was spotted it would have already engaged the enemy with AMRAAMs or *Have Dash 2* stealthy equivalents.

At closer ranges, reheat would be an option – though probably a last resort – for 'turn 'n' burn' dogfighting, though the F-22's unique 2-D nozzles assist with sprightly performance in 'dry' engine settings. However, long before that need arose, it would flip open its weapons bays and unleash a couple of Box Offices or ASRAAM missiles. Closing further still to ranges at which it begins to be detected by more sharply discriminating sensors – visual range in daytime and a few hundred yards by night – it would break a virgin sheath of frangible material or open its cat flap to pour out volleys of lead from a Gatling gun. Forming the apex of a gorilla package of Coalition fighters, it could sweep away most serious aerial opposition within hours of a campaign, leaving lesser aircraft such as the American Teenagers and European fighters to do the mopping-up. A truly stealthy air superiority fighter would also open up options for special operations – such as a covert strike against enemy AWACS and EW/recce platforms (even a cargo transporter carrying VIPs). Stealth thus not only makes such a fighter significantly harder to catch, but makes it significantly more lethal.

The YF-22's almost uncanny manoeuvrability, thanks to its 2-D vectoring nozzles, was entirely convincing too. Full-stick aileron rolls at 50° AoA were demonstrated, along with roll rates in excess of 100° *per se*cond at 120 knots. Riding along at the stall margin at 80 knots with the nose pointing skyward for as long as 1 minute demonstrated little tactical application but did highlight the aircraft's impressive stability and vice-free handling characteristics. Seemingly effortless supercruise at Mach 1.58 and speeds of Mach 2 were also achieved (the Mach 2.2

dash requirement having been deleted as incurring an unnecessary penalty on tailpipe structure, owing to increased EGTs).

Further comparisons with the Air Force's current mainstay air superiority fighter the F-15 are inevitable, and it is perhaps somewhat ironic that the winning design bears an uncanny outward resemblance to the aircraft it is intended to replace. The similarities end there, as the YF-22's established performance keeps the F-15 in its chocks: in mil thrust the audacious newcomer can outperform an afterburning F-15 across the entire height/speed envelope, with full augmented thrust levered-in on the throttle quadrant, it leaves the F-15 struggling for control in ATF jet wash! Interestingly, although the YF-23 was also fast off the mark, it appears that the Northrop/McDonnell Douglas team simply underestimated the inbred desire within the USAF fighter community for 'turn 'n' burn' dogfighter manoeuvrability.

With the exception of the short-lived missileer concepts of the late 1950s and early 1960s, agility has always been deemed paramount both for air combat superiority and for the 'aircrew character-building process', a factor which is all too easily overlooked. Most commanders possess vivid memories of busting blood vessels in a fighter; and not least of all the aggressive self-confidence that their machines imbued in them. In fact, there exists almost a perverse antipathy towards anything that makes a fighter pilot's life easier! To cope with the stresses and strains, the YF-22 introduced a Weber rocker seat to increase resilience to higher g-loads, but this is now to be deleted in favour of a fixed seat plumbed-in for the new service-wide tactical life-support system (TLSS) suit, presently entering service with the F-16 community. TLSS comprises a full torso suit and a positive pressure-breathing oxygen mask. It should ease the transition into the new high-performing beast. The F-23 proposals seem to have in part neglected these factors, though the Evaluation Board candidly stated that all four airframe/engine proposals – there existed two of each airframe design each outrigged with the competing engines – would have offered 'superb' fighters.

Lockheed/Boeing's penchant for innovation was tempered by their willingness to listen to the pilots and embody maximum ergonomics in the cockpit. For example, the touch-activated full-colour liquid crystal cockpit displays (and there will be seven of them) are to be reconfigured with simple push-buttons. Apparently, the test pilots found subtle inputs (such as cranking in radio frequencies) with their chunky gloved digits 'a pain'. A centrally located control column also is replacing the F-16-style sidestick fitted to the PAVs. That the Team One organization were able to incorporate so many of these advanced features into their two demonstrators – nicknamed 'Iron Birds' because of their non-operational avionics suite – was impressive. A final sprinkling of sugar which sweetened the USAF was the YF-22's full-blown canopy hood arrangement which provides unobstructed all-round vision. Many scrutinizing the two competitors side-by-side at Edwards AFB commented that the competing YF-23's otherwise beautiful lines were marred by the canopy bow, dictated by structural loads imposed by the forward-emplaced cockpit. Curiously, the latest European designs similarly retain a canopy bow.

The F-22 is a formidable concept, which rewrites air-to-air combat yet again within the space of a decade, after prolonged stagnation. And it is interesting to reflect that the Russian equivalent the MiG 1.42 – at the time of writing, still sat on the concrete paving, awaiting its new engines – shares much in common with the Lockheed/Boeing design. Resembling the F-22 ATF in some respects, it is not very stealthy but its designation implies supercruise at Mach 1.42, just a tad below that of the American design. It is nonetheless 'scheduled for service entry within the next three to five years', whereas the production-standard F-22A is not now scheduled to fly before January 1997. The MiG and Sukhoi Bureaux are also

creating designs which match the JAS 39 Gripen, Rafale and Eurofighter 2000, as back-up, with a view to entering the world fighter market on a serious basis, using Western avionics in some instances.

However, unlike its less sophisticated but more firmly rooted European counterparts, political considerations continue to cloud the F-22 programme. The original FSD schedule called for the use of nine single-seaters and two twin-seat tubs. The major unresolved obstacle is the age-old issue of cost, particularly as many are beginning to question the need for a brand-new expensive air superiority fighter. Peacetime Europe under threat from the malevolent Russian Bear was for a long time the notional front line which gave so much impetus to previous expensive programmes, but the US presence there is waning rapidly in the aftermath of the Conventional Forces in Europe Treaty. The implosion of the Warsaw Pact and the recent NATO-Russian Partnership-For-Peace deal signed during June 1994 allegedly makes the need for sizeable numbers of F-22As even more questionable.

Additionally, since reunification, Germany's Luftwaffe has assumed exclusive responsibilities for maintaining its own round-the-clock air defence coverage in what until quite recently used to be a USAFE F-15 bastion. American, British and Canadian aircraft ceased *Zulu Alert* QRA duties in

Western Europe's plunge into the dynamic fighter environment of the next century includes the Dassault Rafale, which is being developed for land and carrier operations. It is a good-looking fighter (always a plus with pilots) but Dassault chose this curious charcoal grey-black scheme for the first prototype – perhaps to add to its mystique in the light of the Lockheed F-117A's presence at Le Bourget? (Dassault)

Eurofighter 2000 will use an extremely advanced GEC-Marconi ECR-90 multi-mode radar offering automated stand-off aerial target tracking, close-quarters auto-acquisition and advanced ground mapping. The machine is destined to enter service with the air forces of Great Britain, Germany and Italy, and will likely find additional clients. (BAe via Bob Munro)

Germany on 23:59L on 2 October 1991, creating a watershed. American forces stationed in the Far Eastern sector of the Pacific Rim will similarly dwindle. There are no longer any fighters stationed in the Philippines, nor any requirement for ATFs to be permanently based in South Korea, while the air superiority wing at Kadena AB is fated to follow a similar path to those in USAFE. Other force reductions, decreed as part of the 10-Wing USAF cut (a force equivalent to that used in *Desert Storm!*), will also bite into the numbers, as US forces are gradually pulled back into the Stateside rapid-deployment Central Command structure to be reorganized into the new Superwings.

However, concurrent F-22 engineering, manufacture and development (EMD) is scheduled to continue into the next decade, with IOC tentatively scheduled for the year 2003, by which time the F-15 design will be 35 years old and the operational fleet more than a little dog-eared, with retirement looming. Political swings and roundabouts are such that a pressing need for a new fighter may emerge virtually overnight. Above all, the USAF is not willing to renounce its position at the top of the technological league, and points out that it has enjoyed such supremacy for 50 years. They also take time to remind

the critics that the edge enjoyed by the F-15 lies mainly with its multi-mode radar, allied avionics and missile kit, not its performance. Indeed, economists who argue that the so-called Sale of the Century should amount to no more than a token-sized production run of 100 or so F-22s, are being uncharacteristically myopic.

The Air Force has no doubts that the ATF will remain its top-priority procurement programme at the start of the new millennium and the Service has enjoyed considerable political clout ever since the undeniably successful application of air power in the Gulf (even if 85 per cent of Iraqi air power was destroyed on the ground by INT). The lawmakers on Capitol Hill, for their own part, are supportive so far. They are well aware of the jobs at stake, and the fact that multi-billion dollar overseas sales of American hardware rest largely on their armed forces acting as showcase for the latest technology, even if potential clients are not permitted to buy, or cannot afford the best. Upgrading the existing inventory with derivative Teenage fighters will merely serve to provide the ideal opening for the emerging generation of highly capable European competitors such as the Gripen, Rafale and Eurofighter 2000.

Even if the end product is too expensive for all but

a select few overseas clients, without it, America may not be able to establish command of the air in a future war, which is militarily unpalatable. Apart from brief periods of excessively poor weather which has periodically grounded its air power, such as during the Battle of the Bulge in the wet and foggy December of 1944, the US has enjoyed air superiority in every battle since the débâcle at Kassarine Pass in North Africa two years earlier when the US Army was given a nasty shock by the Deutsches Afrika Korps. It has no desire to repeat this in an age of stand-off, push-button warfare where its hard-pressed ground troops take air supremacy for granted, and where the kinds of losses sustained in those Second World War actions would abruptly signal a political end to American involvement. In the world of fighters, the F-22 is a Big League gamester with which not only future air battles will be won or lost, but the foundations of coalition action will stand firm or collapse.

JAST

One big problem resulting from high unit prices incurred by leading-edge technology fighters is the knock-on effect on training resources, and consequently combat proficiency. There is only so much money to go around, and when it gets tight, training and spares tend to play second fiddle to procurement of new hardware. Only the mass-produced American F-4 and Russian MiG-21 of the 1960s were considered anything like really throwaway at a million pounds each, and only then in combat; and these two types were produced in abundance. However, nowadays, with fighters carrying a price tag of tens of millions of pounds per aircraft and procured in comparatively modest numbers, which aviator is not becoming increasingly mindful of his or her responsibility to the taxpayer? That is, when does the necessary bravado involved in flying a modern fighter become the 'wrong stuff' in the minds of politicians and the public, in turn obliging aviators to err on the side of caution to the detriment of operational prowess? Or fly much-reduced hours, making up the balance of their time in the 'sim'? We are not talking about combat proficiency but actually the raw act of stick-and-rudder airmanship. Purposefully aggressive flying is the cornerstone of military aviation. And if unit costs continue to rise, how long will it be before each and every aircraft has to be locked in a silk-cushioned hangar between sorties, and handled delicately during only occasional flight operations?

Fortunately, this mentality has not yet made too much of a dent in Western fighter operations (as opposed to the new stealth superbomber circuit), and crews continue to 'train like they fight' with vigour. On a lighter note, one aviator recently confided to the author that on the very same morning that he had written out a hefty cheque for the American IRS tax authorities, he suffered a problem shortly after take-off. In order to bring the jet down to a safe recovery weight, he had been obliged to dump fuel worth twice as much as his recent tax bill! However, fighter operations are no longer immune from tight budgetary scrutiny even on a week-to-week basis, as O & M costs are continuously scrutinized by an army of comptrollers and civil servants.

In the US, a concept known as total quality management (TQM) is expected to generate 'more, faster, and for less money'. There's some leeway available by chipping away at gross inefficiencies but the aviators' increasing antipathy towards the army of 'bean-counters' reflects a broader malaise affecting Western adventurousness. Innovation from engineers who might not be sufficiently articulate to argue their case has given way to the briefcase clout of vociferous business people with no technical background, who are sucking up to all the high-powered jobs. This background pressure will mount as newer but fewer, more expensive aircraft become operational over the course of the next decade. Waste must be eliminated, but the whole psyche of fighter operations is under threat from inappropriate commercial management techniques aimed solely at reducing costs. It is apt to create a hollow force: air arms equipped with compromised fighters and sparkling with impressive ready-to-fly readiness rates, but manned by aviators who seldom get the opportunity to wring them out, let alone push the aircraft and themselves to the limits. As a result they may fall short of the mark in actual combat – the boundaries of human spirit thwarted by boardroom economics. The two must be kept apart from one another.

The long-term solution to the very survival of the military fighter tradition, and the vast institutional knowledge it has accrued over the past eight decades, thus appears to rest with commonality. That is, developing a fighter-bomber that, with only minor modifications at the CAD/CAM stage, would be compatible with both shore and ship operations, and be capable of conducting a multitude of tasks. The glaringly obvious argument in its favour is that such would spread the enormous fixed development costs over a longer production run, thus reducing both unit costs and O & M over the aircraft's operational lifetime by simplifying logistics and maintenance support to boot. However, only recently has it become possible to achieve this, owing to the removal of technological limitations which previously burdened the engineering community. A prime example is the recent elusive quest by the United States for a true multi-role, joint-service fighter-bomber: capable of combining stealth with the light weight that is ideal for land-based operations to maximize range and payload, together with the US Navy's need for a beefy design capable of conducting a plethora of tasks from a carrier deck.

The effort has engendered a series of designs since the mid-1980s, all of which have foundered. They have been replaced by the current Joint-Service Advanced Strike Technology (JAST) initiative which

looks like it will make a real go of it. The idea behind JAST (a technology demonstration programme only at this juncture) is to show just how an aircraft sharing around 70 per cent commonality in core systems, despite ostensibly conflicting Service requirements, which will inevitably dictate a diversity of different-looking fighter designs, can be created as a rational concept. The intention is to make this possible by using a common pool of subassemblies such as engines and avionics which now account for at least two thirds of the cost of an aircraft (as opposed to the

The shape of future fighter technology, the F-22 Rapier. The JAST concept is as yet too immature for solid aircraft shapes to emerge, but the artwork is very 'Gerry Anderson' in concept. (Lockheed)

inverse situation resulting from such efforts of three decades ago).

Some scoff at the idea, harking back to the mid-1960s and the saga of TFX/TFX-N, at the time known to the engineers as 'Terrible F***ing Experience', which produced the F-111. This was 'airframe first, avionics added', and took eight years to evolve into its eventual useful role as interdictor. The original, and wholly unrealistic, goal was to create a Fleet defence fighter for the US Navy as well as a fighter-bomber, reconnaissance jet and nuclear attack machine for the USAF, and cheap, off-the-shelf derivatives of these for NATO. Britain, for example, ordered 50 of the more advanced F-111K version and cancelled the indigenous TSR.2 project, while whole Wings of derivatives were envisaged for export to Belgium, Holland and Germany. Cost, weight and complexity spiralled inexorably upwards. The US Navy pulled out of the programme during May 1967 only 30 months after the first prototype flew. By the following summer when the first USAF operational Wing was forming for *Combat Lancer* combat trials at Takhli in South-East Asia, it was clear that the aircraft would only usefully be used for low-level high-speed attack (albeit superbly, and disregarding the fact that it has since evolved into a capable EW and recce platform too).

However, the original proposal was too ambitious. The Navy and Air Force designs were ostensibly very similar but differed massively in terms of their avionics, which were channelled along each Service's requirements. Eventually, the structure also required considerable revision to meet their various needs. Commonality fell to something like 10 per cent from an initial goal of 80 per cent. The avionics of the era simply were not sophisticated enough to cope with more than one task at a time (a factor which plagued the F-4, too, which to some extent in its 'growth' formats eclipsed the TFX and which suffered enormous problems with its radar kit). The advent of high-speed integrated avionics linked to multi-mode search and mapping radars, all managed by digital databuses, have expanded the options considerably. Add monolithic micro-integrated chips contained in today's all-knowing CIPs/SEM-Es and the horizon grows massively. And this is what drives JAST. The same avionics can perform a whole host of tasks using only different software – the all-essential programming that tells the multi-mode avionics what to do – even if the antenna configurations associated with radar and EW remain pretty much identical.

Fringe exemplars of this technology within the existing operational framework are the McDonnell F-15E Eagle DRF and F/A-18C/D Hornet, which can handle ground attack and air combat tasks equally well. However, these are two widely differing designs when it comes to support procedures, as the Eagle DRF will never land on a carrier while the Hornet will never surpass the Mud Hen in terms of range and payload. The two share virtually nothing in common in terms of subsystems, despite vaguely common Hughes radars, part-task trainers and simulators which its angst-ridden engineers in Missouri continually strive to improve. This inevitably results in very different support systems.

The Services themselves are being asked to pool brains and achieve common directives to common problems in the case of JAST – not a concept so out of reach in the light of the recent American 'Bottom-Up' Review of missions and roles, where some radical rethinking is taking place. But for the officer top-heavy air forces of the world, an almost religious feeling of devotion to separatism ingrained in naval forces, and the pyramidal structures of the US Army/Marine Corps which forms an apex with the elite kudos attached to its Special Forces, there still exists a cogent argument for the establishment of a unified 'defence force'. JAST might well ease that painful process, even if it just chips at the edges. The problem lies not with inefficiency, but with unnecessary duplication.

JAST means to take care of the airframe aspect of commonality by using a modular approach within given parameters. The aircraft is to comprise several segments, which can be designed in common or independently, then spliced together in the appropriate fashion to create the desired end product, almost like a snap-together kit: lift-fan a V/STOL aircraft tailored for the peculiar demands of forward land-based or seagoing operations; or even a high-performance land-based or catapult-launched fighter capable of carrying a massive payload. The mature technology offered by FBW and FBL will compensate for the differing configurations, so that the aircraft actually seem to respond and handle in much the same manner, including various stores configurations which can be programmed into the flight control systems.

Avionics, engines and a host of other items will be common to all variants. This will include derivatives which the US Pentagon hopes will be co-developed with friendly overseas countries to help further drive down development and procurement costs, reaching the stage where BAe might produce 'module B', Aérospatiale 'module F' and Japan 'module J'. So the actual outward appearance of JAST, because of this modularity, will differ widely. The current thinking goes 'buy computers and put wings on them': make the different modules talk to one another and just about anything is possible! JAST may well represent the only affordable way forward, even if it has until

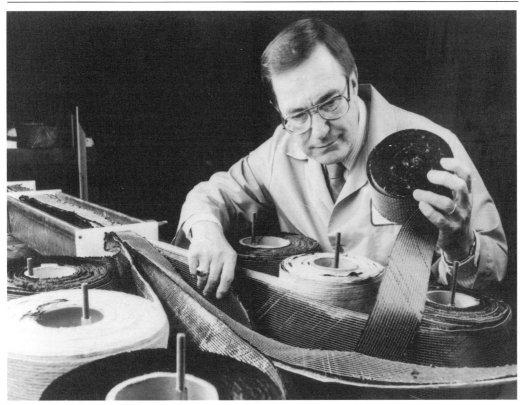

Modern fighters embody a hefty percentage – up to one-third – of composite materials, which offer stealth attributes as well as incredibly light weight and stiffness. Here, thermoplastic strips are laid out at Lockheed's Composite Development Center. Ironed and cut to shape using a high-pressure water jet, the parts are then formed into the definitive format using compression-moulding where the resins bind the ensemble into a single, solid component. Larger assemblies are hand-laid and consolidated in an autoclave. (Lockheed)

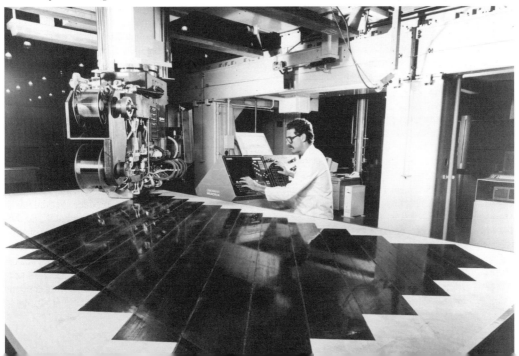

2000 to mature into a set of airworthy demonstrators, and takes another 15 years to develop into a truly multi-national effort as the lynchpin of a peacekeeper of the twenty-first century.

JAST is very ambitious, so how will it really emerge? In terms of structure, thermoplastics will feature strongly. CAD/CAM techniques may also permit more finely tuned airframes to be built. The designs drafted by engineers go straight to the composite material laying and curing 'houses'. Metal-cutting instructions are similarly sent direct to the machine tools so that the assemblers form more of the managerial process. There is a compromise to be worked-in here, and inputs from the ground and air crews may prove the real stickler.

FBW/FBL control systems are nowadays configured for safety; for example, the Panavia Tornado's Spils system prevents the pilot from exerting excessive strain on the structure, but a potential JAST pilot might exclaim that this should be eradicated, and short of getting into a punching match with the stability designer, might introduce all sorts of new demands – move that button there, because it is awkward to reach, and so on. However, using CAD/CAM, designs could be made lighter, and FBW/FBL systems used to maintain airframe integrity by limiting pilot roll commands to avoid overstressing the structure altogether. Pilots rostered through CAD terminals might input their desires between flying sorties, before heading for the bar.

But what happens when a collision is imminent and the right thing to do is roll violently, possibly at the risk of deforming such an optimized structure? Who wins? Does the pilot override the system and lie to the designers or computers? The truth is that aviators' egos are built upon the designs they fly, and the egos in turn sometimes drive engineers crazy! For the most part, they will not form part of the JAST or any other design equation, except by selective feedback. However, already, pilots are coming to rely increasingly on computer-vetted manoeuvring and are abrogating their responsibilities; when something goes wrong, it is usually put down to the FBW system having gone awry, and consequently the supplier or software engineer is blamed. If the 1970s represented the crossover from stick-and-rudder flying to systems management, and the 1980s extended it by adding stand-off sensors linked to precision-guided weaponry, then the 1990s are witnessing the crossover to passive computer technician. Fighter aviation is being remoulded into a new profession behind the backs of those who will actually have to fly the aircraft!

This increasing reliance on the digital number-crunching operator who can type 40 words per minute while being subjected to 9 g extends to targeting, as outlined in the opening chapter in the context of remote off-board sensing. We have already put the case for the F-22 and the manned air superiority fighter, but what of the attack machine? There is at present a drive towards forwarding near real-time images of a target to the cockpit of an attack fighter while it is *en route* to its objective. Derived from SAR or E-O imagery gleaned by HAE UAVs or other sources and processed by the Joint-Service Imagery Processing System (JSIPS), this can be conveyed to suitable fighters equipped with an IDM within 5–6 minutes of its collection. In plain English, this means that TV-type daytime or infrared images, as well as SAR radar maps, gleaned by pilotless aircraft flying deep into enemy airspace, or stand-off JSTARS or U-2Ss, are conveyed to a team of Army, Navy and Air Force personnel running an image-processing shop. These personnel then speedily sift through the material and pass on the relevant imagery to the fighter pilots, enabling them to receive constant target updates.

This is assuming ever greater importance in the ongoing quest to search and destroy mobile TELs, in particular. It is equally applicable to striking a convoy of war *matériel*, stopping an armoured division in its tracks, and even thwarting an amphibious assault. The inherent mobility of the targets means they might have moved miles since the aircrews originally drew up their mission plans. It might also be used to provide BDA imagery of fixed or moving targets to a second wave of fighters, who at that stage would have no idea how well the first wave had performed, and so could adjust their targeting to ensure that the key targets are taken out, or to finish off the remaining ones.

Pilots at the receiving end of this imagery will not get the big-picture image, but rather a patch of it, laced with suitable coordinates (in keeping with the 512 x 512 pixels available on a standard modern MFD display – the increased node of their mental focus). Remarkably, perhaps alarmingly, it has already been shown to work! Using the Advanced Fighter Technology Integration (AFTI) F-16 to demonstrate such evolving new avionics, suitably equipped with an IDM to receive the imagery, a satellite image of a SAM site was passed to the pilot, along with its coordinates. He then succeeded in engaging the target using a HARM missile, despite being stuck 3,500 ft below an 8,000 ft ridge which effectively hid the simulated target complex from his line of sight. It may have far-reaching repercussions for future air combat. At the present time, the imagery being gleaned is usually several hours old or older and so the chances are that the pilot would already have been able to preview it during mission planning. If image-garnering can be speeded up to genuinely near real-time and conveyed to pilots in the cockpit within, say, half an hour or less, then all sorts of possibilities open up – including the truly irksome one of rendering future fighters totally reliant on such off-board sensor data, instead of using it as a simple supplement or update.

Current trends indicate that fighter development will beat a path in one of two principal directions. Taking the extremes, the first is towards medium-weight single-seat fighters which will derive virtually all their target information on a hand-me-down basis over secure data-link via satellite (or command-and-control aircraft, if it is within line of sight). These fighters would feature little in the way of onboard sensors other than those associated with passive navigation and EW. They would be relatively cheap to build, with little risk of them going over budget and time schedules. Their inherent simplicity – clean airframes embedded with receptive microprocessors in their skins – would permit them to be stealthy and to preserve those characteristics because there would be no complicated seams to degrade electrical continuity, nor unsightly bulges accommodating even passive sensors such as FLIR or IRST.

Hermetically sealed shirtsleeve environment cockpit capsules might also make a comeback, as proposed by Boeing for JAST, permitting ejections at up to 750-knot equivalent airspeeds, in which the pilot would use wraparound liquid crystal colour head-up cockpit displays in lieu of g-limiting helmet sights, and the option to black-out the transparency at a flick of a switch to counter harmful lasers. Entry to the cockpit would be through the wheel well, or by plug-in or plug-on Angel Interceptor methods.

The other path (arguably the more desirable, but one which is looking increasingly unlikely) is to build mostly modular twin-seaters in the medium-heavy weight range. These would offer improved mission flexibility by means of an optional extra crewman and would make greater use of onboard autonomous sensors, using off-board sensor input merely as an aid to SA. This approach, on the other hand, is a far more costly proposition, with major potential for running over budget. Numerous programmes following this thinking have already been abandoned, such as the US Navy's A-12 Avenger 2.

There were other 'complicated factors' entering this line of thinking also. For example, if the twin-seat concept was to be retained, some designers and tacticians argue that it would be safer and more convenient to place future navigators on board deep strike jets in a rearwards-facing position, much as the Bristol Beaufighter TF.X and many Luftwaffe and Red Army radio-navigators of the Second World War

were seated. But instead of giving them a machine-gun, equip them with a Schlem or helmet-mounted sight, *Fulcrum*-style, to permit them to engage enemy fighters closing on the tail with rearwards-firing missiles at their fingertips too! A simple toggle on the rails would prevent the weapons from sliding off during normal flight routines.

Some serious thought was given to this during the inception of the aborted Avenger 2 stealth strike machine, but it was abandoned early on in the effort owing to its unorthodox approach. Pilots did not like the idea of nervous, trigger-happy bombardier-navigators taking out stray wingmen or tankers which might all too readily be mistaken for bandits. A hierarchical effect is implied by this reluctance, given that the back-seater would have copious access to a bank of SA-enhancing MFDs, making him a valid sting in the tail. It is interesting to note that in nearly all air arms save the US Navy the pilot remains firmly the AC, irrespective of relative rank; in American seagoing tradition there exists the almost unique concept governed by Martial Law that the higher-ranking officer has the final say. Clearly, F-14 Tomcat and A-6E Intruder pilots, having adopted the habit of being in charge, did not warm to the idea! Clearly also, American Naval aviators can learn to differentiate between law and convention. The latter has a keen edge, if respected.

Again, sensor technology appears to be the key: how these develop for off-board and onboard use, and for use with the emerging range of super smart weapons which may derive their electronic kamikaze mission objectives from either source. Serious consideration is already being given to developing JAST without sophisticated onboard sensors such as radar and FLIR, and making it solely reliant on off-board sensory input. However, as the RAND think-tank have rightly warned of several potential problems. Platforms such as the Tier HAE UAVs, AWACS and JSTARS, upon which the operational versions of JAST and its contemporaries would rely heavily, are still apt to produce targeting ambiguities, and will always be in scarce supply. Sensing satellites are inflexible. Communications satellites, crucial for conveying the data, would be likely quickly to be saturated with wartime traffic.

Neither should Russian developments be overlooked. There is, for example, the Navator Bureau's 202-mile-range KS.172 AAM, which the CIS might sell overseas to select customers in order to earn some hard currency. There is a steady proliferation of highly capable fighters like the Mikoyan Tochka Opori and Sukhoi Zhuravlik, which will be capable of carrying up to seven such weapons at a time. Given such considerations as these, the all-seeing, all-knowing sentinels would either be obliged to move their racetrack orbits so far to the rear as to be ineffectual, or risk destruction early on in a conflict. Even a reasonable-sized force of Tier HAE UAVs would not last long in a high-intensity conflict, nor our old friend the U-2S Dragon Lady.

The former scenario would strip off-board sensor-reliant fighters of much-needed tactical information, while in the aftermath of the latter contingency they might be brought to a standstill in one fell swoop. And who is to blame if the targeting process goes awry? Who is going to write the letters back home when an entire squadron is lost in a day – the commander, who went down with his or her colleagues with the dreaded last words: 'Control, my displays are blank, where are you?'

Alarm bells are ringing in the cockpit. The new designs will also require much-improved physiological support for the hard-pressed aviators destined to fly them. It may soon become necessary for a pilot to cope with a sustained acceleration of up to 15 g, in order to maintain an edge in performance to outmanoeuvre AAMs and SAMs, even with extensive EW protection such as towed decoys. Not so long ago, there was a time when pilots could bend the aircraft; we are rapidly getting to the stage where the aircraft, because of their sprightly performance and extremely tough composite airframes, will bend the pilot if he strains too much on the controls!

The main routes of salvation are threefold: the wider use of positive-pressure-breathing under g (PBG) combined with full anti-g trousers, as is proving successful with the F-16's newly introduced TLSS; and seats that are further reclined. In the former instance, inflatable bladders extended to cover 93 per cent of the lower body would raise average relaxed tolerance to 8.3 g, so that only moderate straining would be required to withstand 9 g, and current techniques would enable well-rehearsed aviators to cope with double figures. However, as the aeromedical researchers point out, when arms are positioned well below the heart level (as they will be in Eurofighter 2000, and also in JAST), arm pain after about 5 seconds of exposure to forces above 6 g can become so intolerable that crews would have to spend a fair amount of time afterwards in vulnerable wings-level flight in order to recover. And nobody spends more than 20 seconds flying so vulnerably during daytime; only night-time would offer that respite.

Combat also requires almost gymnastic head and upper torso movements under high-g (so called rubber-necking), and the instances of severe strain to neck and shoulder muscles are expected to increase once these new high-performance machines enter squadron service. The reclining Martin-Baker Mk.16

ejection seat will help a little. However, worthwhile tolerance enhancements are gained only from seats reclined at more than 75°, which increase relaxed tolerance to over 9 g. Such an arrangement would necessitate cocooning the pilot within the airframe and replacing the blown canopy hood with panoramic displays, suffocating his senses, and going beyond one of the avenues being seriously explored for JAST.

Pilots in these instances would fly using virtual reality techniques. Only off-board sensor technology would be used, processed into 3-D graphics depicting the terrain below, friendly and enemy fighter activity, ground threats as danger-zone hemispheres, a 'highway in the sky' based on the programmed flight-plan on disc or bubble-memory cartridges (adjusted automatically to counter new ground and air threats). There would be no direct visual link to the outside world! Such a pilot, relatively immobile, would sit reclined in an ejection seat plumbed into the virtual reality headset, and use single-source engine bleed air for molecularly sieved oxygen force-fed for high-g PBG, and the option of purified, recycled urine to top-up water reserves, fed via drip-feed or sip-straw. The flightsuit, too, would offer a spacesuit seal for pressure-breathing at altitude (PBA), enabling the gyrating new fighter to be flown up to its maximum ceiling.

The logical extension of this borders on science-fiction: chemicals could be pressure-injected into a pilot to keep him or her awake for extended missions, for resuscitation, and to provide a dose of painkillers. Diodes measuring brain activity might inform the computer of the pilot's mental state of health too, letting it take over if the aviator flunks the test. If these options begin to take shape, might it not be altogether better to produce an unmanned fighter flown by remote control by an 'aviator' using virtual reality in the relative tranquillity of a bunker, with a mug of coffee to hand? Certainly, aerodynamicists still tend to think of pilots and 'fightergators' as nuisances who spoil the outline of their otherwise beautiful designs, and squeeze in cockpits and cap their beloved computer-aided craft with canopy hoods as almost an afterthought. They would much prefer to design a totally clean aircraft, devoid of such far from stealthy bulges. It may not be that far into the future.

All of this is far removed from flying fighters in today's relatively free airspace, with its brash element of kicking the tyres, lighting the 'burners and speeding away in a thundering steed. However, it may be just around the corner. No matter what the aeromedical, airframe, propulsion and avionics people evolve in the quest for the common and bizarre, doubtless fighter pilots will have a thing to say about it all!

GLOSSARY

AA	auto-acquisition	AP	armour piercing
AAA	anti-aircraft artillery	ARCP	AAR control point
AAM	air-to-air missile	ARM	anti-radiation missile
AAR	air-to-air refuelling	ARN	airborne radio navigation
Aardvark	nickname for F-111	ARS	attack radar set
AB	Air Base	ASE	allowable or angular steering error
AC	Aircraft Commander	ASM	air to surface missile
Ace	aviator with five or more enemy aircraft kills	ASRAAM	advanced short-range AAM (AIM-132)
ACEVAL	air combat evaluation	ATARS	Advanced Tactical Aircraft Reconnaissance System
ACC	Air Combat Command (USAF)		
ACM	air combat manoeuvring	ATF	Advanced Tactical Fighter
ACMI	air combat manoeuvring instrumented range	ATHS	automatic target hand-off system
		AUP	Avionics Update Programme
ADI	attitude director indicator	AVTR	airborne videotape recorder
ADIZ	aircraft identification zone	AWACS	Airborne Warning & Control System
ADWC	Air Defense Weapons Center		
AF	Air Force	AWACW	AWACS Wing
AFB	Air Force Base	A-X/AX	Attack Experimental (designation)
AFCS	automatic flight control system	BAe	British Aerospace
AFMSS	Air Force Mission Support System	BAI	battle area interdiction
AFRes	Air Force Reserve (USAF)	BAK	barrier-arrestor cable system
AFV	armoured fighting vehicle·	BDA	bomb damage assessment
AGC	automatic gain control	BDU	bomb, dummy unit
AGL	above ground level	Big Eye	ARS or GMR (INT aircraft ground-map radars)
AGM	air-to-ground missile		
AIM	air intercept missile (AAM)	BIT	built-in test
AIMVAL	AIM evaluation	BLC	boundary-layer control (wing)
ALARM	air-launched ARM	B-scan	boresight scan, looking ahead (radar)
AMP	Avionics Modernization Program		
AMRAAM	advanced medium-range air-to-air missile (AIM-120)	BTH	beyond the horizon (radar coverage)
		BVR	beyond visual range
AN/	airborne system/	C³I	command, control & communications intelligence
ANG	Air National Guard (USAF)		
AoA	angle of attack		

CAD/CAM	computer-aided design/manufacture		DR	dead reckoning
CAI	Chicago Aerial Industries		DRF	dual-role fighter (F-15E)
CAP	combat air patrol		DSC(G)	digital scan converter (Group)
Capper	CAP aircraft or crew		DST	destructor adaptation of an iron
CAS	close air support			bomb to create a mine
CBU	cluster bomb unit		DTM	data transfer module
CCIP	continuously computed impact point		dumb	free-falling unguided bomb; iron
CCRP	continuously computed release point			bomb
CEA	circular error average		ECCM	electronic counter-countermeasures
CEM	combined effects munitions		ECM	electronic countermeasures
CEP	circular error probability		ECR	Electronic Combat Reconnaissance
CFIT	controlled flight into terrain		EFA	European Fighter Aircraft, now
CIA	Central Intelligence Agency			known as Eurofighter 2000
CIP	common integrated processor		EGT	exhaust gas temperature
CNI	communications, navigation,		Elint	electronic intelligence
	interrogation avionics		EMD	engineering, manufacture &
CNN	Cable News Network			development
Cobra Ball	USAF RC-135S optical tracking		EMI	electromagnetic interference
	platform		EMP	electromagnetic pulse
Comint	communications intelligence		E-O	electro-optical
comm-out	communications silence		EOB	electronic order of battle or enemy
	(radio-quiet)			order of battle
CONUS	Continental US		EOGB	electro-optically guided bomb
CP	control point		EOR	end of runway
CPGS	cassette preparation ground		ER/DL	extended-range/data-link
	system/station		E-scan	terrain-following elevation scan
CRPMD	combined radar and projected map		ESM	electronic support measures
	display		ETA	estimated time of arrival
CRT	cathode-ray tube		EW	electronic warfare
CSAR	Combat Search & Rescue		EWO	Electronic Warfare Officer (USAF)
CW	Combat Wing (USAF)		FAC	Forward Air Controller
DACT	dissimilar aircraft combat training		FADECS	full-authority digital engine control
DAFECS	digital authority full engine control			system
	system		FBL	fly-by-light
dB	decibel		FBW	fly-by-wire
DCC	Dedicated Crew Chief (USAF		FFAR	folding-fin aerial rocket
	groundcrew)		FG	Fighter Group
DDD	detail data display		FL	flight level
DDI	detail display indicator		FLIR	forward-looking infrared
DECM	defensive electronic		FLOT	forward line of troops
	countermeasures		FMS	foreign military sales
DEECS	digital electronic engine control		FOD	foreign object damage
	system		FoV	field of view
DIRCM	directed infrared countermeasures		frag	Fragmentary Order
DM	Deputy Commander for		FS	Fighter Squadron
	Maintenance (USAF)		FSD	full-scale development
DMAS	digital modular avionics system		FWIC	Fighter Weapons Instructor Course
DP	destination point		g	acceleration of free fall (acceleration
DO	Deputy Commander for Operations			due to gravity); 9.80665 m s^{-2}
	(USAF)		GBU	guided bomb Unit
DoD	Department of Defense (US)		GC	ground control
DQI	digital quartz inertial		GCI	ground control intercept

GE	General Electric (USA)		Technology
GIB	guy in the back seat	JDAM	Joint-Service Direct Attack Munition
GLOB	ground-loving old bastard (KC-135)	JSOW	Joint-Service Stand-Off Weapon
G-LOC	g-induced loss of consciousness	JSTARS	Joint-Service Surveillance Target
GMR	ground-mapping radar		Attack Radar System
GMT	Greenwich Mean Time	JSS	JSTARS Squadron
GPS	global positioning system Navstar	JTIDS	joint tactical information distribution
gorilla	NATO term for a large gaggle of		system
	aircraft, particularly those engaged	KKV	kinetic-kill vehicle
	on Capping duties	knot	nautical mile per hour
HAE/UAV	High-Altitude, Long-Endurance	ladar	laser radar
	Unmanned Air Vehicle	LADD	low-angle drogue delivery (nuclear)
HALM	high-angle-of-attack low-mach	LANTIRN	low-altitude navigation/targeting
	seeker		infrared for night
HARM	high-speed anti-radiation missile	LARA	low-altitude radar altimeter
	(AGM-88)	LASTE	low-altitude safety & targeting
HAS	hardened aircraft shelter		enhancement (OA/A-10A)
HAWC	homing & warning computer	LCOSS	lead-computing optical sight system
HavCAP	high-value CAP	LGB	laser-guided bomb
heat	heat-seeking AAM	Lead	Flight Leader
HEI	high-explosive incendiary (cannon	LED	light-emitting diode
	shell)	LLLGB	low-level laser-guided bomb
HOTAS	hands on throttle and stick	LLLTV	low light-level television
HRM	high-resolution ground map	LoC	lines of communication
HSD/I	horizontal situation display/indicator	LOROPS	long-range oblique optical system
HTS	HARM Targeting System	LORAN	long-range radio aid to navigation
HUD	head-up display	LPI	low probability of intercept
IBM	International Business Machines Inc	LRI	long-range intercept
ICT	integrated combat turnaround	LRU	line-replaceable unit
ID	identification	LSI	Lear-Siegler Inc.
IDF/AF	Israeli Defence Force/Air Force	LWF	Lightweight Fighter (YF-16 versus
	(Heyl Ha'Avir)		YF-17 fly-off)
IDM	improved data modem	Mach	speed of sound, which differs with
IDS	interdictor-strike (Tornado variant)		altitude (air density)
IFF	identification, friend or foe	MAWS	missile approach warning system
IFR	instrument flight rules	MB	Martin Baker Co.
IIR	imaging infrared	MCR	mission capable rate
IMC	instrument meteorological	MER	multiple ejection rack
	conditions	MFD	multi-function display
IMU	inertial measurement unit	MiGCAP	MiG combat air patrol
INS	inertial navigation set	MMC	metal matrix composites
INT	interdiction	MMH/FH	maintenance man-hours per flight
IOC	initial operational capability		hour
IP	initial point or instructor pilot	MMW	millimetre wave
IRADS	infrared attack & designation system	MRC	major regional conflict
	(F-117A)	MSL	mean sea-level
IRAN	inspect and repair as necessary	MSS	mission support system
IRCM	infrared countermeasures	MTBF	mean-time between failure
IRLS	infrared line-scanner	MTI	moving target indicator/indication
IRST	infrared search & track	NASA	National Aeronautics and Space
JASSM	Joint Air-to-Surface Stand-off Missile		Administration (US)
JAST	Joint-Service Advanced Strike	NATO	North Atlantic Treaty Organization

NFO	Naval Flight Officer (US)
nm	nautical mile (6,076 ft)
NVG	night-vision goggles
OAP	offset aimpoint
OASD	Office of the Assistant Secretary for Defense in the Pentagon
OCU	Operational Conversion Unit or Operational Capability Upgrade
ODR	overland downlook radar (AWACS APY-1/2)
O & M	Operations & Maintenance (Costs)
ORI	Operational Readiness Inspection
PALOMA	Preparation Automatisée Locale des Missions Aériennes (Mirage 2000N/D mission-planning system)
Para	two-aircraft Flight (Russia)
PAV	Prototype Air Vehicle
Pave	precision avionics vectoring equipment
PD	pulse-Doppler radar mode
PDF	Precision Direction Finder
PDM	programmed depot-level maintenance
PGM	precision-guided munition
Photint	photographic intelligence
PI	photo interpreter
PIRATE	Passive Infrared Tracking Equipment
pK	kill probability
POL	petroleum, oil, lubricants (storage facility)
PPI	plan position indicator; God's-eye view
PPIF	photo-processing and interpretation facility
PVO	Voiska Protivovoz Dushnoy Oborini (Russian air defence force)
QRA	quick reaction alert
QRC	quick reaction capability
RAAF	Royal Australian Air Force
RAF	Royal Air Force (UK)
RAM	radar-absorbent material (stealth)
RAND	Research & Development Corporation
RBL	radar boresight line
RHAWS	radar homing & warning system
RIC	reconnaissance intelligence center
Rivet Joint	RC-135V/W Elint platform
RLG	ring-laser gyro
RN	Royal Navy (UK)
RNAS	Royal Naval Air Station (UK)
RoE	Rules of Engagement

ROR	release on range (to target)
rpm	revolutions per minute (engines)
RQ/I	radar-quiet/intercept
RS	Reconnaissance Squadron
RSP	radarscope photography
RTB	return to base
RTT	realistic target training
RTU	replacement training unit
RWR	radar warning receiver
SA	situational awareness
SAL	semi-active laser
SAM	surface-to-air missile
SAR	synthetic aperture radar
SARA	Systéme Aérotransportable de Reconnaissance Aérienne (the French PPIF)
SARH	semi-active radar-homing
SAS	Special Air Service (UK)
Schlem	Russian helmet-mounted sight
SCP	set clearance planes
SEA	South-East Asia
SEAD	suppression of enemy air defences
SEAL	Sea And Land Special Forces (USN)
SEM-E	standard electronics module, E-size (avionics)
Sigint	signals intelligence
sim	simulator
SLAR	sideways-looking airborne radar
SLIR	sideways-looking infrared
smart	see PGM
S/MTD	STOL/Manoeuvre Technology Demonstrator
spm	shells per minute
SOR	specific operational requirement
Stan/Eval	Standardization and Evaluation (checkrides)
STARM	Standard ARM (AGM-78)
STARS	Stored Terrain Access And Retrieval System
SUU	suspension underwing unit
TAB-Vee	theater air base vulnerability shelter (US HAS)
TALD	tactical air-launched decoy (ADM-141)
TARPS	Tactical Airborne Reconnaissance Pod System
TASMO	Tactical Air Support For Maritime Operations
TCA	track crossing angle
TCS	television camera set
TDOA	time difference of arrival
TEC	thermo-electrically cooled

Teenagers	US fighters bearing a numerical suffix in the 14 to 18 range (e.g. the F/A-18 Hornet)
TEL	transporter-erector launcher
TER	triple ejection rack
Terprom	terrain profile matching (BAe TRN system)
TFR	terrain-following radar
TFS	Tactical Fighter Squadron
TFW(P)	Tactical Fighter Wing (Provisional)
TFX/TFX-N	Tactical Fighter Experimental/-Navy (F-111 series)
TI	Texas Instruments Inc.
TIALD	thermal imaging & laser designator
TIC	troops in contact with the enemy
TID	tactical information display
Tier	code-name for a new series of HAE/UAVs
TISEO	Target Identification System Electro-Optical
TLSS	tactical life support system
TMD	tactical munitions dispenser
TOT	time over target
TRN	terrain-referenced navigation system
Tropik	Russian LORAN
TTT	time to target ('bombs away')
TUC	time of useful consciousness
TWS	track while scan
UAV	unmanned aerial vehicle
USAF	United States Air Force
USAFE	United States Air Forces in Europe
USMC	United States Marines Corps
USN	United States Navy
UTM	Universal Transverse Mercator (coordinates)
VID	virtual image display
VMC	visual meteorological conditions
VMCJ-	US Marine Corps Composite Squadron
VFR	visual flight rules
Victor Alert	nuclear strike stand-by
Viper	nickname for the F-16 Fighting Falcon
vis-rep	visual report
V/STOL	vertical/short take-off & landing
V-VS	Voyenno-Vozdushniye Sily (Russian tactical air force)
Warthog	nickname for the A/OA-10A Thunderbolt II
WASP	*Weasel* attack signal processor (F-4G AN/APR-47)
WCP	weapons control panel
Weasel	aviator dedicated to SEAD
Wild Weasel	USAF F-4s dedicated to SEAD
wizzo	*see* WSO
WRCS	weapons release computer system (F-4 ASQ-91)
WSO	Weapons Systems Officer
XST	Experimental Stealth Tactical; *Have Blue*
Zveno	four-aircraft Flight (Russia)
Z/Zulu	Greenwich Mean Time
Zulu Alert	*see* QRA; also known as Zulu Alert India

INDEX

Italics refer to illustrations

AIRCRAFT

A/EA/KA-6 Intruder, *11, 49, 61, 65, 122, 140, 171,* 52, 60, 62, 115, 123, 125, 141, 150

A-7 Corsair II, *119,* 41, 110, 111, 125, 150

A-10 Thunderbolt II, *102, 103,* 12, 24, 99, 100, 103-105, 109, 112, 119, 165

A-12 Avenger II, 193

AH-64 Apache, 71, 101

B-1 Lancer, 126

B-2 Spirit, 126, 179

B-52 Stratofortress, *125,* 11, 79, 126, 162

BO.105, 100

Boeing 707, 52

Boeing 727, 16

Buccaneer S2, 144

EA-6B Prowler, 156

E-2 Hawkeye, 76, 79

E-3 AWACS   *14,* 10, 14-17, 25, 53, 55, 56, 57, 58, 79, 93, 94, 185, 193

E-8 J-STAR, *17, 18,* 16, 17-19, 193

Eurofighter 2000, *187,* 35, 39, 58, 187, 194

EB-66 Destroyer, 11

EC-121 Warning Star, 11, 14

EF-111A Raven, *152, 153,* 12, 20, 135, 156-157, 158

F/RF-4 Phantom II, *10, 11, 37, 42, 45, 49, 64, 66, 67, 80, 91, 97, 104, 108, 109, 110, 172, 176, 177,* 10-12, 20, 24, 26, 27, 29, 31, 38, 39, 41, 43, 45, 48, 55, 57, 63-68, 69, 70, 71, 72, 73, 80, 97, 111, 112, 114, 115, 133, 146, 159, 169, 171, 173, 175, 188, 190

F-5 Tiger, 83, 85

F-14 Tomcat, *41, 76, 77, 78,* 12, 26, 74-77, 79, 80, 82, 90, 177, 193

F-15 Eagle, *35, 54, 81, 82, 84, 85, 89, 148, 153,* *183,* 12, 15, 18, 20, 22, 23, 24, 25, 26, 27-28, 29, 30, 41, 57, 58, 68, 70, 72, 74, 79, 81, 82, 83, 85, 90, 92, 94, 97, 100, 106, 115, 125, 141, 150-152, 154, 159, 177, 185, 186

F-16 Fighting Falcon, *13, 68, 90, 112, 113, 114, 117, 151,* 20, 21, 22, 24, 25, 26, 27, 33, 43, 62, 67-68, 70, 85, 92, 97, 103, 104, 111, 113-119, 120, 122, 124, 147, 157, 170, 175, 192

F/A-18 Hornet, *88, 147, 169,* 16, 23, 25, 87, 93, 125, 161

F-22 ATF, *180, 189,* 25, 26, 58, 87, 93, 97, 100, 166, 179-187

F-84 Thunderstreak, 27

F-104 Starfighter, 27, 179, 183

F-105 Thunderchief, *60,* 10, 60, 67

F/FB-111 Aardvark, *22, 34, 51, 98, 123, 132, 135, 137, 139, 169, 173,* 178, 12, 21-22, 30, 41, 48, 52, 62, 119, 124, 128-131, 132, 133-139, 141, 150, 154, 156, 160, 162, 172, 174, 177, 190

F-117 Nighthawk, *21, 47, 50, 160, 161, 162, 163, 175, Jacket rear,* 19-20, 21, 22, 24, 30, 31-32, 43, 44, 125, 162-166, 171, 174, 175, 181, 184

Gripen, 26, 187

Harrier AV-8B/GR.7, *105,* 12, 31, 96, 99, 106, 122, 124

Hercules, 174

Jaguar, *118,* 24, 31, 120, 122, 129, 158

JAST, 188-190, 192-194

KC-10 Extender, *50,* 51, 52

KC-135 Stratotanker, 11, 51

MH-53J Pave Low IIIE, 71

Mi-8 Hip, 100

Mi-24 Hind, 15

MiG-15, 72

MiG-21 Fishbed, 90, 188

MiG-23/27 Flogger, 58, 90, 94, 106, 162, 173
MiG-25 Foxbat, 28, 77, 90, 94
MiG-29/33 Fulcrum, *92*, 16, 43, 58, 90, 91-92, 94, 96, 99, 100, 157, 174, 193
MiG-31 Foxhound, 77, 79
MiG 1.42, 93, 186
Mirage IVP, 168
Mirage F1, 23, 24, 146
Mirage 2000, *Jacket front, 46, 86*, 32, 42, 168
PQM-102 Pave Deuce, *89*
QF-86 Sabre, 100
Rafale, *186*, 26, 35, 187
RC-135 Rivet Joint/Cobra Ball, 18, 68
Sea Harrier, 85
SR-71A Blackbird, *33, 176*, 23, 34
Super Galeb, 25
Su-17/22 Fitter, 89, 106, 156
Su-24 Fencer, *155*, 154
Su-25 Frogfoot, 105-106, 109
Su-27 Flanker, *92*, 28, 44, 58, 90, 92, 94, 194
Su-33, 28, 79, 92
Su-34, 22, 28
Su-35, 26, 28, 79, 94, 96
Super Etendard, *145, 167*, 146
Tornado F3/GR1/ECR, *53, 69, 86, 96, 141, 143*, 23, 26, 31, 57, 69-70, 71, 79, 85, 98, 125, 129, 141-146, 154, 160, 170, 192
Tristar, 52
TSR.2, 190
Tu-16 Badger, 20, 146
Tu-22 Blinder/Backfire, 146
Tu-95/142 Bear, 75, 146
Tu-160 Blackjack, 126
UH-60 Blackhawk, 15
U-2R/S, 23, 34, 145, 192, 194
VC-10 K-tankers, 52
Viggen, 98
Yak-28 Brewer, 156
YF-17 Cobra, 25, 90
YF-23 Black Widow II, *180*, 93, 179, 181, 183, 185, 186

AIR CREWS
Crew composition, 24-28, 29-30, 68, 114, 154, 193
Physiological factors, *32, 33*, 105, 25, 32-34, 35-38, 72, 185, 188, 193, 194
Situational awareness, 14, 31, 55, 56, 57, 58, 79, 193-194
Training
    ACMI/TACTS ranges, *13*, 188
    Simulators, *26, 152*, 26, 72

AWACS, *14*, 10, 14-17, 25, 53, 55, 56, 57, 58, 79, 93, 94, 150, 185, 193

BOMBS
Conventional general purpose, *43, 61, 109, 119, 132, 134, 140*, 44, 59, 121, 135, 137, 141, 144
Cluster, *118, 134*, 59, 62, 107-108, 109, 112
Dispensers
    JP233, *143*, 144
    LAD, *151*, 145
    CBU canisters, 107-108
    MW-1, 145
Electro-optically-guided, GBU-15, *10, 135*, 121, 139, 140, 141, 150, 151
JDAM, JSOW, 71, 126, 149, 166
Laser-guided
    Arming, 44
    BLU-109-based penetrators, *22, 162*, 138, 165
    CPU-123, *142*, 122, 124, 125, 144
    Deep Throat, 21, 138-139
    Paveway series, *22, 120, 136, 161, 162*, 121, 122-124, 138, 165
Nuclear, *164, 165*, 167-168

COMBAT
Afghanistan, 105-106
Bosnia, 25, 102
Falklands, 89, 102, 124, 146
Gulf War, *17, 18, 20, 22, 64, 66, 67, 141, 142, 143*, 9, 10, 15, 17-18, 19-23, 24, 25, 26, 27, 58, 64-66, 69-70, 83, 103-104, 105-106, 114, 120-121, 124, 125, 126, 137, 138-139, 141-145, 150, 154, 163, 164-166, 178, 187
Israeli, *11*, 67, 94
Libya, *132, 140*, 89, 137-138, 141, 150
Vietnam, *10, 11, 49, 61*, 9-12, 14, 27, 56, 59, 60-62, 109, 112, 123, 137, 172, 178, 190

COUNTERMEASURES & DECOYS
Active electronic, *118*, 58, 156-159
Chaff/flares, 118, 158, 105, 159-161
Laser, 70, 161, 162
Missile Approach Warning, 70, 161
Radar warning receivers, *61*, 57, 59-60, 63, 67, 70, 156, 157-158, 159
Towed/released active decoys, *65*, 64, 161-162

CREW CHIEFS, *34, 35, 43, 44, 143, 163, 164*, 35, 37-38, 39, 43, 44-45, 177, 178, 182

ENGINES, POWERPLANTS
Advanced systems, *38*, 91, 92-93, 166, 184-185
Armour protection, 105-106
Cruise, 48, 72, 184-185
DEECS/DAFICS, 38-39, 56, 77, 93
EJ200, *38*
FOD hazards, 44
J79-GEs, *39*, 38, 47-48

Principles, 37-39
Shut-down, 176-177
Start-up, *37*, 37-39
Supercruise, 185

EJECTION SEATS, *36-37*, 35, 194

EXERCISES
Flags, 12, 128
Gunsmoke, 114-115
Vigilant Warrior, 126
Zealous Pursuit, 18

GUNS
Gatling type, *97, 98, 111*, 99, 100, 103, 104, 105, 109
Cannon, 111, 98-100, 109

FATIGUE LIVES, AIRCRAFT, 72

IFF, 44, 11, 15, 50 (See also AWACS;
   NAVIGATION AIDS, JTIDS)

INFRA-RED SYSTEMS
Air-to-air IRSTS, *91*, 57-58, 72, 88, 94-96, 181, 184
Mapping/targeting FLIR, *114, 117, 132, 142, Jacket
   rear*, 115-117, 118, 124, 133-134, 144, 151, 154,
   163-164

J-STARS, E-8, *17, 18*, 16, 17-19, 193

MISSILES
Arming, 44
Air-to-air, heat-seeking
   Archer R-73, *95*, 94-96
   ASRAAM AIM-132, *96*, 96-97, 185
   Magic 550, *86*
   Python III, 96
   Sidewinder AIM-9, *54, 80, 88, 90, 118*, 58, 83, 85,
      87, 88-89, 97-98, 185
Air-to-air, radar-guided
   Alamo R-27, 94
   Amos R-33, 79
   AMRAAM AIM-120, *85*, 15, 25, 79, 82-83, 85,
      87, 94, 159, 183, 185
   Amraamski R-77, 87
   Aspide, 81, 86
   Have Dash 2, 87, 185
   KS.172, 79, 94, 193
   MICA, 87
   Phoenix AIM-54, *76, 78*, 12, 75-77, 83
   Skyflash, *53, 80*
   Sparrow AIM-7, *54, 81*, 11, 58, 79, 80-81, 82
   Super 530D, *86*
Air-to-surface, anti-radar
   ALARM, *69*, 69-70, 125, 147

HARM AGM-88, *66*, 12, 20, 62-63, 64, 65, 67,
   68, 70, 71, 125, 149, 192
Kh-31P, 94
Shark, 71
Shrike AGM-45, 59, 62, 149
Standard ARM AGM-78, *61*, 62
Tacit Rainbow AGM-136, 69
Air-to-surface, anti-ship
   Exocet AM.39, *145*, 79, 146
   Gabriel III, 146
   Harpoon AGM-84, *134*, 149-150
   Kormoran, 125, 146
   Penguin, 146, 147
   Sea Eagle, 146
   Skipper II AGM-123, *122*
Air-to-surface, electro-optically-aided
   AGM-130, *139*, 141, 151
   Maverick AGM-65, *104*, 103, 104-105, 115, 120,
      139
   Popeye AGM-142, *125*
   SLAM AGM-84E, *147*, 150
Air-to-surface, nuclear
   Aerospatiale ASMP, *165*, 168
Surface/Sea-to-surface, conventional
   SCUD, 18, 22, 23, 144, 154
   Tomahawk, *20*, 55

MISSION PROFILES
   Aerial refuelling, *49, 50, 51*, 48-52, 170
   Air-to-air, *56, 73, 75, 78, 81, 82, 87, 89, 90, 95*,
      53-58, 70-100
   Anti-shipping, *122, 147*, 146-147, 149-150
   BAI, *114, 119, 120*, 101, 106-107, 112-124
   Brief/debrief, 29, 32, 177-178
   Close-air-support, *109, 110, 111*, 101-112
   End-of-runway procedures, *44*, 43-45
   Engine start, 37-39
   Emergency landings, *169, 172, 174*, 172
   FACs, Fast-FACS, 102-103, 105
   Interdiction, *127, 130, 132, 136, 140, 142*, 101,
      124-146, 150-152, 154, 162-168
   Jamming, *158*, 156-159
   Laser-bombing, *136, 140, 142, 162*, 120-124, 138-
      139, 164, 165
   Launch, *44, 45, 46, 47*, 42-48
   Nuclear attack, *165*, 166-168
   Pre-flight checks, 35, 39, 41-42
   Radar attack, over land, *127, 130*, 128-131, 133-
      135, 150-151
   Recovery, *171, 172, 173, 174, 175, 176*, 170-175
   Runway denial, *143*, 137, 141, 144, 145
   SEAD, *60, 61, 64, 65, 66, 67, 68, 69*, 59-71

NAVIGATION & ATTACK AIDS
Airborne radio

ARNs, 31, 114, 133
Navstar, *131*, 19, 131, 133, 150
ATHS, 19, 102-103
Designators – refer to **WEAPONS**
Digital storage systems, 31-32, 41, 110-111, 113, 117-118, 130, 141, 163, 177
Electro-optic aids, *114, 117, 132, 142, Jacket rear,* 115-117, 118, 124, 133-134, 144, 151, 154, 163-164
Inertially-aided, *40*, 39-41, 114, 130-131, 133, 164, 166
J-TIDS, *56*, 15, 57, 70, 80
Mission-planning, 29-32
Moving-map, 31
Radar, radar-updating, *127*, 130, 113-114, 130, 131, 135, 141
Terrain-referenced, 117-119, 145-146
Powell, Colin, Gen., US JCS Chairman, *20*, 166

RADARS, AIRBORNE
(see also AWACS; J-STARS)
Air-to-air, *75, 77, 112*, 56, 72, 73-77, 79, 80, 81, 82, 182
Air-to-surface navigation and mapping, *127, 130*, 113-114, 130-131, 135, 141
Horizon, 146-147
HOTAS-SWITCHING, *73*, 12, 72, 74, 80, 81, 82, 88, 117, 152
Predictions, 30
SAR, *18*, 17-18, 150-151, 154, 164
Sea-search modes, 147

Terrain-following, 116, 117-118, 119, 128-129

ROCKETS, *110*, 109, 110

Schwarzkopf, Norman, Gen., Commander, 23

STEALTH (see also **AIRCRAFT, F–117A**), 105, 165, 166, 181-182

UNMANNED AIR VEHICLES, *23*, 23, 24, 192, 193, 194

WEAPONS
Data-links, *135*, 77, 85, 139, 141, 150
Designators
    ATLIS 2, 120-121
    IRADS – refer to AIRCRAFT, F-117A
    LANTIRN, *113, 114*, 24, 70, 115-118, 122, 124, 151, 152, 154
    Pave Light AVQ-9, 123
    Pave Knife AVQ-10, *11*, 123
    Pave Tack AVQ-26, *130, 132*, 136, 133-134, 135, 138, 141
    TIALD, *141, 142*, 24, 144
    TRIM, *140*, 115, 123
    TRAM AAS-33, *140*, 123, 141, 150
See also BOMBS, MISSILES

WEATHER, 9, 12

WILD WEASELS – see MISSION PROFILES, SEAD